5 STEPS TO A 5™

AP Physics C

2020

5 STEPS TO A 5™

AP Physics C

2020

Greg Jacobs

Mc
Graw
Hill

New York   Chicago   San Francisco   Athens   London   Madrid
Mexico City   Milan   New Delhi   Singapore   Sydney   Toronto

1 2 3 4 5 6 7 8 9   LHS   24 23 22 21 20 19

ISBN   978-1-260-45475-8
MHID   1-260-45475-4

e-ISBN   978-1-260-45476-5
e-MHID   1-260-45476-2

The series editor was Grace Freedson, and the project editor was Del Franz.

Series design by Jane Tenenbaum.

McGraw-Hill Education products are available at special quantity discounts to use as premiums and sales promotions, or for use in corporate training programs. To contact a representative, please visit the Contact Us pages at www.mhprofessional.com.

CONTENTS

STEP 4   **Review the Knowledge You Need to Score High**

STEP 5   **Build Your Test-Taking Confidence**

Appendixes

ACKNOWLEDGMENTS

I extend my thanks to Grace Freedson, who was the driving force behind this book's publication, and especially to Don Reis, who was not only a superb editor but also an unwavering source of support. I also appreciate Ruth Mills's awesome work on the second edition and Bev Weiler and Clara Wente's careful and thorough editing of the questions and example problems for the 2010–2011 edition.

Thank you to Chat Hull and Jessica Broaddus, veterans of my 2002 Physics B class, who provided the idea for two free-response questions.

My 2004 students at Woodberry Forest School were extremely helpful in the development of this book. It was they who served as guinea pigs, reading chapters for clarity and correctness, making suggestions, and finding mistakes. They are Andrew Burns, Jordan Crittenden, David Fulton, Henry Holderness, Michael Ledwith, Johnny Phillips, Rob Sellers, and Chris Straka from Physics C; Wes Abcouwer, Wyatt Bone, Matt Brown, David Goodson, Bret Holbrook, Mike Johnson, Rich Lane, Jake Miller, Jake Reeder, Charles Shackelford, Beau Thomas, David Badham, Marks Brewbaker, Charlton deSaussure, Palmer Heenan, Wilson Kieffer, Brian McCormick, Eli Montague, Christian Rizzuti, Pierre Rodriguez, and Frazier Stowers from Physics B; and Andy Juc, Jamie Taliaferro, Nathan Toms, Matt Laughridge, Jamie Gardiner, Graham Gardiner, Robbie Battle, William Crosscup, Jonas Park, Billy Butler, Bryan May, Fletcher Fortune, and Stuart Coleman from the general physics class. Although Josh and I bear responsibility for all errors in the text, the folks mentioned above deserve credit for minimizing our mistakes.

The idea for the Four-Minute Drill came originally from Keen Johnson Babbage, my seventh-grade social studies teacher. I've borrowed the idea from him for over two decades of teaching AP. Thank you!

The faculty and administration at Woodberry, in particular Jim Reid, the science department chairman, deserve mention. They have been so supportive of me professionally.

Additional thanks go to members of my 2009 AP physics classes who helped edit the practice tests: Min SuKim, Cannon Allen, Collins MacDonald, Luke Garrison, Chris Cirenza, and Landon Biggs. And to later students: Michael Bauer, Vinh Hoang, and Evan Sun.

Most important, I'd like to thank Shari and Milo Cebu for putting up with me during all of my writing projects.

ABOUT THE AUTHOR

GREG JACOBS teaches AP Physics C, AP Physics 1, and conceptual physics at Woodberry Forest School, the nation's premier boarding school for boys. He is a reader and consultant for the College Board—this means he grades the AP Physics exams, and he runs professional development seminars for other AP teachers. Greg is president of the USAYPT, a nonprofit organization promoting physics research at the high school level. Greg was honored as an AP Teacher of the Year by the Siemens Foundation. Outside the classroom, Greg has coached baseball, football, and debate. He umpires high school baseball. He is the lead broadcaster for Woodberry football, baseball, soccer, and basketball. Greg writes a physics teaching blog available at **www.jacobsphysics.blogspot.com**.

INTRODUCTION: THE FIVE-STEP PROGRAM

Welcome!

I know that preparing for the Advanced Placement (AP) Physics exam can seem like a daunting task. There's a lot of material to learn, and some of it can be rather challenging. But I also know that preparing for the AP exam is much easier—and much more enjoyable—if you do it with a friendly guide. So let me introduce myself; my name is Greg, and I'll be your friendly guide for this journey.

Why This Book?

To understand what makes this book unique, you should first know a little bit about who I am. I have taught all versions of AP Physics over the past two decades, helping more than 90% of my Physics C students garner 5s on the exam. I am also an AP Physics table leader—which means I set the rubrics for the AP exams and supervise their scoring.

I know, from my own experiences and from talking with countless other students and teachers, what you *don't* need in a review book. You don't need to be overwhelmed with unimportant, technical details; you don't need to read confusing explanations of arcane topics; you don't need to be bored with a dull text.

Instead, what I think you do need—and what this book provides—are the following:

- A text that's written in clear, simple language.
- A thorough review of every topic you need to know for the AP exam.
- Lots of problem-solving tips and strategies.

Organization of the Book: The Five-Step Program

You will be taking a lengthy, comprehensive exam this May. You want to be well prepared enough that the exam takes on the feel of a command performance, not a trial by fire. Following the Five-Step program is the best way to structure your preparation.

Step 1: Set Up Your Study Program

Physics does not lend itself well to cramming. Success on the AP exam is invariably the result of diligent practice over the course of months, not the result of an all-nighter on the eve of exam day. Step 1 gives you the background and structure you need before you even start exam preparation.

Step 2: Determine Your Test Readiness

I have included a diagnostic test, of course, broken down by topic. But more important to your preparation are the *fundamentals quizzes* in Chapter 4. These quizzes, a unique feature of the *5 Steps to a 5* program, are different from test-style problems.

A problem on the AP exam usually requires considerable problem solving or critical thinking skills. Rare is the AP question that asks about straightforward facts that you can memorize—you'll get maybe two of those on the entire 70-question multiple-choice test. Rather than asking you to spit out facts, the AP exam asks you to use the facts you know to reason deeply about a physical situation. But if you don't know the fundamental facts, you certainly won't be able to reason deeply about anything!

Thus, a good place to start your test preparation is by quizzing yourself. Find out what fundamental facts you know, and which you need to know. The *5 Steps* fundamentals quizzes will diagnose your areas of strength and weakness. Once you can answer every question on a fundamentals quiz quickly and accurately, you are ready for deeper questions that will challenge you on the AP exam.

Step 3: Develop Strategies for Success

Yes, yes, I know you've been listening to general test-taking advice for most of your life. Yet, I have *physics-specific* advice for you. An AP physics test requires a dramatically different approach than does a state standards test or an SAT.

I start you with the secret weapon in attacking an AP test: memorizing equations. I explain *why* you should memorize, then I suggest some ways to make the learning process smoother. Next, I move on to discuss the major types of questions you'll see on the AP exam, and how to approach each with confidence.

Finally, I present you with drills on some of the most common physics situations tested on the AP exams. These exercises will allow you to conquer any fear or uncertainty you may have about your skills.

Step 4: Review the Knowledge You Need to Score High

This is a comprehensive review of all the topics on the AP exam. Now, you've probably been in an AP Physics class all year; you've likely read[1] your textbook. This review is meant to be just that—*review*, in a readable format, and focused exclusively on the AP exam.

These review chapters are appropriate both for quick skimming, to remind yourself of salient points, and for in-depth study, working through each practice problem. I do not go into nearly as much detail as a standard textbook; but the advantage of this lack of detail is that you can focus only on those issues germane to the AP Physics exams.

Step 5: Build Your Test-Taking Confidence

Here is your full-length practice test. Unlike other practice tests you may take, this one comes with thorough explanations. One of the most important elements in learning physics is making, and then learning from, mistakes. I don't just tell you what you got wrong; I explain why your answer is wrong, and how to do the problem correctly. It's okay to make a mistake here, because if you do, you won't make that same mistake again on that Monday in mid-May.

---

[1]Or at least tried to read.

The Graphics Used in This Book

To emphasize particular skills and strategies, I use several icons throughout this book. An icon in the margin will alert you that you should pay particular attention to the accompanying text. I use these three icons:

1. This icon points out a very important concept or fact that you should not pass over.

2. This icon calls your attention to a problem-solving strategy that you may want to try.

3. This icon indicates a tip that you might find useful.

Boldfaced words indicate terms that are included in the glossary at the end of the book. Boldface is also used to indicate the answer to a sample problem discussed in the test.

5 STEPS TO A 5™

AP Physics C

2020

STEP 1

Set Up Your Study Program

CHAPTER 1

How to Approach Your AP Physics Course

IN THIS CHAPTER

Summary: Recognize the difference between truly understanding physics and just doing well in your physics class.

Key Ideas

KEY IDEA

✪ Focus on increasing your knowledge of physics, not on pleasing your teacher.
✪ Don't spend more than 10 minutes at one time on a problem without getting anywhere—come back to it later if you don't get it.
✪ Form a study group; your classmates can help you learn physics better.
✪ If you don't understand something, ask your teacher for help.
✪ Don't cram; although you can memorize equations, the skills you need to solve physics problems can't be learned overnight.

Before we even dive into the nitty-gritty of the AP Physics exam, it's important for you to know that the AP exam is an *authentic* physics test. What this means is that it's not possible to "game" this test—in order to do well, *you must know your physics*. Therefore, the purpose of this book is twofold:

(1) to teach you the ways in which the AP exam tests your physics knowledge, and
(2) to give you a review of the physics topics that will be tested—and to give you some hints on how to approach these topics.

Everyone who takes the AP exam has just completed an AP Physics course. **Recognize that your physics course is the place to start your exam preparation!** Whether or not you are satisfied with the quality of your course or your teacher, the best way to start preparing for the exam is by doing careful, attentive work in class all year long.

Okay, for many readers, we're preaching to the choir. You don't want to hear about your physics class; you want the specifics about the AP exam. If that's the case, go ahead and turn to Chapter 2, and get started on your exam-specific preparation. But we think that you can get even more out of your physics class than you think you can. Read these pieces of time-tested advice, follow them, and we promise you'll feel more comfortable about your class *and* about the AP exam.

Ignore Your Grade

This must be the most ridiculous statement you've ever read. But it may also be the most important of these suggestions. Never ask yourself or your teacher "Can I have more points on this assignment?" or "Is this going to be on the test?" You'll worry so much about giving the teacher merely what she or he wants that you won't learn physics in the way that's best for you. Whether your score is perfect or near zero, ask, "Did I really understand all aspects of these problems?"

Remember, the AP exam tests your physics knowledge. If you understand physics thoroughly, you will have no trouble at all on the AP test. But, while you may be able to argue yourself a better grade in your physics *class,* even if your comprehension is poor, the AP readers are not so easily moved.

If you take this advice—if you really, truly ignore your grade and focus on physics—your grade will come out in the wash. You'll find that you got a very good grade after all, because you understood the subject so well. But you *won't care,* because you're not worried about your grade!

Don't Bang Your Head Against a Brick Wall

Our meaning here is figurative, although there are literal benefits also. Never spend more than 10 minutes or so staring at a problem without getting somewhere. If you honestly have no idea what to do at some stage of a problem, STOP. Put the problem away. Physics has a way of becoming clearer after you take a break.

On the same note, if you're stuck on some algebra, don't spend forever trying to find what you know is a trivial mistake, say a missing negative sign or some such thing. Put the problem away, come back in an hour, and start from scratch. This will save you time in the long run.

And finally, if you've put forth a real effort, you've come back to the problem many times and you still can't get it: relax. Ask the teacher for the solution, and allow yourself to be enlightened. You will not get a perfect score on every problem. But you don't care about your grade, remember?

Work with Other People

When you put a difficult problem aside for a while, it always helps to discuss the problem with others. Form study groups. Have a buddy in class with whom you are consistently comparing solutions.

Although you may be able to do all your work in every other class without help, we have never met a student who is capable of solving every physics problem on his or her own.

It is not shameful to ask for help. Nor is it dishonest to seek assistance—as long as you're not copying, or allowing a friend to carry you through the course. Group study is permitted and encouraged in virtually every physics class around the globe.

Ask Questions When Appropriate

We know your physics teacher may seem mean or unapproachable, but in reality, physics teachers do want to help you understand their subject. If you don't understand something, don't be afraid to ask. Chances are that the rest of the class has the same question. If your question is too basic or requires too much class time to answer, the teacher will tell you so.

Sometimes the teacher will not answer you directly, but will give you a hint, something to think about so that you might guide yourself to your own answer. Don't interpret this as a refusal to answer your question. You must learn to think for yourself, and your teacher is helping you develop the analytical skills you need for success in physics.

Keep an Even Temper

A football team should not give up because they allow an early field goal. Similarly, you should not get upset at poor performance on a test or problem set. No one expects you to be perfect. Learn from your mistakes, and move on—it's too long a school year to let a single physics assignment affect your emotional state.

On the same note, however, a football team should not celebrate victory because it scores a first-quarter touchdown. You might have done well on this test, but there's the rest of a nine-month course to go. Congratulate yourself, then concentrate on the next assignment.

Don't Cram

Yes, we know that you got an "A" on your history final because, after you slept through class all semester, you studied for 15 straight hours the day before the test and learned everything. And, yes, we know you are willing to do the same thing this year for physics. We warn you, both from our and from others' experience: *it won't work.* Physics is not about memorization and regurgitation. Sure, there are some equations you need to memorize. But problem-solving skills cannot be learned overnight.

Furthermore, physics is cumulative. The topics you discuss in December rely on the principles you learned in September. If you don't understand basic vector analysis and free-body diagrams, how can you understand the relationship between an electric field (which is a vector quantity) and an electric force, or the multitude of other vector quantities that you will eventually study?

So, the answer is to keep up with the course. Spend some time on physics every night, even if that time is only a couple of minutes, even if you have no assignment due the next day. Spread your "cram time" over the entire semester.

Never Forget, Physics Is "Phun"

The purpose of all these problems, these equations, and these exams is to gain knowledge about physics—a deeper understanding of how the natural world works. Don't be so caught up in the grind of your coursework that you fail to say "Wow!" occasionally. Some of the things you're learning are truly amazing. Physics gives insight into some of humankind's most critical discoveries, our most powerful inventions, and our most fundamental technologies. Enjoy yourself. You have an opportunity to emerge from your physics course with wonderful and useful knowledge, and unparalleled intellectual insight. Do it.

CHAPTER 2

What You Need to Know About the AP Physics C Exams

IN THIS CHAPTER

Summary: Learn what topics are tested, how the test is scored, and basic test-taking information.

Key Ideas
✪ Most colleges will award credit for a score of 4 or 5, some for a 3.
✪ Multiple-choice questions account for half of your final score.
✪ There is no penalty for guessing on the multiple-choice questions. You should answer every question.
✪ Free-response questions account for half of your final score.
✪ Your composite score on the two test sections is converted to a score on the 1-to-5 scale.

Background Information

The AP Physics exam was first offered by the College Board in 1954. Since then, the number of students taking the test has grown rapidly. In 2015, more than 70,000 students took at least one of the AP Physics C exams, and those numbers go up every year.

Some Frequently Asked Questions About the AP Physics C Exams

Why Should I Take an AP Physics Exam?

Many of you take the AP Physics exam because you are seeking college credit. The majority of colleges and universities will award you some sort of credit for scoring a 4 or a 5. A smaller number of schools will even accept a 3 on the exam. This means you are one or two courses closer to graduation before you even start college!

Therefore, one compelling reason to take the AP exam is economic. How much does a college course cost, even at a relatively inexpensive school? You're talking several thousand dollars. If you can save those thousands of dollars by paying less than a hundred dollars now, why not do so?

Even if you do not score high enough to earn college credit, the fact that you elected to enroll in AP courses tells admission committees that you are a high achiever and serious about your education. In recent years, about 60% of students have scored a 3 or higher on their AP Physics C exam.

You'll hear a whole lot of misinformation about AP credit policies. Don't believe anything a friend (or even an adult) tells you; instead, find out for yourself. A good way to learn about the AP credit policy of the school you're interested in is to look it up on the College Board's official Web site, at http://collegesearch.collegeboard.com/apcreditpolicy/index.jsp. Even better, contact the registrar's office or the physics department chairman at the college directly.

What Are the Different AP Physics Courses?

You can take various AP Physics courses. They differ in both the range of topics covered and the level at which those topics are tested. Here's the rundown:

Physics 1 and Physics 2 (Algebra Based)

Physics 1 is intended to simulate the first semester of the standard algebra-based college physics course. It covers classical mechanics, waves, and circuits. Physics 2 is intended to simulate the second semester of the college course, covering electromagnetism, thermodynamics, fluids, and atomic physics. Although they mimic semester courses in college, each of these is a full-year high school course.

When the College Board says "algebra based," they mean it—not only is no calculus necessary, but no mathematics beyond definitions of the basic trig functions are required. Most of the Physics 1 and 2 exams require verbal, not mathematical, responses.

Physics 1 in particular is ideal for ALL college-bound high school students. For those who intend to major in math or the heavy-duty sciences, Physics 1 and Physics 2 serve as perfect introduction to college-level work. For those who want nothing to do with physics after high school, Physics 1 and Physics 2 are terrific terminal courses—you get exposure to many facets of physics at a rigorous yet understandable level.

Physics C

These courses are ONLY for those who have already taken a solid introductory physics course and are considering a career in math or science. Some schools teach Physics C as a follow-up to Physics 1, but as long as you've had a rigorous introduction to the subject, that introduction does not have to be at the AP level.

Physics C is two separate courses: (1) Newtonian Mechanics, and (2) Electricity and Magnetism. Of course, the Physics 1 and 2 courses cover these topics as well. However, the C courses go into greater depth and detail. The problems are more involved, and they demand a higher level of conceptual understanding. You can take either or both 90-minute Physics C exams.

The C courses require some calculus. Although much of the material can be handled without it, you should be taking a good calculus course concurrently.

Is Physics C Better Than Physics 1/2? Should I Take More Than One Exam?

We strongly recommend taking only the exam that your high school AP course prepared you for. Physics C is not considered "better" than Physics 1 in the eyes of colleges and scholarship committees; they are different courses with different intended audiences. It is far better to do well on the exam that your class prepared you for than to do poorly on multiple exams.

What Is the Format of the Exam?

Table 2.1 summarizes the format of the AP Physics C exams.

Table 2.1 AP Physics C exams

AP Physics C – Mechanics

SECTION	NUMBER OF QUESTIONS	TIME LIMIT
I. Multiple-Choice Questions	35	45 minutes
II. Free-Response Questions	3	45 minutes

AP Physics C – Electricity and Magnetism

SECTION	NUMBER OF QUESTIONS	TIME LIMIT
I. Multiple-Choice Questions	35	45 minutes
II. Free-Response Questions	3	45 minutes

Who Writes the AP Physics Exam?

Development of each AP exam is a multiyear effort that involves many education and testing professionals and students. At the heart of the effort is the AP Physics Development Committee, a group of college and high-school physics teachers who are typically asked to serve for three years. The committee and other physics teachers create a large pool of multiple-choice questions. With the help of the testing experts at Educational Testing Service (ETS), these questions are then pre-tested with college students for accuracy, appropriateness, clarity, and assurance that there is only one possible answer. The results of this pre-testing allow each question to be categorized by degree of difficulty. After several more months of development and refinement, Section I of the exam is ready to be administered.

The free-response questions that make up Section II go through a similar process of creation, modification, pre-testing, and final refinement so that the questions cover the necessary areas of material and are at an appropriate level of difficulty and clarity. The committee also makes a great effort to construct a free-response exam that will allow for clear and equitable grading by the AP readers.

At the conclusion of each AP reading and scoring of exams, the exam itself and the results are thoroughly evaluated by the committee and by ETS. In this way, the College Board can use the results to make suggestions for course development in high schools and to plan future exams.

What Topics Appear on the Exam?

The College Board, after consulting with physics teachers at all levels, develops a curriculum that covers material that college professors expect to cover in their first-year classes. Based on this outline of topics, the multiple-choice exams are written such that those topics are covered in proportion to their importance to the expected understanding of the student.

Confused? Suppose that faculty consultants agree that, say, atomic and nuclear physics is important to the physics curriculum, maybe to the tune of 10%. If 10% of the curriculum is devoted to atomic and nuclear physics, then you can expect roughly 10% of the exam will address atomic and nuclear physics. This includes both the multiple-choice and the free-response sections—so a topic that is not tested in the free-response section will have *extra* multiple-choice questions to make up the difference.

The following are the general outlines for the AP Physics curriculum and exams. Remember this is just a guide, and each year the exam differs slightly in the percentages.

AP PHYSICS C, MECHANICS

A.	Kinematics	18%
B.	Newton's Laws	20%
C.	Work, Energy, Power	14%
D.	Linear Momentum	12%
E.	Rotational Motion	18%
F.	Oscillations and Gravitation	18%

AP PHYSICS C, ELECTRICITY AND MAGNETISM

A.	Electrostatics	30%
B.	Conductors, Capacitors, Dielectrics	14%
C.	Electric Circuits	20%
D.	Magnetic Fields	20%
E.	Electromagnetism	16%

What Types of Questions Are Asked on the Exam?

The multiple-choice questions tend to focus either on your understanding of concepts or on your mastery of equations and their meaning. Here's an example of a "concept" multiple-choice question.

Which of the following is an expression of conservation of charge?

(A) Kirchoff's loop rule
(B) Kirchoff's junction rule
(C) Ohm's law
(D) Snell's law
(E) Kinetic theory of gases

The answer is **B**. Kirchoff's junction rule states that whatever charge comes in must come out. If you don't remember Kirchoff's junction rule, turn to Chapter 19, Circuits.

And here's an example of an "equation" multiple-choice question.

If the separation between plates in a parallel-plate capacitor is tripled, what happens to the capacitance?

(A) It is reduced by a factor of 9.
(B) It is reduced by a factor of 3.
(C) It remains the same.
(D) It increases by a factor of 3.
(E) It increases by a factor of 9.

The answer is **B**. For this kind of question, you either remember the equation for the capacitance of a parallel-plate capacitor,

$$C = \frac{\varepsilon_0 A}{d}$$

or you don't. For help, turn to Chapter 6, Memorizing Equations in the Shower.

You are given a sheet that contains a bunch of physical constants (like the mass of a proton), SI units, and trigonometric values (like "tan 45° = 1"). All in all, this sheet is pretty useless—you'll probably only refer to it during the course of the test if you need to look up an obscure constant. That doesn't happen as often as you might think.

The free-response questions take 15 minutes apiece to answer, and they test both your understanding of concepts and your mastery of equations. Some of the free-response questions ask you to design or interpret the results of an experimental setup; others are more theoretical. Luckily, in addition to the constant sheet, you will also get a sheet that contains every equation you will ever need. You still need to have your equations memorized! It is not useful to hunt through the equation sheet trying to find the one you need, any more than it's a useful writing strategy to hunt randomly through the dictionary trying to find an appropriate word.

We talk in much more detail about both the multiple-choice and the free-response sections of the test later, in Step 5, so don't worry if this is all a bit overwhelming now.

Who Grades My AP Physics Exam?

Every June, a group of physics teachers gathers for a week to assign grades to your hard work. Each of these "readers" spends a day or so getting trained on one question—and one question only. Because each reader becomes an expert on that question, and because each exam book is anonymous, this process provides a consistent and unbiased scoring of that question.

During a typical day of grading, a random sample of each reader's scores is selected and crosschecked by other experienced "Table Leaders" to ensure that the consistency is maintained throughout the day and the week. Each reader's scores on a given question are also statistically analyzed, to make sure they are not giving scores that are significantly higher or lower than the mean scores given by other readers of that question. All measures are taken to maintain consistency and fairness for your benefit.

Will My Exam Remain Anonymous?

Absolutely. Even if your high-school teacher happens to randomly read your booklet, there is virtually no way he or she will know it is you. To the reader, each student is a number, and to the computer, each student is a bar code.

What About That Permission Box on the Back?

The College Board uses some exams to help train high-school teachers so that they can help the next generation of physics students to avoid common mistakes. If you check this box, you simply give permission to use your exam in this way. Even if you give permission, your anonymity is still maintained.

How Is My Multiple-Choice Section Scored?

The multiple-choice section of each physics exam is worth half of your final score. Your answer sheet is run through the computer, which adds up your correct responses. Effective with the May 2011 AP exam, the guessing penalty (which involved subtracting a fraction of a point for incorrect responses) has been eliminated. Now the number of correct responses is your raw score on the multiple-choice section.

If I Don't Know the Answer, Should I Guess?

Yes. There is no penalty for guessing.

How Is My Free-Response Section Scored?

Your performance on the free-response section is also worth half of your final score. On the Physics C exams, this section consists of three questions, worth 15 points each. Your score on the free-response section is simply the sum of your scores on each problem.

How Is My Final Grade Determined and What Does It Mean?

Each section counts for 50% of the exam. The total composite score is thus a weighted sum of the multiple-choice and the free-response sections. In the end, when all of the numbers have been crunched, the Chief Faculty Consultant converts the range of composite scores to the 5-point scale of the AP grades. This conversion is not a true curve—it's not that there's some target percentage of 5s to give out. This means you're not competing against other test takers. Rather, the 5-point scale is adjusted each year to reflect the same standards as in previous years. The goal is that students who earn 5s this year are just as strong as those who earned 5s in 2000 or 2010.

The tables at the end of the practice exams in this book give you a rough example of a conversion, and as you complete the practice exams, you should use this to give yourself a hypothetical grade. Keep in mind that the conversion changes slightly every year to adjust for the difficulty of the questions—but, generally, it takes only about 60% of the available points to earn a 5.

Finally, you should receive your grade in early July.

How Do I Register and How Much Does It Cost?

If you are enrolled in AP Physics in your high school, your teacher will provide all of these details, but a quick summary here can't hurt. After all, you do not have to enroll in the AP course to register for and complete the AP exam. When in doubt, the best source of information is the College Board's Web site: www.collegeboard.com.

In 2016, the fee for taking the exams was $92. (This means $92 *each* for Physics C Mechanics and for Physics C Electricity and Magnetism.) Students who demonstrate financial need may receive a refund to offset the cost of testing. The amount of the fee and the refund changes a little from year to year. You can learn more about the exam fee and fee reductions and subsidies from the coordinator of your AP program or by checking specific information on the official website: www.collegeboard.com.

I know that seems like a lot of money just for a test. But, you should think of this $92 as the biggest bargain you'll ever find. Why? Most colleges will give you a few credit hours for a good score. Do you think you can find a college that offers those credit hours for less than $92? Usually you're talking hundreds of dollars per credit hour! You're probably saving thousands of dollars by earning credits via AP.

There are also several optional fees that must be paid if you want your scores rushed to you or if you wish to receive multiple-grade reports. Don't worry about doing that unless your college demands it. (What, you think your scores are going to change if you don't find them out right away?)

The coordinator of the AP program at your school will inform you where and when you will take the exam. If you live in a small community, your exam may not be administered at your school, so be sure to get this information.

What If My School Only Offers Physics 1/2 and Not AP Physics C, or Vice Versa? Or, What If My School Doesn't Offer AP Physics at All?

Ideally, you should enroll in the AP class for the exam you wish to take. But, not every school offers exactly what you want to take.

If your school offers one exam or the other, you are much better off taking the exam for which your teacher prepared you. Sure, if you are an absolute top Physics 1 student, you can probably pass the Physics C exam with some extra preparation; but if you're a top Physics 1 student, why not just earn your 5 on the 1 exam rather than take a chance at merely passing the C exam? Or, if you've been preparing for Physics C, you might think you have a better chance for success on the "easier" 1 exam. But, the 1 exam tests different topics and is in a completely different style than Physics C so you're still most likely better off on the exam your class taught toward.

If your school doesn't offer either AP course, then you should look at the content outline and talk to your teacher. Chances are, you will want to take the 1 exam, and chances are you will have to do a good bit of independent work to learn the topics that your class didn't discuss. But, if you are a diligent student in a rigorous course, you will probably be able to do fine.

What Should I Bring to the Exam?

On exam day, I suggest bringing the following items:

- Several pencils and an eraser that doesn't leave smudges.
- Black or blue colored pens for the free-response section.[1]
- A ruler or straightedge.
- A scientific calculator with fresh batteries. (A graphing calculator is not necessary.)
- A watch so that you can monitor your time. You never know if the exam room will have a clock on the wall. Make sure you turn off the beep that goes off on the hour.

---

[1]You may use a pencil, but there's no need . . . you should not erase incorrect work, you should cross it out. Not only does crossing out take less time than erasing, but if you erase by mistake, you lose all your work. But, if you change your mind about crossing something out, just circle your work and write the reader a note: "Grade this!"

- Your school code.
- Your photo identification and Social Security number.
- Tissues.
- Your quiet confidence that you are prepared.

What Should I NOT Bring to the Exam?

Leave the following at home:

- A cell phone, PDA, or walkie-talkie.
- Books, a dictionary, study notes, flash cards, highlighting pens, correction fluid, etc., *including this book*. Study aids won't help you the morning of the exam . . . end your studying in the very early evening the night before.
- Portable music of any kind. No iPods, MP3 players, CD players, cassette players, or record players.
- Clothing with any physics terminology or equations on it.
- Panic or fear. It's natural to be nervous, but you can comfort yourself that you have used this book well and that there is no room for fear on your exam.

CHAPTER 3

How to Plan Your Time

IN THIS CHAPTER

Summary: What to study for the Physics C exam, plus three schedules to help you plan.

Key Ideas
✪ Focus your attention and study time on those topics that are most likely to increase your score.
✪ Study the topics that you're afraid will appear, and relax about those that you're best at.
✪ Don't study so widely that you don't get good at some specific type of problem.

The AP Physics exam is held on a Monday afternoon in mid-May. You may think that you just started your exam preparation today, when you opened this book . . . but, in reality, you have been getting ready for the AP test all year. The AP exam is an authentic test of your physics knowledge and skills. Your AP Physics *class* presumably is set up to teach those skills. So, don't give your class short shrift. Diligent attention to your class lectures, demonstrations, and assignments can only save you preparation time in the long run.

Of course, you may not be satisfied with the quantity or quality of your in-class instruction. And even if your class is the best in the country, you will still need a reminder of what you covered way back at the beginning of the year. That's where this book, and extracurricular AP exam preparation, are useful.

What Should I Study?

You will hear plenty of poorly-thought-out advice about how to deal with the vast amounts of material on the AP Physics exams, especially if you are taking both Mechanics and E and M.

Fact is, in the month or two before the exam, you do not have enough time to re-teach yourself the entire course. So, you ask a presumed expert, "What should I study?"

Bad Answer Number 1: *"Everything."*

This logic says, every topic listed in the AP course description is guaranteed to show up somewhere on the exam, whether in the free-response or the multiple-choice sections. So, you must study everything. That's ridiculous, I say to my students. You've been studying "everything" all year. You need to focus your last-month study on those topics that are most likely to increase your score.

Bad Answer Number 2: *"Let me use my crystal ball to tell you exactly what types of problems will show up on this year's free-response exam. Study these."*

I know teachers who think they're oracles . . . "An RC circuit was on last year's test, so it won't be on this year's. And, we haven't seen point charges for two straight years, so we'll definitely see one this year."[1] Suffice it to say that a teacher who is not on the test development committee has no possible way of divining which specific types of problems will appear on the exam, any more than a college basketball "expert" can say with confidence which teams will make the final four. And, even if you *did* know which topics would be covered on the free-response section, all of the other topics must appear on the multiple-choice section! So don't choose your study strategy based on an oracle's word.

Good Answer: *Do a Cost-Benefit Analysis*

You know how much time you have left. Use that limited time to study the topics that are most likely to increase your score. The trick is identifying those topics. Start with honest, hyperbole-free answers to two questions, in the following manner.

Imagine that the AP Physics Genie[2] has granted you two boons. You may choose one type of problem that *will* be tested on the free-response exam; and you may choose one type of problem that will *not* appear on the free response. Now, answer:

1. What topic or problem type do you ask the genie to put on the exam?
2. What topic or problem type do you forbid the genie to put on the exam?

If you are extremely comfortable, say, solving kinematics and projectile problems, why would you spend any time on those? It won't hurt to give yourself a quick reminder of fundamental concepts, but in-depth study of what you know well is a waste of valuable time. On the other hand, if you're *un*comfortable with, say, Energy-Position diagrams, then spend a couple of evenings learning how to deal with them. Study the topics you're afraid will appear; relax about those you're best at.[3]

This is an important point—don't study so broadly that you don't get good at some specific type of problem. Use Chapter 8's drill exercises, or the end-of-chapter examples in this book, or some similar handout from your teacher, or a subset of your textbook's

---

[1] A moment's thought will find some inconsistency in the above logic.

[2] . . . who is not a real person . . .

[3] I know many wiseguys will say, "There's nothing I'm comfortable with; I'm bad at everything." That's called defeatism, and you shouldn't tolerate that from yourself. If you were to tell your softball coach, "Hey, I'm going to strike out at the plate, let grounders go through my legs, and drop all the fly balls hit to me," would the coach let you play? More likely, he or she would kick you off the team! When you pretend that you can't do anything in physics, you do yourself a tremendous disservice. Pick *something* that you can figure out, *some* topic you can develop confidence in, and go from there.

end-of-chapter problems, to keep practicing until you actually are *hoping* to see certain types of problems on your test. That's far more useful than just skimming around.

For the mechanics exam, focus your preparation on Chapter 16, Rotational Motion. For the E&M exam, understand how to use Gauss's law and the time-varying circuits: RC, RL, and LC.

Though there are other subtopics that are unique to Physics C, extra preparation on these topics will probably benefit you the most, because they are (a) far enough removed from first-year material that they truly require extra work and (b) understandable with a reasonable amount of supplemental study.

Have a Plan for the Exam

When it comes to the last few days before the exam, think about your mental approach. You can do very well on the exam even if you have difficulty with a few of the topics. But, know ahead of time which topics you are weak on. If you have trouble, say, with electric fields, plan on skipping electric fields multiple-choice questions so as to concentrate on those that you'll have more success on. Don't fret about this decision—just make it ahead of time, and follow your plan. On the free-response test, though, be sure to approach every problem. Sure, it's okay to decide that you will not waste time on electric fields due to point charges. But if you read the entire problem, you might find that parts (d) and (e) are simple $F = qE$ questions, or ask about some aspect of electricity that you understand just fine.

Understand Physics First, Then AP Physics C

Be sure you understand physics before preparing specifically for the AP Physics C exams.

I've taught Physics C with great success for many years. But, not just anyone can sign up for my Physics C class. I only take students who have completed Physics 1, and for good reason. The C course is very deep. It requires that you have not just an idea about, but a true *mastery* of, Physics 1- and 2-level material.

Now, your first physics course might not have formally been labeled "Advanced Placement." Any rigorous introductory class is sufficient preparation for Physics C. Nevertheless, before you even begin to discuss a calculus-based approach to problem-solving, you MUST have a solid conceptual understanding of physics at the introductory level.

My advice to my Physics C students has always been to know the basics. An average difficulty Physics C question is equivalent to an above-average (and more calculational) Physics 1 or 2 question. Someone who knows physics cold at the 1/2 level could do reasonably well on the Physics C exam.

Therefore, you start your preparation by answering the following with brutal honesty: "Could I solve *any* Physics 1 level mechanics, or Physics 2 E&M, problem? Would I recognize the appropriate equations, relationships, and definitions instantly, without wrinkling my forehead for more than a few seconds?"

If the answer is "no," then the most efficient way to improve your Physics C performance is to learn the fundamentals. Use your algebra-based physics textbook or *5 Steps to a 5: AP Physics 1*. There's no substitute for a thorough knowledge of basic physics principles. Don't worry about calculus concepts, don't worry about the special Physics C–specific material, just work until you have the material down at the introductory level. Even if this is the only exam preparation you have time for, you will be far better served by shoring up your fundamentals than by grasping at more difficult concepts.

Once you are rock-solid on your algebra-based physics, then it's time to think about the advanced topics on the C exam.

A Word About Calculus

Yes, Physics C is "calculus-based" physics. And yes, you will be asked to evaluate a few integrals and/or derivatives here and there. But it is vitally important that you understand that Physics C is *not* a math course. The development committee is not trying to find out whether you know how to evaluate $\int \sin x \cdot dx$. Rather, they are looking to see whether you understand how to apply calculus concepts to physics problems. What do we mean by calculus concepts? Two things.

1. Recognizing When a Calculus Approach Is Necessary

In algebra-based physics you learned that the work done by a force is equal to that force times parallel displacement. You will use that relationship in Physics C, too. However, in Physics C, you must recognize the limitations of that relationship: you can only multiply force times parallel displacement *when the force is constant*. If the force is changing, you must use calculus concepts, knowing that work is the integral of force with respect to distance.

Physics 1-style situations, in which calculus is not necessary, *will* appear on the Physics C exam. Your challenge is to recognize when a quantity is changing in such a way that calculus must be used.

2. Understanding the Conceptual and Graphical Meanings of Integrals and Derivatives

On a graph, an integral is the area under the graph; a derivative is the slope of a graph at a given point. Consider a problem in which you're asked to find the work done by a non-constant force. If you're given a graph of that force vs. position, then all you've got to do is find the area under the graph—*no integration necessary*.

You should have an idea of the meaning of a derivative or integral, even without evaluating it, or without graphing the function in question. This isn't as hard as it looks! Consider the following multiple-choice problem:

A box is pushed across a frictionless table a distance of 9 m. The horizontal force pushing the box obeys the function $F(x) = 50(5 - \sqrt{x})$, where F is in newtons and x is in meters. How much work is done by the pushing force?

(A) 2500 J
(B) 1350 N
(C) 900 J
(D) 250 J
(E) 90 J

"Whoa," you say. "This is a nasty calculus problem, especially without a calculator." Your first instinct is to take the integral $\int_{0}^{9} 50(5 - \sqrt{x}) \, dx$. That becomes nasty toot sweet. No chance you can get that done in the minute or so you have on a multiple-choice problem. So, what to do?

You know in your bones that if this force were constant, then all you'd have to do is multiply the force by 9 m. This force is not constant. But, we can approximate an *average* force from the function, can't we? Sure . . . the initial force is $50(5 - 0) = 250$ N. The force at the end of the push is $50(5 - \sqrt{9}) = 100$ N. So, the average force is somewhere in between 100 N

and 250 N.[4] Guess that this average force is between 150 N and 200 N. That gives work done between (150 N)(9 m) and (200 N)(9 m), or between 1350 N and 1800 N. Only choice B fits.

Note that ANY kind of estimate of the average force would still get you close to the correct answer. This is a classic calculus *concepts* question . . . it's not about evaluating the integral, it's about understanding the meaning of work.

What Specific Calculus Methods Do I Have to Know?

You will be expected to evaluate straightforward integrals and derivatives. Remember, this is not a math test—the exam is not trying to test your math skills but rather your ability to apply calculus to physical situations. This means the actual integrals and derivatives will not be from the most difficult questions on your AP Calculus BC test!

You should know:

- Derivatives and integrals of polynomial functions
- Derivatives and integrals of sin x and cos x—but we've never seen questions that require trigonometric identities on the exam
- Derivatives and integrals with ln x or e^x
- Derivatives using the chain rule
- Integration with u-substitution

If you need a review of these topics, take a look at your calculus book or at *5 Steps to a 5: AP Calculus AB*.

Two other mathematical techniques are necessary on the Physics C exam:

- Basic first- and second-order differential equations
- Integrals involving linear density

These topics are covered briefly in this book.

Three Different Study Schedules

MONTH	PLAN A: FULL SCHOOL YEAR	PLAN B: ONE SEMESTER	PLAN C: 6 WEEKS
September–October	Chapters 1–5	——	——
November	Chapters 9–10, Chapter 6	——	——
December	Chapters 11–13	——	——
January	Chapters 14–15	Chapters 2–6	——
February	Chapters 16–17	Chapters 9–13	——
March	Chapters 18–19	Chapters 14–17	——
April	Chapter 20 Chapters 7–8	Chapters 18–20	Skim Chapters 9–18, Chapter 6
May	Review everything; Practice Exams	Chapters 7–8; Review everything; Practice Exams	Skim Chapters 19–20, Chapters 7–8; Practice Exams

---

[4]Not *exactly* in between, because this function is not linear. However, you'll see that any approximation of the average force will do here.

Plan A: You Have a Full School Year to Prepare

Although its primary purpose is to prepare you for the AP Physics exam you will take in May, this book can enrich your study of physics, your analytical skills, and your problem-solving abilities.

SEPTEMBER–OCTOBER (Check off the activities as you complete them.)
— Determine the study mode (A, B, or C) that applies to you.
— Carefully read Steps 1 and 2 of this book.
— Work through the diagnostic exam.
— Get on the web and take a look at the AP Web site(s).
— Skim Step 4. (Reviewing the topics covered in this section will be part of your year-long preparation.)
— Buy a few color highlighters.
— Flip through the entire book. Break the book in. Write in it. Highlight it.
— Get a clear picture of what your own school's AP Physics curriculum is.
— Begin to use this book as a resource to supplement the classroom learning.

NOVEMBER (The first 10 weeks have elapsed.)
— Read and study Chapter 9, A Bit About Vectors.
— Read and study Chapter 10, Free-Body Diagrams and Equilibrium.
— Read Chapter 6, Memorizing Equations in the Shower.

DECEMBER
— Read and study Chapter 11, Kinematics.
— Read and study Chapter 12, Newton's Second Law, $F_{net} = ma$.
— Read and study Chapter 13, Momentum.
— Review Chapters 9–10.

JANUARY (20 weeks have elapsed.)
— Read and study Chapter 14, Energy Conservation.
— Read and study Chapter 15, Gravitation and Circular Motion.
— Review Chapters 9–13.

FEBRUARY
— Read and study Chapter 16, Rotational Motion (for Physics C students only).
— Read and study Chapter 17, Simple Harmonic Motion.
— Review Chapters 9–15.

MARCH (30 weeks have now elapsed.)
— Read and study Chapter 18, Electrostatics.
— Read and study Chapter 19, Circuits.
— Review Chapters 9–20.

APRIL
— Read and study Chapter 20, Magnetism.
— Review Chapters 9–19.
— Read Chapters 7–8 carefully!

MAY (first 2 weeks) (THIS IS IT!)
— Review Chapters 9–20—all the material!!!
— Take the Practice Exams, and score yourself.
— Get a good night's sleep before the exam. Fall asleep knowing that you are well prepared.

GOOD LUCK ON THE TEST.

Plan B: You Have One Semester to Prepare

Working under the assumption that you've completed one semester of your physics course, the following calendar will use those skills you've been practicing to prepare you for the May exam.

JANUARY–FEBRUARY
— Carefully read Steps 1 and 2 of this book.
— Work through the diagnostic exam.
— Read and study Chapter 9, A Bit About Vectors.
— Read and study Chapter 10, Free-Body Diagrams and Equilibrium.
— Read and study Chapter 11, Kinematics.
— Read and study Chapter 12, Newton's Second Law, $F_{net} = ma$.
— Read and study Chapter 13, Momentum.
— Read Chapter 6, Memorizing Equations in the Shower.

MARCH (10 weeks to go.)
— Read and study Chapter 14, Energy Conservation.
— Read and study Chapter 15, Gravitation and Circular Motion.
— Read and study Chapter 16, Rotational Motion.

— Read and study Chapter 17, Simple Harmonic Motion.
— Review Chapters 9–13.

APRIL
— Read and study Chapter 18, Electrostatics.
— Read and study Chapter 19, Circuits.
— Read and study Chapter 20, Magnetism.
— Review Chapters 9–17.

MAY (first 2 weeks) (THIS IS IT!)
— Review Chapters 9–20—all the material!!!
— Read Chapters 7–8 carefully!
— Take the Practice Exams and score yourself.
— Get a good night's sleep before the exam. Fall asleep knowing that you are well prepared.

GOOD LUCK ON THE TEST.

Plan C: You Have Six Weeks to Prepare

At this point, we assume that you have been building your physics knowledge base for more than six months (if you're a Physics C student, you've probably been studying physics for more than a year). You will, therefore, use this book primarily as a specific guide to the AP Physics exam. Given the time constraints, now is not the time to try to expand your AP Physics knowledge. Rather, you should focus on and refine what you already do know.

APRIL 1–15
— Skim Steps 1 and 2 of this book.
— Skim Chapters 9–13.
— Skim and highlight the Glossary at the end of the book.
— Read Chapter 6, and work on memorizing equations.

APRIL 16–MAY 1
— Skim Chapters 14–18.
— Continue to work on memorizing equations.

MAY (first 2 weeks) (THIS IS IT!)
— Skim Chapters 19–20.
— Carefully go over the Rapid Review sections of Chapters 10–20.
— Read Chapter 7.
— Take the Practice Exams and score yourself.
— Get a good night's sleep before the exam. Fall asleep knowing that you are well prepared.

GOOD LUCK ON THE TEST.

STEP **2**

Determine Your Test Readiness

CHAPTER 4

Fundamentals Quizzes

IN THIS CHAPTER

Summary: To test your readiness for the exam, take these short quizzes on these two fundamental topics of AP Physics.

Key Ideas

✪ Find out what you know—and what you don't know—about mechanics.

✪ Find out what you know—and what you don't know—about electricity and magnetism.

✪ Focus your exam preparation time only on the areas you don't already know well.

These short quizzes may be helpful if you're looking for some additional review of the most fundamental topics in AP Physics. If you can get all these right, you are READY for the exam! The answers are printed at the end of this chapter.

Mechanics Quiz

1. What is the mass of a block with weight 100 N?

2. Give the equations for two types of potential energy, identifying each.

3. When an object of mass m is on an incline of angle θ, one must break the weight of an object into components parallel and perpendicular to the incline.
   i.   What is the component of the weight parallel to the incline?_____
   ii. What is the component of the weight perpendicular to the incline?_____

4. Write two expressions for work, including the definition of work and the work-energy principle.

5. Quickly identify as a vector or a scalar:

   _____ acceleration   _____ force   _____ momentum
   _____ velocity   _____ speed   _____ displacement
   _____ work   _____ mass   _____ kinetic energy

6. Name at least four things that can NEVER go on a free-body diagram.

7. Write two expressions for impulse. What are the units of impulse?

8. In what kind of collision is momentum conserved? In what kind of collision is kinetic energy conserved?

9. What is the mass of a block with weight W?

10. A ball is thrown straight up. At the peak of its flight, what is the ball's acceleration? Be sure to give both magnitude and direction.

11. A mass experiences a force vector with components 30 N to the right, 40 N down. Explain how to determine the magnitude and direction (angle) of the force vector.

12. Write the definition of the coefficient of friction, μ. What are the units of μ?

13. How do you find acceleration from a velocity-time graph?

14. How do you find displacement from a velocity-time graph?

15. How do you find velocity from a position-time graph?

16. An object has a positive acceleration. Explain *briefly* how to determine whether the object is speeding up, slowing down, or moving with constant speed.

17. Given the velocity of an object, how do you tell which direction that object is moving?

18. When is the gravitational force on an object mg? When is the gravitational force Gm_1m_2/r^2?

19. What is the direction of the net force on an object that moves in a circle at constant speed?

20. Under what conditions is the equation $x - x_0 = v_0t + \frac{1}{2}at^2$ valid? Give a specific situation in which this equation might seem to be valid, but is NOT.

Electricity and Magnetism Quiz

1. Given the charge of a particle and the electric field experienced by that particle, give the equation to determine the electric force acting on the particle.

2. Given the charge of a particle and the magnetic field experienced by that particle, give the equation to determine the magnetic force acting on the particle.

3. What are the units of magnetic flux? What are the units of EMF?

4. A wire carries a current to the left, as shown below. What is the direction and magnitude of the magnetic field produced by the wire at point P?

5. When is the equation kQ/r^2 valid? What is this an equation for?

6. The electric field at point P is 100 N/C; the field at point Q, 1 meter away from point P, is 200 N/C. A point charge of +1 C is placed at point P. What is the magnitude of the electric force experienced by this charge?

7. Can a current be induced in a wire if the flux through the wire is zero? Explain.

8. True or false: In a uniform electric field pointing to the right, a negatively charged particle will move to the left. If true, justify with an equation; if false, explain the flaw in reasoning.

9. Which is a vector and which is a scalar: electric field and electric potential?

10. Fill in the blank with either "parallel" or "series":

   a. Voltage across resistors in _____ must be the same for each.
   b. Current through resistors in _____ must be the same for each.
   c. Voltage across capacitors in _____ must be the same for each.
   d. Charge stored on capacitors in _____ must be the same for each.

11. A uniform electric field acts to the right. In which direction will each of these particles accelerate?

   a. proton
   b. positron (same mass as electron, but opposite charge)
   c. neutron
   d. anti-proton (same mass as proton, but opposite charge)

12. A uniform magnetic field acts to the right. In which direction will each of these particles accelerate, assuming they enter the field moving toward the top of the page?

   a. proton
   b. positron (same mass as electron, but opposite charge)
   c. neutron
   d. anti-proton (same mass as proton, but opposite charge)

13. How do you find the potential energy of an electric charge?

Answers to Mechanics Quiz

1. Weight is mg. So, mass is weight divided by g, which would be 100 N/(10 N/kg) = 10 kg.

2. PE = mgh, gravitational potential energy;
   PE = $\frac{1}{2} kx^2$, potential energy of a spring.

3. i. $mg \sin \theta$ is parallel to the incline.
   ii. $mg \cos \theta$ is perpendicular to the incline.

4. The definition of work is work = force times parallel displacement. The work-energy principle states that net work = change in kinetic energy.

5. vectors: acceleration, force, momentum, velocity, displacement

   scalars: speed, work, mass, kinetic energy

6. Only forces acting on an object and that have a single, specific source can go on free-body diagrams. Some of the things that cannot go on a free-body diagram but that students often put there by mistake:

motion	mass	acceleration	*ma*
centripetal force	velocity	inertia	

7. Impulse is force times time interval, and also change in momentum. Impulse has units either of newton·seconds or kilogram·meters/second.

8. Momentum is conserved in *all* collisions. Kinetic energy is conserved only in elastic collisions.

9. Using the reasoning from question #1, if weight is *mg*, then $m = W/g$.

10. The acceleration of a projectile is *always g*; i.e., 10 m/s², downward. Even though the velocity is instantaneously zero, the velocity is still changing, so the acceleration is *not* zero. (By the way, the answer "−10 m/s²" is wrong unless you have clearly and specifically defined the down direction as negative for this problem.)

11. The magnitude of the resultant force is found by placing the component vectors tip-to-tail. This gives a right triangle, so the magnitude is given by the Pythagorean theorem, 50 N. The angle of the resultant force is found by taking the inverse tangent of the vertical component over the horizontal component, $\tan^{-1}(40/30)$. This gives the angle measured from the horizontal.

12.
$$\mu = \frac{F_f}{F_n}$$

   friction force divided by normal force. μ has no units.

13. Acceleration is the slope of a velocity-time graph.

14. Displacement is the area under a velocity-time graph (i.e., the area between the graph and the horizontal axis).

15. Velocity is the slope of a position-time graph. If the position-time graph is curved, then instantaneous velocity is the slope of the tangent line to the graph.

16. Because acceleration is not zero, the object *cannot* be moving with constant speed. If the signs of acceleration and velocity are the same (here, if velocity is positive), the object is speeding up. If the signs of acceleration and velocity are different (here, if velocity is negative), the object is slowing down.

17. An object *always* moves in the direction indicated by the velocity.

18. Near the surface of a planet, *mg* gives the gravitational force. Newton's law of gravitation, Gm_1m_2/r^2, is valid everywhere in the universe. (It turns out that *g* can be found by calculating GM_{planet}/R_{planet}^2, where R_{planet} is the planet's radius.)

19. An object in uniform circular motion experiences a *centripetal,* meaning "center seeking," force. This force must be directed to the center of the circle.

20. This and all three kinematics equations are valid only when acceleration is constant. So, for example, this equation can NOT be used to find the distance travelled by a mass attached to a spring. The spring force changes as the mass moves; thus, the acceleration of the mass is changing, and kinematics equations are not valid. (On a problem where kinematics equations aren't valid, conservation of energy usually is what you need.)

Answers to Electricity and Magnetism Quiz

1. $F = qE$.

2. $F = qvB \sin \theta$.

3. Magnetic flux is BA, so the units are tesla·meters^2 (or, alternatively, webers). EMF is a voltage, so the units are volts.

4. Point your right thumb in the direction of the current, i.e., to the left. Your fingers point in the direction of the magnetic field. This field wraps around the wire, pointing into the page above the wire and out of the page below the wire. Since point P is below the wire, the field points out of the page.

5. This equation is only valid when a point charge produces an electric field. (Careful—if you just said "point charge," you're not entirely correct. If a point charge experiences an electric field produced by something else, this equation is irrelevant.) It is an equation for the electric field produced by the point charge.

6. Do *not* use $E = kQ/r^2$ here because the electric field is known. So, the source of the electric field is irrelevant—just use $F = qE$ to find that the force on the charge is (1 C)(100 N/C) = 100 N. (The charge is placed at point P, so anything happening at point Q is irrelevant.)

7. Yes! Induced EMF depends on the *change* in flux. So, imagine that the flux is changing rapidly from one direction to the other. For a brief moment, flux will be zero; but flux is still changing at that moment. (And, of course, the induced current will be the EMF divided by the resistance of the wire.)

8. False. The negative particle will be *forced* to the left. But the particle could have entered the field while moving to the right . . . in that case, the particle would continue moving to the right, but would slow down.

9. Electric field is a vector, so fields produced in different directions can cancel. Electric potential is a scalar, so direction is irrelevant.

10. Voltage across resistors in parallel must be the same for each.
    Current through resistors in series must be the same for each.
    Voltage across capacitors in parallel must be the same for each.
    Charge stored on capacitors in series must be the same for each.

11. The positively charged proton will accelerate with the field, to the right.
    The positively charged positron will accelerate with the field, to the right.
    The uncharged neutron will not accelerate.
    The negatively charged anti-proton will accelerate against the field, to the left.

12. Use the right-hand rule for each:
The positively charged proton will accelerate into the page.
The positively charged positron will accelerate into the page.
The uncharged neutron will not accelerate.
The negatively charged anti-proton will accelerate out of the page.

13. If you know the electric potential experienced by the charge, $PE = qV$.

What Do I Know, and What Don't I Know?

I'll bet you didn't get every question on both of these fundamentals quizzes correct. That's okay. The whole point of these quizzes is for you to determine where to focus your study.

It's a common mistake to "study" by doing 20 problems on a topic on which you are already comfortable. But that's not studying . . . that's a waste of time. You don't need to drill yourself on topics you already understand! It's also probably a mistake to attack what for you is the toughest concept in physics right before the exam. Virtually every student has that one chapter they just don't get, however hard they try. That's okay.

The fundamentals quizzes that you just took can tell you exactly what you should and should not study. Did you give correct answers with full confidence in the correctness of your response? In that case, you're done with that topic. No more work is necessary. The place to focus your efforts is on the topics where either you gave wrong answers that you thought were right, or right answers that you weren't really sure about.

Now, take the diagnostic test. Once you've used the fundamentals quizzes and diagnostic test to identify the specific content areas you want to work on, proceed to the review in Chapters 9–20. Read a chapter, work through the examples in the chapter, and attempt some of the problems at the end of the chapter. Then come back to these fundamentals quizzes. When you respond to every question confidently, you are ready.

CHAPTER 5

Take a Diagnostic Test

IN THIS CHAPTER

Summary: Assess your strengths and weaknesses by answering some sample questions and then reading the answers and explanations, so you'll know where to focus your efforts when preparing for the exam.

› Diagnostic Test

Kinematics

1. Which of the following must be true of an object that is slowing down?

   (A) Its acceleration must be negative.
   (B) Its velocity must be smaller than its acceleration.
   (C) It must experience more than one force.
   (D) Its acceleration and its velocity must be in opposite directions.
   (E) Its velocity must be negative.

2. A baseball is thrown straight up. It reaches a peak height of 15 m, measured from the ground, in a time of 1.7 s. Treating "up" as the positive direction, what is the acceleration of the ball when it reaches its peak height?

   (A) 0 m/s^2
   (B) $+8.8 \text{ m/s}^2$
   (C) -8.8 m/s^2
   (D) $+9.8 \text{ m/s}^2$
   (E) -9.8 m/s^2

Newton's laws

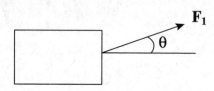

3. What is the vertical component of $\mathbf{F}_1$ in the above diagram?

   (A) $\frac{1}{2}\mathbf{F}_1$
   (B) $\mathbf{F}_1$
   (C) $\mathbf{F}_1 \cos \theta$
   (D) $\mathbf{F}_1 \sin \theta$
   (E) $\mathbf{F}_1 \tan \theta$

4. The box pictured above moves at constant speed to the left. Which of the following is correct?

   (A) The situation is impossible. Because more forces act right, the block must move to the right.
   (B) $T_3 > T_1 + T_2$
   (C) $T_3 < T_1 + T_2$
   (D) $T_3 = T_1 + T_2$
   (E) A relationship among the three tensions cannot be determined from the information given.

The following diagram relates to Questions 5 and 6.

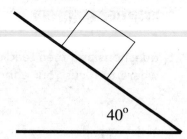

A block of mass m is sliding up a frictionless incline, as shown above. The block's initial velocity is 3 m/s up the plane.

5. What is the component of the weight parallel to the plane?

   (A) mg
   (B) $mg \cos 40°$
   (C) $mg \sin 40°$
   (D) $g \sin 40°$
   (E) $g \cos 40°$

6. What is the acceleration of the mass?

   (A) 3 m/s^2, up the plane
   (B) $mg \sin 40°$, up the plane
   (C) $mg \sin 40°$, down the plane
   (D) $g \sin 40°$, up the plane
   (E) $g \sin 40°$, down the plane

GO ON TO THE NEXT PAGE

Work/Energy

7. Which of the following is a scalar?

   (A) velocity
   (B) acceleration
   (C) displacement
   (D) kinetic energy
   (E) force

8. A 500-g block on a flat tabletop slides 2.0 m to the right. If the coefficient of friction between the block and the table is 0.1, how much work is done on the block by the table?

   (A) 0.5 J
   (B) 1.0 J
   (C) 0 J
   (D) 100 J
   (E) 50 J

9. A block has 1500 J of potential energy and 700 J of kinetic energy. Ten seconds later, the block has 100 J of potential energy and 900 J of kinetic energy. Friction is the only external force acting on the block. How much work was done on this block by friction?

   (A) 600 J
   (B) 200 J
   (C) 1400 J
   (D) 1200 J
   (E) 120 J

Momentum

10. Two identical small balls are moving with the same speed toward a brick wall. After colliding with the wall, ball 1 sticks to the wall while ball 2 bounces off the wall, moving with almost the same speed that it had initially. Which ball experiences greater impulse?

    (A) ball 1
    (B) ball 2
    (C) Both experience the same impulse.
    (D) The answer cannot be determined unless we know the time of collision.
    (E) The answer cannot be determined unless we know the force each ball exerts on the wall.

11. Ball *A* moves to the right with a speed of 5.0 m/s; Ball *B* moves to the left with speed 2.0 m/s. Both balls have mass 1.0 kg. What is the total momentum of the system consisting only of balls *A* and *B*?

    (A) 7.0 N·s to the right
    (B) 3.0 N·s to the right
    (C) zero
    (D) 7.0 N·s to the left
    (E) 3.0 N·s to the left

12. Momentum of an isolated system always remains constant. However, in a collision between two balls, a ball's momentum might change from, say, +1 kg m/s to −1 kg m/s. How can this be correct?

    (A) It is *not* correct. Momentum conservation means that the momentum of an object must remain the same.
    (B) A force outside the two-ball system must have acted.
    (C) Friction is responsible for the change in momentum.
    (D) Although one ball's momentum changed, the momentum of *both* balls in total remained the same.
    (E) Momentum is conserved because the magnitude of the ball's momentum remained the same.

Circular motion

13. Which of the following must be true of an object in uniform circular motion?

    (A) Its velocity must be constant.
    (B) Its acceleration and its velocity must be in opposite directions.
    (C) Its acceleration and its velocity must be perpendicular to each other.
    (D) It must experience a force away from the center of the circle.
    (E) Its acceleration must be negative.

Harmonic motion

14. A mass on a spring has a frequency of 2.5 Hz and an amplitude of 0.05 m. What is the period of the oscillations?

    (A) 0.4 s
    (B) 0.2 s
    (C) 8 s
    (D) 20 s
    (E) 50 s

GO ON TO THE NEXT PAGE

15. A mass m oscillates on a horizontal spring of constant k with no damping. The amplitude of the oscillation is A. What is the potential energy of the mass at its maximum displacement?

(A) zero
(B) mgh
(C) kA
(D) $\frac{1}{2}mv^2$
(E) $\frac{1}{2}kA^2$

Rotational motion

16. A ball of mass m is spinning about a diameter. If it were instead to make twice as many rotations per second, what would happen to the ball's rotational inertia and its angular momentum?

	Moment of inertia	Angular momentum
(A)	remains the same	quadruples
(B)	doubles	remains the same
(C)	doubles	quadruples
(D)	doubles	doubles
(E)	remains the same	doubles

Gravitation

17. A satellite orbits the moon far from its surface in a circle of radius r. If a second satellite has a greater speed, yet still needs to maintain a circular orbit around the moon, how should the second satellite orbit?

(A) with a radius r
(B) with a radius greater than r
(C) with a radius less than r
(D) Only an eccentric elliptical orbit can be maintained with a larger speed.
(E) No orbit at all can be maintained with a larger speed.

Electrostatics

18. Which of the following statements about electric potential is correct?

(A) A proton experiences a force from a region of low potential to a region of high potential.
(B) The potential of a negatively charged conductor must be negative.
(C) If the electric field is zero at point P, then the electric potential at P must also be zero.
(D) If the electric potential is zero at point P, then the electric field at P must also be zero.
(E) The electric potential with respect to earth ground can be less than zero at all points on an isolated wire conductor.

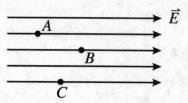

19. A uniform electric field points to the right, as shown above. A test charge can be placed at one of three points as shown in the above diagram. At which point does the test charge experience the greatest force?

(A) point A
(B) point B
(C) point C
(D) The charge experiences the greatest force at two of these three points.
(E) The charge experiences the same force at all three points.

20. An electron in an electric field is suspended above the earth's surface. Which of the following diagrams correctly shows the forces acting on this electron?

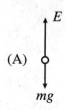

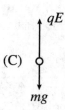

GO ON TO THE NEXT PAGE

Circuits

21. Which of the following will increase the capacitance of a parallel plate capacitor?

(A) increasing the charge stored on the plates
(B) decreasing the charge stored on the plates
(C) increasing the separation between the plates
(D) decreasing the separation between the plates
(E) decreasing the area of the plates

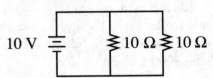

22. A 10-V battery is connected to two parallel 10-Ω resistors, as shown above. What is the current through and voltage across each resistor?

	Current	Voltage
(A)	1 A	5 V
(B)	1 A	10 V
(C)	0.5 A	5 V
(D)	2 A	10 V
(E)	2 A	5 V

Magnetic fields and force

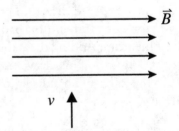

23. A positive point charge enters a uniform rightward magnetic field with a velocity v, as diagramed above. What is the direction of the magnetic force on the charge?

(A) in the same direction as v
(B) to the right
(C) to the left
(D) out of the page
(E) into the page

24. A long wire carries a current I toward the top of the page. What is the direction of the magnetic field produced by this wire to the left of the wire?

(A) into the page
(B) out of the page
(C) toward the bottom of the page
(D) toward the top of the page
(E) to the right

Electromagnetism

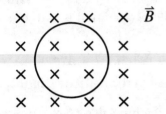

25. A circular loop of wire in the plane of the page is placed in a magnetic field pointing into the page, as shown above. Which of the following will NOT induce a current in the loop?

(A) moving the wire to the right in the plane of the page
(B) increasing the area of the loop
(C) increasing the strength of the magnetic field
(D) rotating the wire about a diameter
(E) turning the magnetic field off

END OF DIAGNOSTIC TEST

❯ Answers and Explanations

1. **D**—Choices A and E don't make sense because the direction of an object's acceleration or velocity is essentially arbitrary—when solving a problem, you can usually pick the "positive" direction based on convenience. So neither value *must* be negative. We can rule out choice B because we know that a fast moving object can slow down very gradually. And there's no reason why you need multiple forces to make an object slow down, so that gets rid of choice C.

2. **E**—When an object is thrown in the absence of air resistance near the surface of the Earth, its acceleration in the vertical direction is always *g*, the acceleration due to gravity, which has a magnitude of 9.8 m/s². The acceleration due to gravity is directed down, toward the Earth. So the ball's acceleration is −9.8 m/s².

3. **D**—The vertical component of a vector is the magnitude of the vector times the sine of the angle measured to the horizontal; in this case, $\mathbf{F}_1 \sin \theta$.

4. **D**—Something that moves in a straight line at constant speed is in equilibrium. So, the sum of left forces has to equal the sum of right forces.

5. **C**—On an incline, the weight vector parallel to the plane goes with the sine of the plane's angle. *g* sin 40° is an acceleration, not a weight.

6. **E**—Because the weight is the only force acting parallel to the plane, $mg \sin 40° = ma$, so $a = g \sin 40°$. This acceleration is down the plane, in the direction of the net force. Yes, the block is moving up the plane, but the block is *slowing down*, and so the acceleration must be in the opposite direction from the velocity.

7. **D**—All forms of energy are scalar quantities: potential energy, kinetic energy, work, internal energy of a gas. Energy doesn't have direction.

8. **B**—Work is force times parallel displacement. The force acting here is the force of friction, and the displacement is 2.0 m parallel to the force of friction. The friction force is equal to the coefficient of friction (0.10) times the normal force. The normal force in this case is equal to the block's weight of 5 N (because no other vertical forces act). Combining all these equations, the work done is (2.0 m) (0.1)(5 N) = 1.0 J.

9. **D**—Look at the total energy of the block, which is equal to the potential energy plus the kinetic energy. Initially, the total energy was 2200 J. At the end, the total energy was 1000 J. What happened to the extra 1200 J? Because friction was the only external force acting, friction must have done 1200 J of work.

10. **B**—Impulse is equal to the change in an object's momentum. Ball 1 changes its momentum from something to zero. But ball 2 changes its momentum from something to zero, and *then* to something in the other direction. That's a bigger momentum change than if the ball had just stopped. (If we had been asked to find the force on the ball, then we'd need the time of collision, but the impulse can be found without reference to force or time.)

11. **B**—Momentum is a *vector*, meaning direction is important. Call the rightward direction positive. Ball A has +5 kg·m/s of momentum; ball B has −2 kg·m/s of momentum. Adding these together, we get a total of +3 kg·m/s. This answer is equivalent to 3 N·s to the right. (The units kg·m/s and N·s are identical.)

12. **D**—The law of conservation of momentum requires that *all* objects involved in a collision be taken into account. An object can lose momentum, as long as that momentum is picked up by some other object.

13. **C**—"Uniform" circular motion means that an object's *speed* must be constant. But *velocity* includes direction, and the direction of travel changes continually. The velocity of the object is always along the circle, but the acceleration is centripetal; i.e., center-seeking. The direction toward the center of the circle is perpendicular to the path of the object everywhere.

14. **A**—Period is equal to 1/frequency, regardless of the amplitude of harmonic motion.

15. E—The maximum displacement is the amplitude. Energy of a spring is $\frac{1}{2}kx^2$. So, at $x = A$, the energy is $\frac{1}{2}kA^2$.

16. E—An object's rotational inertia can be thought of as a rotational equivalent of mass; rotational inertia, like mass, is a property of an object and the axis about which it rotates. Rotational inertia does not depend on the speed of rotation. Angular momentum, equal to rotational inertia times angular velocity, *does* depend on the speed of rotation. Because the rotation rate doubled, so did angular momentum.

17. C—In an orbit, gravity provides a centripetal force. So, $GmM/r^2 = mv^2/r$. Solving for v,

$$v = \sqrt{\frac{GM}{r}}$$

where M is the mass of the moon. If the speed gets bigger, then the radius of orbit (in the denominator) must get smaller to compensate.

18. E—Most of these statements drive at the fundamental principle that the value of an electric potential can be set to anything; it is only the *difference* in electric potential between two points that has a physical usefulness. Usually potential is set to zero either at the ground or, for isolated point charges, a very long distance away from the charges. But potential can, in fact, be set to zero anywhere, meaning that the potential could easily be less than zero everywhere on a wire. (And a proton, a positive charge, is forced from high to low potential, not the other way around.)

19. E—This is a *uniform* electric field. The force on a charge in an electric field is given by $F = qE$. Therefore, as long as the electric field is the same at all three points, the force on the charge is the same as well.

20. C—Only forces can go on free-body diagrams, and the electric field is not itself a force. The force *provided by* an electric field is qE; the weight of the electron is mg.

21. D—Capacitance is a property of the structure of the capacitor. Changing the charge on (or the voltage across) a capacitor does not change the capacitance. The capacitance of a parallel-plate capacitor is given by the equation

$$C = \frac{\varepsilon_0 A}{d}$$

Decreasing d, the distance between the plates, will increase the capacitance.

22. B—These resistors are in parallel with the battery; thus, they *both* must take the voltage of the battery, 10 V. The total current in the circuit is 2.0 A, but that current splits between the two resistors, leaving 1.0 A through each. This can also be determined by a direct application of Ohm's law—because we know both the voltage and resistance for each resistor, divide V/R to get the current.

23. E—Use the right-hand rule for the force on a charged particle in a magnetic field: point your right hand in the direction of the velocity, curl your fingers toward the magnetic field, and your thumb points into the page. The charge is positive, so your thumb points in the direction of the force.

24. B—This question uses the right-hand rule for the magnetic field produced by a current-carrying wire. Point your thumb in the direction of the current; your fingers wrap around the wire in the direction of the magnetic field. To the wire's left, your fingers point out of the page.

25. A—Only a changing magnetic flux induces a current. Flux is given by $BA\cos\theta$, where B is the magnetic field, and A is the area of the loop of wire. Obviously, then, choices B, C, and E change the flux and induce a current. Choice D produces a flux by changing θ, the angle at which the field penetrates the loop of wire. In choice A, no current is induced because the field doesn't change and always points straight through the loop.

Interpretation: How Ready Are You?

Now that you have finished the diagnostic exam and checked your answers, it is time to try to figure out what it all means. First, remember that getting only about 60% of the answers correct will give you a 5 on the AP exam; about 30–40% correct is the criterion for a qualifying score of 3. You're not supposed to get 90% correct! So relax and evaluate your performance dispassionately.

Next, see if there are any particular areas in which you struggled. For example, were there any questions that caused you to think something such as, "I learned this . . . *when?!?*" or "What the heck is *this?!?*" If so, put a little star next to the chapter that contains the material in which this occurred. You may want to spend a bit more time on that chapter during your review for this exam. It is quite possible that you *never* learned some of the material in this book. Not every class is able to cover all the same information.

In general, try to interpret your performance on this test in a productive manner. If you did well, that's terrific . . . but don't get overconfident now. There's still a lot of material to review before you take the Practice Exams in Step 5—let alone the real AP exam. If you don't feel good about your performance, now is the time to turn things around. You have a great opportunity here—time to prepare for the real exam, a helpful review book, and a sense of what topics you need to work on most—so use it to its fullest. Good luck!

STEP 3

Develop Strategies for Success

Memorizing Equations in the Shower

IN THIS CHAPTER

Summary: Learn how to memorize all the equations you absolutely need to know to ace the AP Physics exam.

Key Ideas
✪ Learn why memorizing equations is so critical.
✪ Learn equations by using them: practice solving problems without looking up the equations you need.
✪ Use mnemonic devices to help you remember.
✪ Practice speed: see how many equations you can say in four minutes.
✪ Use visual reminders: put a copy of the equation sheet somewhere you'll see it often.

Can You Ace This Quiz?

Instructions: We'll give you a prompt, you tell us the equation. Once you've finished, check your answers with the key at the end of this chapter.

1. Coefficient of friction in terms of F_f
2. Momentum
3. Two equations for impulse
4. Two equations for mechanical power
5. Two equations for work
6. Period of a mass on a spring
7. Three kinematics equations for constant acceleration
8. Centripetal acceleration
9. Kinetic energy
10. Gravitational force of one planet on another
11. Ohm's Law
12. Power in a circuit
13. Magnetic force on a charge
14. Magnetic force on a wire
15. Electric force on a charge
16. Electric potential energy
17. Magnetic field around a long, straight, current-carrying wire
18. Time constant for an RC circuit
19. Resistance of a wire in terms of its dimensions
20. Electric field due to a point charge

So, How Did You Do?

Grade yourself according to this scale.

20 right	Excellent
0–19 right	Start studying

You may think we're joking about our grading system, but we're completely serious. Knowing your equations is absolutely imperative. Even if you missed one question on the quiz, you need to study your equations. Right now! A student who is ready to take the AP exam is one who can ace an "equations quiz" without even thinking about it. How ready are you?

Equations Are Crucial

It's easy to make an argument against memorizing equations. For starters, you're given all the equations you need on the exam. And besides, you can miss a whole bunch of questions on the test and still get a 5.

But equations are the nuts and bolts of physics. They're the fundamentals. They should be the foundation on which your understanding of physics is built. Not knowing an equation—even one—shows that your knowledge of physics is incomplete. And every question on the AP exam assumes *complete* knowledge of physics.

Now you get equation sheets on the multiple choice section, too.

What About the Free-Response Section?

The free-response questions test your ability to solve complex, multistep problems. They also test your understanding of equations. You need to figure out which equations to use when and how. The makers of the test are being nice by giving you the equation sheet— they're reminding you of all the equations you already know in case you cannot think of that certain equation that you *know* would be just perfect to solve a certain problem. But the sheet is intended to be nothing more than a reminder. It will not tell you when to use an equation or which equation would be best in solving a particular problem. You have to know that. And you will know that only if you have intimate knowledge of every equation.

Exam tip from an AP Physics veteran:
Don't use the equation sheet to "hunt and peck." The sheet can remind you of subtle things; for example, does the magnetic field due to a wire have an r or an r^2 in the denominator? But if you don't have the general idea that the magnetic field depends on current and gets weaker farther away from a wire, then you won't recognize

$$B = \frac{\mu_0 I}{2\pi r}$$

even if you go hunting for it.

—*Wyatt, college freshman in engineering*

Some Examples

We mentioned in Step 2 that some questions on the AP exam are designed solely to test your knowledge of equations. If you know your equations, you will get the question right. Here's an example.

A pendulum of length L swings with a period of 3 s. If the pendulum's length is increased to $2L$, what will its new period be?

(A) $3/\sqrt{2}$ s

(D) 6 s

(B) 3 s

(E) 12 s

(C) $3\sqrt{2}$ s

The answer is (C). The equation for a pendulum's period is

$$T = 2\pi\sqrt{\frac{L}{g}}$$

since L is in the numerator and under the square root, multiplying L by 2 multiplies the period by $\sqrt{2}$.

Of course, the multiple-choice section will not be the only part of the exam that tests your knowledge of equations. Often, a part of a free-response question will also test your ability to use an equation. For example, check out this problem.

Four charges $+Q$ are arranged in a square of side length l.

(a) What is the magnitude of the electric field due to just one of these charges at the center of the square?

Yes, later in the problem you'll be asked to add vectors to find E due to a bunch of charges. But you can still score some easy points here if you simply remember that old standby, $E = \left(\dfrac{1}{4\pi\varepsilon_0}\right)\dfrac{Q}{r^2}$.

Memorizing equations will earn you points. It's that simple.

Treat Equations Like Vocabulary

Think about how you would memorize a vocabulary word: for example, "boondoggle." There are several ways to memorize this word. The first way is to say the word out loud and then spell it: "Boondoggle: B-O-O-N-D-O-G-G-L-E." The second way is to say the word and then say its definition: "Boondoggle: An unproductive or impractical project, often involving graft." If you were to use the first method of memorizing our word, you would become a great speller, but you would have no clue what "boondoggle" means. As long as you are not preparing for a spelling bee, it seems that the second method is the better one.

This judgment may appear obvious. Who ever learned vocabulary by spelling it? The fact is, this is the method most people use when studying equations.

Let's take a simple equation, $v_f = v_o + at$. An average physics student will memorize this equation by saying it aloud several times, and that's it. All this student has done is "spelled" the equation.

But you're not average.[1] Instead, you look at the equation as a whole, pronouncing it like a sentence: "*Vf* equals *v* naught plus *at*." You then memorize what it means and when to use it: "This equation relates initial velocity with final velocity. It is valid only when acceleration is constant." If you are really motivated, you will also try to develop some intuitive sense of why the equation works. "Of course," you say, "this makes perfect sense! Acceleration is just the change in velocity divided by the time interval. If acceleration is multiplied by the time interval, then all that's left is the change in velocity

$$\frac{\Delta v}{\Delta t} \cdot \Delta t = \Delta v$$

So the final velocity of an object equals its initial velocity plus the change in velocity."

The first step in memorizing equations, then, is to learn them as if you were studying for a vocabulary test, and not as if you were studying for a spelling bee.

Helpful Tips

Memorizing equations takes a lot of time, so you cannot plan on studying your equations the night before the AP exam. If you want to really know your equations like the back of your hand, you will have to spend months practicing. But it's really not that bad. Here are four tips to help you out.

Tip 1: Learn through use. Practice solving homework problems without looking up equations.

Just as with vocabulary words, you will only learn physics equations if you use them on a regular basis. The more you use your equations, the more comfortable you will be with them, and that comfort level will help you on the AP test.

The reason you should try solving homework problems without looking up equations is that this will alert you to trouble spots. When you can look at an equations sheet, it's easy to fool yourself into a false sense of confidence: "Oh, yeah, I *knew* that spring potential energy is ½kx^2." But when you don't have an equations sheet to look at, you realize that either you know an equation or you don't. So if you solve homework problems without looking up equations, you'll quickly figure out which ones you know and which you don't; and then you can focus your studying on those equations that need more review.

Tip 2: Use mnemonic devices.

Use whatever tricks necessary to learn an equation. For example, it is often hard to remember that the period of a pendulum is

$$T = 2\pi \sqrt{\frac{L}{g}}$$

---

[1]In fact, just because you bought this book, we think that you're way better than average. "Stupendous" comes to mind. "Extraordinary, Gullible." Er . . . uh . . . cross that third one out.

[2]We've included a copy of this sheet at the end of the book, along with a sheet of prompts to guide you through a four-minute drill.

and **not**

$$T = 2\pi\sqrt{\frac{g}{L}}$$

So make up some trick, like "The terms go in backward alphabetical order: **Two-pi root *L* over *g*.**" Be creative.

> **Tip 3:** The Four-Minute Drill.

Practice speed. Say the equations as fast as you can, then say them faster. Start at the top of the AP equations sheet[2] and work your way down. Have someone quiz you. Let that person give you a lead, like "Period of a pendulum," and you respond "Two-pi root *L* over *g*." See how many equations you can rattle off in four minutes. We call it the Four-Minute Drill.

This is much more fun with a group; for example, try to persuade your teacher to lead the class in a four-minute drill. Not only will you get out of four minutes of lecture, but you may also be able to bargain with your teacher: "Sir, if we can rattle off 50 equations in the Four-Minute Drill, will you exempt us from doing tonight's problems?"[3]

> **Tip 4:** Put a copy of the equations sheet somewhere visible.

See how the equations sheet looks next to your bathroom mirror. Or in your shower (laminated, of course). Or taped to your door. Or hung from your ceiling. You'd be surprised how much sparkle it can add to your décor. You'd also be surprised how easy it will be to memorize equations if you are constantly looking at the equations sheet.

So what are you waiting for? Start memorizing!

---

[3]"No."

❯ Answer Key to Practice Quiz

1. $\mu = \dfrac{F_f}{F_n}$

2. $p = mv$

3. $I = \Delta p$ and $I = F\Delta t$

4. $P = Fv$ and $P = \dfrac{W}{t}$

5. $W = Fd$ and $W_{net} = \Delta KE$

6. $T = 2\pi\sqrt{\dfrac{m}{k}}$

7. $\begin{cases} v_f = v_o + at \\ x - x_0 = v_0 t + \frac{1}{2}at^2 \\ v_f^2 = v_0^2 + 2a(x - x_0) \end{cases}$

8. $a_c = \dfrac{v^2}{r}$

9. $KE = \frac{1}{2}mv^2$

10. $F = \dfrac{Gm_1 m_2}{r^2}$

11. $V = IR$

12. $P = IV$

13. $F = qvB \sin\theta$

14. $F = ILB \sin\theta$

15. $F = qE$

16. $U = qV$

17. $B = \dfrac{\mu_0 I}{2\pi r}$

18. $\tau = RC$

19. $R = \dfrac{\rho L}{A}$

20. $E = \dfrac{kQ}{r^2}$

CHAPTER 7

How to Approach Each Question Type

IN THIS CHAPTER

Summary: Become familiar with the three types of questions on the exam: multiple-choice, free-response, and lab questions. Pace yourself, and know when to skip a question.

Key Ideas

✪ You don't need a calculator to figure out multiple choice questions, even though you are allowed a calculator.

✪ There are five categories of multiple-choice questions. Two of these involve numbers: easy calculations and order-of-magnitude estimates. The other three don't involve numbers at all: proportional reasoning questions, concept questions, and questions asking for the direct solution with variables only.

✪ Free-response questions test your understanding of physics, not obscure theories or technical terms.

✪ You can get partial credit on free-response questions.

✪ Each free-response section will contain at least one question that involves experiment design and analysis—in other words, a lab question.

✪ Check out our six steps to answering lab questions successfully.

How to Approach the Multiple-Choice Section

The AP exam is very, very straightforward. There are no trick questions, no unreasonably difficult problems, no math beyond the clearly articulated scope of the course. The multiple choice questions test your physics knowledge in a variety of ways—a glance through the practice exam in this book, as well as reading through this section, can give you a sense of the types of questions asked.

Until 2015, calculators and the equation sheet were not provided during the multiple choice section. Now, though, you can use calculators and equation sheets on the whole exam.

Important point: *The content and style of questions did not change, even though the calculator policy did.*

The point is, you do not need to use a calculator on the multiple choice section. No multiple choice question requires significant number crunching. More importantly, though, understand that

> Physics is NOT about numbers.

Yes, you must use numbers occasionally. Yet you must understand that the number you get in answer to a question is always subordinate to what that number represents.

Many misconceptions about physics start in math class. There, your teacher shows you how to do a type of problem, then you do several variations of that same problem for homework. The answer to one of these problems might be 30,000,000, another 16.5. It doesn't matter . . . in fact, the book (or your teacher) probably made up random numbers to go into the problem to begin with. The "problem" consists of manipulating these random numbers a certain way to get a certain answer.

In physics, though, *every number has meaning*. Your answer will not be 30,000,000; the answer may be 30,000,000 electron-volts, or 30,000,000 seconds, but not just 30,000,000. If you don't see the difference, you're missing the fundamental point of physics.

We use numbers to represent REAL goings on in nature. 30,000,000 eV (or, 30 MeV) is an energy; this could represent the energy of a particle in a multibillion-dollar accelerator, but it's much too small to be the energy of a ball dropped off of a building. 30,000,000 seconds is a time; not a few hours or a few centuries, but about one year. These two "30,000,000" responses mean entirely different things. If you simply give a number as an answer, you're doing a math problem. It is only when you can explain the meaning of any result that you may truly claim to understand physics.

So How Do I Deal with All the Numbers on the Test?

You see, in virtually all cases the test authors still assume that you have no calculator. Thus, a large majority of the multiple-choice questions involve *no numbers at all!* And those questions that do use numbers will never require more than the simplest manipulations. Here is a question you will **never** see on the AP test:

> What is the magnitude of the magnetic field a distance of 1.5 m away from a long, straight wire that carries 2.3 A of current?
>
> (A) 3.066×10^{-6} T
> (B) 3.166×10^{-6} T
> (C) 3.102×10^{-6} T
> (D) 2.995×10^{-6} T
> (E) 3.109×10^{-6} T

Yes, we know you might have seen this type of problem in class. But it will *not* be on the AP exam. Why not? Plugging numbers into a calculator is not a skill being tested by this examination. (You should have recognized that the equation necessary to solve this problem is $B = \dfrac{\mu_0 I}{2\pi r}$ though.) We hope you see that, without a calculator, it is pointless to try to get a precise numerical answer to this kind of question.

Fine . . . Then What Kinds of Questions *Will* Be Asked on the Multiple-Choice Section?

Fair enough. We break down the kinds of questions into five categories. First, the categories of questions that involve numbers:

1. easy calculations
2. order of magnitude estimates

Most questions, though, do NOT involve numbers at all. These are:

3. proportional reasoning
4. concept questions, subdivided into
    a. "Why?" questions, and
    b. diagram questions
5. direct solution with variables

Okay, let's take a look at a sample of each of these.

Easy Calculations

These test your knowledge of formulas.

A ball is dropped from a 45-m-high platform. Neglecting air resistance, how much time will it take for this ball to hit the ground?

(A) 1.0 s
(B) 2.0 s
(C) 3.0 s
(D) 4.0 s
(E) 5.0 s

You should remember the kinematics equation: $x - x_0 = v_0 t + \frac{1}{2} at^2$. Here the initial velocity is zero because the ball was "dropped." The distance involved is 45 meters, and the acceleration is caused by gravity, 10 m/s^2. The solution must be found without a calculator, but notice how easy they have made the numbers:

$$45 \text{ m} = 0t + \frac{1}{2}(10 \text{ m/s}^2) \cdot t^2$$

$$90 = 10t^2$$

$$9 = t^2$$

$$t = 3.0 \text{ s}$$

Everything here can be done easily without a calculator, especially if you remember to use 10 m/s^2 for g. No problem!

Order of Magnitude Estimates

These test your understanding of the size of things, measurements, or just numbers.

Which of the following best approximates the gravitational force experienced by a high school student due to the student sitting in an adjacent seat?

(A) 10^1 N
(B) 10^{-8} N
(C) 10^{-18} N
(D) 10^{-28} N
(E) 10^{-38} N

Wow, at first you have no idea. But let's start by looking at the answer choices. Notice how widely the choices are separated. The second choice is a hundred millionth of a newton; the third choice is a billionth of a billionth of a newton. Clearly no kind of precise calculation is necessary here.

The answer can be calculated with Newton's law of gravitation $G\dfrac{m_1 m_2}{r^2}$. You complain:

"They didn't give me any information to plug in. It's hopeless!" Certainly not. The important thing to remember is that you have very little need for precision here. This is a rough estimate! *Just plug in a power of 10 for each variable.* Watch:

1. G: The table of information says that the constant G is 6.67×10^{-11} N·m²/kg². So we just use 10^{-11} in standard units.
2. m_1, m_2: It doesn't say whether this is Olympic gymnast Shawn Johnson (41 kg) or football offensive lineman John Urschel (137 kg). What do I do? Just use 10^1 or 10^2 kg. If you're really concerned, you can make one 10^1 kg and one 10^2 kg. It won't matter.
3. r: The distance between desks in any classroom will be more than a few tens of centimeters, but less than a few tens of meters. Call it 10^0 meters and be done with it.

Okay, we're ready for our quick calculation:

$$F = G\frac{m_1 m_2}{r^2} = (10^{-11})(10^1)(10^2)/(10^0)^2 = 10^{-8} \text{ N}$$

(You remember that to multiply powers of 10, just add the exponents; to divide, subtract the exponents.)

You still object, "But when I use my calculator and plug in more precise values, I get 3.67×10^{-7} N. Or, if I use both masses as Shawn Johnson's, I get 1.1×10^{-7} N." Look at the choices again; the second answer choice is still the best answer. We got that without a calculator—and a lot quicker, too.

Proportional Reasoning

These also test your knowledge of how to use equations, except that you don't have to plug in numerical values to solve them.

Planet X is twice as massive as Earth, but its radius is only half of Earth's radius. What is the acceleration due to gravity on Planet X in terms of g, the acceleration due to gravity on Earth?

(A) $\frac{1}{4}g$
(B) $\frac{1}{2}g$
(C) g
(D) $4g$
(E) $8g$

First we need to know what equation to use. We know that the force that a planet exerts on a small mass m_1 near its surface is

$$F = \frac{GM_{planet}m_1}{R_{planet}^2}$$

Using Newton's second law ($F_{net} = ma$), we know that the acceleration of the small mass is simply

$$a = \frac{GM_{planet}}{R_{planet}^2}$$

One method of solution would be to plug in the actual mass and radius of the new planet. But no fair, you say, the mass of the Earth isn't given on the constants sheet. How do I find the mass of the planet?

You don't!

Use proportional reasoning skills instead, so:

"The mass of the planet is twice that of the Earth. Since mass is in the numerator of the equation for acceleration, doubling the mass of the planet must double the acceleration.

"Okay, but the radius of this planet is also different. Radius is in the denominator, so a smaller radius means a bigger acceleration. The radius of the new planet is half of the radius of the Earth. Therefore, the acceleration must be doubled. Almost there . . . because the radius is SQUARED in the denominator, the acceleration must be doubled AGAIN.

"So what is my final answer? The mass causes acceleration to double. The radius causes the acceleration to double, and then to double again. So the total acceleration is multiplied by a factor of 8. The acceleration on this planet is 8 g."

In the much more concise language of algebra, your reasoning might look like this:

$$a = \frac{2}{\left(\frac{1}{2}\right)^2}g = 8g$$

What if the answer choices had been like this:

(A) 2.5 m/s²
(B) 4.9 m/s²
(C) 9.8 m/s²
(D) 19.6 m/s²
(E) 78.4 m/s²

Is the problem any different? (Answer: no.)

Concept Questions: "WHY?"

Many multiple-choice questions involve no calculations and no formulas. These test your understanding of vocabulary and explanations for physical phenomena.

Two identical train cars move toward each other, each with the same speed as the other. When the train cars collide, they stick together and remain at rest. Which of the following fundamental physics principles can best be used to explain why the attached cars cannot move after the collision?

(A) Conservation of mechanical energy
(B) Conservation of linear momentum
(C) Conservation of angular momentum
(D) Conservation of mass
(E) Conservation of rotational energy

The direct answer to this question is B: conservation of linear momentum applies to all collisions. The cars had equal momentum in opposite directions, so the net momentum before collision was zero; thus, the cars may not have any momentum after collision. Kinetic energy is a scalar, having no direction, and so kinetic energy of two moving objects cannot cancel to zero. Mechanical energy was not conserved, because kinetic energy was lost in the collision.

But even if you have a hesitation about the difference between momentum and kinetic energy conservation, you can still get close to the right answer by eliminating obvious "stupidicisms." Look at E: perhaps you recognize that there's no such thing as "conservation of rotational energy." Or likely you see right away that conservation of mass, while a legitimate concept, is usually relevant in a chemical process or fluid dynamics and can have little bearing on the speed of train cars in a collision.

Concept Questions: Diagrams

These ask you a simple question based (obviously) on a diagram.

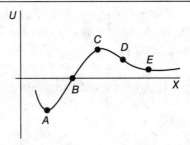

A particle experiences a potential energy U as a function of position x as shown in the diagram above. At which position is the particle in a state of unstable equilibrium?

(A) A
(B) B
(C) C
(D) D
(E) E

For these, you either know what to do with the diagram or you don't. Here you, of course, remember that equilibrium is represented on an energy-position diagram by a horizontal slope and that unstable equilibrium requires the energy-position diagram to be at a maximum. Thus, the answer is C.

Three Things You Can Do with a Graph

You could see so, so many graphs on the AP exam. . . . It's often difficult to remember which graph means what. But if you know your equations, you can usually figure out how to interpret any graph you are faced with. Why? Because there are pretty much ONLY three things you can do with a graph:

1. Take the slope.
2. Find the area under the graph.
3. Read off an axis.

For example, an AP Physics C exam question described an experiment in which a solenoid was stretched to vary the number of turns per length, n. At constant current, the magnetic field inside was plotted as a function of n; the question asked for an experimental value of the permeability of free space μ_0. Chances are that you've never done this experiment and that you've never seen this particular graph. But you do remember your equations: the magnetic field of a solenoid is $B = \mu_0 n I$. Solving for μ_0, $\mu_0 = \left(\dfrac{B}{n}\right)\left(\dfrac{1}{I}\right)$.

The slope of this graph is $\left(\dfrac{B}{n}\right)$. Therefore, μ_0 must be the **slope** of the graph divided by the current in the solenoid.

Similarly, imagine a graph of force vs. time on a question that asks for impulse. Since impulse is equal to force times time interval ($\Delta p = F \Delta t$), then impulse must be the **area** under the graph.

Finally, if you're totally clueless about what to do with a graph, just try taking a slope or an area, and see what happens! You might experience a revelation.

Other diagram questions might ask you to:

- use the right-hand rule to determine the direction of a magnetic force on a particle
- identify the direction of an electric or magnetic field
- analyze the properties of a circuit
- recognize the correct free-body diagram of an object
- interpret motion graphs

Many other diagram questions are possible. Try making one yourself—pick your favorite diagram from your textbook, and ask a question about it. Chances are, you have just written an AP multiple-choice question.

Direct Solution with Variables

Because the AP test writers can't ask you to do any kind of difficult number crunching on the multiple-choice section, often they will ask you to do your problem-solving using variables only.

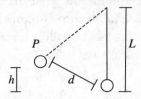

A pendulum of length L is drawn back to position P, as shown in the above diagram, and released from rest. The linear distance from P to the lowest point in the pendulum's swing is d; the vertical distance from P to the lowest point in the swing is h. What is the maximum speed of this pendulum in terms of the above variables and fundamental constants?

(A) $\sqrt{2gL}$　　　　　　　(D) $\sqrt{\dfrac{2gd}{L}}$

(B) $\sqrt{2gd}$　　　　　　　(E) $\sqrt{\dfrac{2gh}{L}}$

(C) $\sqrt{2gh}$

"Ugh . . . too many letters!" you say. We disagree. Solving this problem is no different than solving the same problem with numbers given. In fact, if the variables bother you, try solving with made-up numbers first:

> Let's say the height h is 5 meters, and the mass of the bob is 2 kg . . . well, we use conservation of energy. Energy at the top of the swing is all potential, all mgh. So that's $2 \times 10 \times 5 = 100$ J of potential energy.
>
> At the bottom, all this energy is kinetic. So $100\ \text{J} = \frac{1}{2}mv^2$. Solving, $v = 10$ m/s.
>
> Now how did we get that? We set $mgh = \frac{1}{2}mv^2$, and solved for v. The masses cancelled, so $v =$ square root of $2gh$. Lo and behold, that's an answer choice!

When Should You Skip a Question?

Never. There is no penalty for guessing, so guess away!

Some Final Advice on Multiple-Choice Questions

- Know your pace. Take the practice exams under test conditions (45 minutes for 35 questions, or some fraction thereof). Are you getting to all the questions? If not, you are going to need to decide your strengths and weaknesses. Know before the exam which types of problems you want to attempt first. Then, when you take your exam, FOLLOW YOUR PLAN!
- The multiple-choice questions do not necessarily start easy and get harder, as do SAT questions. So if you suspect from your practice that you may be pressed for time, know that problems on your strong topics may be scattered throughout the exam. Problem 35 might be easier for you than problem 5, so look at the whole test.

- Speaking of time, the AP test authors know the time limit of the exam—you must average a minute and a half per question in order to answer everything. So they are not going to write a question that really takes three or four minutes to solve! You must always look for the approach to a problem that will let you solve quickly. If your approach won't get you to a solution in less than two minutes, then either look for another approach or move on.

- One other alternative if you don't see a reasonable direct approach to a problem: look at the answer choices. Some might not make any sense; for example, you can eliminate any choice for a speed that is faster than light, or a couple of answer choices to concept questions might contain obvious errors. Guess from the remaining choices, and move on.

- Correct your practice exam. For any mistakes, write out an explanation of the correct answer and why you got it wrong. Pledge to yourself that you will never make the same mistake twice.

How to Approach the Free-Response Section

The best thing about the free-response section of the AP exam is this: you've been preparing for it *all year long!* "Really?" you ask. "I don't remember spending much time preparing for it."

But think about the homework problems you've been doing throughout the year. Every week, you probably answer a set of questions, each of which might take a few steps to solve, and we bet that your teacher always reminds you to show your work. This sounds like the AP free-response section to us!

The key to doing well on the free-response section is to realize that, first and foremost, these problems test your *understanding* of physics. The purpose is not to see how good your algebra skills are, how many fancy-sounding technical terms you know, or how many obscure theories you can regurgitate. So all we're going to do in this section is give you a few suggestions about how, when you work through a free-response question, you can communicate to the AP readers that you understand the concepts being tested. If you can effectively communicate your understanding of physics, you will get a good score.

What Do the Readers Look For?

Before grading a single student's exam, the high school and college physics teachers who are responsible for scoring the AP free-response section make a "rubric" for each question. A rubric is a grading guide; it specifies exactly what needs to be included for an answer to receive full credit, and it explains how partial credit should be awarded.

For example, consider part of a free-response question:

A student pulls a 1.0-kg block across a table to the right, applying a force of 8.0 N. The coefficient of kinetic friction between the block and the table is 0.20. Assume the block is at rest when it begins its motion.

(a) Determine the force of friction experienced by the block.
(b) Calculate the speed of the block after 1.5 s.

Let's look just at part (b). What do you think the AP readers are looking for in a correct answer? Well, we know that the AP free-response section tests your understanding of physics. So the readers probably want to see that you know how to evaluate the forces acting on an object and how to relate those forces to the object's motion.

In fact, if part (b) were worth 4 points, the readers might award 1 point for each of these elements of your answer:

1. Applying Newton's second law, $F_{net} = ma$, to find the block's acceleration.
2. Recognizing that the net force is not 8.0 N, but rather is the force of the student minus the force of friction [which was found in (a)], 8.0 N − 2.0 N = 6.0 N.
3. Using a correct kinematics equation with correct substitutions to find the final velocity of the block; i.e., $v_f = v_o + at$, where $v_o = 0$ and $a = 6.0$ N/1.0 kg = 6.0 m/s².
4. Obtaining a correct answer with correct units, 9.0 m/s.

Now, we're not suggesting that you try to guess how the AP readers will award points for every problem. Rather, we want you to see that the AP readers care much more about your understanding of physics than your ability to punch numbers into your calculator. Therefore, *you* should care much more about demonstrating your understanding of physics than about getting the right final answer.

Partial Credit

Returning to part (b) from the example problem, it's obvious that you can get lots of partial credit even if you make a mistake or two. For example:

- If you forgot to include friction, and just set the student's force equal to *ma* and solved, you could still get 2 out of 4 points.

- If you solved part (a) wrong but still got a reasonable answer, say 4.5 N for the force of friction, and plugged that in correctly here, you would still get either 3 or 4 points in part (b)! Usually the rubrics are designed not to penalize you twice for a wrong answer. So if you get part of a problem wrong, but your answer is consistent with your previous work, you'll usually get full or close to full credit.

- That said, if you had come up with a 1000 N force of friction, which is clearly unreasonable, you probably will not get credit for a wrong but consistent answer, unless you indicate the ridiculousness of the situation. You'll still get probably 2 points, though, for the correct application of principles!

- If you got the right answer using a shortcut—say, doing the calculation of the net force in your head—you would not earn full credit but you would at least get the correct answer point. However, if you did the calculation *wrong* in your head, then you would *not* get any credit—AP readers can read what's written on the test, but they're not allowed to read your mind. Moral of the story: communicate with the readers so you are sure to get all the partial credit you deserve.

- Notice how generous the partial credit is. You can easily get 2 or 3 points without getting the right answer and 50–75% is in the 4–5 range when the AP test is scored!

You should also be aware of some things that will NOT get you partial credit:

- You will not get partial credit if you write multiple answers to a single question. If AP readers see that you've written two answers, they will grade the one that's wrong. In other words, you will lose points if you write more than one answer to a question, even if one of the answers you write is correct.

- You will not get partial credit by including unnecessary information. There's no way to get extra credit on a question, and if you write something that's wrong, you could lose points. Answer the question fully, then stop.

The Tools You Can Use

You can use a calculator. Most calculators are acceptable—the acceptable calculator list is the same as for the SAT or the AP calculus exam. The obvious forbidden calculators are those with a keyboard, cell phones used as a calculator, or those calculators that make noise or print their answers onto paper.[1] You also cannot share a calculator with anyone during the exam.

The real question, though, is whether a calculator will really help you. The short answer is "Yes": you will be asked questions on the exam that require you to do messy calculations (for example, you might need to divide a number by π, or multiply something by the universal gravitation constant). The longer answer, though, is "Yes, but it won't help very much." To see what we mean, look back at the hypothetical grading rubric for part (b) of the example problem we discussed earlier. Two of the four possible points are awarded for using the right equations, one point is awarded for finding the magnitude of a force using basic arithmetic, and the last point is awarded for solving a relatively simple equation. So you would get half-credit if you did no math at all, and you would get full credit just by doing some very elementary math. You probably wouldn't need to touch your calculator!

So definitely bring a calculator to the exam, but don't expect that you'll be punching away at it constantly.

The other tool you can use on the free-response section is the equations sheet. You will be given a copy of this sheet in your exam booklet. It's a handy reference because it lists all the equations that you're expected to know for the exam.

However, the equations sheet can also be dangerous. Too often, students interpret the equations sheet as an invitation to stop thinking: "Hey, they tell me everything I need to know, so I can just plug-and-chug through the rest of the exam!" Nothing could be further from the truth.

First of all, you've already *memorized* the equations on the sheet. It might be reassuring to look up an equation during the AP exam, just to make sure that you've remembered it correctly. And maybe you've forgotten a particular equation, but seeing it on the sheet will jog your memory. This is exactly what the equations sheet is for, and in this sense, it's pretty nice to have around. But beware of the following:

- Don't look up an equation unless you know *exactly* what you're looking for. It might sound obvious, but if you don't know what you're looking for, you won't find it.
- Don't go fishing. If part of a free-response question asks you to find an object's momentum, and you're not sure how to do that, don't just rush to the equations sheet and search for every equation with a "*P*" in it.

Math and the Physics C Exam

Physics C students often worry about the math they're expected to know for the AP exam, because some of the material covered in the Physics C curriculum involves pretty complicated calculus. Maxwell's equations, for example, involve concepts that are well beyond the scope of most high school calculus classes.

---

[1] Does anyone actually use printing calculators anymore?

Whether or not you are carrying an A in your AP Calculus course is irrelevant. Most importantly, you must have a strong understanding of the physical meaning behind the mathematics. The problems that might seem to involve calculus—those that use an integral or derivative equation from the equations sheet—can often be approached with algebraic methods. Remember, an integral is just the area under a graph; a derivative is just the slope of a graph. If you have to, set up an integral and don't solve it. Or explain in words what your answer should look like. Also, note that many of the equations that appear on the equations sheet as calculus expressions rarely or never need calculus. For instance, Gauss's law has a nasty integral in it, but when used correctly, Gauss's law rarely requires any calculus. Whatever you do, it is *not* worth the time and frustration to focus exclusively on the tough calculus—this isn't a math exam, and the point distribution in the rubrics reflects this fact.

Other Advice About the Free-Response Section

- Always show your work. If you use the correct equation to solve a problem but you plug in the wrong numbers, you will probably get partial credit, but if you just write down an incorrect answer, you will definitely get no partial credit.

- If you don't know precisely how to solve a problem, simply explain your thinking process to the grader. If a problem asks you to find the centripetal acceleration of a satellite orbiting a planet, for example, and you don't know what equations to use, you might write something like this: "The centripetal force points toward the center of the satellite's orbit, and this force is due to gravity. If I knew the centripetal force, I could then calculate the centripetal acceleration using Newton's second law." This answer might earn you several points, even though you didn't do a single calculation.

- However, don't write a book. Keep your answers succinct.

- Let's say that part (b) of a question requires you to use a value calculated in part (a). You didn't know how to solve part (a), but you know how to solve part (b). What should you do? We can suggest two options. First, make up a reasonable answer for part (a), and then use that answer for part (b). Or, set some variable equal to the answer from part (a) (write a note saying something like, "Let *v* be the velocity found in part (a)"). Then, solve part (b) in terms of that variable. Both of these methods should allow you to get partial or even full credit on part (b).

- If you make a mistake, cross it out. If your work is messy, circle your answer so that it's easy to find. Basically, make sure the AP readers know what you want them to grade and what you want them to ignore.

- If you're stuck on a free-response question, try another one. Question #3 might be easier for you than question #1. Get the easy points first, and then only try to get the harder points if you have time left over.

- Always use units where appropriate.

- It may be helpful to include a drawing or a graph in your answer to a question, but make sure to label your drawings or graphs so that they're easy to understand.

- No free-response question should take you more than about 15 minutes to solve. They're not designed to be outrageously difficult, so if your answer to a free-response problem is outrageously complicated, you should look for a new way to solve the problem, or just skip it and move on.

Lab Questions

It is all well and good to be able to solve problems and calculate quantities using the principles and equations you've learned. However, the true test of any physics theory is whether or not it WORKS.

The AP development committee is sending a message to students that laboratory work is an important aspect of physics. To truly understand physics, you must be able to design and analyze experiments. Thus, *each free-response section will contain at least one question that involves experiment design and analysis.*

Here's an example:

In the laboratory, you are given a metal block, about the size of a brick. You are also given a 2.0-m-long wooden plank with a pulley attached to one end. Your goal is to determine experimentally the coefficient of kinetic friction, μ_k, between the metal block and the wooden plank.

(a) Draw a labeled diagram showing how the plank, the metal block, and the additional equipment you selected will be used to measure μ_k.

(b) Briefly outline the procedure you will use, being explicit about what measurements you need to make and how these measurements will be used to determine μ_k.

To answer a lab question, just follow these steps:

1. **Follow the directions.**
   Sounds simple, doesn't it? When the test says, "Draw a diagram," it means they want you to draw a diagram. And when it says, "Label your diagram," it means they want you to label your diagram. You will likely earn points just for these simple steps.

Exam tip from an AP Physics veteran:
On the 1999 AP test, I forgot to label point B on a diagram, even though I obviously knew where point B was. This little mistake cost me several points!

—*Zack, college senior and engineer*

---

2. **Use as few words as possible.**
   Answer the question, then stop. You can lose credit for an incorrect statement, even if the other 15 statements in your answer are correct. The best idea is to keep it simple.

3. **There is no single correct answer.**
   Most of the lab questions are open-ended. There might be four or more different correct approaches. So don't try to "give them the answer they're looking for." Just do something that seems to make sense—you might well be right!

4. **Don't assume you have to use all the stuff they give you.**
   It might sound fun to use a force probe while determining the time constant of an RC circuit, but really! A force probe!?!

5. **Don't over-think the question.**
   They're normally not too complicated. Remember, you're supposed to take only 15 minutes to write your answer. You're not exactly designing a subatomic particle accelerator.

6. **Don't state the obvious.**
   You may assume that basic lab protocols will be followed. So there's no need to tell the reader that you recorded your data carefully, nor do you need to remind the reader to wear safety goggles.

Now Put It All Together

Here are two possible answers to the sample question. Look how explicit we were about what quantities are measured, how each quantity is measured, and how μ_k is determined. We aren't *artistes*, so our diagram doesn't look so good. But for the AP exam, we believe in substance over style. All the necessary components are there, and that's all that matters.

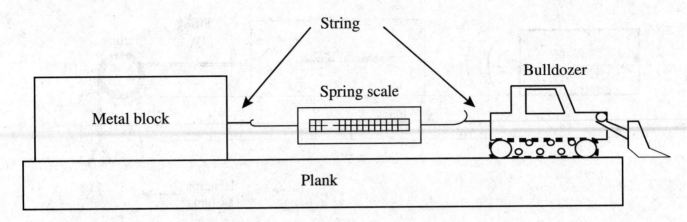

Answer #1

In the laboratory, you are given a metal block, about the size of a brick. You are also given a 2.0-m-long wooden plank with a pulley attached to one end. Your goal is to determine experimentally the coefficient of kinetic friction, μ_k, between the metal block and the wooden plank.

(a) Draw a labeled diagram showing how the plank, the metal block, and the additional equipment you selected will be used to measure μ_k.

(b) Briefly outline the procedure you will use, being explicit about what measurements you need to make and how these measurements will be used to determine μ_k.

Use the balance to determine the mass, m, of the metal block. The weight of the block is mg. Attach the spring scale to the bulldozer; attach the other end of the spring scale to the metal block with string. Allow the bulldozer to pull the block at constant speed.

The block is in equilibrium. So, the reading of the spring scale while the block is moving is the friction force on the block; the normal force on the block is equal to its weight. The coefficient of kinetic friction is equal to the spring scale reading divided by the block's weight.

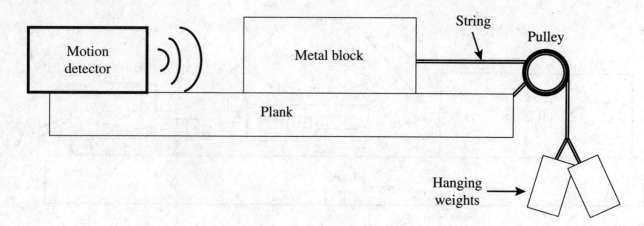

Answer #2

In the laboratory, you are given a metal block, about the size of a brick. You are also given a 2.0-m-long wooden plank with a pulley attached to one end. Your goal is to determine experimentally the coefficient of kinetic friction, μ_k, between the metal block and the wooden plank.

(a) Draw a labeled diagram showing how the plank, the metal block, and the additional equipment you selected will be used to measure μ_k.

(b) Briefly outline the procedure you will use, being explicit about what measurements you need to make and how these measurements will be used to determine μ_k.

Determine the mass, m, of the block with the balance. The weight of the block is mg. Attach a string to the block and pass the string over the pulley. Hang masses from the other end of the string, changing the amount of mass until the block can move across the plank at constant speed. Use the motion detector to verify that the speed of the block is as close to constant as possible.

The block is in equilibrium. So, the weight of the hanging masses is equal to the friction force on the block; the normal force on the block is equal to its weight. The coefficient of kinetic friction is thus equal to the weight of the hanging masses divided by the block's weight.

CHAPTER 8

Extra Drill on Difficult but Frequently Tested Topics

IN THIS CHAPTER

Summary: Drills in five types of problems that you should spend extra time reviewing, with step-by-step solutions.

Key Ideas
- ✪ Tension problems
- ✪ Electric and magnetic fields problems
- ✪ Inclined plane problems
- ✪ Motion graph problems
- ✪ Simple circuits problems

Practice problems and tests cannot possibly cover every situation that you may be asked to understand in physics. However, some categories of topics come up again and again, so much so that they might be worth some extra review. And that's exactly what this chapter is for—to give you a focused, intensive review of a few of the most essential physics topics.

We call them "drills" for a reason. They are designed to be skill-building exercises, and as such, they stress repetition and technique. Working through these exercises might remind you of playing scales if you're a musician or of running laps around the field if you're an athlete. Not much fun, maybe a little tedious, but very helpful in the long run.

The questions in each drill are all solved essentially the same way. *Don't* just do one problem after the other . . . rather, do a couple, check to see that your answers are right,[1] and then, half an hour or a few days later, do a few more, just to remind yourself of the techniques involved.

---

[1]For numerical answers, it's okay if you're off by a significant figure or so.

Tension

How to Do It

Use the following steps to solve these kinds of problems: (1) Draw a free-body diagram for each block; (2) resolve vectors into their components; (3) write Newton's second law for each block, being careful to stick to your choice of positive direction; and (4) solve the simultaneous equations for whatever the problem asks for.

The Drill

In the diagrams below, assume all pulleys and ropes are massless, and use the following variable definitions.

$$F = 10 \text{ N}$$
$$M = 1.0 \text{ kg}$$
$$\mu = 0.2$$

Find the tension in each rope and the acceleration of the set of masses.
(For a greater challenge, solve in terms of F, M, and μ instead of plugging in values.)

1. Frictionless

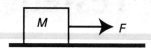

2. Frictionless

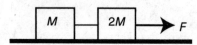

3. Frictionless

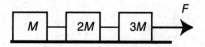

4. Coefficient of Friction μ

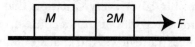

5.

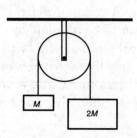

6.

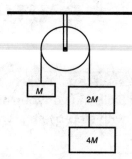

7. Frictionless

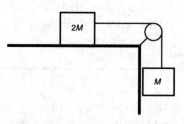

8. Frictionless

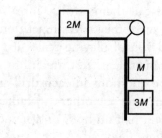

9. Frictionless

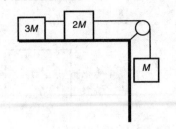

12. Frictionless

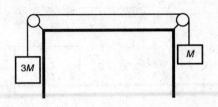

10. Coefficient of Friction μ

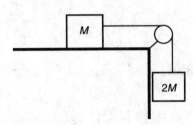

13. Frictionless

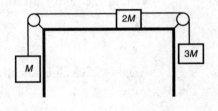

11. Coefficient of Friction μ

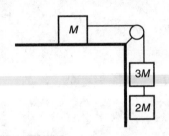

14. Coefficient of Friction μ

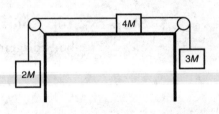

〉 The Answers
(Step-by-Step Solutions to #2 and #5 Are on the Next Page.)

1. $a = 10$ m/s^2

2. $a = 3.3$ m/s^2
$T = 3.3$ N

3. $a = 1.7$ m/s^2
$T_1 = 1.7$ N
$T_2 = 5.1$ N

4. $a = 1.3$ m/s^2
$T = 3.3$ N

5. $a = 3.3$ m/s^2
$T = 13$ N

6. $a = 7.1$ m/s^2
$T_1 = 17$ N
$T_2 = 11$ N

7. $a = 3.3$ m/s^2
$T = 6.6$ N

8. $a = 6.7$ m/s^2
$T_1 = 13$ N
$T_2 = 10$ N

9. $a = 1.7$ m/s^2
$T_1 = 5.1$ N
$T_2 = 8.3$ N

10. $a = 6.0$ m/s^2
$T = 8.0$ N

11. $a = 8.0$ m/s^2
$T_1 = 10$ N
$T_2 = 4.0$ N

12. $a = 5.0$ m/s^2
$T = 15$ N

13. $a = 3.3$ m/s^2
$T_1 = 13$ N
$T_2 = 20$ N

14. $a = 0.22$ m/s^2
$T_1 = 20$ N
$T_2 = 29$ N

Step-by-Step Solution to #2:

Step 1: Free-body diagrams:

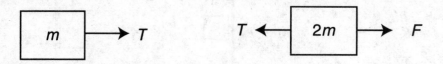

No components are necessary, so on to *Step 3:* write Newton's second law for each block, calling the rightward direction positive:

$$T - 0 = ma.$$
$$F - T = (2m)a.$$

Step 4: Solve algebraically. It's easiest to add these equations together, because the tensions cancel:

$$F = (3m)a, \text{ so } a = F/3m = (10 \text{ N})/3(1 \text{ kg}) = 3.3 \text{ m/s}^2.$$

To get the tension, just plug back into $T - 0 = ma$ to find $T = F/3 = 3.3$ N.

Step-by-Step Solution to #5:

Step 1: Free-body diagrams:

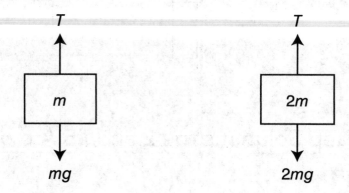

No components are necessary, so on to *Step 3:* write Newton's second law for each block, calling clockwise rotation of the pulley positive:

$$(2m)g - T = (2m)a.$$
$$T - mg = ma.$$

Step 4: Solve algebraically. It's easiest to add these equations together, because the tensions cancel:

$$mg = (3m)a, \text{ so } a = g/3 = 3.3 \text{ m/s}^2.$$

To get the tension, just plug back into $T - mg = ma$: $T = m (a + g) = (4/3)mg = 13$ N.

Electric and Magnetic Fields

How to Do It

The force of an electric field is $F = qE$, and the direction of the force is in the direction of the field for a positive charge. The force of a magnetic field is $F = qvB \sin\theta$, and the direction of the force is given by the right-hand rule.

The Drill

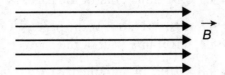

The magnetic field above has magnitude 3.0 T. For each of the following particles placed in the field, find (a) the force exerted by the magnetic field on the particle, and (b) the acceleration of the particle. Be sure to give magnitude *and direction* in each case.

1. an e- at rest
2. an e- moving ↑ at 2 m/s
3. an e- moving ← at 2 m/s
4. a proton moving ⊙ at 2 m/s
5. an e- moving up and to the right, at an angle of 30° to the horizontal, at 2 m/s
6. an e- moving up and to the left, at an angle of 30° to the horizontal, at 2 m/s
7. a positron moving up and to the right, at an angle of 30° to the horizontal, at 2 m/s
8. an e- moving → at 2 m/s
9. a proton moving ⊗ at 2 m/s

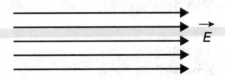

The electric field above has magnitude 3.0 N/C. For each of the following particles placed in the field, find (a) the force exerted by the electric field on the particle, and (b) the acceleration of the particle. Be sure to give magnitude *and direction* in each case.

10. an e- at rest
11. a proton at rest
12. a positron at rest
13. an e- moving ↑ at 2 m/s
14. an e- moving → at 2 m/s
15. a proton moving ⊙ at 2 m/s
16. an e- moving ← at 2 m/s
17. a positron moving up and to the right, at an angle of 30° to the horizontal, at 2 m/s

〉 The Answers
(Step-by-Step Solutions to #2 and #10 Are on the Next Pages.)

1. No force or acceleration, $v = 0$.

2. $F = 9.6 \times 10^{-19}$ N, out of the page.
$a = 1.1 \times 10^{12}$ m/s², out of the page.

3. No force or acceleration, $\sin \theta = 0$.

4. $F = 9.6 \times 10^{-19}$ N, toward the top of the page.
$a = 5.6 \times 10^8$ m/s², toward the top of the page.

5. $F = 4.8 \times 10^{-19}$ N, out of the page.
   $a = 5.3 \times 10^{11}$ m/s², out of the page.

6. $F = 4.8 \times 10^{-19}$ N, out of the page.
   $a = 5.3 \times 10^{11}$ m/s², out of the page.

7. $F = 4.8 \times 10^{-19}$ N, into the page.
   $a = 5.3 \times 10^{11}$ m/s², into the page.

8. No force or acceleration, $\sin \theta = 0$.

9. $F = 9.6 \times 10^{-19}$ N, toward the bottom of the page.
   $a = 5.6 \times 10^{8}$ m/s², toward the bottom of the page.

10. $F = 4.8 \times 10^{-19}$ N, left.
    $a = 5.3 \times 10^{11}$ m/s², left.

11. $F = 4.8 \times 10^{-19}$ N, right.
    $a = 2.8 \times 10^{8}$ m/s², right.

12. $F = 4.8 \times 10^{-19}$ N, right.
    $a = 5.3 \times 10^{11}$ m/s², right.

13. $F = 4.8 \times 10^{-19}$ N, left.
    $a = 5.3 \times 10^{11}$ m/s², left.
    Velocity does not affect electric force.

14. $F = 4.8 \times 10^{-19}$ N, left.
    $a = 5.3 \times 10^{11}$ m/s², left.

15. $F = 4.8 \times 10^{-19}$ N, right.
    $a = 2.8 \times 10^{8}$ m/s², right.

16. $F = 4.8 \times 10^{-19}$ N, left.
    $a = 5.3 \times 10^{11}$ m/s², left.

17. $F = 4.8 \times 10^{-19}$ N, right.
    $a = 5.3 \times 10^{11}$ m/s², right.

Step-by-Step Solution to #2:

(a) The magnetic force on a charge is given by $F = qvB \sin \theta$. Since the velocity is perpendicular to the magnetic field, $\theta = 90°$, and $\sin \theta = 1$. The charge q is the amount of charge on an electron, 1.6×10^{-19} C. v is the electron's speed, 2 m/s. B is the magnetic field, 3 T.

$$F = (1.6 \times 10^{-19} \text{ C})(2 \text{ m/s})(3 \text{ T})(1) = 9.6 \times 10^{-19} \text{ N}$$

The direction is given by the right-hand rule. Point your fingers in the direction of the electron's velocity, toward the top of the page; curl your fingers in the direction of the magnetic field, to the right; your thumb points into the page. Since the electron has a negative charge, the force points opposite your thumb, or out of the page.

(b) Even though we're dealing with a magnetic force, we can still use Newton's second law. Since the magnetic force is the only force acting, just set this force equal to ma and solve. The direction of the acceleration must be in the same direction as the net force.

$$9.6 \times 10^{-19} \text{ N} = (9.1 \times 10^{-31} \text{ kg})a$$
$$a = 1.1 \times 10^{12} \text{ m/s}^2, \text{ out of the page}$$

Step-by-Step Solution to #10:

(a) The electric force on a charge is given by $F = qE$. The charge q is the amount of charge on an electron, 1.6×10^{-19} C. E is the electric field, 3 N/C.

$$F = (1.6 \times 10^{-19} \text{ C})(3 \text{ N/C}) = 4.8 \times 10^{-19} \text{ N}$$

Because the electron has a negative charge, the force is opposite the electric field, or right.

(b) Even though we're dealing with an electric force, we can still use Newton's second law. Since the electric force is the only force acting, just set this force equal to ma and solve. The direction of the acceleration must be in the same direction as the net force.

$$4.8 \times 10^{-19} \text{ N} = (9.1 \times 10^{-31} \text{ kg})a$$
$$a = 2.8 \times 10^{8} \text{ m/s}^2, \text{ left}$$

Inclined Planes

How to Do It

Use the following steps to solve these kinds of problems: 1) Draw a free-body diagram for the object (the normal force is perpendicular to the plane; the friction force acts along the plane, opposite the velocity); 2) break vectors into components, where the parallel component of weight is $mg(\sin \theta)$; 3) write Newton's second law for parallel and perpendicular components; and 4) solve the equations for whatever the problem asks for.

Don't forget, the normal force is NOT equal to mg when a block is on an incline!

The Drill

Directions: For each of the following situations, determine:

    (a) the acceleration of the block down the plane
    (b) the time for the block to slide to the bottom of the plane

In each case, assume a frictionless plane unless otherwise stated; assume the block is released from rest unless otherwise stated.

1.

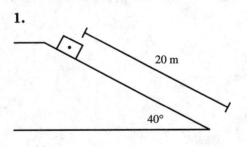

2.

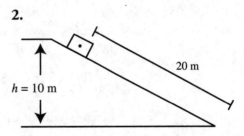

3.

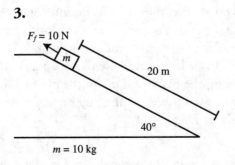

4.

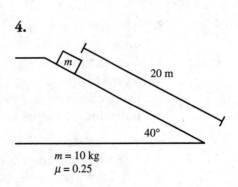

5.

6.

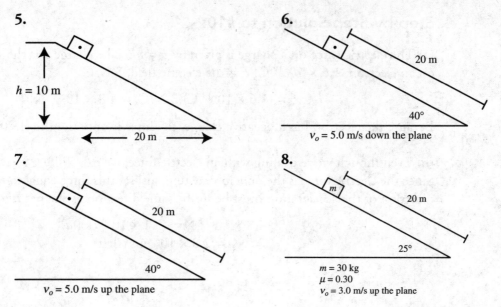

$h = 10$ m

20 m

20 m

40°

$v_o = 5.0$ m/s down the plane

7.

8.

20 m

m

20 m

40°

25°

$v_o = 5.0$ m/s up the plane

$m = 30$ kg
$\mu = 0.30$
$v_o = 3.0$ m/s up the plane

Careful—this one's tricky.

› The Answers
(A Step-by-Step Solution to #1 Is on the Next Page.)

1. $a = 6.3$ m/s^2, down the plane.
   $t = 2.5$ s

2. $a = 4.9$ m/s^2, down the plane.
   $t = 2.9$ s

3. $a = 5.2$ m/s^2, down the plane.
   $t = 2.8$ s

4. $a = 4.4$ m/s^2, down the plane.
   $t = 3.0$ s

5. Here the angle of the plane is 27° by trigonometry, and the distance along the plane is 22 m.
   $a = 4.4$ m/s^2, down the plane.
   $t = 3.2$ s

6. $a = 6.3$ m/s^2, down the plane.
   $t = 1.8$ s

7. $a = 6.3$ m/s^2, down the plane.
   $t = 3.5$ s

8. This one is complicated. Since the direction of the friction force changes depending on whether the block is sliding up or down the plane, the block's acceleration is NOT constant throughout the whole problem. So, unlike problem #7, this one can't be solved in a single step. Instead, in order to use kinematics equations, you must break this problem up into two parts: up the plane and down the plane. During each of these individual parts, the acceleration is constant, so the kinematics equations are valid.

   • up the plane:
     $a = 6.8$ m/s^2, down the plane.
     $t = 0.4$ s before the block turns around to come down the plane.

- down the plane:
  $a = 1.5$ m/s^2, down the plane.
  $t = 5.2$ s to reach bottom.

So, a total of $t = 5.6$ s for the block to go up and back down.

Step-by-Step Solution to #1:

Step 1: Free-body diagram:

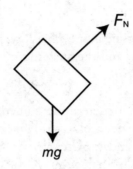

Step 2: Break vectors into components. Because we have an incline, we use inclined axes, one parallel and one perpendicular to the incline:

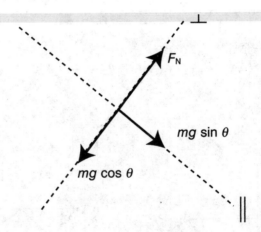

Step 3: Write Newton's second law for each axis. The acceleration is entirely directed parallel to the plane, so perpendicular acceleration can be written as zero:

$$mg \sin \theta - 0 = ma.$$
$$F_N - mg \cos \theta = 0.$$

Step 4: Solve algebraically for a. This can be done without reference to the second equation. (In problems with friction, use $F_f = \mu F_N$ to relate the two equations.)

$$a = g \sin \theta = 6.3 \text{ m/s}^2$$

To find the time, plug into a kinematics chart:

$$v_o = 0$$
$$v_f = \text{unknown}$$
$$\Delta x = 20 \text{ m}$$
$$a = 6.3 \text{ m/s}^2$$
$$t = ???$$

Solve for t using the second star equation for kinematics (**): $\Delta x = v_o t + \frac{1}{2}at^2$, where v_o is zero;

$$t = \sqrt{\frac{2\Delta x}{a}} = \sqrt{\frac{2(20 \text{ m})}{6.3 \text{ m/s}^2}} = 2.5 \text{ s}$$

Motion Graphs

How to Do It

For a position–time graph, the slope is the velocity. For a velocity–time graph, the slope is the acceleration, and the area under the graph is the displacement.

The Drill

Use the graph to determine something about the object's speed. Then play "Physics *Taboo*": suggest what object might reasonably perform this motion and explain in words how the object moves. Use everyday language. In your explanation, you may *not* use any words from the list below:

velocity
acceleration
positive
negative
increase
decrease
object
constant

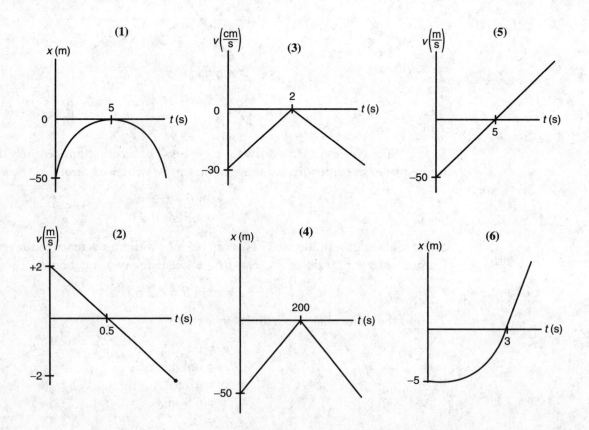

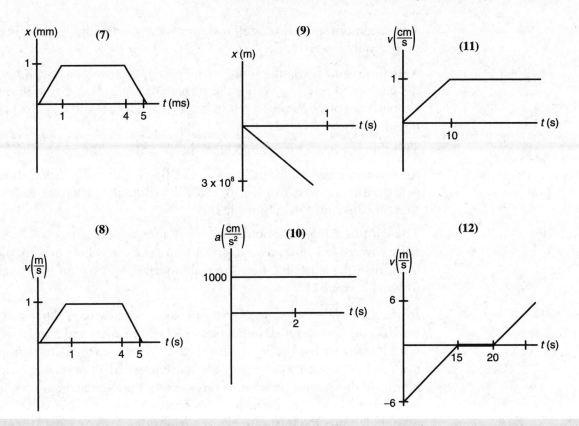

› The Answers

Note that our descriptions of the moving objects reflect our own imaginations. You might have come up with some very different descriptions, and that's fine . . . provided that your answers are conceptually the same as ours.

1. The average speed over the first 5 s is 10 m/s, or about 22 mph. So:

   Someone rolls a bowling ball along a smooth road. When the graph starts, the bowling ball is moving along pretty fast, but the ball encounters a long hill. So, the ball slows down, coming to rest after 5 s. Then, the ball comes back down the hill, speeding up the whole way.

2. This motion only lasts 1 s, and the maximum speed involved is about 5 mph. So:

   A biker has been cruising up a hill. When the graph starts, the biker is barely moving at jogging speed. Within half a second, and after traveling only a meter up the hill, the bike turns around, speeding up as it goes back down the hill.

3. The maximum speed of this thing is 30 cm/s, or about a foot per second. So:

   A toy racecar is moving slowly along its track. The track goes up a short hill that's about a foot long. After 2 s, the car has just barely reached the top of the hill, and is perched there momentarily; then, the car crests the hill and speeds up as it goes down the other side.

4. The steady speed over 200 s (a bit over 3 minutes) is 0.25 m/s, or 25 cm/s, or about a foot per second.

   A cockroach crawls steadily along the school's running track, searching for food. The cockroach starts near the 50 yard line of the football field; around three minutes later, the cockroach reaches the goal line and, having found nothing of interest, turns around and crawls at the same speed back toward his starting point.

5. The maximum speed here is 50 m/s, or over a hundred mph, changing speed dramatically in only 5 or 10 s. So:

   A small airplane is coming in for a landing. Upon touching the ground, the pilot puts the engines in reverse, slowing the plane. But wait! The engine throttle is stuck! So, although the plane comes to rest in 5 s, the engines are still on. The plane starts speeding up backwards! Oops . . .

6. This thing covers 5 meters in 3 seconds, speeding up the whole time.

   An 8-year-old gets on his dad's bike. The boy is not really strong enough to work the pedals easily, so he starts off with difficulty. But, after a few seconds he's managed to speed the bike up to a reasonable clip.

7. Though this thing moves quickly—while moving, the speed is 1 m/s—the total distance covered is 1 mm forward, and 1 mm back; the whole process takes 5 ms, which is less than the minimum time interval indicated by a typical stopwatch. So we'll have to be a bit creative:

   In the Discworld novels by Terry Pratchett, wizards have developed a computer in which living ants in tubes, rather than electrons in wires and transistors, carry information. (Electricity has not been harnessed on the Discworld.) In performing a calculation, one of these ants moves forward a distance of 1 mm; stays in place for 3 ms; and returns to the original position. If this ant's motion represents two typical "operations" performed by the computer, then this computer has an approximate processing speed of 400 Hz times the total number of ants inside.

8. Though this graph *looks* like #7, this one is a velocity–time graph, and so indicates completely different motion.

   A small child pretends he is a bulldozer. Making a "brm-brm-brm" noise with his lips, he speeds up from rest to a slow walk. He walks for three more seconds, then slows back down to rest. He moved forward the entire time, traveling a total distance (found from the area under the graph) of 4 m.

9. This stuff moves 300 million meters in 1 s at a constant speed. There's only one possibility here: electromagnetic waves in a vacuum.

   Light (or electromagnetic radiation of any frequency) is emitted from the surface of the moon. In 1 s, the light has covered about half the distance to Earth.

10. Be careful about axis labels: this is an *acceleration*–time graph. Something is accelerating at 1000 cm/s² for a few seconds. 1000 cm/s² = 10 m/s², about Earth's gravitational acceleration. Using kinematics, we calculate that if we drop something from rest near Earth, after 4 s the thing has dropped 80 m.

    One way to simulate the effects of zero gravity is to drop an experiment from the top of a high tower. Then, because everything that was dropped is speeding up at the same rate, the effect is just as if the experiment were done in the Space Shuttle—at least until everything hits the ground. In this case, an experiment is dropped from a 250-ft tower, hitting the ground with a speed close to 90 mph.

11. 1 cm/s is ridiculously slow. Let's use the world of slimy animals:

    A snail wakes up from his nap and decides to find some food. He speeds himself up from rest to his top speed in 10 s. During this time, he's covered 5 cm, or about the length of your pinkie finger. He continues to slide along at a steady 1 cm/s, which means that a minute later he's gone no farther than a couple of feet. Let's hope that food is close.

12. This one looks a bit like those up-and-down-a-hill graphs, but with an important difference—this time the thing stops not just for an instant, but for five whole seconds, before continuing back toward the starting point.

A bicyclist coasts to the top of a shallow hill, slowing down from cruising speed (~15 mph) to rest in 15 s. At the top, she pauses briefly to turn her bike around; then, she releases the brake and speeds up as she goes back down the hill.

Simple Circuits

How to Do It

Think "series" and "parallel." The current through series resistors is the same, and the voltage across series resistors adds to the total voltage. The current through parallel resistors adds to the total current, and the voltage across parallel resistors is the same.

The Drill

For each circuit drawn below, find the current through and voltage across each resistor.

Note: Assume each resistance and voltage value is precise to two significant figures.

1.

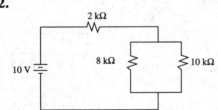

2.

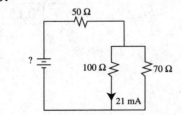

3.

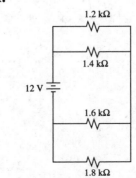

4.

5.

6.

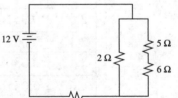

7.

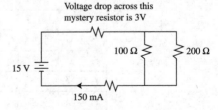

› The Answers
(A Step-by-Step Solution to #2 Is on the Next Page.)

1.

V	I	R
12 V	0.40 A	30 Ω
12 V	0.60 A	20 Ω
12 V	1.2 A	10 Ω
12 V	2.2 A	5.5 Ω

2.

V	I	R
3.2 V	1.6 mA	2 kΩ
6.8 V	0.9 mA	8 kΩ
6.8 V	0.7 mA	10 kΩ
10 V	1.6 mA	6.4 kΩ

(Remember, a kΩ is 1000 Ω, and a mA is 10^{-3} A.)

3.

V	I	R
2.5 V	0.051 A	50 Ω
2.1 V	0.021 A	100 Ω
2.1 V	0.030 A	70 Ω
4.6 V	0.051 A	91 Ω

4.

V	I	R
5.2 V	4.3 mA	1.2 kΩ
5.2 V	3.7 mA	1.4 kΩ
6.8 V	4.2 mA	1.6 kΩ
6.8 V	3.8 mA	1.8 kΩ
12 V	8.0 mA	1.5 kΩ

5.

V	I	R
3.4 V	0.034 A	100 Ω
6.8 V	0.034 A	200 Ω
10 V	0.025 A	400 Ω
10 V	0.059 A	170 Ω

6.

V	I	R
1.8 V	0.90 A	2.0 Ω
0.7 V	0.13 A	5.0 Ω
0.8 V	0.13 A	6.0 Ω
10.3 V	1.03 A	10.0 Ω
12.0 V	1.03 A	11.7 Ω

7.

V	I	R
3 V	0.15 A	20 Ω
10 V	0.10 A	100 Ω
10 V	0.05 A	200 Ω
2 V	0.15 A	13 Ω
15 V	0.15 A	100 Ω

Step-by-Step Solution to #2:

Start by simplifying the combinations of resistors. The 8 kΩ and 10 kΩ resistors are in parallel. Their equivalent resistance is given by

$$\frac{1}{R_{eq}} = \frac{1}{8 \text{ k}\Omega} + \frac{1}{10 \text{ k}\Omega}$$

which gives $R_{eq} = 4.4$ kΩ.

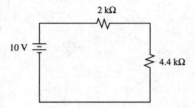

Next, simplify these series resistors to their equivalent resistance of 6.4 kΩ.

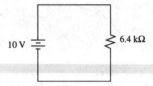

6.4 kΩ (i.e., 6400 Ω) is the total resistance of the entire circuit. Because we know the total voltage of the entire circuit to be 10 V, we can use Ohm's law to get the total current

$$I_{total} = \frac{V_{total}}{R_{total}} = \frac{10 \text{ V}}{6400 \text{ }\Omega} = 0.0016 \text{ A}$$

(more commonly written as 1.6 mA).

Now look at the previous diagram. The same current of 1.6 mA must go out of the battery, into the 2 kΩ resistor, and into the 4.4 kΩ resistor. The voltage across each resistor can thus be determined by $V = (1.6 \text{ mA})R$ for each resistor, giving 3.2 V across the 2 kΩ resistor and 6.8 V across the 4.4 kΩ resistor.

The 2 kΩ resistor is on the chart. However, the 4.4 kΩ resistor is the equivalent of two parallel resistors. Because voltage is the same for resistors in parallel, there are 6.8 V across *each* of the two parallel resistors in the original diagram. Fill that in the chart, and use Ohm's law to find the current through each:

$$I_{8k} = 6.8 \text{ V}/8000 \text{ }\Omega = 0.9 \text{ mA}$$
$$I_{10k} = 6.8 \text{ V}/10,000 \text{ }\Omega = 0.7 \text{ mA}$$

STEP 4

Review the Knowledge You Need to Score High

CHAPTER 9

Free-Body Diagrams and Equilibrium

IN THIS CHAPTER

Summary: Free-body diagrams can help you see forces as vectors, and we'll review torque as well as a variety of forces: normal force, tension, friction, forces operating on inclined planes, and static and kinetic friction.

Key Ideas

✪ A free-body diagram is a picture that represents an object, along with the forces acting on that object.
✪ When the net force on an object equals zero, that object is in equilibrium.
✪ The normal force is *not* always equal to the weight of an object.
✪ Tension is a force applied by a rope or string.
✪ Friction is only found when there is contact between two surfaces.
✪ When an object is on an incline, use tilted axes, one parallel to the incline, one perpendicular.
✪ Torque occurs when a force is applied to an object, and that force can cause the object to rotate.

Relevant Equations

When the angle θ is measured from the horizontal, any force can be broken into components:

$$F_x = F\cos\theta \qquad F_y = F\sin\theta$$

On an inclined plane—*only* when an object is on an incline—the weight can be broken into components:

$$mg_\perp = mg(\cos\theta) \qquad mg_\parallel = mg(\sin\theta)$$

The force of friction is given by

$$F_f = \mu F_N$$

Physics, at its essence, is all about simplification. The universe is a complicated place, and if you want to make sense of it—which is what physicists try to do—you need to reduce it to some simplified representation: for example, with free-body diagrams.

We will refer regularly to forces. A force refers to a push or a pull applied to an object. Something can experience many different forces simultaneously—for example, you can push a block forward while friction pulls it backward, but the net force is the vector sum of all of the individual forces acting on the block. By "vector" sum we mean, direction matters. Add forces that act in the same direction, subtract forces acting in the opposite direction.

Net Force: The vector sum of all the forces acting on an object

---

What Is a Free-Body Diagram?

A free-body diagram is a picture that represents one or more objects, along with the forces acting on those objects. The objects are almost always drawn as rectangles or circles, just for the sake of simplicity, and the forces are always shown as arrows, where the arrow starts on the object and points away from the object in the direction that the force acts. Figure 9.1 shows a few examples.

Let's look at the two examples in Figure 9.1. In the first, a force is directed down. This force, which is the force of gravity, was labeled in the diagram as "weight." The force of gravity on the hippo (that is, the hippo's weight) pulls downward. In the second example, a force is directed to the right. The pineapple is being pulled by a rope to the right.

Weight: The force due to gravity, equal to the mass of an object times g, the gravitational field (about 10 N/kg on Earth)

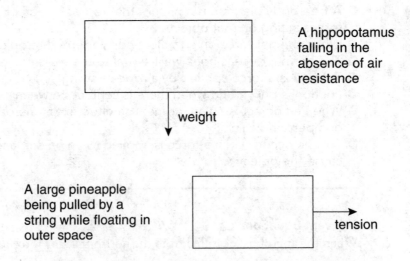

**Figure 9.1   Two examples of free-body diagrams.
As you see, there is no need to be artistic on the AP exam.**

You'll often see weight abbreviated as *mg*. Just be careful that the mass you use is in kilograms.

For the rest of this chapter, we focus on objects in equilibrium.

Equilibrium

When the net force on an object equals zero, that object is in equilibrium. At equilibrium, an object is either at rest or *moving with a constant velocity*, but it is not accelerating.

You've heard of Newton's first law, of course: an object maintains its velocity unless acted upon by a net force. Well, an object in equilibrium is obeying Newton's first law.

How to Solve Equilibrium Problems

We have a tried-and-true method. Follow it every time you see an equilibrium situation.

1. Draw a proper free-body diagram.
2. Resolve force vectors into *x* and *y* components, if necessary. (We'll show you how to do that on page 86.)
3. Write an expression setting the left forces equal to the right forces. Then write an expression setting the up forces equal to the down forces.
4. Solve the resulting algebraic equations.

A Brief Interlude: UNITS!

Before we lose ourselves in the excitement of free-body diagrams, we need to pay tribute to the unit of force: the newton. One N (as newtons are abbreviated) equals one kg·m/s². We discuss why 1 newton equals 1 kg·m/s² in a future chapter. For now, let it suffice that any force can be measured in newtons.

A Really Simple Equilibrium Problem

For those of you who prefer to splash your toes in the metaphorical swimming pool of physics before getting all the way in, this section is for you. Look at this situation:

Three astronauts tug horizontally on a satellite. The first astronaut tugs to the left with 30 N of force. The second astronaut tugs to the right with 20 N of force. What force should the third astronaut apply to keep the satellite at rest?

The solution to this problem is painfully obvious, but we'll go through the steps just to be thorough.

Step 1: Draw a proper free-body diagram.

We can skip Step 2 because these vectors already line up with each other, so they do not need to be resolved into components.

Step 3: Write equilibrium equations: up = down, left = right. The problem involves only left-right forces so we only need one expression.

$$F_1 = F_2 + F_3$$

The problem asks us to solve for F_3. Since we know F_1 and F_2, we have one equation with only one unknown—the physics is done, and what's left is just math.

Step 4: Solve.

$$(30 \text{ N}) = (20 \text{ N}) + F_3$$

Therefore, **F_3 = 10 N.**

Very good. Now, let's see how closely you were paying attention. Here's the same problem, with a slightly different twist.

> Three astronauts tug horizontally on a satellite. The first astronaut tugs to the left with 30 N of force. The second astronaut tugs to the right with 20 N of force. What force should the third astronaut apply to keep the satellite moving at a constant speed of 20 m/s?

Think for a moment. Does the third astronaut have to apply more, less, or the same force as compared to the previous problem?

The third astronaut applies *exactly the same force* as in the previous problem! An object moving with constant velocity is in equilibrium, just as if the object were still. This is a central concept in Newtonian mechanics.

Normal Force

Let's return to Earth for a moment.

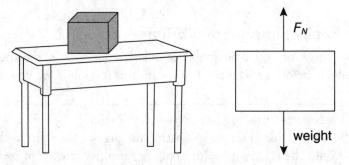

Figure 9.2   Normal force.

In Figure 9.2, a box is sitting on a table. The force of gravity pulls downward (as with the hippo, we've labeled this force "weight"). We know from experience that boxes sitting on tables do not accelerate downward; they remain where they are. Some force must oppose the downward pull of gravity.

This force is called the normal force,[1] and it is abbreviated F_N. In fact, whenever you push on a hard surface, that surface pushes back on you—it exerts a normal force. So, when you stand on the floor, the floor pushes up on you with the same amount of force with which gravity pulls you down, and, as a result, you don't fall through the floor.

> **Normal Force:** A force that acts perpendicular to the surface on which an object rests

---

[1]When physicists say "normal," they mean "perpendicular." The word "normal" in its conventional meaning simply does not apply to physicists.

The normal force is *not* always equal to the weight of an object! Think about this before we get to the practice problems.

Tension

Tension is a force applied by a rope or string. Here are two of our favorite tension problems. The first is super easy, but a good introduction to tension; the second is more involved.

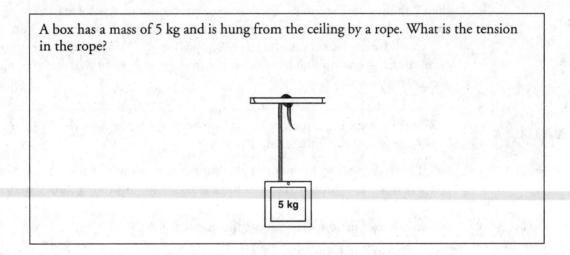

A box has a mass of 5 kg and is hung from the ceiling by a rope. What is the tension in the rope?

Step 1: Free-body diagram.

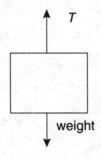

Step 2: Vector components.
Hey! These vectors already line up. On to Step 3.

Step 3: Equations.
Remember, weight is equal to mass times the gravitational field, or *mg*.

$$T = mg$$

Step 4: Solve.

$$T = (5 \text{ kg})(10 \text{ N/kg})$$

So **T = 50 N.**

The same box is now hung by two ropes. One makes a 45-degree angle with the ceiling; the other makes a 30-degree angle with the ceiling. What is the tension in each rope?

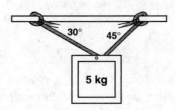

Step 2 in the equilibrium problem-solving procedure says, resolve force vectors into *x* and *y* components, where necessary. Here's a situation in which components are necessary.

Consider the tension in the left rope—call it T_1. This force can be represented by two components—one pulling left (called the *horizontal component*), one pulling up (called the *vertical component*).

Whenever breaking a force vector into components, be sure the angle θ of the force is measured from the horizontal. Then:

- The horizontal component of the force is the amount of force times cos θ.
- The vertical component of the force is the amount of force times sin θ.

Now, let's use the four-step problem solving-process.

Step 1: Free-body diagram.

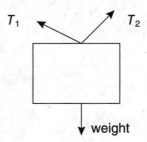

Step 2: Break forces into components.

Step 3: Equations

In the *x* direction, $T_1\cos30 = T_2\cos45$.

In the *y* direction, $T_1\sin30 + T_2\sin45 = mg$.

Do we have enough information to solve? We need to find T_1 and T_2. But we know the sines and cosines by plugging into a calculator. We know $m = 5$ kg, and $g = 10$ N/kg. So we have two unknowns ... but also two equations. The problem is solvable. The physics is done.

Step 4: Solve.
We can solve Equation 1 and Equation 2 simultaneously and find T_1 and T_2. We'll let you do this on your own,[2] but in case you want to check your answers, $T_1 = 37$ N and $T_2 = 45$ N. (These are reasonable answers, as the tension in each rope is the same power of 10 as the 50 N weight of the box.)

Steps 1, 2, and 3 are the important steps. Step 4 only involves math. "ONLY math?!?" you ask, incredulous. "That's the toughest part!"

Well, maybe for some people. Getting the actual correct answer does depend on your algebra skills. But, and this is important, *this is AP Physics, NOT AP Algebra.* The graders of the AP exam will assign most of the credit just for setting up the problem correctly! If you're stuck on the algebra, skip it! Come up with a reasonable answer for the tensions, and move on!

We're not kidding. Look at Chapter 7, which discusses approaches to the free-response section, for more about the relative importance of algebra.

Friction

Friction is only found when there is contact between two surfaces.

Friction: A force acting parallel to two surfaces in contact. If an object moves, the friction force always acts opposite the direction of motion.

For example, let's say you slide a book at a constant speed across a table. The book is in contact with the table, and, assuming your table isn't frictionless, the table will exert a friction force on the book opposite its direction of motion. Figure 9.3 shows a free-body diagram of that situation.

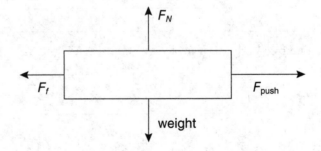

Figure 9.3   Free-body diagram of a book sliding on a table.

---

[2]Try solving the *x*-axis equation for T_1, then plug that into the *y*-axis equation:

$$T_1 = T_2 \frac{\cos 45°}{\cos 30°}$$

$$\left(T_2 \frac{\cos 45°}{\cos 30°} \right) \sin 30° + (T_2 \sin 45°) - (50 \text{ N}) = 0$$

Plug in the value of cos 45°, cos 30°, sin 30°, sin 45° ... and now it's easy to solve for $T_2 = 45$ N.

We know that because the book represented in Figure 9.3 is not being shoved through the table or flying off it, F_N must equal the book's weight. And because the book moves at constant velocity, the force you exert by pushing the book, F_{push}, equals the force of friction, F_f. *Remember, being in equilibrium does not necessarily mean that the book is at rest. It could be moving at a constant velocity.*

How do we find the magnitude of F_f?

$$F_f = \mu \, F_N$$

Mu (μ) is the coefficient of friction. This is a dimensionless number (that is, it doesn't have any units) that describes how big the force of friction is between two objects. It is found experimentally because it differs for every combination of materials (for example, if a wood block slides on a glass surface), but it will usually be given in AP problems that involve friction.

And if μ isn't given, it is easy enough to solve for—just rearrange the equation for μ algebraically:

$$\mu = \frac{F_f}{F_N}.$$

Remember, when solving for F_f, do not assume that F_N equals the weight of the object in question. Here's a problem where this reminder comes in handy:

A floor buffer consists of a heavy base ($m = 15$ kg) attached to a very light handle. A worker pushes the buffer by exerting a force P directly down the length of the handle. If the coefficient of friction between the buffer and the floor is $\mu = 0.36$, what is the magnitude of the force P needed to keep the buffer moving at a constant velocity?

The free-body diagram looks like this:

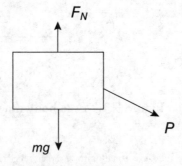

Exam tip from an AP Physics veteran:
When drawing a free-body diagram, put the tail of the force vectors on the object, with the arrow pointing away from the object. Never draw a force vector pointing into an object, even when something is pushing, as with the P force in this example.

—*Chris, high school junior*

Now, in the vertical direction, there are three forces acting: F_N acts up; weight and the vertical component of P act down.

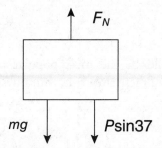

Notice that when we set up the equilibrium equation in the vertical direction, $F_N = mg + P\sin37$, we find that F_N is greater than mg.

Let's finish solving this problem together. We've already drawn the vertical forces acting on the buffer, so we just need to add the horizontal forces to get a complete free-body diagram with the forces broken up into their components (Steps 1 and 2):

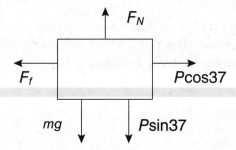

Step 3 calls for equations in the vertical and horizontal directions:

$$F_f = P\cos37$$

$$F_N = mg + P\sin37$$

Step 4 asks for a mathematical solution. At first this seems impossible—we have two equations, but three unknown values, F_f, F_N, and P. All the algebra in the world won't help without a third equation.

The friction force equation is the third equation we need: $F_f = \mu F_N$. We know μ from the problem statement.

Substitue μF_N into the top equation, and then solve the remaining equations for P and F_N. The final solution should be that $\boldsymbol{P = 93 \text{ N}}$.

Static and Kinetic Friction

You may have learned that the coefficient of friction takes two forms: **static** and **kinetic** friction. Use the coefficient of static friction if something is stationary, and the coefficient of kinetic friction if the object is moving. The equation for the force of friction is essentially the same in either case: $F_f = \mu F_N$.

The only strange part about static friction is that the coefficient of static friction is a *maximum* value. Think about this for a moment . . . if a book just sits on a table, it doesn't need any friction to stay in place. But that book won't slide if you apply a very small horizontal pushing force to it, so static friction can act on the book. To find the maximum coefficient of static friction, find out how much horizontal pushing force will just barely cause the book to move; then use $F_f = \mu F_N$.

Inclined Planes

These could be the most popular physics problems around. You've probably seen way too many of these already in your physics class, so we'll just give you a few tips on approaching them.

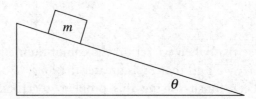

Figure 9.4   Generic inclined-plane situation.

In Figure 9.4 we have a block of mass m resting on a plane elevated an angle θ above the horizontal. The plane is not frictionless. We've drawn a free-body diagram of the forces acting on the block in Figure 9.5a.

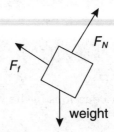

Figure 9.5a   Forces acting on the block in Figure 9.4.

F_f is directed parallel to the surface of the plane, and F_N is, by definition, directed perpendicular to the plane. It would be a pain to break these two forces into x- and y-components, so instead we will break the "weight" vector into components that "line up" with F_f and F_N, as shown in Figure 9.5b.

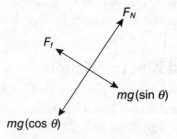

Figure 9.5b   Forces acting on the block in Figure 9.4, with the weight vector resolved into components that line up with the friction force and the normal force.

Memorize this

> As a rule of thumb, in virtually all inclined-plane problems, you can always break the weight vector into components parallel and perpendicular to the plane, where the component parallel to (pointing down) the plane = mg(sin θ) and the component perpendicular to the plane = mg(cos θ).

This rule always works, as long as the angle of the plane is measured from the horizontal.

Even Physics C Students Must Use Free-Body Diagrams

It must be emphasized that even Physics C students must go through the four-step problem-solving process described in this chapter. Frequently, Physics C students try to take shortcuts, thinking that equilibrium problems are easy, only to miss something important. If free-body diagrams are good enough for professional physicists to use, they are good enough for you.

Torque

Torque occurs when a force is applied to an object, and that force can cause the object to rotate.

$$\textbf{Torque} = Fd$$

In other words, the torque exerted on an object equals the force exerted on that object (F) multiplied by the distance between where the force is applied and the fulcrum (d) as long as the force acts perpendicular to the object.

> **Fulcrum:** The point about which an object rotates

Figure 9.6 shows what we mean:

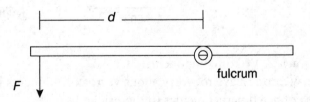

Figure 9.6   The torque applied to this bar equals *Fd*.

The unit of torque is the newton-meter.

Here's an example.

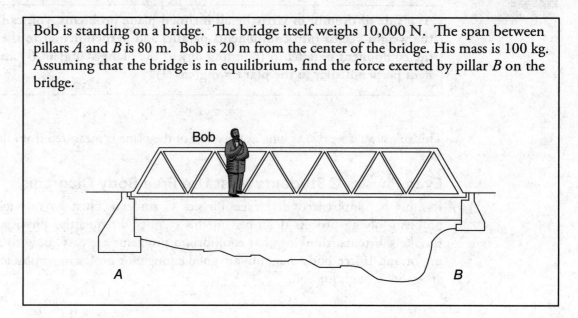

Bob is standing on a bridge. The bridge itself weighs 10,000 N. The span between pillars *A* and *B* is 80 m. Bob is 20 m from the center of the bridge. His mass is 100 kg. Assuming that the bridge is in equilibrium, find the force exerted by pillar *B* on the bridge.

Step 1: Free-body diagram.

We'll use point *A* as the fulcrum to start with. Why? In a static equilibrium situation, since the bridge isn't *actually* rotating, any point on the bridge could serve as a fulcrum. But we have two unknown forces here, the forces of the supports *A* and *B*. We choose the location of one of these supports as the fulcrum, because now that support provides zero torque—the distance from the fulcrum becomes zero! Now all we have to do is solve for the force of support *B*.

The diagram below isn't a true "free-body diagram," because it includes both distance and forces, but it is useful for a torque problem. Bob's weight acts downward right where he stands.

The bridge's weight is taken into account with a force vector acting at the bridge's center of mass; that is, 40 m to the right of pillar *A*. This is a generally valid approach—replace the weight of an extended object with a single weight vector acting at the center of mass.

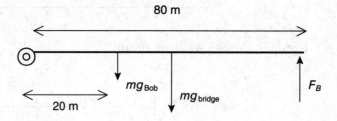

Step 2: Vector components.

We don't have to worry about vector components here. (We would have if the forces had not acted perpendicular to the bridge.)

Step 3: Equations.

counterclockwise torque = clockwise torque
$$F_B(80 \text{ m}) = (1000 \text{ N})(20 \text{ m}) + (10,000 \text{ N})(40 \text{ m})$$

Step 4: Solve. $F_B = 5300$ N

This is reasonable because pillar *B* is supporting *less* than half of the 11,000 N weight of the bridge and Bob. Because Bob is closer to pillar *A*, and otherwise the bridge is symmetric, *A* should bear the majority of the weight.

The Physics C exam will often expect you to find the torque provided by a force that acts at an angle. For example, consider a force *F* acting on a bar at an angle θ, applied a distance *x* from a pivot. How much torque does this force provide? See Figure 9.7.

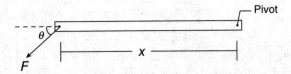

Figure 9.7   Force F acting on a bar at an angle θ.

To solve, break the force vector into horizontal and vertical components, as shown in Figure 9.8.

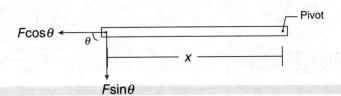

Figure 9.8   Break the force vector into horizontal and vertical components.

The vertical component of *F* applies a torque of $(F \sin \theta)x$. The horizontal component of *F* does not apply any torque, because it could not cause the bar to rotate. So, the total torque provided by *F* is $(F \sin \theta)x$.

Lever Arm

The "lever arm" for a force is the closest distance from the fulcrum to the line of that force. Then, the torque provided by a force is the force times the lever arm.

Consider Figure 9.9, which represents the same situation as Figure 9.7. Instead of breaking *F* into components, continue the line of the force. The torque is *F* times the lever arm shown in the diagram. By trigonometry, you can see that the lever arm is equal to $x \sin \theta$. No matter how you look at it, the torque provided by *F* is still $(F \sin \theta)x$.

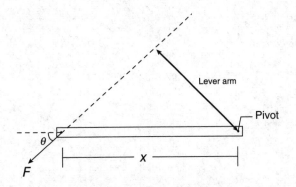

Figure 9.9   Force F acting on a bar at an angle θ.

› Practice Problems

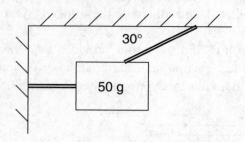

1. A 50-g object is hung by string as shown in the picture above. The left-hand string is horizontal; the angled string measures 30° to the horizontal. What is the tension in the angled string?

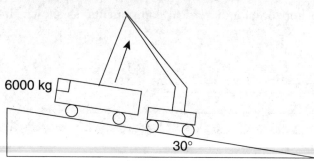

2. A 6000-kg bus sits on a 30° incline. A crane attempts to lift the bus off of the plane. The crane pulls perpendicular to the plane, as shown in the diagram. How much force must the crane apply so that the bus is suspended just above the surface? [cos 30° = 0.87, sin 30° = 0.50]

(A) 52,000 N
(B) 30,000 N
(C) 6000 N
(D) 5200 N
(E) 300 N

3. Give two examples of a situation in which the normal force on an object is less than the object's weight. Then give an example of a situation in which there is NO normal force on an object.

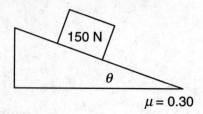

4. A 150-N box sits motionless on an inclined plane, as shown above. What is the angle of the incline?

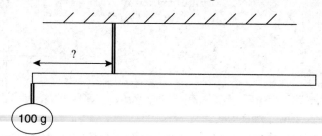

5. A 50-g meterstick is to be suspended by a single string. A 100-g ball hangs from the left-hand edge of the meterstick. Where should the string be attached so that the meterstick hangs in equilibrium?

(A) at the left-hand edge
(B) 40 cm from left-hand edge
(C) 30 cm from right-hand edge
(D) 17 cm from left-hand edge
(E) at the midpoint of the meterstick

› Solutions to Practice Problems

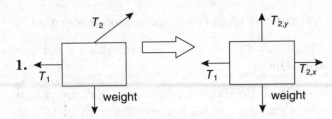

1.

Call the tension in the angled rope T_2. In the y-direction, we have $T_{2,y} = T_2(\sin 30°)$ acting up, and mg acting down. Set "up" forces equal to "down" forces and solve for tension: $T_2 = mg/(\sin 30°)$. Don't forget to use the mass in KILOgrams, i.e., 0.050 kg. The tension thus is $(0.050 \text{ kg})(10 \text{ N/kg})/(0.5) = 1.0$ N. This is reasonable because the tension is about the same order of magnitude as the weight of the mass.

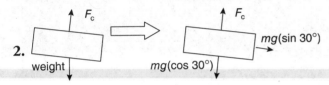

2.

A—Because the force of the crane, F_c, acts perpendicular to the plane, the parallel-to-the-plane direction is irrelevant. So all we need to do is set F_c equal to $mg(\cos 30°) = (6000 \text{ kg})(10 \text{ N/kg})(.87)$ and plug in. $F_c = 52,000$ N. This is a reasonable answer because it is less than—but on the same order of magnitude as—the weight of the bus.

3. When a block rests on an inclined plane, the normal force on the block is less than the block's weight, as discussed in the answer to #2. Another example in which the normal force is less than an object's weight occurs when you pull a toy wagon.

In any situation where an object does not rest on a surface (for example, when something floats in space), there is no normal force.

4. This free-body diagram should be very familiar to you by now.

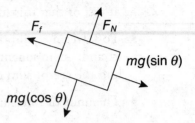

The box is in equilibrium, so F_f must equal $mg(\sin \theta)$, and F_N must equal $mg(\cos \theta)$.

$$\mu \cdot F_N = \mu \cdot mg(\cos \theta) = mg(\sin \theta).$$

Plugging in the values given in the problem we find that $\mu = 17°$. This answer seems reasonable because we'd expect the incline to be fairly shallow.

5. D—This is a torque problem, and the fulcrum is wherever the meterstick is attached to the string. We know that the meterstick's center of mass is at the 50-cm mark, so we can draw the following picture.

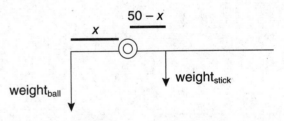

Because the stick is in equilibrium, the clockwise torques equal the counterclockwise torques: $(1 \text{ N})(x) = (0.5 \text{ N})(50 - x)$. So $x =$ something in the neighborhood of $25/1.5 \sim 17$ cm. This answer is less than 50 cm, and is closer to the edge with the heavy mass, so it makes sense.

❯ Rapid Review

- A free-body diagram is a simplified representation of an object and the forces acting on it.

- When the net force on an object is zero, it is in equilibrium. This means that it is either at rest or that it is moving at a constant velocity.

- To solve an equilibrium problem, draw a good free-body diagram, resolve all forces into x- and y-components, and then set the vector sum of the x-components equal to zero and the vector sum of the y-components equal to zero.

- The units of force are newtons, where $1 \text{ N} = 1 \text{ kg·m/s}^2$.

- Torque equals the force exerted on an object multiplied by the distance between where that force is applied and the fulcrum (the point about which an object can rotate). When an object is in equilibrium, the counterclockwise torques equal the clockwise torques.

- A "normal force" means the force of a solid surface pushing perpendicular to that surface. The normal force is NOT always equal to an object's weight.

CHAPTER 10

Kinematics

IN THIS CHAPTER

Summary: As soon as an object's velocity changes, you need to analyze the problem using kinematics, which deals with aspects of motion separate from considerations of mass and force.

Key Ideas

- ✪ Kinematics problems involve five variables: initial velocity, final velocity, displacement, acceleration, and time interval.
- ✪ Use the three kinematics equations whenever acceleration is constant.
- ✪ Average speed is the total distance in a given time divided by the time it takes you to travel that distance.
- ✪ Velocity is just like speed, except it's a vector.
- ✪ Acceleration is the change in velocity divided by a time interval.
- ✪ Displacement is the vector equivalent of distance.
- ✪ The key rule of projectile motion is that an object's motion in one dimension does not affect its motion in any other dimension.

Relevant Equations

The constant-acceleration kinematics equations, which we refer to as the "star" equations:

$$* \; v_f = v_0 + at$$

$$** \; \Delta x = v_0 t + \tfrac{1}{2}at^2$$

$$*** \; v_f^2 = v_0^2 + 2a\Delta x$$

The equilibrium problems we saw in the last chapter all had something in common: there was no acceleration. Sure, an object can move at a constant velocity and still be in equilibrium, but as soon as an object's velocity changes, you need a new set of tricks to analyze the situation. This is where kinematics comes in.

Velocity, Acceleration, and Displacement

We'll start with a few definitions.

Average Speed: $\dfrac{\Delta x}{\Delta t}$ The units for speed are m/s.

In this definition, Δx means "displacement" and Δt means "time interval." Average speed is the total displacement you travel in a straight line in a given time divided by the time it takes you to travel that distance. This is different from "instantaneous speed," which is your speed at any given moment. WARNING: The formula you learned in seventh grade, "speed = distance/time" is ONLY valid for an average speed, or when something is moving with constant speed. If an object speeds up or slows down, and you want to know its speed at some specific moment, don't use this equation![1]

Velocity: Just like speed, except it's a vector

Questions on the AP exam tend to focus on velocity more than speed, because velocity says more about an object's motion. (Remember, velocity has both magnitude and direction.) Acceleration occurs when an object changes velocity.

Acceleration: $\dfrac{\Delta v}{\Delta t}$ The units of acceleration are meters per second per second, also written as m/s/s or "m/s^2".

The symbol Δ means "change in." So $\Delta v = v_f - v_0$, where v_f means "final velocity" and v_0 means "initial velocity" and is pronounced "v-naught." Similarly, Δt is the time interval during which this change in velocity occurred.

Just as velocity is the vector equivalent of speed, displacement is the vector equivalent of distance—it has both magnitude and direction.

Displacement: The vector equivalent of distance

So, let's say that you head out your front door and walk 20 m south. If we define north to be the positive direction, then your displacement was "–20 m." If we had defined south to be the positive direction, your displacement would have been "+20 m." Regardless of which direction was positive, the *distance* you traveled was just "20 m." (Or consider this: If you walk 20 m north, followed by 5 m back south, your displacement is 15 m, north. Your displacement is *not* 25 m.)

---

[1]Use the "star equations," which we will address in detail momentarily.

Constant-Acceleration Kinematics Equations

Putting all of these definitions together, we can come up with some important lists. First, we have our five variables:

Variables
1. v_0 (initial velocity)
2. v_f (final velocity)
3. Δx (displacement)
4. a (acceleration)
5. t (time interval)

Using just these five variables, we can write the three most important kinematics equations. An important note: *The following equations are valid ONLY when acceleration is constant. We repeat: ONLY WHEN ACCELERATION IS CONSTANT.* Which is most of the time.[2]

Equations
$$*v_f = v_0 + at$$
$$**\Delta x = v_0 t + \tfrac{1}{2}at^2$$
$$***v_f^2 = v_0^2 + 2a\Delta x$$

We call these equations the "star equations." You don't need to call them the "star equations," but just be aware that we'll refer to the first equation as "*," the second as "**," and the third as "***" throughout this chapter.

These are the only equations you really need to memorize for kinematics problems.

Constant-Acceleration Kinematics Problem-Solving

Step 1: Write out all five variables in a table. Fill in the known values, and put a "?" next to the unknown values.

Step 2: Count how many known values you have. If you have three or more, move on to Step 3. If you don't, find another way to solve the problem (or to get another known variable).

Step 3: Choose the "star equation" that contains all three of your known variables. Plug in the known values, and solve.

Be sure that you have committed these steps to memory. Now, let's put them into action.

A rocket-propelled car begins at rest and accelerates at a constant rate up to a velocity of 120 m/s. If it takes 6 s for the car to accelerate from rest to 60 m/s, how long does it take for the car to reach 120 m/s, and how far does it travel in total?

---

[2]When *can't* you use kinematics, you ask? The most common situations are when a mass is attached to a spring, when a roller coaster travels on a curvy track, or when a charge is moving in a non-uniform electric field produced by other charges. To approach these problems, use conservation of energy, as discussed in Chapter 13.

Before we solve this problem—or any problem, for that matter—we should think about the information it provides. The problem states that acceleration is constant, so that means we can use our kinematics equations. Also, it asks us to find two values, a time and a distance. Based on the information in the problem, we know that the time needed for the car to reach 120 m/s is greater than 6 s because it took 6 s for the car just to reach 60 m/s. Moreover, we can estimate that the car will travel several hundred meters in total, because the car's *average* velocity must be less than 120 m/s, and it travels for several seconds.

So now let's solve the problem. We'll use our four-step method.

Step 1: Describe what part of the motion you're considering. Fill in the known values for all five variables in a table, and put a "?" next to the unknown values.

The car begins at rest, so $v_0 = 0$ m/s. The final velocity of the car is 120 m/s. We're solving for time and displacement, so those two variables are unknown. And, at least for right now, we don't know what the acceleration is.

v_0	0 m/s
v_f	120 m/s
Δx	?
a	?
t	?

This table represents the car's entire motion.

Step 2: Count variables.
We only have two values in our chart, but we need three values in order to use our kinematics equations. Fortunately, there's enough information in the problem for us to solve for the car's acceleration.

Acceleration is defined as a change in velocity divided by the time interval during which that change occurred. The problem states that in the first 6 s, the velocity went from 0 m/s to 60 m/s.

$$\Delta v = v_f - v_0 = 60 \text{ m/s} - 0 = 60 \text{ m/s}$$

$$a = \frac{\Delta v}{\Delta t} = \frac{60 \text{ m/s}}{6\text{s}} = 10 \text{ m/s}^2$$

v_0	0 m/s
v_f	120 m/s
Δx	?
a	10 m/s^2
t	?

Chart for car's entire motion.

We now have values for three of our variables, so we can move to Step 3.

Step 3: Use "star equations" to solve.
All three of our known values can be plugged into *, which will allow us to solve for *t*.

$$* \ v_f = v_0 + at$$
$$120 \text{ m/s} = 0 + (10 \text{ m/s}^2)t$$
$$t = 12 \text{ s}$$

Now that we know *t*, we can use either ** or *** to solve for displacement. Let's use **:

$$** \ \Delta x = v_0 t + \tfrac{1}{2}at^2$$
$$\Delta x = 0(12 \text{ s}) + \tfrac{1}{2}(10 \text{ m/s}^2)(12 \text{ s})^2$$
$$\Delta x = 720 \text{ m}$$

Always remember units! And make sure that your units are sensible—if you find that an object travels a distance of 8 m/s, you've done something screwy. In our case, the answers we found have sensible units. Also, our answers seem reasonable based on the initial estimates we made: It makes sense that the car should travel a bit more than 6 s, and it makes sense that it should go several hundred meters (about half a mile) in that time.

Freefall

An object is in freefall if the only force acting on it is the force of gravity. This includes objects moving up or moving down!

> *g*: The acceleration of an object in freefall near Earth, about 10 m/s/s

Falling-object problems should be solved using the method we outlined above. However, you have to be really careful about choosing a positive direction and sticking to it. That is, figure out before you solve the problem whether you want "up" to be positive (in which case *a* equals −10 m/s²) or "down" to be positive (where *a* would therefore equal +10 m/s²). Here's a practice problem:

> **Exam tip from an AP Physics veteran:**
> You may remember that a more precise value for *g* is 9.80 m/s². That's correct. But estimating *g* as 10 m/s² is encouraged by the AP readers to make calculation quicker.
>
> —*Jake, high school junior*

Begin by defining the positive direction. We will call "up" positive. Then use the four-step

> You are standing on a cliff, 30 m above the valley floor. You throw a watermelon vertically upward at a velocity of 3 m/s. How long does it take until the watermelon hits the valley floor?
>
>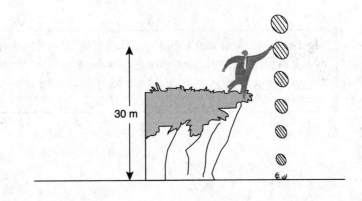

method to solve the problem.

Step 1: Table of variables.

v_0	3 m/s
v_f	?
Δx	−30 m
a	−10 m/s²
t	?

Melon's entire motion

Why do we always indicate what part of the motion the kinematics chart is for? Well, this problem *could* be solved instead by making two separate charts: one for the upward motion (where v_f would be zero), and one for the downward motion (where v_0 would be zero). Be crystal clear how much of an object's motion you are considering with a chart.

Remember that displacement is a vector quantity. Even though the melon goes up before coming back down, the displacement is simply equal to the height at which the melon ends its journey (0 m) minus its initial height (30 m). Another way to think about displacement: In total, the melon ended up 30 m BELOW where it started. Because down is the negative direction, the displacement is −30 m.

Step 2: Count variables.
Three! We can solve the problem.

Step 3: Solve.
The rest of this problem is just algebra. Yes, you have to do it right, but setting up the problem correctly and coming up with an answer that's reasonable is more important than getting the exact right answer. Really! If this part of an AP free-response problem is worth 5 points, you might earn 4 of those points just for setting up the equation and plugging in values correctly, even if your final answer is wrong.

But which equation do you use? We have enough information to use ** $(x − x_0 = v_0t + \frac{1}{2}at^2)$ to solve for t. Note that using ** means that we'll have to solve a quadratic equation; you can do this with the help of the quadratic formula.[3] Or, if you have a graphing calculator, you can use it to solve. But almost always there's a way to avoid the quadratic.

Algebra hint: You can avoid quadratics in all constant acceleration kinematics problems by solving in a roundabout way. Try solving for the velocity when the watermelon hits the ground using *** $[v_f^2 = v_0^2 + 2a(x − x_0)]$; then plug into * $(v_f = v_0 + at)$. This gives you the same answer.

$$** \ x − x_0 = v_0t + \frac{1}{2}at^2$$
$$(−30 \text{ m}) = (3 \text{ m/s})t + \frac{1}{2}(−10 \text{ m/s}^2)t^2$$
$$t = 2.8 \text{ s}$$

---

[3] $x = \dfrac{-b \pm \sqrt{b^2 - 4a \cdot c}}{2a}$

What If Acceleration Isn't Constant?

A typical Physics C kinematics question asks you to use calculus to find position, velocity, or acceleration functions. Then you can solve a motion problem even if acceleration is not constant. The way to remember what to do is, first and foremost, to understand graphical kinematics as discussed in the section below. Then, we know that the slope of a graph is related to the *derivative* of a function; the area under a graph is related to the *integral* of a function. Therefore:

- To find velocity from a position function, take the derivative with respect to time: $v = \dfrac{dx}{dt}$

- To find acceleration from a velocity function, also take the time derivative: $a = \dfrac{dv}{dt}$

- To find position from a velocity function, take the integral with respect to time: $x = \int v\, dt$

- To find velocity from an acceleration function, take the time integral: $v = \int a\, dt$

Most of the time, even on the Physics C exam, you'll be able just to use the star equations to solve a kinematics problem. Reserve your use of calculus for those problems that explicitly include an unusual function for position, velocity, or acceleration.

Projectile Motion

Things don't always move in a straight line. When an object moves in two dimensions, we look at vector components.

The super-duper-important general rule is this: *An object's motion in one dimension does not affect its motion in any other dimension.*

The most common kind of two-dimensional motion you will encounter is projectile motion. The typical form of projectile-motion problems is the following:

> *"A ball is shot at a velocity v from a cannon pointed at an angle θ above the horizontal . . ."*

No matter what the problem looks like, remember these rules:

- The vertical component of velocity, v_y, equals $v(\sin \theta)$.
- The horizontal component of velocity, v_x, equals $v(\cos \theta)$ when θ is measured relative to the horizontal.
- Horizontal velocity is constant.
- Vertical acceleration is g, directed downward.

Here's a problem that combines all of these rules:

A ball is shot at a velocity 25 m/s from a cannon pointed at an angle $\theta = 30°$ above the horizontal. How far does it travel before hitting the level ground?

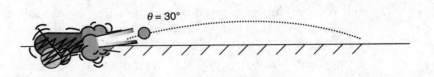

We begin by defining "up" to be positive and writing our tables of variables, one for horizontal motion and one for vertical motion.

Horizontal		Vertical	
v_0	$v(\cos\theta) = 22\,\text{m/s}$	v_0	$v(\sin\theta) = 13\,\text{m/s}$
v_f	$v(\cos\theta) = 22\,\text{m/s}$	v_f	?
Δx	?	Δx	0 m
a	$0\,\text{m/s}^2$	a	$-10\,\text{m/s}^2$
t	?	t	?

Entire motion of cannonball

Note that because horizontal velocity is constant, on the horizontal table, $v_f = v_0$, and $a = 0$. Also, because the ball lands at essentially the same height it was launched from, $\Delta x = 0$ on the vertical table. You should notice, too, that we rounded values in the tables to two significant figures (for example, we said that v_0 in the vertical table equals 13 m/s, instead of 12.5 m/s). We can do this because the problem is stated using only two significant figures for all values, so rounding to two digits is acceptable, and it makes doing the math easier for us.

We know that t is the same in both tables—the ball stops moving horizontally at the same time that it stops moving vertically (when it hits the ground). We have enough information in the vertical table to solve for t by using equation **.

$$** \ x - x_0 = v_0 t + \tfrac{1}{2}at^2$$
$$0 = (13\ \text{m/s})t + \tfrac{1}{2}(-10\ \text{m/s}^2)t^2$$
$$t = 2.6\ \text{s}$$

Using this value for t, we can solve for $x - x_0$ in the horizontal direction, again using **.

$$** \ x - x_0 = v_0 t + \tfrac{1}{2}at^2$$
$$x - x_0 = (22\ \text{m/s})(2.6\ \text{s}) + 0$$
$$x - x_0 = 57\ \text{m}$$

The cannonball traveled 57 m, about half the length of a football field.

You may have learned in your physics class that the range of a projectile (which is what we just solved for) is

$$R = \frac{v^2 \sin 2\theta}{g}$$

If you feel up to it, you can plug into this equation and show that you get the same answer we just got. There's no need to memorize the range equation, but it's good to know the conceptual consequences of it: the range of a projectile on *level earth* depends only on the initial speed and angle, and the maximum range is when the angle is 45°.

A Final Word About Kinematics Charts

The more you practice kinematics problems using our table method, the better you'll get at it, and the quicker you'll be able to solve these problems. Speed is important on the AP exam, and you can only gain speed through practice. So use this method on all your homework problems, and when you feel comfortable with it, you might want to use it on quizzes and tests. The other benefit to the table method, besides speed, is consistency; it forces you to set up every kinematics problem the same way, every time. This is a time-tested strategy for success on the AP exam.

Motion Graphs

You may see some graphs that relate to kinematics on the AP test. They often look like those in Figure 10.1. We call these graphs by the names of their axes: For example, the top graph in Figure 10.1 is a "position–time graph" and the second one is a "velocity–time graph."

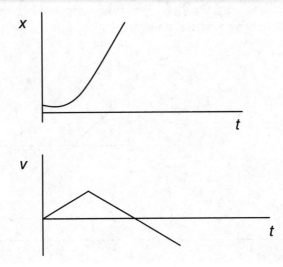

Figure 10.1 Typical motion graphs. (As an excercise, you may want to describe the motion these represent; answers are at the end of this section.)

Here are some rules to live by:

- The slope of a position–time graph at any point is the velocity of the object at that point in time.
- The slope of a velocity–time graph at any point is the acceleration of the object at that point in time.
- The area under a velocity–time graph between two times is the displacement of the object during that time interval.

It's sometimes confusing what is meant by the area "under" a graph. In the velocity–time graphs below, the velocity takes on both positive and negative values. To find the object's displacement, we first find the area above the *t*-axis; this is positive displacement. Then we subtract the area below the *t*-axis, which represents negative displacement. The correct area to measure is shown graphically in Figure 10.2a. Whatever you do, *don't* find the area as shown in Figure 10.2b! When we say "area," we measure that area to the *t*-axis only.

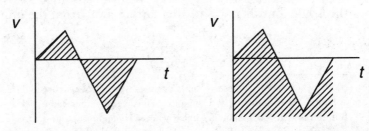

Figure 10.2a: Do this.   **Figure 10.2b: Don't do this.**

Problems involving graphical analysis can be tricky because they require you to think abstractly about an object's motion. For practice, let's consider one of the most common velocity–time graphs you'll see:

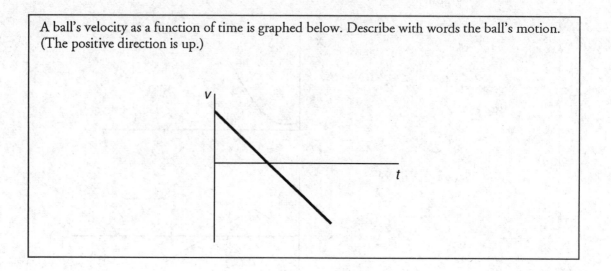

A ball's velocity as a function of time is graphed below. Describe with words the ball's motion. (The positive direction is up.)

Whenever you have to describe motion in words, do so in everyday language, not physics-speak. Don't say the word "it"; instead, give the object some specificity. Never say "positive" or "negative"; + and − merely represent directions, so name these directions.[4]

In this case, let's consider a ball going up (positive) and down (negative). Here's how we'd answer the question:

"At first the ball is moving upward pretty fast, but the ball is slowing down while going upward. (I know this because the speed is getting closer to zero in the first part of the graph.) The ball stops for an instant (because the v–t graph crosses the horizontal axis); then the ball begins to speed up again, but this time moving downward."

Now, no numerical values were given in the graph. But would you care to hazard a guess as to the likely slope of the graph's line if values *were* given?[5]

Figure 10.1 Graphs

The position–time graph has a changing slope, so the speed of the object is changing. The object starts moving one way, then stops briefly (where the graph reaches its minimum, the slope, and thus the speed is zero). The object then speeds up in the other direction. How did I know the object's velocity changed direction? The position was at first *approaching* the origin, but then was getting farther away from the origin.

---

[4]Why *shouldn't* I say "positive" and "negative," you ask? Well, how do these directions to the store sound: "Define north as positive. Start from zero, and go positive 20 constantly; then come back at −20, also constantly." You'd never say that! But, this is what you'll sound like unless you use common language.

[5]−10m/s², if we're on Earth.

The second graph is a velocity–time graph, and it must be analyzed differently. The object starts from rest, but speeds up; the second part of the motion is just like the example shown before, in which the object slows to a brief stop, turns around, and speeds up.

For more practice interpreting motion graphs, see page 72.

Air Resistance and the First-Order Differential Equation

The force of air resistance is usually negligible in kinematics problems. You probably don't believe me, though. After all, unless you're on the moon, or unless your teacher is using a vacuum chamber for demonstrations, air is all around us. And if I dropped a piece of paper simultaneously and from the same height as a lead weight, the weight would hit the ground first—and by a huge margin. Certainly. Obviously.

Why don't you try it? But be sure you *crinkle up the paper first* and drop it from about waist height. Notice how the lead weight hits the ground WAY before . . .

Oops.

The weight and the paper hit the ground essentially at the same time. If the weight did hit first, the difference wasn't anything you could reliably time or even be sure enough to gamble on.

Conclusion: As long as we're not throwing objects out of our car on the freeway, air resistance is not important in kinematics.

The most common questions asked:

When *is* air resistance important? And how should it be dealt with?

Air resistance should only be considered when the problem explicitly says so. Usually, a problem will suggest that the force of air acts opposite to an object's velocity, and is equal to a constant times the velocity: $F_{air} = bv$.[6]

---

1. **Find the terminal speed.** Terminal speed means that, after a long time, the object's speed becomes constant. To find that terminal speed, do an equilibrium problem: Free body, set up forces equal down forces, and left forces equal right forces. If something's falling straight down with no other forces, usually you'll get $bv = mg$. Then solve for v. That's the terminal speed.

2. **Sketch a graph of the speed of the object as a function of time.** Perhaps the problem will say the object was dropped from rest, or give an initial velocity. Well, you can plot that point at time $t = 0$. Then you can find the terminal velocity using the method above—the terminal speed is the constant velocity after a long time. Plot a horizontal line for the terminal velocity near the right-hand side of the t-axis.

    In between the initial velocity and the terminal velocity, just know that the velocity function will look like an exponential function, changing rapidly at first, and changing less rapidly as time goes on. Sketch a curve in between the point and the line you drew. Done.

---

[6] Occasionally you might see a different form, $F_{air} = bv^2$. In this case, you might be asked about the terminal speed, but you will NOT have to solve a differential equation.

3. **Describe the motion in words, including what's happening to the acceleration and/or the velocity.** Be sure to use a free-body diagram, and to separate the motion if necessary into parts when the object is moving up, and moving down. When the speed is zero, the force of air resistance is zero. This doesn't mean no acceleration, of course. When the speed is not zero, use a free body to figure out the amount and direction of the net force. Remind yourself of the basics of kinematics—the net force is the direction of acceleration. If the acceleration is in the direction of motion, the object speeds up; if the acceleration is opposite motion, the object slows down.

4. **Solve a differential equation to find an expression for the velocity as a function of time.** Again, start with a free-body diagram, and write $F_{net} = ma$. Now, though, you'll need to do some calculus: acceleration $a = \dfrac{dv}{dt}$. Perhaps your Newton's second law equation might say something like $mg - bv = ma$.

Okay, solve for a and write the calculus expression for a: $\dfrac{dv}{dt} = g - \dfrac{b}{m}v$. This type of equation is called a differential equation, where a derivative of a function is proportional to the function itself. Specifically, since the *first* derivative is involved, this is called a "first order" differential equation.

Your calculus class may well have taught you how to solve this equation by a technique known as separation of variables: put all the v terms on one side, the t terms on the other, and integrate. If you know how to do that, great; if not, it's complex enough not in any way to be worth learning in order to possibly—*possibly*—earn yourself one or two points. Everyone, though, should be able to recognize and write the answer using the knowledge that **the solution to a first-order differential equation will involve an exponential function.** You can use facts about the initial velocity and the terminal velocity to write this function without an algorithmic solution.

Imagine that a ball was dropped from rest in the presence of air resistance $F_{air} = bv$. Writing the second law gives you the equation shown above. What's the solution? Well, the initial velocity is zero; the terminal velocity can be found by setting acceleration to zero, meaning $v_{term} = \dfrac{mg}{b}$. The answer will *always* be something like $v(t) = Ae^{-kt}$ or $v(t) = A(1 - e^{-kt})$. Start by figuring out which: does the speed start large, and get small? If so, use the first expression. Or, does the speed start small, and get larger? If so, use the second expression. In this case, the speed starts from zero and ends up faster. So we use $v(t) = A(1 - e^{-kt})$. Generally, the k term is going to be whatever's multiplying the v in the original equation. In this case, then, $k = b/m$.

Now, look at the initial and final conditions to find the value of A. At time $t = 0$, $v = 0$; that works no matter the value of A, because $e^0 = 1$. But after a long time, we know the terminal velocity is mg/b. And in the equation, e^{-kt} goes to zero for large t. Meaning: after a long time, the velocity function equals A. This A must be the terminal velocity!

So our final equation looks like: $v(t) = \dfrac{mg}{b}(1 - e^{-\frac{b}{m}t})$.

› Practice Problems

Multiple Choice:

1. A firework is shot straight up in the air with an initial speed of 50 m/s. What is the maximum height it reaches?

(A) 12.5 m
(B) 25 m
(C) 125 m
(D) 250 m
(E) 1250 m

2. On a strange, airless planet, a ball is thrown downward from a height of 17 m. The ball initially travels at 15 m/s. If the ball hits the ground in 1 s, what is this planet's gravitational acceleration?

(A) 2 m/s²
(B) 4 m/s²
(C) 6 m/s²
(D) 8 m/s²
(E) 10 m/s²

3. An object moves such that its position is given by the function $x(t) = 3t^2 - 4t + 1$. The units of t are seconds, and the units of x are meters. After 6 s, how fast and in what direction is this object moving?

(A) 32 m/s in the original direction of motion
(B) 16 m/s in the original direction of motion
(C) 0 m/s
(D) 16 m/s opposite the original direction of motion
(E) 32 m/s opposite the original direction of motion

Free Response:

4. An airplane attempts to drop a bomb on a target. When the bomb is released, the plane is flying upward at an angle of 30° above the horizontal at a speed of 200 m/s, as shown below. At the point of release, the plane's altitude is 2.0 km. The bomb hits the target.

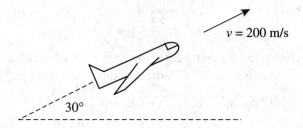

(a) Determine the magnitude and direction of the vertical component of the bomb's velocity at the point of release.
(b) Determine the magnitude and direction of the horizontal component of the bomb's velocity at the point when the bomb contacts the target.
(c) Determine how much time it takes for the bomb to hit the target after it is released.
(d) At the point of release, what angle below the horizontal does the pilot have to look in order to see the target?

› Solutions to Practice Problems

1. Call "up" the positive direction, and set up a chart. We know that $v_f = 0$ because, at its maximum height, the firework stops for an instant.

v_0	+50 m/s
v_f	0
Δx	?
a	−10 m/s
t	?

Solve for Δx using equation ***: $v_f^2 = v_0^2 + 2a(\Delta x)$. The answer is (C) 125 m, or about skyscraper height.

2. Call "down" positive, and set up a chart:

v_0	+15 m/s
v_f	?
Δx	+17 m
a	?
t	1 s

Plug straight into ** ($\Delta x = v_0 t + \frac{1}{2}at^2$) and you have the answer. This is NOT a quadratic, because this time t is a known quantity. The answer is (B) 4 m/s², less than half of Earth's gravitational field, but close to Mars's gravitational field.

3. First find the velocity function by taking the derivative of the position function: $v(t) = 6t - 4$. Now plug in $t = 6$ to get the velocity after 6 s; you get 32 m/s. Note that this velocity is positive. Was the object originally moving in the positive direction? Plug in $t = 0$ to the velocity formula to find out . . . you find the initial velocity to be −4 m/s, so the object was originally moving in the negative direction, and has reversed direction after 6 s. The answer is (E).

4. (a) Because the angle 30° is measured to the horizontal, the magnitude of the vertical component of the velocity vector is just (200 m/s)(sin 30°), which is 100 m/s. The direction is "up," because the plane is flying up.

(b) The horizontal velocity of a projectile is constant. Thus, the horizontal velocity when the bomb hits the target is the same as the horizontal velocity at release, or (200 m/s)(cos 30°) = 170 m/s, to the right.

(c) Let's call "up" the positive direction. We can solve this projectile motion problem by our table method.

Horizontal		Vertical	
v_0	+170 m/s	v_0	+100 m/s
v_f	+170 m/s	v_f	?
Δx	?	Δx	−2000 m
a	0	a	−10 m/s²
t	?	t	?

Don't forget to convert to meters, and be careful about directions in the vertical chart.

The horizontal chart cannot be solved for time; however, the vertical chart can. Though you could use the quadratic formula or your fancy calculator to solve $x - x_0 = v_0 t + \frac{1}{2}at^2$, it's much easier to start with ***, $v_f^2 = v_0^2 + 2a(x - x_0)$, to find that v_f vertically is −220 m/s (this velocity must have a negative sign because the bomb is moving down when it hits the ground). Then, plug in to *($v_f = v_0 + at$) to find that the bomb took 32 s to hit the ground.

(d) Start by finding how far the bomb went horizontally. Because horizontal velocity is constant, we can say distance = velocity × time. Plugging in values from the table, distance = (170 m/s)(32 s) = 5400 m. Okay, now look at a triangle:

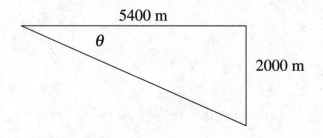

By geometry, tan θ = 2000 m/5400 m. The pilot has to look down at an angle of 20°.

› Rapid Review

- Average speed is total distance divided by total time. Instantaneous speed is your speed at a particular moment. On a position-time graph, instantaneous speed is the slope of a tangent to the graph.

- Velocity is the vector equivalent of speed.

- Acceleration is a change in velocity divided by the time during which that change occurred.

- Displacement is the vector equivalent of distance.

- The three "star equations" are valid only when acceleration is constant.

- To solve any constant-acceleration kinematics problem, follow these four steps:
  - Write out a table containing all five variables—v_0, v_f, $x - x_0$, a, t—and fill in whatever values are known.
  - Count variables. If you have three known values, you can solve the problem.
  - Use the "star equation" that contains your known variables.
  - Check for correct units.

- When an object is in free-fall—meaning, no forces act other than gravity—it experiences an acceleration of g, about 10 m/s^2. It's particularly important for problems that involve falling objects to define a positive direction before solving the problem.

- An object's motion in one dimension does not affect its motion in any other dimension.

- Projectile motion problems are solved by breaking the object's motion into "horizontal" and "vertical" vector components.

- The slope of a position-time graph is velocity.

- The slope of a velocity–time graph is acceleration.

- The area under a velocity–time graph is displacement.

CHAPTER 11

Newton's Second Law, $F_{net} = ma$

IN THIS CHAPTER

Summary: Chapter 9 explained how to deal with objects in equilibrium, that is, with zero acceleration. The same problem-solving process can be used with accelerating objects.

Key Ideas

✪ Only a NET force, not an individual force, can be set equal to *ma*.

✪ Use a free-body diagram and the four-step problem-solving process when a problem involves forces.

✪ When two masses are connected by a rope, the rope has the same tension throughout. (One rope = one tension.)[1]

✪ Newton's third law: force pairs must act on different objects.

Relevant Equations

Um, the chapter title says it all . . .

$$F_{net} = ma$$

What this means is that *the net force acting on an object is equal to the mass of that object multiplied by the object's acceleration*. And that statement will help you with all sorts of problems.

---

[1]But if the rope is attached across a massive pulley, the tension is different on each side of the pulley. See Chapter 15.

The Four-Step Problem-Solving Process

If you decide that the best way to approach a problem is to use $F_{net} = ma$, then you should solve the problem by following these four steps.

1. Draw a proper free-body diagram.
2. Resolve forces into their components.
3. For each axis, set up an expression for F_{net}, and set it equal to ma.
4. Solve your system of equations.

Note the marked similarity of this method to that discussed in the chapter on equilibrium.

Following these steps will get you majority credit on an AP free-response problem even if you do not ultimately get the correct answer. In fact, even if you only get through the first one or two steps, it is likely that you will still get some credit.

Only *Net* Force Equals *ma*

THIS IS REALLY IMPORTANT. Only F_{net} can be set equal to *ma*. You cannot set any old force equal to *ma*. For example, let's say that you have a block of mass *m* sitting on a table. The force of gravity, *mg*, acts down on the block. But that does not mean that you can say, "$F = mg$, so the acceleration of the block is *g*, or about 10 m/s²." Because we know that the block isn't in free fall! Instead, we know that the table exerts a normal force on the block that is equal in magnitude but opposite in direction to the force exerted by gravity. So the NET force acting on the block is 0. You can say "$F_{net} = 0$, so the block is not accelerating."

A Simple Example

A block of mass $m = 2$ kg is pushed along a frictionless surface. The force pushing the block has a magnitude of 5 N and is directed at $\theta = 30°$ below the horizontal.
(a) What is the block's acceleration? (b) What is the normal force of the surface on the block?

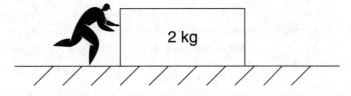

We follow our four-step process. First, draw a proper free-body diagram.

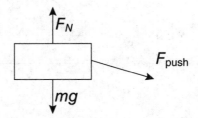

Second, we break the F_{push} vector into components that line up with the horizontal and vertical axes.

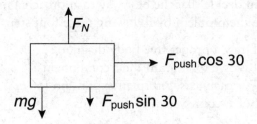

We can now move on to Step 3, writing equations for the net force in each direction:

$$F_N - (mg + F_{push}\sin 30) = ma_y$$

$$F_{push}\cos 30 = ma_x$$

In the vertical direction, the block is in equilibrium—it is neither flying off nor burrowing into the surface—so $a_y = 0$. We therefore know the value of all the variables in the two preceding equations, except for F_N and a_x. The physics is done—the two-variable, two-equation system can be solved.

Use the horizontal equation to solve for acceleration:

$$(5 \text{ N})\cos 30 = (2 \text{ kg})a_x$$

$$a_x = 2.2 \text{ m/s}^2$$

Then use the vertical equation to get the normal force of the surface on the block:

$$F_N - ((20 \text{ N}) + (5 \text{ N})\sin 30) = 0$$

$$F_N = 22.5 \text{ N}$$

F_{net} on Inclines

A block of mass m is placed on a plane inclined at an angle θ. The coefficient of friction between the block and the plane is μ. What is the acceleration of the block down the plane?

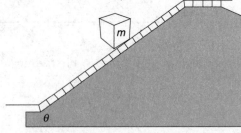

This is a really boring problem. But it's also a really common problem, so it's worth looking at.[2]

Note that no numbers are given, just variables. That's okay. It just means that our answer should be in variables. Only the given variables—in this case m, θ, and μ—and constants such as g can be used in the solution. And you shouldn't plug in any numbers (such as 10 m/s² for g), even if you know them.

Step 1: Free-body diagram.

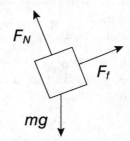

Step 2: Break vectors into components.

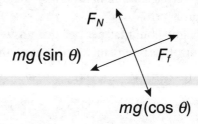

If you don't know where we got those vector components, refer back to Chapter 9.

Step 3: Write equations for the net force in each direction.
Note that the block is in equilibrium in the direction perpendicular to the plane, so the equation for $F_{net, \, perpendicular}$ (but not the equation for $F_{net, \, down \, the \, plane}$) can be set equal to 0.

$$F_{net, \, perpendicular} = mg(\cos\theta) - F_N = 0$$
$$mg(\cos\theta) = F_N$$
$$F_{net, \, down \, the \, plane} = mg(\sin\theta) - F_f = ma_{down \, the \, plane}$$

Step 4: Solve.
We can rewrite F_f, because

$$F_f = \mu F_N = \mu \, mg(\cos\theta)$$

Plugging this expression for F_f into the "$F_{net, \, down \, the \, plane}$" equation, we have

$$ma_{down \, the \, plane} = mg(\sin\theta - \mu \cos\theta)$$

$$\text{Answer: } a_{down \, the \, plane} = g(\sin\theta - \mu \cos\theta)$$

---

[2] If you want to make this problem more interesting, just replace the word "block" with the phrase "maniacal tobogganist" and the word "plane" with the phrase "highway on-ramp."

It always pays to check the reasonability of the answer. First, the answer doesn't include any variables that weren't given. Next, the units work out: g has acceleration units; neither the sine or cosine of an angle nor the coefficient of friction has any units.

Second, compare the answer to something familiar. Note that if the plane were vertical, $\theta = 90°$, so the acceleration would be g—yes, the block would then be in free fall! Also, note that friction tends to make the acceleration smaller, as you might expect.

For this particular incline, what coefficient of friction would cause the block to slide with constant speed?

Constant speed means $a = 0$. The solution for F_N in the perpendicular direction is the same as before: $F_N = mg(\cos\theta)$. But in the down-the-plane direction, no acceleration means that $F_f = mg(\sin\theta)$. Because $\mu = F_f/F_N$,

$$\mu = \frac{mg\sin\theta}{mg\cos\theta}$$

Canceling terms and remembering that $\sin/\cos = \tan$, you find that $\mu = \tan\theta$ when acceleration is zero.

You might note that neither this answer nor the previous one includes the mass of the block, so on the same plane, both heavy and light masses move the same way!

F_{net} for a Pulley

Before we present our next practice problem, a few words about tension and pulleys are in order. Tension in a rope is the same *everywhere* in the rope, even if the rope changes direction (such as when it goes around a pulley) or if the tension acts in different directions on different objects. ONE ROPE = ONE TENSION. If there are multiple ropes in a problem, each rope will have its own tension. TWO ROPES = TWO TENSIONS.[3]

When masses are attached to a pulley, the pulley can only rotate one of two ways. Call one way positive, the other, negative.

A block of mass M and a block of mass m are connected by a thin string that passes over a light frictionless pulley. Find the acceleration of the system.

We arbitrarily call counterclockwise rotation of the pulley "positive."

---

[3]Except for the Physics C corollary, when the pulley is massive—this situation is discussed in Chapter 15.

Step 1: Free-body diagrams.

The tension T is the same for each block—ONE ROPE = ONE TENSION. Also, note that because the blocks are connected, they will have the same acceleration, which we call *a*.

Step 2: Components.
The vectors already line up with one another. On to Step 3.

Step 3: Equations.

$$\text{Block } M: F_{net} = Mg - T = Ma$$
$$\text{Block } m: F_{net} = T - mg = ma$$

Notice how we have been careful to adhere to our convention of which forces act in the positive and negative directions.

Step 4: Solve.
Let's solve for *T* using the first equation:

$$T = Mg - Ma.$$

Plugging this value for *T* into the second equation, we have

$$(Mg - Ma) - mg = ma$$

Our answer is

$$a = g\left(\frac{M - m}{M + m}\right)$$

A 2-kg block and a 5-kg block are connected as shown on a frictionless surface. Find the tension in the rope connecting the two blocks. Ignore any friction effects.

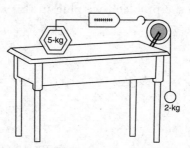

Why don't you work this one out for yourself? We have included our solution on the following page.

Solution to Example Problem

Step 1: Free-body diagrams.

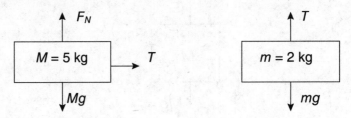

Step 2: Components.

Again, our vectors line up nicely, so on to Step 3.

Step 3: Equations.

Before we write any equations, we must be careful about signs: we shall call counterclockwise rotation of the pulley "positive."

For the more massive block, we know that, because it is not flying off the table or tunneling into it, it is in equilibrium in the up–down direction. But it is not in equilibrium in the right–left direction.

$$F_{\text{net},y} = (F_N - Mg) = 0$$
$$F_{\text{net},x} = (0 - T) = Ma$$

For the less massive block, we only have one direction to concern ourselves with: the up–down direction.

$$F_{\text{net}} = T - mg = ma$$

We can solve for T from the "$F_{\text{net},x}$" equation for the more massive block and plug that value into the "F_{net}" equation for the less massive block, giving us

$$(-Ma) - mg = ma$$

We rearrange some terms to get

$$a = \frac{-mg}{m + M}$$

Now we plug in the known values for M and m to find that

$$a = -\frac{2}{7}g$$

To finish the problem, we plug in this value for a into the "$F_{\text{net},x}$" equation for the more massive block.

$$-T = Ma$$
$$-T = (5)\left(-\frac{2}{7}g\right)$$
$$T = 14 \text{ N}$$

More Thoughts on $F_{\text{net}} = ma$

The four example problems in this chapter were all solved using only $F_{\text{net}} = ma$. Problems you might face on the AP exam will not always be so straightforward. Here's an example: imagine that this last example problem asked you to find the speed of the blocks after 2 seconds had elapsed, assuming that the blocks were released from rest. That's a kinematics problem, but to solve it, you have to know the acceleration of the blocks. You would first have to use $F_{net} = ma$ to find the acceleration, and then you could use a kinematics equation to find the final speed. We suggest that you try to solve this problem: it's good practice.

Also, remember in Chapter 9 when we introduced the unit of force, the newton, and we said that $1\ N = 1\ kg \cdot m/s^2$? Well, now you know why that conversion works: the units of force must be equal to the units of mass multiplied by the units of acceleration.

> **Exam tip from an AP Physics veteran:**
> Newton's second law works for *all* kinds of forces, not just tensions, friction, and such. Often what looks like a complicated problem with electricity or magnetism is really just an $F_{net} = ma$ problem, but the forces might be electric or magnetic in nature.
>
> —*Jonas, high school senior*

Newton's Third Law

We're sure you've been able to quote the Third Law since birth, or at least since fifth grade, something like "Forces come in equal and opposite action-reaction pairs." That's true. But it's not as simple as you think.

A force's action-reaction pair is not just any old equal force acting in an opposite direction. For example, consider a block sitting at rest on a table. What's the action-reaction pair to the weight of the block? It's NOT the normal force! Yes, I know the normal force is equal and opposite to the block's weight. But a Newton's Third Law force pair cannot both act on the same object.

> To find the action-reaction pair to a force, reverse the objects exerting and experiencing the force.

What object exerts the force we call "weight?" Well, that would be the entire Earth. The block's weight is the force of Earth on the block. So, the action-reaction pair is **the force of the block on the Earth.**

Similarly, the normal force is the force of the table on the block. Its action-reaction pair is the force of the block on the table.

Now, ask yourself one of the most important conceptual questions in first-year physics: "If all forces cause reaction forces, then how can anything ever accelerate?" Pull a little lab cart horizontally across the table . . . you pull on the cart, the cart pulls on you, so don't these forces cancel out, prohibiting acceleration?

Well, obviously, things can move. The trick is, Newton's third law force pairs *must act on different objects*, and so can never cancel each other.

> When writing $F_{net} = ma$, only consider the forces acting on the object in question. Do not include forces exerted *by* the object.

Consider the lab cart. The only horizontal force that it experiences is the force of your pull. So, it accelerates toward you. Now, you experience a force from the cart, but you also experience a whole bunch of other forces that keep you in equilibrium; thus, you don't go flying into the cart.

This Chapter Was Not as Easy as You Thought

Be careful with this chapter. Most Physics C students say, "Oh, come on, this stuff is easy . . . let's move on to something challenging." Okay, you're right—if you're at the level you need to be for Physics C, basic Newton's second law problems need to be easy for you. What you must remember from this and the equilibrium chapter is the **absolute necessity** of free-body diagrams.

No matter how easy or hard an F_{net} problem may seem, you must start the problem with a free-body diagram. Points are awarded for the free-body diagram, and that diagram will ensure that you don't make minor mistakes on the rest of the problem. My own Physics C students frequently mess up on what should be straightforward problems when they try to take shortcuts. If you draw the FBD and follow the four-step problem-solving procedure, it's hard to go wrong. Even professional physicists use free-body diagrams. You must, too.

› Practice Problems

Multiple Choice:

1. A 2.0-kg cart is given a shove up a long, smooth 30° incline. If the cart is traveling 8.0 m/s after the shove, how much time elapses until the cart returns to its initial position?

(A) 1.6 s
(B) 3.2 s
(C) 4.0 s
(D) 6.0 s
(E) 8.0 s

2. A car slides up a frictionless inclined plane. How does the normal force of the incline on the car compare with the weight of the car?

(A) The normal force must be equal to the car's weight.
(B) The normal force must be less than the car's weight.
(C) The normal force must be greater than the car's weight.
(D) The normal force must be zero.
(E) The normal force could have any value relative to the car's weight.

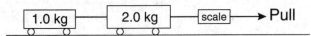

3. In the diagram above, a 1.0-kg cart and a 2.0-kg cart are connected by a rope. The spring scale reads 10 N. What is the tension in the rope connecting the two carts? Neglect any friction.

(A) 30 N
(B) 10 N
(C) 6.7 N
(D) 5.0 N
(E) 3.3 N

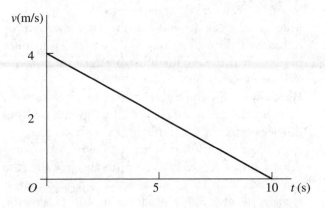

4. The velocity–time graph above represents the motion of a 5-kg box. The only force applied to this box is a person pushing. Assuming that the box is moving to the right, what is the magnitude and direction of the force applied by the person pushing?

(A) 2.0 N, right
(B) 2.0 N, left
(C) 0.4 N, right
(D) 0.4 N, left
(E) 12.5 N, left

Free Response:

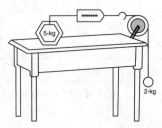

5. A 2-kg block and a 5-kg block are connected as shown above. The coefficient of friction between the 5-kg block and the flat surface is $\mu = 0.2$.

(A) Calculate the magnitude of the acceleration of the 5-kg block.
(B) Calculate the tension in the rope connecting the two blocks.

6. Bert, Ernie, and Oscar are discussing the gas mileage of cars. Specifically, they are wondering whether a car gets better mileage on a city street or on a freeway. All agree (correctly) that the gas mileage of a car depends on the force that is produced by the car's engine—the car gets fewer miles per gallon if the engine must produce more force. Whose explanation is completely correct?

Bert says: Gas mileage is better on the freeway. In town the car is always speeding up and slowing down because of the traffic lights, so because $F_{net} = ma$ and acceleration is large, the engine must produce a lot of force. However, on the freeway, the car moves with constant velocity, and acceleration is zero. So the engine produces no force, allowing for better gas mileage.

Ernie says: Gas mileage is better in town. In town, the speed of the car is slower than the speed on the freeway. Acceleration is velocity divided by time, so the acceleration in town is smaller. Because $F_{net} = ma$, then, the force of the engine is smaller in town giving better gas mileage.

Oscar says: Gas mileage is better on the freeway. The force of the engine only has to be enough to equal the force of air resistance—the engine doesn't have to accelerate the car because the car maintains a constant speed. Whereas in town, the force of the engine must often be greater than the force of friction and air resistance in order to let the car speed up.

❯ Solutions to Practice Problems

1. **B**—"Smooth" usually means, "ignore friction." So the only force acting along the plane is a component of gravity, $mg(\sin 30°)$. The F_{net} equation becomes $mg(\sin 30°) - 0 = ma$. The mass cancels, leaving the acceleration as 5 m/s². What's left is a kinematics problem. Set up a chart, calling the direction down the plane as positive:

v_0	−8.0/s
v_f	?
$x - x_0$	0 (cart comes back to starting point)
a	+5.0 m/s²
t	??? what we're looking for

Use ** ($\Delta x = v_0 t + \frac{1}{2}at^2$) to find that the time is 3.2 s.

2. **B**—The normal force exerted on an object on an inclined plane equals $mg(\cos \theta)$, where θ is the angle of the incline. If θ is greater than 0, then $\cos \theta$ is less than 1, so the normal force is less than the object's weight.

3. **E**—Consider the forces acting on each block separately. On the 1.0-kg block, only the tension acts, so $T = (1.0 \text{ kg})a$. On the 2.0-kg block, the tension acts left, but the 10 N force acts right, so $10 \text{ N} - T = (2.0 \text{ kg})a$. Add these equations together (noting that the tension in the rope is the same in both equations), getting $10 \text{ N} = (3.0 \text{ kg})a$; acceleration is 3.3 m/s². To finish, $T = (1.0 \text{ kg})a$, so tension is 3.3 N.

4. **B**— The acceleration is given by the slope of the v–t graph, which has magnitude 0.4 m/s². $F_{net} = ma$, so 5 kg × 0.4 m/s² = 2.0 N. This force is to the left because acceleration is negative (the slope is negative), and negative was defined as left.

5. The setup is the same as in the chapter's example problem, except this time there is a force of friction acting to the left on the 5-kg block. Because this block is in equilibrium vertically, the normal force is equal to the block's weight, 50 N. The friction force is μF_N, or 10 N.

Calling the down-and-right direction positive, we can write two equations, one for each block:

$$(2 \text{ kg})g - T = (2 \text{ kg})a.$$
$$T - F_f = (5 \text{ kg})a.$$

(A) To solve for acceleration, just add the two equations together. The tensions cancel. We find the acceleration to be 1.4 m/s².

(B) Plug back into either equation to find the final answer, that the tension is 17 N. This is more than the 14 N we found for the frictionless situation, and so makes sense. We expect that it will take more force in the rope to overcome friction on the table.

6. Although Bert is right that acceleration is zero on the freeway, this means that the NET force is zero; the engine still must produce a force to counteract air resistance. This is what Oscar says, so his answer is correct. Ernie's answer is way off—acceleration is not velocity/time, acceleration is a CHANGE in velocity over time.

› Rapid Review

- The net force on an object equals the mass of the object multiplied by the object's acceleration.

- To solve a problem using $F_{net} = ma$, start by drawing a good free-body diagram. Resolve forces into vector components. For each axis, the vector sum of forces along that axis equals ma_i, where a_i is the acceleration of the object along that axis.

- When an object is on an inclined plane, resolve its weight into vector components that point parallel and perpendicular to the plane.

- For problems that involve a massless pulley, remember that if there's one rope, there's one tension.

CHAPTER 12

Momentum

IN THIS CHAPTER

Summary: The impulse–momentum relationship can explain how force acts in a collision. Momentum is conserved in all collisions, allowing a prediction of objects' speeds before and after a collision.

Key Ideas

- ✪ Impulse can be expressed both as force times a time interval, *and* as a change in momentum.
- ✪ The total momentum of a set of objects before a collision is equal to the total momentum of a set of objects after a collision.
- ✪ Momentum is a vector, so leftward momentum can "cancel out" rightward momentum.

Relevant Equations

The definition of momentum:

$$p = mv$$

The impulse–momentum theorem:

$$\Delta p = F\Delta t$$

Location of the center of mass:

$$Mx_{cm} = m_1 x_1 + m_2 x_2 + \cdots$$

If an object is moving, it has momentum. The formal definition of momentum[1] is that it's equal to an object's mass multiplied by that object's velocity. However, a more intuitive way to think about momentum is that it corresponds to the amount of "oomph" an object has in a collision. Regardless of how you think about momentum, the key is this: the momentum of a system upon which no net external force acts is always conserved.

Momentum and Impulse

$$\boxed{\textbf{Momentum: } mv}$$

The units of momentum are kg·m/s, which is the same as N·s. Momentum is a vector quantity, and it is often abbreviated with a p.

$$\boxed{\textbf{Impulse: } \Delta p = F\Delta t}$$

Impulse (designated as I) is an object's change in momentum. It is also equal to the force acting on an object multiplied by the time interval over which that force was applied. The above equation is often referred to as the "impulse–momentum theorem."

The $F\Delta t$ definition of impulse explains why airbags are used in cars and why hitting someone with a pillow is less dangerous than hitting him or her with a cement block. The key is the Δt term. An example will help illustrate this point.

A man jumps off the roof of a building, 3.0 m above the ground. His mass is 70 kg. He estimates (while in free fall) that if he lands stiff-legged, it will take him 3 ms (milliseconds) to come to rest. However, if he bends his knees upon impact, it will take him 100 ms to come to rest. Which way will he choose to land, and why?

This is a multistep problem. We start by calculating the man's velocity the instant before he hits the ground. That's a kinematics problem, so we start by choosing a positive direction—we'll choose "down" to be positive—and by writing out our table of variables.

v_0	0
v_f	?
Δx	3.0 m
a	10 m/s^2
t	?

We have three variables with known values, so we can solve for the other two. We don't care about time, t, so we will just solve for v_f.

$$v_f^2 = v_0^2 + 2a(x - x_0)$$
$$v_f = 7.7 \text{ m/s}$$

Now we can solve for the man's momentum the instant before he hits the ground.

$$p = mv = (70)(7.7) = 540 \text{ kg·m/s}$$

---

[1]This chapter deals only with *linear* momentum. Angular momentum is covered in Chapter 15.

Once he hits the ground, the man quickly comes to rest. That is, his momentum changes from 540 kg·m/s to 0.

$$I = \Delta p = P_f - p_0$$
$$I = -540 \text{ N·s} = F\Delta t$$

If the man does not bend his knees, then

$$-540 = F(0.003 \text{ s})$$
$$F = -180,000 \text{ N}$$

The negative sign in our answer just means that the force exerted on the man is directed in the negative direction: up.

Now, what if he had bent his knees?

$$I = -540 = F\Delta t$$
$$-540 = F(0.10 \text{ seconds})$$
$$F = -5400 \text{ N}$$

If he bends his knees, he allows for his momentum to change more slowly, and as a result, the ground exerts a lot less force on him than had he landed stiff-legged. More to the point, hundreds of thousands of newtons applied to a person's legs will cause major damage—this is the equivalent of almost 20 tons sitting on his legs. So we would assume that the man would bend his knees upon landing, reducing the force on his legs by a factor of 30.

Calculus Version of the Impulse–Momentum Theorem

Conceptually, you should think of impulse as change in momentum, also equal to a force multiplied by the time during which that force acts. This is sufficient when the force in question is constant, or when you can easily define an average force during a time interval.

But what about when a force is changing with time? The relationship between force and momentum in the language of calculus is

$$F = \frac{dp}{dt}, \text{ which then implies that Impulse} = \int F\, dt$$

A common AP question, then, gives momentum of an object as a function of time, and asks you to take the derivative to find the force on the object.

It's also useful to understand this calculus graphically. Given a graph of momentum vs. time, the slope of the tangent to the graph gives the force at that point in time. Given a graph of force vs. time, the area under that graph is impulse, or change in momentum during that time interval.

Conservation of Momentum

Momentum in an isolated system, where no net external forces act, is always conserved. A rough approximation of a closed system is a billiard table covered with hard tile instead of felt. When the billiard balls collide, they transfer momentum to one another, but the total momentum of all the balls remains constant.

The key to solving conservation of momentum problems is remembering that momentum is a vector.

A satellite floating through space collides with a small UFO. Before the collision, the satellite was traveling at 10 m/s to the right, and the UFO was traveling at 5 m/s to the left. If the satellite's mass is 70 kg, and the UFO's mass is 50 kg, and assuming that the satellite and the UFO bounce off each other upon impact, what is the satellite's final velocity if the UFO has a final velocity of 3 m/s to the right?

Let's begin by drawing a picture.

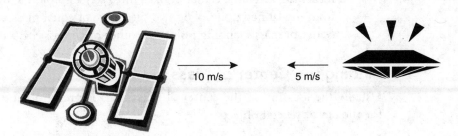

Momentum is conserved, so we write

$$p_{\text{satellite}} + p_{\text{UFO}} = p'_{\text{satellite}} + p'_{\text{UFO}}$$
$$(m_s)(v_s) + (m_{\text{UFO}})(v_{\text{UFO}}) = (m_s)(v_s)' + (m_{\text{UFO}})(v_{\text{UFO}})'$$

The tick marks on the right side of the equation mean "after the collision." We know the momentum of each space traveler before the collision, and we know the UFO's final momentum. So we solve for the satellite's final velocity. (Note that we must define a positive direction; because the UFO is moving to the left, its velocity is plugged in as negative.)

$$(70 \text{ kg})(+10 \text{ m/s}) + (50 \text{ kg})(-5 \text{ m/s}) = (70 \text{ kg})v_s' + (50 \text{ kg})(+3 \text{ m/s})$$
$$v_s' = 4.3 \text{ m/s to the right}$$

Now, what if the satellite and the UFO had stuck together upon colliding? We can solve for their final velocity easily:

$$p_{\text{satellite}} + p_{\text{UFO}} = p'_{\text{satellite \& UFO}}$$
$$(m_s)(v_s) + (m_{\text{UFO}})(v_{\text{UFO}}) = (m_{s \text{ \& UFO}})(v_{s \text{ \& UFO}})'$$
$$(70 \text{ kg})(+10 \text{ m/s}) + (50 \text{ kg})(-5 \text{ m/s}) = (70 \text{ kg} + 50 \text{ kg})(v_{s \text{ \& UFO}})'$$
$$v'_{s \text{ \& UFO}} = 3.8 \text{ m/s to the right}$$

Motion of the Center of Mass

The center of mass of a system of objects obeys Newton's second law. Two common examples might illustrate the point:

(1) Imagine that an astronaut on a spacewalk throws a rope around a small asteroid, and then pulls the asteroid toward him. Where will the asteroid and the astronaut collide?

Answer: at the center of mass. Since no forces acted except due to the astronaut and asteroid, the center of mass must have no acceleration. The center of mass started at rest, and stays at rest, all the way until the objects collide.

(2) A toy rocket is in projectile motion, so that it is on track to land 30 m from its launch point. While in the air, the rocket explodes into two identical pieces, one of which lands 35 m from the launch point. Where does the first piece land?

Answer: 25 m from the launch point. Since the only external force acting on the rocket is gravity, the center of mass must stay in projectile motion, and must land 30 m from the launch point. The two pieces are of equal mass, so if one is 5 m beyond the center of mass's landing point, the other piece must be 5 m short of that point.

Finding the Center of Mass

Usually the location of the center of mass (cm) is pretty obvious . . . the formal equation for the cm of several objects is

$$Mx_{cm} = m_1 x_1 + m_2 x_2 + \cdots$$

Multiply the mass of each object by its position, and divide by the total mass M, and voila, you have the position of the center of mass. What this tells you is that the cm of several equal-mass objects is right in between them; if one mass is heavier than the others, the cm is closer to the heavy mass.

Very rarely, you might have to find the center of mass of a continuous body (like a baseball bat) using calculus. The formula is

$$Mx_{cm} = \int r \, dm$$

Do not use this equation unless (a) you have plenty of extra time to spend, and (b) you know exactly what you're doing. In the highly unlikely event it's necessary to use this equation to find a center of mass, you will usually be better off just guessing at the answer and moving on to the rest of the problem. (If you want to find out how to do such a problem thoroughly, consult your textbook. This is not something worth reviewing if you don't know how to do it already.)

Elastic and Inelastic Collisions

This brings us to a couple of definitions.

> **Elastic Collision:** A collision in which kinetic energy is conserved

If you're unfamiliar with the concept of kinetic energy (KE), take a few minutes to skim Chapter 13 right now.

When the satellite and the UFO bounced off each other, they experienced a perfectly elastic collision. If kinetic energy is lost to heat or anything else during the collision, it is called an inelastic collision.

> **Inelastic Collision:** A collision in which KE is not conserved

The extreme case of an inelastic collision is called a perfectly inelastic collision.

> **Perfectly Inelastic Collision:** The colliding objects stick together after impact

The second collision between the satellite and the UFO was a perfectly inelastic collision. BUT, MOMENTUM IS STILL CONSERVED, EVEN IN A PERFECTLY INELASTIC COLLISION!

Two-Dimensional Collisions

The key to solving a two-dimensional collision problem is to remember that momentum is a vector, and as a vector it can be broken into x and y components. Momentum in the x-direction is always conserved, and momentum in the y-direction is always conserved.

Maggie has decided to go ice-skating. While cruising along, she trips on a crack in the ice and goes sliding. She slides along the ice at a velocity of 2.5 m/s. In her path is a penguin. Unable to avoid the flightless bird, she collides with it. The penguin is initially at rest and has a mass of 20 kg, and Maggie's mass is 50 kg. Upon hitting the penguin, Maggie is deflected 30° from her initial path, and the penguin is deflected 60° from Maggie's initial path. What is Maggie's velocity, and what is the penguin's velocity, after the collision?

We want to analyze the x-component of momentum and the y-component of momentum separately. Let's begin by defining "right" and "up" to be the positive directions. Now we can look at the x-component.

$$(m_{\text{Maggie}})(v_{\text{Maggie},x}) + (m_{\text{penguin}})(v_{\text{penguin},x}) = (m_M)(v_{M,x})' + (m_p)(v_{p,x})'$$
$$(50 \text{ kg})(+2.5 \text{ m/s}) + (20 \text{ kg})(0) = (50 \text{ kg})(+v'_M \cos 30°) + (20 \text{ kg})(+v'_p \cos 60°)$$
$$125 \text{ kg} \cdot \text{m/s} = (50 \text{ kg})(+v'_M)(\cos 30°) + (20 \text{ kg})(+v'_p)(\cos 60°)$$

We can't do much more with the x-component of momentum, so now let's look at the y-component.

$$(m_{\text{Maggie}})(v_{\text{Maggie}, y}) + (m_{\text{penguin}})(v_{\text{penguin}, y}) = (m_M)(v_{M,y})' + (m_p)(v_{p,y})'$$
$$(50 \text{ kg})(0) + (20 \text{ kg})(0) = (50 \text{ kg})(-v'_M \sin 30°) + (20 \text{ kg})(+v'_p \sin 60°)$$

(Note the negative sign on Maggie's y-velocity!)

$$0 = (50 \text{ kg})(-v'_M \sin 30°) + (20 \text{ kg})(+v'_p \sin 60°)$$

Okay. Now we have two equations and two unknowns. It'll take some algebra to solve this one, but none of it is too hard. We will assume that you can do the math on your own, but we will gladly provide you with the answer:

$$v'_M = 2.2 \text{ m/s}$$
$$v'_p = 3.1 \text{ m/s}.$$

The algebra is not particularly important here. Get the conceptual physics down—in a two-dimensional collision, you must treat each direction separately. If you do so, you will receive virtually full credit on an AP problem. If you combine vertical and horizontal momentum into a single conservation equation, you will probably not receive any credit at all.

› Practice Problems

Multiple Choice:

<u>First two questions:</u> A ball of mass M is caught by someone wearing a baseball glove. The ball is in contact with the glove for a time t; the initial velocity of the ball (just before the catcher touches it) is v_0.

1. If the time of the ball's collision with the glove is doubled, what happens to the force necessary to catch the ball?

(A) It doesn't change.
(B) It is cut in half.
(C) It is cut to one-fourth of the original force.
(D) It quadruples.
(E) It doubles.

2. If the time of collision remains t, but the initial velocity is doubled, what happens to the force necessary to catch the ball?

(A) It doesn't change.
(B) It is cut in half.
(C) It is cut to one-fourth of the original force.
(D) It quadruples.
(E) It doubles.

before collision

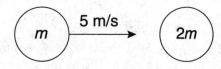

3. Two balls, of mass m and $2m$, collide and stick together. The combined balls are at rest after the collision. If the ball of mass m was moving 5 m/s to the right before the collision, what was the velocity of the ball of mass $2m$ before the collision?

(A) 2.5 m/s to the right
(B) 2.5 m/s to the left
(C) 10 m/s to the right
(D) 10 m/s to the left
(E) 1.7 m/s to the left

4. Two identical balls have initial velocities $v_1 = 4$ m/s to the right and $v_2 = 3$ m/s to the left, respectively. The balls collide head-on and stick together. What is the velocity of the combined balls after the collision?

(A) ½ m/s to the right
(B) ⅔ m/s to the right
(C) ½ m/s to the right
(D) ⅖ m/s to the right
(E) 1 m/s to the right

Free Response:

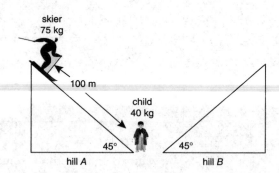

5. A 75-kg skier skis down a hill. The skier collides with a 40-kg child who is at rest on the flat surface near the base of the hill, 100 m from the skier's starting point, as shown above. The skier and the child become entangled. Assume all surfaces are frictionless.

(a) How fast will the skier be moving when he reaches the bottom of the hill? Assume the skier is at rest when he begins his descent.
(b) What will be the speed of the skier and child just after they collide?
(c) If the collision occurs in half a second, how much force will be experienced by each person?

› Solutions to Practice Problems

1. **B**—Impulse is force times the time interval of collision, and is also equal to an object's change in momentum. Solving for force, $F = \Delta p/\Delta t$. Because the ball still has the same mass, and still changes from speed v_0 to speed zero, the ball's momentum change is the same, regardless of the collision time. The collision time, in the denominator, doubled; so the entire expression for force was cut in half.

2. **E**—Still use $F = \Delta p/\Delta t$, but this time it is the numerator that changes. The ball still is brought to rest by the glove, and the mass of the ball is still the same; but the doubled velocity upon reaching the glove doubles the momentum change. Thus, the force doubles.

3. **B**—The total momentum after collision is zero. So the total momentum before collision must be zero as well. The mass m moved 5 m/s to the right, giving it a momentum of $5m$ units; the right-hand mass must have the same momentum to the left. It must be moving half as fast, 2.5 m/s, because its mass it twice as big; then its momentum is $(2m)(2.5) = 5m$ units to the left.

4. **C**—Because the balls are identical, just pretend they each have mass 1 kg. Then the momentum conservation tells us that

$$(1 \text{ kg})(+4 \text{ m/s}) + (1 \text{ kg})(-3 \text{ m/s}) = (2 \text{ kg})(v').$$

The combined mass, on the right of the equation above, is 2 kg; v' represents the speed of the combined mass. Note the negative sign indicating the direction of the second ball's velocity. Solving, $v' = +0.5$ m/s, or 0.5 m/s to the right.

5. (a) This part is not a momentum problem, it's a Newton's second law and kinematics problem. (Or it's an energy problem, if you've studied energy.) Break up forces on the skier into parallel and perpendicular axes—the net force down the plane is $mg(\sin 45°)$. So by Newton's second law, the acceleration down the plane is $g(\sin 45°) = 7.1$ m/s². Using kinematics with intitial velocity zero and distance 100 m, the skier is going 38 m/s (!).

   (b) Now use momentum conservation. The total momentum before collision is $(75 \text{ kg})(38 \text{ m/s}) = 2850$ kg·m/s. This must equal the total momentum after collision. The people stick together, with combined mass 115 kg. So after collision, the velocity is 2850 kg·m/s divided by 115 kg, or about 25 m/s.

   (c) Change in momentum is force multiplied by time interval . . . the child goes from zero momentum to $(40 \text{ kg})(25 \text{ m/s}) = 1000$ kg·m/s of momentum. Divide this change in momentum by 0.5 seconds, and you get 2000 N, or a bit less than a quarter ton of force. Ouch!

› Rapid Review

- Momentum equals an object's mass multiplied by its velocity. However, you can also think of momentum as the amount of "oomph" a mass has in a collision.

- Impulse equals the change in an object's momentum. It also equals the force exerted on an object multiplied by the time it took to apply that force.

- Momentum is always conserved. When solving conservation of momentum problems, remember that momentum is a vector quantity.

- In an elastic collision, kinetic energy is conserved. When two objects collide and bounce off each other, without losing any energy (to heat, sound, etc.), they have engaged in an elastic collision. In an inelastic collision, kinetic energy is not conserved. The extreme case is a perfectly inelastic collision. When two objects collide and stick together, they have engaged in a perfectly inelastic collision.

CHAPTER 13

Energy Conservation

IN THIS CHAPTER

Summary: While kinematics can be used to predict the speeds of objects with constant acceleration, energy conservation is a more powerful tool that can predict how objects will move even with a changing acceleration.

Key Ideas

- ✪ Work is related to kinetic energy through the work–energy theorem.
- ✪ There are many types of potential energy. Two (due to gravity and due to a spring) are discussed in this chapter.
- ✪ To use conservation of energy, add potential + kinetic energy at two positions in an object's motion. This sum must be the same everywhere.
- ✪ A potential energy function can be derived for any conservative force.

Relevant Equations

The definition of work:

$$W = F \cdot d_{\parallel}$$

The work–energy theorem:

$$W_{\text{net}} = \Delta K$$

The force of a spring:

$$F = -kx$$

Two different types of potential energy:

$$\text{Gravitational PE} = mgh$$
$$\text{Spring PE} = \tfrac{1}{2}kx^2$$

Power:

$$\text{Power} = \frac{\text{work}}{\text{time}} = Fv$$

Relationship between a conservative force F and the potential energy U it creates:

$$F = -\frac{dU}{dx}; U = -\int F dx$$

As with momentum, the energy of an isolated system is always conserved. It might change form—potential energy can be converted to kinetic energy, or kinetic energy can be converted to heat—but it'll never simply disappear.

Conservation of energy is one of the most important, fundamental concepts in all of physics . . . translation: it's going to show up all over the AP exam. So read this chapter carefully.

Kinetic Energy and the Work-Energy Theorem

We'll start with some definitions.

Energy: The ability to do work

Work: $F \cdot d_\parallel$

What this second definition means is that work equals the product of the distance an object travels and the component of the force acting on that object directed parallel to the object's direction of motion. That sounds more complicated than it really is: an example will help.

A box is pulled along the floor, as shown in Figure 13.1. It is pulled a distance of 10 m, and the force pulling it has a magnitude of 5 N and is directed 30° above the horizontal. So, the force component that is PARALLEL to the 10 m displacement is (5 N)(cos 30°).

$$W = (5 \cos 30° \text{ N})(10 \text{ m})$$
$$W = 43 \text{ N} \cdot \text{m}$$

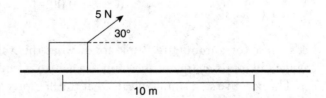

Figure 13.1   Box is pulled along the floor.

One newton·meter is called a joule, abbreviated as 1 J.

- Work is a scalar. So is energy.
- The units of work and of energy are joules.
- Work can be negative . . . this just means that the force is applied in the direction opposite displacement.

> **Kinetic Energy:** Energy of motion, abbreviated K

$$K = \tfrac{1}{2}mv^2$$

This means that the kinetic energy of an object equals one-half the object's mass times its speed squared.

> **Work-Energy Theorem:** $W_{net} = \Delta K$

The net work done on an object is equal to that object's change in kinetic energy. Here's an application:

A train car with a mass of 200 kg is traveling at 20 m/s. How much force must the brakes exert in order to stop the train car in a distance of 10 m?

200 kg   20 m/s

Here, because the only horizontal force is the force of the brakes, the work done by this force is W_{net}.

$$W_{net} = \Delta KE = KE_f - KE_0$$

$$W = \tfrac{1}{2}mv_f^2 - \tfrac{1}{2}mv_0^2$$

$$W = (0) - \tfrac{1}{2}(200 \text{ kg})(20 \text{ m/s})^2$$

$$W = -40{,}000 \text{ J}$$

Let's pause for a minute to think about what this value means. We've just calculated the change in kinetic energy of the train car, which is equal to the net work done on the train car. The negative sign simply means that the net force was opposite the train's displacement. To find the force:

$$-40{,}000 \text{ N} = \text{Force} \cdot \text{distance}$$

$$-40{,}000 \text{ N} = F(10 \text{ m})$$

$$F = -4000 \text{ N, which means 4000 N opposite the}$$
$$\text{direction of displacement}$$

Potential Energy

> **Potential Energy**: Energy of position, abbreviated U

Potential energy comes in many forms: there's gravitational potential energy, spring potential energy, electrical potential energy, and so on. For starters, we'll concern ourselves with gravitational potential energy.

Gravitational PE is described by the following equation:

$$U = mgh$$

In this equation, m is the mass of an object, g is the gravitational field of 10 N/kg on Earth, and h is the height of an object above a certain point (called "the zero of potential").[1] That point can be wherever you want it to be, depending on the problem. For example, let's say a pencil is sitting on a table. If you define the zero of potential to be the table, then the pencil has no gravitational PE. If you define the floor to be the zero of potential, then the pencil has PE equal to mgh, where h is the height of the pencil above the floor. Your choice of the *zero* of potential in a problem should be made by determining how the problem can most easily be solved.

REMINDER: h in the potential energy equation stands for *vertical* height above the zero of potential.

Conservation of Energy: Problem-Solving Approach

Solving energy-conservation problems is relatively simple, as long as you approach them methodically. The general approach is this: write out all the terms for the initial energy of the system, and set the sum of those terms equal to the sum of all the terms for the final energy of the system. Let's practice.

> A block of mass m is placed on a frictionless plane inclined at a 30° angle above the horizontal. It is released from rest and allowed to slide 5 m down the plane. What is its final velocity?
>
>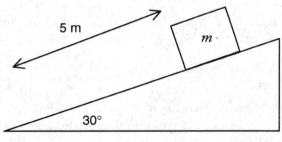

If we were to approach this problem using kinematics equations (which we could), it would take about a page of work to solve. Instead, observe how quickly it can be solved using conservation of energy.

---

[1] Note that 10 N/kg is exactly the same as 10 m/s².

$$K_i + U_i = K_f + U_f \left(\begin{array}{l} i = \text{initial, at the top} \\ f = \text{final, at the bottom} \end{array} \right)$$

$$\tfrac{1}{2}mv_i^2 + mgh_i = \tfrac{1}{2}mv_f^2 + mgh_f$$

We will define our zero of potential to be the height of the box after it has slid the 5 m down the plane. By defining it this way, the PE term on the right side of the equation will cancel out. Furthermore, because the box starts from rest, its initial KE also equals zero.

$$0 + mgh_i = \tfrac{1}{2}mv_f^2 + 0$$

The initial height can be found using trigonometry: $h_i = (5\text{m})(\sin 30°) = 2.5$ m.

$$mg(2.5\,\text{m}) = \tfrac{1}{2}mv_f^2$$
$$50(\text{m/s})^2 = v_f^2$$
$$v_f = 7\,\text{m/s}$$

In general, the principle of energy conservation can be stated mathematically like this:

$$\boxed{K_i + U_i + W = K_f + U_f}$$

The term W in this equation stands for work done on an object. For example, if there had been friction between the box and the plane in the previous example, the work done by friction would be the W term. When it comes to the AP exam, *you will include this W term only when there is friction (or some other exteral force) involved*. When friction is involved, $W = F_f d$, where F_f is the force of friction on the object, and d is the distance the object travels.

Let's say that there was friction between the box and the inclined plane.

A box of mass m is placed on a plane inclined at a 30° angle above the horizontal. The coefficient of friction between the box and the plane is 0.20. The box is released from rest and allowed to slide 5.0 m down the plane. What is its final velocity?

We start by writing the general equation for energy conservation:

$$K_i + U_i + W = E_f + U_f$$

W equals $F_f d$, where F_f is the force of friction, and d is 5 m.[2]

$$W = -F_f d = -\mu F_N d$$
$$F_N = (mg \cos\theta), \text{where } \theta = 30°$$

The value for W is negative because friction acts opposite displacement. You may want to draw a free-body diagram to understand how we derived this value for F_N.

Now, plugging in values we have

$$\tfrac{1}{2}mv_i^2 + mgh_i \pm 0.2(mg\cos 30°)(5\,\text{m}) = \tfrac{1}{2}mv_f^2 + mgh_f$$

$$0 + mg(2.5\,\text{m}) - 0.2(mg)(.87)(5\,\text{m}) = \tfrac{1}{2}mv_f^2$$

---

[2]Note this difference carefully. Although potential energy involves only a vertical height, work done by friction includes the *entire* distance the box travels.

We rearrange some terms and cancel out m from each side to get

$$v_f = 5.7 \text{ m/s}$$

This answer makes sense—friction on the plane *reduces* the box's speed at the bottom.

Springs

Gravitational potential energy isn't the only kind of PE around. Another frequently encountered form is spring potential energy.

The force exerted by a spring is directly proportional to the amount that the spring is compressed. That is,

$$\boxed{F_{spring} = -kx}$$

In this equation, k is a constant (called the spring constant), and x is the distance that the spring has been compressed or extended from its equilibrium state. The negative sign is simply a reminder that the force of a spring always acts opposite to displacement—an extended spring pulls back toward the equilibrium position, while a compressed spring pushes toward the equilibrium position. We call this type of force a restoring force, and we discuss it more in Chapter 16 on simple harmonic motion. However, we can ignore this sign unless we are doing calculus.

When a spring is either compressed or extended, it stores potential energy. The amount of energy stored is given as follows.

$$\boxed{U_{spring} = \frac{1}{2}kx^2}$$

Similarly, the work done by a spring is given by $W_{spring} = \frac{1}{2}kx^2$. Here's an example problem.

A block with a mass of 2 kg is attached to a spring with $k = 1$ N/m. The spring is compressed 10 cm from equilibrium and then released. How fast is the block traveling when it passes through the equilibrium point? Neglect friction.

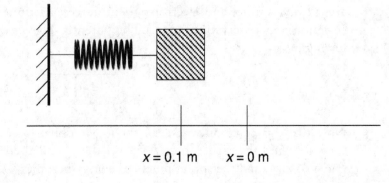

$x = 0.1$ m $x = 0$ m

It's important to recognize that we CANNOT use kinematics to solve this problem! Because the force of a spring changes as it stretches, the block's acceleration is not constant. When acceleration isn't constant, try using energy conservation.

We begin by writing our statement for conservation of energy.

$$K_i + U_i + W = K_f + U_f$$

Now we fill in values for each term. PE here is just in the form of spring potential energy, and there's no friction, so we can ignore the W term. Be sure to plug in all values in meters!

$$0 + \tfrac{1}{2}(k)(0.1\,\mathrm{m})^2 = \tfrac{1}{2}mv_f^2 + 0$$

$$v_f = \sqrt{\frac{k}{m}(0.1\,\mathrm{m})^2}$$

Plugging in values for k and m, we have

$$v_f = 0.07 \text{ m/s, that is, 7 cm/s}$$

Power

Whether you walk up a mountain or whether a car drives you up the mountain, the same amount of work has to be done on you. (You weigh a certain number of newtons, and you have to be lifted up the same distance either way!) But clearly there's something different about walking up over the course of several hours and driving up over several minutes. That difference is power.

> **Power:** work/time

Power is, thus, measured in units of joules/second, also known as watts. A car engine puts out hundreds of horsepower, equivalent to maybe 100 kilowatts; whereas, you'd work hard just to put out a power of a few hundred watts.

Potential Energy vs. Displacement Graphs

A different potential energy function can actually be derived for ANY conservative force. (A conservative force means that energy is conserved when this force acts . . . examples are gravity, spring, and electromagnetic forces; friction and air resistance are the most common nonconservative forces.) The potential energy U for a force is given by the following integral:

$$\boxed{U = -\int F\,dx}$$

Note that this equation works for the gravitational force $F = -mg$ (where − is the down direction) and the spring force $F = -kx$; the potential energy attributable to gravity integrates to mgh, and the spring potential energy becomes $\tfrac{1}{2}kx^2$.

Chris on a Skateboard

Once a potential energy of an object is found as a function of position, making a U vs. x graph tells a lot about the long-term motion of the object. Consider the potential energy of a spring, $\tfrac{1}{2}kx^2$. A graph of this function looks like a parabola, as shown in Figure 13.2.

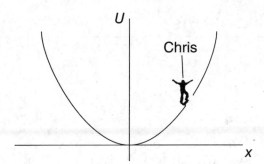

Figure 13.2 Potential energy vs. displacement graph for a spring.

You can get a general feel for how the mass on a spring moves by imagining that Chris is riding a skateboard on a ramp shaped like the graph. A ramp shaped like this looks like a half-pipe. If he starts from some height above the bottom, Chris will oscillate back and forth, going fastest in the middle, and turning around when he runs out of energy at the right or left end. Although this is not precisely how a mass on a spring moves—the mass only moves back and forth, for example—the long-term properties of Chris's motion and the motion of the mass on a spring are the same. The mass oscillates back and forth, with its fastest speed in the middle, just like Chris does.

Thinking about Chris on a skateboard works for all U vs. x graphs. Consider a model of the energy between two atoms that looks like the graph in Figure 13.3.

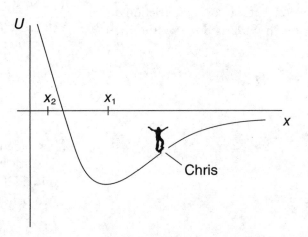

Figure 13.3 Potential energy vs. displacement graph for two atoms.

If Chris on his skateboard released himself from rest near position x_1, he'd just oscillate back and forth, much like in the mass on a spring problem. But if he were to let go near the position labeled x_2, he'd have enough energy to keep going to the right as far as he wants; in fact, he'd make it off the page, never coming back. This is what happens to the atoms in molecules, too. If a second atom is placed pretty close to a distance x_1 from the first atom, it will just oscillate back and forth about that position. However, if the second atom is placed very close to the first atom, it will gain enough energy to escape to a faraway place.

› Practice Problems

Multiple Choice:

Questions 1 and 2

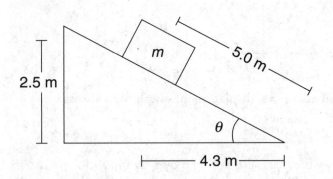

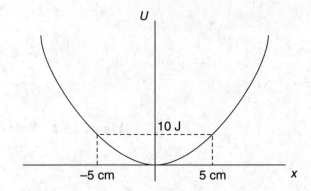

A block of weight $mg = 100$ N slides a distance of 5.0 m down a 30-degree incline, as shown above.

1. How much work is done on the block by gravity?

   (A) 500 J
   (B) 430 J
   (C) 100 J
   (D) 50 J
   (E) 250 J

2. If the block experiences a constant friction force of 10 N, how much work is done by the friction force?

   (A) −43 J
   (B) −25 J
   (C) −500 J
   (D) −100 J
   (E) −50 J

3. A mass experiences a potential energy U that varies with distance x as shown in the graph above. The mass is released from position $x = 0$ with 10 J of kinetic energy. Which of the following describes the long-term motion of the mass?

   (A) The mass eventually comes to rest at $x = 0$.
   (B) The mass slows down with constant acceleration, stopping at $x = 5$ cm.
   (C) The mass speeds up with constant acceleration.
   (D) The mass oscillates, never getting farther than 5 cm from $x = 0$.
   (E) The mass oscillates, never getting farther than 10 cm from $x = 0$.

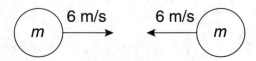

4. Two identical balls of mass $m = 1.0$ kg are moving towards each other, as shown above. What is the initial kinetic energy of the system consisting of the two balls?

   (A) 0 joules
   (B) 1 joules
   (C) 12 joules
   (D) 18 joules
   (E) 36 joules

Free Response:

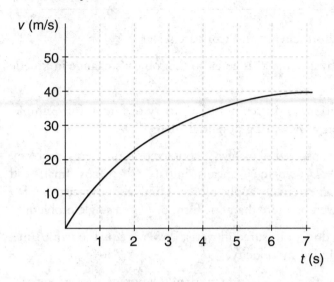

5. A 1500-kg car moves north according to the velocity–time graph shown.

(a) Determine the change in the car's kinetic energy during the first 7 s.

(b) To determine how far the car traveled in these 7 s, the three basic kinematics equations can not be used. Explain why not.

(c) Use the velocity–time graph to estimate the distance the car traveled in 7 s.

(d) What was the net work done on the car in these 7 s?

(e) Determine the average power necessary for the car to perform this motion.

› Solutions to Practice Problems

1. **E**—The force of gravity is straight down and equal to 100 N. The displacement parallel to this force is the *vertical* displacement, 2.5 m. Work equals force times parallel displacement, 250 J.

2. **E**—The force of friction acts up the plane, and displacement is down the plane, so just multiply force times distance to get 50 J. The negative sign indicates that force is opposite displacement.

3. **D**—Think of Chris on a skateboard—on this graph, he will oscillate back and forth about $x = 0$. Because he starts with a KE of 10 J, he can, at most, have a potential energy of 10 J, which corresponds on the graph to a maximum displacement of 5 cm. (The mass cannot have constant acceleration because constant acceleration only occurs for a constant force; a constant force produces an energy graph that is linear. The mass will not come to rest because we are assuming a conservative force, for which KE can be converted to and from PE freely.)

4. **E**—Kinetic energy is a scalar, so even though the balls move in opposite directions, the KEs cannot cancel. Instead, kinetic energy $\frac{1}{2}(1 \text{ kg})(6 \text{ m/s})^2$ attributable to different objects adds together algebraically, giving 36 J total.

5. (a) The car started from rest, or zero KE. The car ended up with $\frac{1}{2}(1500 \text{ kg})(40 \text{ m/s})^2 = 1.2 \times 10^6$ J of kinetic energy. So its change in KE is 1.2×10^6 J.

(b) The acceleration is not constant. We know that because the velocity–time graph is not linear.

(c) The distance traveled is found from the area under the graph. It is easiest to approximate by counting boxes, where one of the big boxes is 10 m. There are, give-or-take, 19 boxes underneath the curve, so the car went 190 m.

(d) We cannot use work = force × distance here, because the net force is continually changing (because acceleration is changing). But $W_{net} = \Delta KE$ is always valid. In part (a) the car's change in KE was found to be 1.2×10^6 J; so the net work done on the car is also 1.2×10^6 J.

(e) Power is work divided by time, or 1.2×10^6 J/7 s = 170 kW. This can be compared to the power of a car, 220 horsepower.

› Rapid Review

- Energy is the ability to do work. Both energy and work are scalars.

- The work done on an object (or by an object) is equal to that object's change in kinetic energy.

- Potential energy is energy of position, and it comes in a variety of forms; for example, there's gravitational potential energy and spring potential energy.

- The energy of a closed system is conserved. To solve a conservation of energy problem, start by writing $K_i + U_i + W = K_f + U_f$, where "$i$" means "initial," "$f$" means "final," and W is the work done by friction or an externally applied force. Think about what type of U you're dealing with; there might even be more than one form of U in a single problem!

- Power is the rate at which work is done, measured in watts. Power is equal to work/time, which is equivalent to force multiplied by velocity.

- If the functional form of a conservative force is known, then the potential energy attributable to that force is given by

$$U = -\int F\,dx$$

When this U is graphed against displacement, the motion of an object can be predicted by imagining "Chris on a skateboard" skating on the graph.

CHAPTER 14

Gravitation and Circular Motion

IN THIS CHAPTER

Summary: When an object moves in a circle, it is accelerating toward the center of the circle. Any two massive objects attract each other due to gravity.

Key Ideas
- Centripetal (center-seeking) acceleration is equal to $\frac{v^2}{r}$.
- Circular motion (and gravitation) problems still require a free-body diagram and the four-step problem-solving process.
- The gravitational force between two objects is bigger for bigger masses, and smaller for larger separations between the objects.
- Kepler's laws apply to the orbits of planets.

Relevant Equations

Centripetal acceleration:

$$a = \frac{v^2}{r}$$

Gravitational force between any two masses:

$$F = \frac{Gm_1m_2}{r^2}$$

Gravitational potential energy a long way from a planet:

$$U = -\frac{Gm_1m_2}{r}$$

It might seem odd that we're covering gravitation and circular motion in the same chapter. After all, one of these topics relates to the attractive force exerted between two massive objects, and the other one relates to, well, swinging a bucket over your head.

However, as you're probably aware, the two topics have plenty to do with each other. Planetary orbits, for instance, can be described only if you understand both gravitation and circular motion. And, sure enough, the AP exam frequently features questions about orbits.

So let's look at these two important topics, starting with circular motion.

Velocity and Acceleration in Circular Motion

Remember how we defined acceleration as an object's change in velocity in a given time? Well, velocity is a vector, and that means that an object's velocity can change either in magnitude or in direction (or both). In the past, we have talked about the magnitude of an object's velocity changing. Now, we discuss what happens when the direction of an object's velocity changes.

When an object maintains the same speed but turns in a circle, the magnitude of its acceleration is constant and directed **toward the center** of the circle. This means that the acceleration vector is perpendicular to the velocity vector at any given moment, as shown in Figure 14.1.

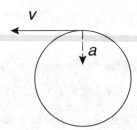

Figure 14.1   Velocity and acceleration of an object traveling in uniform circular motion.

The velocity vector is always directed tangent to the circle, and the acceleration vector is always directed toward the center of the circle. There's a way to prove that statement mathematically, but it's complicated, so you'll just have to trust us. (You can refer to your textbook for the complete derivation.)

Centripetal Acceleration

On to a few definitions.

> **Centripetal acceleration:** The acceleration keeping an object in uniform circular motion, abbreviated a_c

We know that the net force acting on an object is related to the object's acceleration by $F_{net} = ma$. And we know that the acceleration of an object in circular motion points toward the center of the circle. So we can conclude that the centripetal force acting on an object also points toward the center of the circle.

The formula for centripetal acceleration is

$$a_c = \frac{v^2}{r}$$

In this equation, v is the object's velocity, and r is the radius of the circle in which the object is traveling.

> **Centrifugal acceleration:** As far as you're concerned, nonsense. Acceleration in circular motion is always **toward**, not away from, the center.

Centripetal acceleration is real; centrifugal acceleration is nonsense, unless you're willing to read a multipage discussion of "non-inertial reference frames" and "fictitious forces." So for our purposes, there is no such thing as a centrifugal (center-fleeing) acceleration. *When an object moves in a circle, the acceleration (and also the net force) must point to the center of the circle.*

The main thing to remember when tackling circular motion problems is that a *centripetal force is simply whatever force is directed toward the center of the circle in which the object is traveling.* So, first label the forces on your free-body diagram, and then find the net force directed toward the center of the circle. That net force is the centripetal force. But NEVER label a free-body diagram with "F_c."

> **Exam tip from an AP Physics veteran:**
> On a free-response question, do not label a force as "centripetal force," even if that force does act toward the center of a circle; you will not earn credit. Rather, label with the actual source of the force; i.e., tension, friction, weight, electric force, etc.
>
> *—Mike, high school junior*

Mass on a String

A block of mass M = 2 kg is swung on a rope in a vertical circle of radius r at constant speed v. When the block is at the top of the circle, the tension in the rope is measured to be 10 N. What is the tension in the rope when the block is at the bottom of the circle?

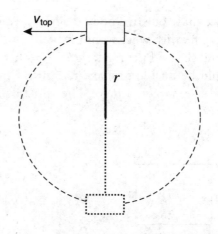

Let's begin by drawing a free-body diagram of the block at the top of the circle and another of the block at the bottom of the circle.

TOP   BOTTOM

Next, we write Newton's second law for each diagram. Acceleration is always toward the center of the circle.

$$Mg + T_{\text{top}} = Ma \qquad T_{\text{bottom}} - Mg = Ma$$

The acceleration is centripetal, so we can plug in v^2/r for both accelerations.

$$Mg + T_{\text{top}} = Mv^2/r \qquad T_{\text{bottom}} - Mg = Mv^2/r$$

At both top and bottom, the speed v and the radius r are the same. So Mv^2/r has to be the same at both the top and bottom, allowing us to set the left side of each equation equal to one another.

$$Mg + T_{\text{top}} = T_{\text{bottom}} - Mg$$

With $M = 2$ kg and $T_{\text{top}} = 10$ N, we solve to get $T_{\text{bottom}} = 50$ N.

Car on a Curve

This next problem is a bit easier than the last one, but it's still good practice.

> A car of mass m travels around a flat curve that has a radius of curvature r. What is the necessary coefficient of friction such that the car can round the curve with a velocity v?

Before we draw our free-body diagram, we should consider how friction is acting in this case. Imagine this: what would it be like to round a corner quickly while driving on ice? You would slide off the road, right? Another way to put that is to say that without friction, you would be unable to make the turn. Friction provides the centripetal force necessary to round the corner. Bingo! The force of friction must point in toward the center of the curve.

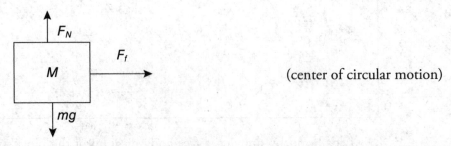

(center of circular motion)

We can now write some equations and solve for μ, the coefficient of friction.

The net force in the horizontal direction is F_f, which can be set equal to mass times (centripetal) acceleration.

$$F_f = ma$$

$$F_f = ma = m\left(\frac{v^2}{r}\right)$$

We also know that $F_f = \mu F_N$. So,

$$\mu F_N = \frac{mv^2}{r}$$

Furthermore, we know that the car is in vertical equilibrium—it is neither flying off the road nor being pushed through it—so $F_N = mg$.

$$\mu mg = \frac{mv^2}{r}$$

Solving for μ we have

$$\mu = \frac{v^2}{gr}$$

Note that this coefficient doesn't depend on mass. Good—if it did, we'd need tires made of different materials depending on how heavy the car is.

Newton's Law of Gravitation

We now shift our focus to gravity. Gravity is an amazing concept—you and the Earth attract each other just because you both have mass!—but at the level tested on the AP exam, it's also a pretty easy concept. In fact, there are only a couple equations you need to know. The first is for gravitational force:

$$F_G = \frac{Gm_1m_2}{r^2}$$

This equation describes the gravitational force that one object exerts on another object. m_1 is the mass of one of the objects, m_2 is the mass of the other object, r is the distance between the center of mass of each object, and G is called the "Universal Gravitational Constant" and is equal to 6.67×10^{-11} (G does have units—they are $N \cdot m^2/kg^2$—but most problems won't require your knowing them). The negative sign indicates that the force is attractive. We can leave it off unless we are doing calculus with the equation.

> The mass of the Earth, M_E, is 5.97×10^{24} kg. The mass of the sun, M_S, is 1.99×10^{30} kg. The two objects are about 154,000,000 km away from each other. How much gravitational force does Earth exert on the sun?

This is simple plug-and-chug (remember to convert km to m).

$$F_G = \frac{GM_EM_S}{r^2}$$

$$F_G = \frac{6.67 \times 10^{-11}(5.97 \times 10^{24})(1.99 \times 10^{30})}{(1.54 \times 10^{11})^2}$$

$$F_G = 3.3 \times 10^{22} N$$

Notice that the amount of force that the Earth exerts on the sun is exactly the same as the amount of force the sun exerts on the Earth.

We can combine our knowledge of circular motion and of gravity to solve the following type of problem.

> What is the speed of the Earth as it revolves in orbit around the sun?

The force of gravity exerted by the sun on the Earth is what keeps the Earth in motion—it is the centripetal force acting on the Earth.

$$F_G = M_E a = M_E \left(\frac{v^2}{r} \right)$$

$$\frac{GM_E M_S}{r^2} = \frac{M_E v^2}{r}$$

$$\frac{GM_S}{r} = v^2$$

$$v = \sqrt{\frac{GM_S}{r}}$$

$v = 29,000$ m/s. (Wow, fast . . . that converts to about 14 miles every second—much faster than, say, a school bus.)

Along with the equation for gravitational force, you need to know the equation for gravitational potential energy.

$$U_G = \frac{-Gm_1 m_2}{r}$$

Why negative? Objects tend get pushed toward the lowest available potential energy. A long way away from the sun, the r term gets big, so the potential energy gets close to zero. But, since a mass is *attracted* to the sun by gravity, the potential energy of the mass must get lower and lower as r gets smaller.

We bet you're thinking something like, "Now hold on a minute! You said a while back that an object's gravitational potential energy equals *mgh*. What's going on?"

Good point. An object's gravitational PE equals *mgh* when that object is near the surface of the Earth. But it equals $\frac{-Gm_1 m_2}{r}$ no matter where that object is.

Similarly, the force of gravity acting on an object equals *mg* (the object's weight) only when that object is near the surface of the Earth.

The force of gravity on an object, however, *always* equals $\frac{Gm_1 m_2}{r^2}$ regardless of location.

Kepler's Laws

Johannes Kepler, the late 1500s theorist, developed three laws of planetary motion based on the detailed observations of Tycho Brahe. You need to understand each law and its consequences.

1. *Planetary orbits are ellipses, with the sun at one focus.* Of course, we can apply this law to a satellite orbiting Earth, in which case the orbit is an ellipse, with Earth at one focus. (We mean the center of the Earth—for the sake of Kepler's laws, we consider the orbiting bodies to be point particles.) In the simple case of a circular orbit, this law still applies because a circle is just an ellipse with both foci at the center.

2. *An orbit sweeps out equal areas in equal times.* If you draw a line from a planet to the sun, this line crosses an equal amount of area every minute (or hour, or month, or whatever)—see Figure 14.2. The consequence here is that when a planet is close to the sun, it must speed up, and when a planet is far from the sun, it must slow down. This applies to the Earth as well. In the northern hemisphere winter, when the Earth is slightly closer to the sun,[1] the Earth moves faster in its orbit. (You may have noticed that the earliest sunset in wintertime occurs about two weeks before the solstice—this is a direct consequence of Earth's faster orbit.)

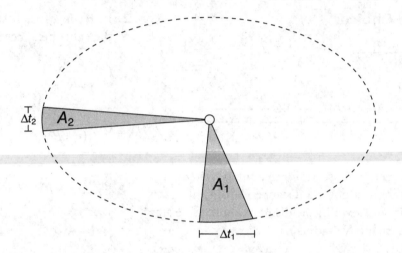

Figure 14.2   Kepler's second law. The area "swept out" by a planet in its orbit is shaded. In equal time intervals Δt_1 and Δt_2, these swept areas A_1 and A_2 are the same.

3. *A planet's orbital period squared is proportional to its orbital radius cubed.* In mathematics, we write this as $T^2 = cR^3$. Okay, how do we define the "radius" of a non-circular orbit? Well, that would be average distance from the sun. And what is this constant c? It's a different value for every system of satellites orbiting a single central body. Not worth worrying about, except that you can easily derive it for the solar system by solving the equation above for c and plugging in data from Earth's orbit: $c = 1$ year²/AU³, where an "AU" is the distance from Earth to the sun. If you *really* need to, you can convert this into more standard units, but we wouldn't bother with this right now.

Energy of Closed Orbits

When an object of mass m is in orbit around the sun, its potential energy is $U = -\dfrac{GMm}{r}$, where M is the mass of the sun, and r is the distance between the centers of the two masses.

The kinetic energy of the orbiting mass, of course, is $K = \frac{1}{2}mv^2$. The total mechanical energy of the mass in orbit is defined as $U + K$. When the mass is in a stable orbit, the total

---

[1]*Please* don't say you thought the Earth must be farther away from the sun in winter because it's cold. When it's winter in the United States, it's summer in Australia, and we're all the same distance from the sun!

mechanical energy must be less than zero. A mass with positive total mechanical energy can escape the "gravitational well" of the sun; a mass with negative total mechanical energy is "bound" to orbit the sun.[2]

All of the above applies to the planets orbiting in the solar system. It also applies to moons or satellites orbiting planets, when (obviously) we replace the "sun" by the central planet. A useful calculation using the fact that total mechanical energy of an object in orbit is the potential energy plus the kinetic energy is to find the "escape speed" from the surface of a planet . . . at r equal to the radius of the planet, set kinetic plus potential energy equal to zero, and solve for v. This is the speed that, if it is attained at the surface of the planet (neglecting air resistance), will cause an object to attain orbit.

❯ Practice Problems

Multiple Choice:

Questions 1 and 2:

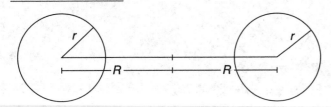

Two stars, each of mass M, form a binary system. The stars orbit about a point a distance R from the center of each star, as shown in the diagram above. The stars themselves each have radius r.

1. What is the force each star exerts on the other?

(A) $G\dfrac{M^2}{(2r+2R)^2}$

(B) $G\dfrac{M^2}{(R+r)^2}$

(C) $G\dfrac{M^2}{R^2}$

(D) $G\dfrac{M^2}{4R^2}$

(E) $G\dfrac{M^2}{2R^2}$

2. In terms of each star's tangential speed v, what is the centripetal acceleration of each star?

(A) $\dfrac{v^2}{2R}$

(B) $\dfrac{v^2}{(r+R)}$

(C) $\dfrac{v^2}{2(r+R)}$

(D) $\dfrac{v^2}{2r}$

(E) $\dfrac{v^2}{R}$

Questions 3 and 4: In the movie *Return of the Jedi*, the Ewoks throw rocks using a circular-motion device. A rock is attached to a string. An Ewok whirls the rock in a horizontal circle above his head, then lets go, sending the rock careening into the head of an unsuspecting stormtrooper.

3. What force provides the rock's centripetal acceleration?

(A) The vertical component of the string's tension
(B) The horizontal component of the string's tension
(C) The entire tension of the string
(D) The gravitational force on the rock
(E) The horizontal component of the gravitational force on the rock

---

[2]It can be shown that for a planet in a stable, *circular* orbit, the kinetic energy is half the absolute value of the potential energy. This isn't something important enough to memorize, but it might help you out sometime if you happen to remember.

4. The Ewok whirls the rock and releases it from a point above his head and to his right. The rock initially goes straight forward. Which of the following describes the subsequent motion of the rock?

(A) It will continue in a straight line forward, while falling due to gravity.
(B) It will continue forward but curve to the right, while falling due to gravity.
(C) It will continue forward but curve to the left, while falling due to gravity.
(D) It will fall straight down to the ground.
(E) It will curve back toward the Ewok and hit him in the head.

5. A Space Shuttle orbits Earth 300 km above the surface. Why can't the Shuttle orbit 10 km above Earth?

(A) The Space Shuttle cannot go fast enough to maintain such an orbit.
(B) Kepler's laws forbid an orbit so close to the surface of the Earth.
(C) Because r appears in the denominator of Newton's law of gravitation, the force of gravity is much larger closer to the Earth; this force is too strong to allow such an orbit.
(D) The closer orbit would likely crash into a large mountain such as Everest because of its elliptical nature.
(E) Much of the Shuttle's kinetic energy would be dissipated as heat in the atmosphere, degrading the orbit.

Free Response:

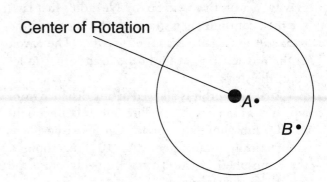

Center of Rotation

6. Consider two points on a rotating turntable: Point A is very close to the center of rotation, while point B is on the outer rim of the turntable. Both points are shown above. A penny could be placed on the turntable at either point A or point B.

(a) In which case would the speed of the penny be greater, if it were placed at point A, or if it were placed at point B? Explain.
(b) At which point would the penny require the larger centripetal force to remain in place? Justify your answer.
(c) Point B is 0.25 m from the center of rotation. If the coefficient of friction between the penny and the turntable is $\mu = 0.30$, calculate the maximum linear speed the penny can have there and still remain in circular motion.

› Solutions to Practice Problems

1. D—In Newton's law of gravitation,

$$F = G\frac{m_1 m_2}{r^2},$$

the distance used is the distance between the centers of the planets; here that distance is $2R$. But the denominator is squared, so $(2R)^2 = 4R^2$ in the denominator here.

2. E—In the centripetal acceleration equation

$$a_c = \frac{v^2}{r},$$

the distance used is the radius of the circular motion. Here, because the planets orbit around

a point right in between them, this distance is simply R.

3. B—Consider the vertical forces acting on the rock. The rock has weight, so mg acts down. However, because the rock isn't falling down, something must counteract the weight. That something is the vertical component of the rope's tension. The rope must not be perfectly horizontal, then. Because the circle is horizontal, the centripetal force must be horizontal as well. The only horizontal force here is the horizontal component of the tension. (Gravity acts *down*, last we checked, and so cannot have a horizontal component.)

4. **A**—Once the Ewok lets go, no forces (other than gravity) act on the rock. So, by Newton's first law, the rock continues in a straight line. Of course, the rock still must fall because of gravity. (The Ewok in the movie who got hit in the head forgot to let go of the string.)

5. **E**—A circular orbit is allowed at any distance from a planet, as long as the satellite moves fast enough. At 300 km above the surface Earth's atmosphere is practically nonexistent. At 10 km, though, the atmospheric friction would quickly cause the Shuttle to slow down.

6. (a) Both positions take the same time to make a full revolution. But point B must go farther in that same time, so the penny must have bigger speed at point B.

   (b) The coin needs more centripetal force at point B. The centripetal force is equal to mv^2/r. However, the speed itself depends on the radius of the motion, as shown in part (a). The speed of a point at radius r is the circumference divided by the time for one rotation T, $v = 2\pi r/T$. So the net force equation becomes, after algebraic simplification, $F_{net} = 4m\pi^2 r/T^2$. Because both positions take equal times to make a rotation, the coin with the larger distance from the center needs more centripetal force.

   (c) The force of friction provides the centripetal force here, and is equal to μ times the normal force. Because the only forces acting vertically are F_N and mg, $F_N = mg$. The net force is equal to mv^2/r, and also to the friction force μmg. Setting these equal and solving for v,

   $$v = \sqrt{\mu rg}$$

   Plug in the values given ($r = 0.25$ m, $\mu = 0.30$) to get $v = 0.87$ m/s. If the speed is faster than this, then the centripetal force necessary to keep the penny rotating increases, and friction can no longer provide that force.

❯ Rapid Review

- When an object travels in a circle, its velocity vector is directed tangent to the circle, and its acceleration vector points toward the center of the circle.

- A centripetal force keeps an object traveling in a circle. The centripetal force is simply whatever net force is directed toward the center of the circle in which the object is traveling.

- Newton's law of gravitation states that the gravitational force between two objects is proportional to the mass of the first object multiplied by the mass of the second divided by the square of the distance between them. This also means that the gravitational force felt by one object is the same as the force felt by the second object.

- Predictions of Kepler's laws: Planets undergo elliptical orbits with the sun at one focus; at points in an orbit closer to the sun, a planet moves faster; the smaller a planet's mean distance from the sun, the shorter its orbital period, by $T^2 \propto R^3$. (The symbol "$\propto$" means "is proportional to.")

CHAPTER 15

Rotational Motion

IN THIS CHAPTER

Summary: The mechanics of rotating objects make up a significant chunk of the AP Physics C exam. But, rotational motion has many direct analogs from linear motion. If you understand the mechanics unit from your first-year physics course, rotational motion can be learned by analogy.

Key Ideas

✪ Rotational kinematics uses essentially the same equations as kinematics, but distances, speeds, and accelerations are rotational quantities expressed with radians instead of with meters.

✪ The rotational inertia defines an object's resistance to rotation. It is the rotational analog of mass.

✪ An object can possess rotational kinetic energy in addition to translational kinetic energy.

✪ Angular momentum is conserved anytime no external torque acts on a system of objects. This includes planets in orbit.

Relevant Equations

Rotational kinematics equations.
First, for constant angular acceleration:

$$\omega_f = \omega_o + at$$
$$\Delta\theta = \omega_o t + \tfrac{1}{2}at^2$$
$$\omega_f^2 = \omega_o^2 + 2a\Delta\theta$$

And, in all cases:

$$\theta = \int \omega \, dt$$

$$\omega = \frac{d\theta}{dt} = \int a \, dt$$

$$a = \frac{d\omega}{dt}$$

Conversion between linear and rotational variables:

$$x = r\theta$$
$$v = r\omega$$
$$a = ra$$

Rotational inertia:

$$I = mr^2 \qquad \text{for a point particle}$$
$$I = \int r^2 \, dm \qquad \text{for a continuous body}$$

Newton's second law for rotation:

$$\tau_{net} = Ia$$

Rotational kinetic energy:

$$K_{rot} = \tfrac{1}{2}I\omega^2$$

Angular momentum:

$$L = I\omega = mvr$$

Okay, you now have thoroughly studied how an object moves; that is, if the object can be treated as a point particle. But what happens when an object is spinning? How does that affect motion? Now is the time to learn.

You'll find clear similarities between the material in this chapter and what you already know. In fact, you'll see that every concept, every variable, every equation for rotational motion has an analog in our study of translational motion. The best way to understand rotational motion is simply to apply the concepts of linear motion to the case of a spinning object.

Rotational Kinematics

For an object moving in a straight line, we defined five variables.

v_0	initial velocity
v_f	final velocity
Δx	displacement
a	acceleration
t	time interval

Now consider a fixed object spinning, like a compact disc. The relevant variables become the following:

ω_0 initial *angular* velocity, measured in radians per second
ω_f final *angular* velocity, measured in radians per second
$\Delta\theta$ the total *angle* through which the spinning object rotates, measured in radians
a *angular* acceleration, telling how *angular* velocity changes with time
t time interval

These variables are related via the following three equations. Obviously, these equations differ from the "star equations" used for kinematics . . . but they're nonetheless very similar:

$$\omega_f = \omega_0 + at$$

$$\Delta\theta = \omega_0 t + \tfrac{1}{2}at^2$$

$$\omega_f^2 = \omega_0^2 + 2a\Delta\theta$$

So try this example:

A bicycle has wheels with radius 50 cm. The bike starts from rest, and the wheels speed up uniformly to 200 revolutions per minute in 10 seconds. How far does the bike go?

In any linear kinematics problem the units should be in meters and seconds; in rotational kinematics, the units MUST be in RADIANS and seconds. So convert revolutions per minute to radians per second. To do so, recall that there are 2π radians in every revolution:

200 rev/min $\times$ 2π rad/rev $\times$ 1 min/60 s = 21 rad/s.

Now identify variables in a chart:

ω_0	0 rad/s
ω_f	21 rad/s
$\Delta\theta$	?
a	?
t	10 s

We want to solve for $\Delta\theta$ because if we know the angle through which the wheel turns, we can figure out how far the edge of the wheel has gone. We know we can solve for $\Delta\theta$, because we have three of the five variables. Plug and chug into the rotational kinematics equations:

$$\omega_f = \omega_0 + at$$

$$a = 2.1\,\text{rad}/\text{s}^2$$

$$\Delta\theta = \omega_0 t + \tfrac{1}{2}at^2$$

$$\Delta\theta = 105\ \text{radians}$$

What does this answer mean? Well, if there are 2π (that is, 6.2) radians in one revolution, then 105 radians is about 17 revolutions through which the wheel has turned.

Now, because the wheel has a radius of 0.50 m, the wheel's circumference is $2\pi r = 3.1$ m; every revolution of the wheel moves the bike 3.1 meters forward. And the wheel made 17 revolutions, giving a total distance of about 53 meters.

Is this reasonable? Sure—the biker traveled across about half a football field in 10 seconds.

There are a few other equations you should know. If you want to figure out the linear position, speed, or acceleration of a spot on a spinning object, or an object that's rolling without slipping, use these three equations:

$$x = r\theta$$
$$v = r\omega$$
$$a = r\alpha$$

where r represents the distance from the spot you're interested in to the center of the object.

So in the case of the bike wheel above, the top speed of the bike was $v = (0.5$ m$)$ $(21$ rad/s$) = 11$ m/s, or about 24 miles per hour—reasonable for an average biker. *Note: To use these equations, angular variable units must involve radians, not degrees or revolutions!!!*

The rotational kinematics equations, just like the linear kinematics equations, are only valid when acceleration is constant. If acceleration is changing, then the same calculus equations that were used for linear kinematics apply here:

$$\theta = \int \omega \, dt$$
$$\omega = \frac{d\theta}{dt} = \int a \, dt$$
$$a = \frac{d\omega}{dt}$$

Rotational Inertia

Newton's second law states that $F_{net} = ma$; this tells us that the greater the mass of an object, the harder it is to accelerate. This tendency for massive objects to resist changes in their velocity is referred to as inertia.

Well, spinning objects also resist changes in their *angular* velocity. But that resistance, that rotational inertia, depends less on the mass of an object than on how that mass is distributed. For example, a baseball player often warms up by placing a weight on the outer end of the bat—this makes the bat more difficult to swing. But he does not place the weight on the bat handle, because extra weight in the handle hardly affects the swing at all.

The rotational inertia, I, is the rotational equivalent of mass. It tells how difficult it is for an object to speed up or slow its rotation. For a single particle of mass m a distance r from the axis of rotation, the rotational inertia is

$$I = mr^2 \qquad I \text{ for a point object.}$$

To find the rotational inertia of several masses—for example, two weights connected by a thin, light rod—just add the I due to each mass.

For a complicated, continuous body, like a sphere or a disk, I can be calculated through integration:

$$I = \int r^2 \, dm \qquad I \text{ for a continuous body.}$$

Exam tip from an AP Physics veteran:
On the AP exam, you will only very occasionally have to use calculus to derive a rotational inertia. Usually you will either be able to sum the *I* due to several masses, or you will be given *I* for the object in question.

—*Joe, college physics student and Physics C alumnus*

Newton's Second Law for Rotation

For linear motion, Newton says $F_{net} = ma$; for rotational motion, the analog to Newton's second law is

$$\tau_{net} = I\alpha$$

where τ_{net} is the net torque on an object. Perhaps the most common application of this equation involves pulleys with mass.

A 2.0-kg block on a smooth table is connected to a hanging 3.0-kg block with a light string. This string passes over a pulley of mass 0.50 kg, as shown in the diagram below. Determine the acceleration of the masses. (The rotational inertia for a solid disc of mass *m* and radius *r* is $\frac{1}{2}mr^2$.)

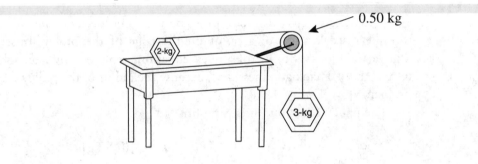

We learned how to approach this type of problem in Chapter 11—draw a free-body diagram for each block, and use $F_{net} = ma$. So we start that way.

The twist in this problem is the massive pulley, which causes two changes in the problem-solving approach:

1. We have to draw a free-body diagram for the pulley as well as the blocks. Even though it doesn't move, it still requires torque to accelerate its spinning speed.
2. We oversimplified things in Chapter 11 when we said, "One rope = one tension." The Physics C corollary to this rule says, ". . . unless the rope is interrupted by a mass." Because the pulley is massive, the tension in the rope may be *different* on each side of the pulley.

The Physics C corollary means that the free-body diagrams indicate T_1 and T_2, which must be treated as different variables. The free-body diagram for the pulley includes only these two tensions:

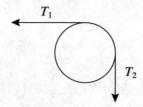

Now, we write Newton's second law for each block:

$$T_1 - 0 = (2 \text{ kg})a$$

$$(3 \text{ kg})g - T_2 = (3 \text{ kg})a.$$

For the pulley, because it is *rotating*, we write Newton's second law for rotation. The torque provided by each rope is equal to the tension in the rope times the distance to the center of rotation; that is, the radius of the pulley. (We're not given this radius, so we'll just call it R for now and hope for the best.)

$$T_2 R - T_1 R = \frac{1}{2}(0.5 \text{ kg})R^2 a$$

The acceleration of each block must be the same because they're connected by a rope; the linear acceleration of a point on the edge of the pulley must also be the same as that of the blocks. So, in the pulley equation, replace a by a/R. Check it out, all the R terms cancel! Thank goodness, too, because the radius of the pulley wasn't even given in the problem.

The pulley equation, thus, simplifies to

$$T_2 - T_1 = \frac{1}{2}(0.5 \text{ kg})a$$

Now we're left with an algebra problem: three equations and three variables (T_1, T_2, and a). Solve using addition or substitution. Try adding the first two equations together—this gives a $T_1 - T_2$ term that meshes nicely with the third equation.

The acceleration turns out to be 5.6 m/s². If you do the problem neglecting the mass of the pulley (try it!) you get 5.9 m/s². This makes sense—the more massive the pulley, the harder it is for the system of masses to speed up.

Rotational Kinetic Energy

The pulley in the last example problem had kinetic energy—it was moving, after all—but it didn't have *linear* kinetic energy, because the velocity of its center of mass was zero. When an object is rotating, its rotational kinetic energy is found by the following equation:

$$\boxed{KE_{\text{rotational}} = \frac{1}{2}I\omega^2}$$

Notice that this equation is very similar to the equation for linear kinetic energy. But, because we're dealing with rotation here, we use rotational inertia in place of mass and angular velocity in place of linear velocity.

If an object is moving linearly at the same time that it's rotating, its total kinetic energy equals the sum of the linear KE and the rotational KE.

$$KE_{total} = KE_{linear} + KE_{rotational}$$

Let's put this equation into practice. Try this example problem.

A ball of mass m sits on an inclined plane, with its center of mass at a height h above the ground. It is released from rest and allowed to roll without slipping down the plane. What is its velocity when it reaches the ground? $I_{ball} = (2/5)mr^2$.

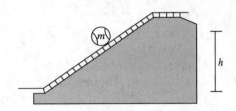

This is a situation you've seen before, except there's a twist: this time, when the object moves down the inclined plane, it gains both linear and rotational kinetic energy. However, it's still just a conservation of energy problem at heart. Initially, the ball just has gravitational potential energy, and when it reaches the ground, it has both linear kinetic and rotational kinetic energy.

$$mgh = \frac{1}{2}mv^2 + \frac{1}{2}I\omega^2$$

$$mgh = \frac{1}{2}mv^2 + \frac{1}{2}(2/5 \ mr^2)(v/r)^2$$

A bit of algebra, and we find that

$$v = \sqrt{\frac{10}{7}gh}$$

If the ball in this problem hadn't rolled down the plane—if it had just slid—its final velocity would have been $\sqrt{2gh}$. (Don't believe us? Try the calculation yourself for practice!) So it makes sense that the final velocity of the ball when it *does* roll down the plane is less than $\sqrt{2gh}$; only a fraction of the initial potential energy is converted to linear kinetic energy.

Angular Momentum and Its Conservation

It probably won't surprise you by this point that momentum, too, has a rotational form. It's called angular momentum (abbreviated, oddly, as L), and it is found by this formula:

$$L = I\omega$$

This formula makes intuitive sense. If you think of angular momentum as, roughly, the amount of effort it would take to make a rotating object stop spinning, then it should seem logical that an object with a large rotational inertia or with a high angular velocity (or both) would be pretty tough to bring to rest.

For a point particle, this formula can be rewritten as

$$L = mvr$$

where v is linear velocity, and r is either (1) the radius of rotation, if the particle is moving in a circle, or (2) distance of closest approach if the particle is moving in a straight line. (See Figure 15.1.)

Figure 15.1   Angular momentum.

Wait a minute! How can an object moving in a straight line have *angular* momentum?!? Well, for the purposes of the AP exam, it suffices just to know that if a particle moves in a straight line, then relative to some point P not on that line, the particle has an angular momentum. But if you want a slightly more satisfying—if less precise—explanation, consider this image. You're standing outside in an open field, and an airplane passes high overhead. You first see it come over the horizon far in front of you, then it flies toward you until it's directly over where you're standing, and then it keeps flying until it finally disappears beneath the opposite horizon. Did the plane fly in an arc over your head or in a straight path? It would be hard for you to tell, right? In other words, when a particle moves in a straight line, an observer who's not on that line would think that the particle sort of looked like it were traveling in a circle.

As with linear momentum, angular momentum is conserved in a closed system; that is, when no external torques act on the objects in the system. Among the most famous examples of conservation of angular momentum is a satellite's orbit around a planet. As shown in Figure 15.2, a satellite will travel in an elliptical orbit around a planet. This means that the satellite is closer to the planet at some times than at others.

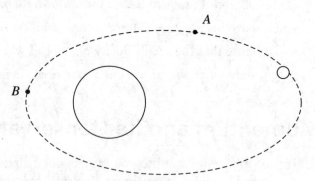

Figure 15.2   Elliptical orbit.

Obviously, at point A, the satellite is farther from the center of rotation than at point B. Conservation of angular momentum tells us that, correspondingly, the angular speed at point A must be less than at point B.[1]

---

[1]Note the consistency with Kepler's law of equal areas in equal times, as discussed in Chapter 14.

The other really famous example of conservation of angular momentum involves a spinning figure skater. When a skater spinning with his or her arms outstretched suddenly brings the arms in close to the body, the speed of rotation dramatically increases. Rotational inertia decreased, so angular speed increased.

You can demonstrate this phenomenon yourself! Sit in a desk chair that spins, and with your legs outstretched, push off forcefully and start spinning. Then tuck in your feet. Dizzying, isn't it?

› Practice Problems

Multiple Choice:

1. All of the objects mentioned in the choices below have the same total mass and length. Which has the greatest rotational inertia about its midpoint?

(A) a very light rod with heavy balls attached at either end
(B) a uniform rod
(C) a nonuniform rod, with the linear density increasing from one end to the other
(D) a nonuniform rod, with the linear density increasing from the middle to the ends
(E) a very light rod with heavy balls attached near the midpoint

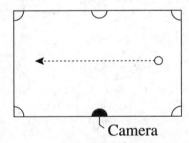

2. A pool ball is struck at one end of the table; it moves at constant speed to the far end of the table. A camera is mounted at the side pocket at the table's midpoint, as shown. From the camera's point of view, the pool ball travels from right to left. At which point in its motion does the ball have the greatest angular momentum about the camera's position?

(A) when the ball was first struck
(B) at the midpoint of the table
(C) the angular momentum is the same throughout the motion
(D) at the far end of the table
(E) one-quarter of the way across the table, and then again three-quarters of the way across the table

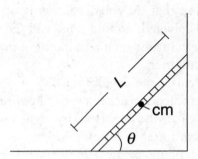

3. A ladder of length L leans against a wall at an angle of θ from the horizontal, as shown above. The normal force F_N applied from the ground on the ladder applies what torque about the ladder's center of mass?

(A) $F_N \cdot (L/2)$
(B) $F_N \cdot L \cos \theta$
(C) $F_N \cdot L \sin \theta$
(D) $F_N \cdot (L/2) \cos \theta$
(E) $F_N \cdot (L/2) \sin \theta$

4. The front wheel on an ancient bicycle has a radius of 0.5 m. It moves with angular velocity given by the function $\omega(t) = 2 + 4t^2$, where t is in seconds. About how far does the bicycle move between $t = 2$ and $t = 3$ seconds?

(A) 36 m
(B) 27 m
(C) 21 m
(D) 14 m
(E) 7 m

Free Response:

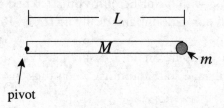

5. A stick of mass M and length L is pivoted at one end. A small mass $m \ll M$ is attached to the right-hand end of the stick. The stick is held horizontally and released from rest.

   (a) Given that the rotational inertia of a uniform rod pivoted around one end is $(1/3)ML^2$, determine the rotational inertia of the described contraption.
   (b) Calculate the angular velocity of the contraption when it reaches a vertical position.
   (c) Calculate the linear velocity of the small mass m when it is at its lowest position.
   (d) The figure below represents the stick at its lowest position. On this figure, draw a vector to represent the net force on the rod's center of mass at this point. Justify your answer.

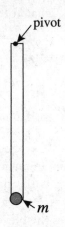

> Solutions to Practice Problems

1. **A**—The farther the mass from the midpoint, the larger its contribution to the rotational inertia. In choice A the mass is as far as possible from the midpoint; because all items have the same mass, A must have the largest I.

2. **C**—The angular momentum of a point particle moving in a straight line about a position near the particle is mvr, where r is the distance of closest approach. This value is constant as long as the particle keeps going in a straight line, which our pool ball does.

3. D—Torque is force times the distance to the fulcrum. The force in question is F_N, and acts straight up at the base of the ladder. The distance used is the distance *perpendicular* to the normal force; this must be $(L/2) \cos \theta$, as shown below:

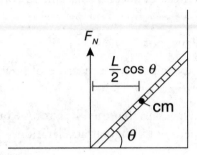

4. D—The angular position function is given by the integral of the angular velocity function with respect to time. The limits on the integral are 2 and 3 seconds:

$$\int_{2}^{3}(2+4t^2)dt = 2t+\frac{4t^3}{3}\Big|_{2}^{3}$$

this evaluates to approximately 27 radians. Using $x = r\theta$, the distance traveled is closest to 14 m.

5. (a) The rotational inertia of the entire contraption is the sum of the moments of inertia for each part. I for the rod is given; I for a point mass a distance L from the pivot is mL^2. So, $I_{total} = (1/3)ML^2 + mL^2$. Be sure to differentiate between M and m.

(b) Rotational kinematics won't work here because angular acceleration isn't constant. We must use energy.

$$U_1 + K_1 = U_2 + K_2$$

Define $U = 0$ at the bottom of the contraption when it hangs vertically. Then, U_2 is only caused by the rod's mass, which is concentrated $L/2$ above the zero point, so $U_2 = MgL/2$. U_1 is due to all of the mass, concentrated L above the zero point: $U_1 = (M + m)gL$. $K_1 = 0$, and K_2 is unknown.

$$(M + m)gL + 0 = MgL/2 + \tfrac{1}{2}I\omega^2.$$

Plug in I from part (*a*) and solve for ω to get

$$\omega = \sqrt{\frac{g}{L}\left(\frac{M+2m}{\frac{1}{3}M+m}\right)}$$

(c) Just use $v = r\omega$. Here $r = L$ because the center of rotation is L away from the mass.

$$\text{Answer: } v = \sqrt{gL\left(\frac{M+2m}{\frac{1}{3}M+m}\right)}$$

(d) At this position, the mass is instantaneously in uniform circular motion. So, acceleration (and therefore net force) must be centripetal. Net force is straight up, toward the center of rotation.

❯ Rapid Review

- Rotational kinematics is very similar to linear kinematics. But instead of linear velocity, you work with angular velocity (in radians/s); instead of linear acceleration, you work with angular acceleration (in radians/s²); and instead of linear displacement, you work with angular displacement (in radians).

- When doing rotation problems, work in radians, not degrees.

- Rotational inertia is the rotational equivalent of mass—it's a measure of how difficult it is to start or stop an object spinning.

- The rotational equivalent of Newton's second law says that the NET torque on an object equals that object's rotational inertia multiplied by its angular acceleration.

- To solve problems involving a massive pulley, make sure you draw a free-body diagram of the pulley. Also, when a rope passes over a massive pulley, the tension in the rope on one side of the pulley won't be the same as the tension on the other side.

- The total kinetic energy of a rolling object is equal to the sum of its linear kinetic energy and its rotational kinetic energy.

- Angular momentum in a closed system is conserved. An object doesn't necessarily need to travel in a circle to have angular momentum.

CHAPTER 16

Simple Harmonic Motion

IN THIS CHAPTER

Summary: An object whose position–time graph makes a sine or cosine function is in simple harmonic motion. The period of such motion can be calculated.

Key Ideas

✪ There are three conditions for something to be in simple harmonic motion. All are equivalent.

1. The object's position–time graph is a sine or cosine graph.
2. The restoring force on the object is proportional to its displacement from equilibrium.
3. The energy vs. position graph is parabolic, or nearly so.

✪ The mass on a spring is the most common example of simple harmonic motion.
✪ The pendulum is in simple harmonic motion for small amplitudes.

Relevant Equations

Period of a mass on a spring:

$$T = 2\pi \sqrt{\frac{m}{k}}$$

Period of a pendulum:

$$T = 2\pi \sqrt{\frac{L}{g}}$$

Relationship between period and frequency:

$$T = \frac{1}{f}$$

What's so simple about simple harmonic motion (SHM)? Well, the name actually refers to a type of movement—regular, back and forth, and tick-tock tick-tock kind of motion. It's simple compared to, say, a system of 25 springs and masses and pendulums all tied to one another and waggling about chaotically.

The other reason SHM is simple is that, on the AP exam, there are only a limited number of situations in which you'll encounter it. Which means only a few formulas to memorize, and only a few types of problems to really master. We hope you'll agree that most of this material is, relatively, simple.

Amplitude, Period, and Frequency

Simple harmonic motion is the study of oscillations. An **oscillation** is motion of an object that regularly repeats itself over the same path. For example, a pendulum in a grandfather clock undergoes oscillation: it travels back and forth, back and forth, back and forth . . . Another term for oscillation is "periodic motion."

Objects undergo oscillation when they experience a **restoring force**. This is a force that restores an object to the equilibrium position. In the case of a grandfather clock, the pendulum's equilibrium position—the position where it would be if it weren't moving—is when it's hanging straight down. When it's swinging, gravity exerts a restoring force: as the pendulum swings up in its arc, the force of gravity pulls on the pendulum, so that it eventually swings back down and passes through its equilibrium position. Of course, it only remains in its equilibrium position for an instant, and then it swings back up the other way. A restoring force doesn't need to bring an object to rest in its equilibrium position; it just needs to make that object pass through an equilibrium position.

If you look back at the chapter on conservation of energy (Chapter 13), you'll find the equation for the force exerted by a spring, $F = -kx$. The negative sign simply signifies that F is a restoring force: It tries to pull or push whatever is on the end of the spring back to the spring's equilibrium position. So if the spring is stretched out, the restoring force tries to squish it back in, and if the spring is compressed, the restoring force tries to stretch it back out.

One repetition of periodic motion is called a **cycle**. For the pendulum of a grandfather clock, one cycle is equal to one back-and-forth swing.

The maximum displacement from the equilibrium position during a cycle is the **amplitude**. In Figure 16.1, the equilibrium position is denoted by "0," and the maximum displacement of the object on the end of the spring is denoted by "A."

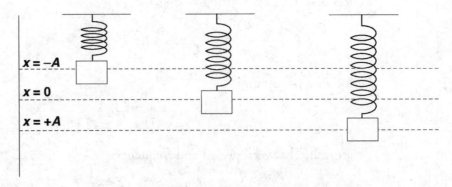

Figure 16.1 Periodic motion of a mass connected to a spring.

The time it takes for an object to pass through one cycle is the period, abbreviated T. Going back to the grandfather clock example, the period of the pendulum is the time it takes to go back and forth once: one second. Period is related to frequency, which is the number of cycles per second. The frequency of the pendulum of the grandfather clock is $f = 1$ cycle/s, where f is the standard abbreviation for frequency; the unit of frequency, the cycle per second, is called a hertz, abbreviated Hz. Period and frequency are related by this equation:

$$T = \frac{1}{f}$$

Vibrating Mass on a Spring

A mass attached to the end of a spring will oscillate in simple harmonic motion. The period of the oscillation is found by this equation:

$$T = 2\pi \sqrt{\frac{m}{k}}$$

In this equation, m is the mass of the object on the spring, and k is the "spring constant." As far as equations go, this is one of the more difficult ones to memorize, but once you have committed it to memory, it becomes very simple to use.

A block with a mass of 10 kg is placed on the end of a spring that is hung from the ceiling. When the block is attached to the spring, the spring is stretched out 20 cm from its rest position. The block is then pulled down an additional 5 cm and released. What is the block's period of oscillation, and what is the speed of the block when it passes through its rest position?

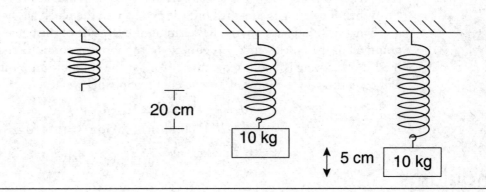

Let's think about how to solve this problem methodically. We need to find two values, a period and a speed. Period should be pretty easy—all we need to know is the mass of the block (which we're given) and the spring constant, and then we can plug into the formula. What about the speed? That's going to be a conservation of energy problem—potential energy in the stretched-out spring gets converted to kinetic energy—and here again, to calculate the potential energy, we need to know the spring constant. So let's start by calculating that.

First, we draw our free-body diagram of the block.

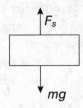

We'll call "up" the positive direction. Before the mass is oscillating, the block is in equilibrium, so we can set F_s equal to mg. (Remember to convert centimeters to meters!)

$$kx = mg$$
$$k(0.20 \text{ m}) = (10 \text{ kg})(10 \text{ m/s}^2)$$
$$k = 500 \text{ N/m}$$

Now that we have solved for k, we can go on to the rest of the problem. The period of oscillation can be found by plugging into our formula.

$$T = 2\pi\sqrt{\frac{m}{k}}$$

$$T = 2\pi\sqrt{\frac{10 \text{ kg}}{500 \text{ N/m}}}$$

$$T = 0.89 \text{ s}$$

To compute the velocity at the equilibrium position, we can now use conservation of energy.

$$K_a + U_a = K_b + U_b$$

When dealing with a vertical spring, it is best to define the rest position as $x = 0$ in the equation for potential energy of the spring. If we do this, then gravitational potential energy can be ignored. Yes, gravity still acts on the mass, and the mass changes gravitational potential energy. So what we're really doing is taking gravity into account in the spring potential energy formula by redefining the $x = 0$ position, where the spring is stretched out, as the resting spot rather than where the spring is unstretched.

In the equation above, we have used a subscript "a" to represent values when the spring is stretched out the extra 5 cm, and "b" to represent values at the rest position.

When the spring is stretched out the extra 5 cm, the block has no kinetic energy because it is being held in place. So, the KE term on the left side of the equation will equal 0. At this point, all of the block's energy is entirely in the form of potential energy. (The equation for the PE of a spring is $\frac{1}{2}kx^2$, remember?) And at the equilibrium position, the block's energy will be entirely in the form of kinetic energy. Solving, we have

$$\frac{1}{2}mv_a^2 + \frac{1}{2}kx_a^2 = \frac{1}{2}mv_b^2 + \frac{1}{2}kx_b^2$$
$$0 + \frac{1}{2}(500 \text{ N/m})(0.05 \text{ m})^2 = \frac{1}{2}(10 \text{ kg})v^2 + 0$$
$$v = 0.35 \text{ m/s}.$$

Pendulums

Simple Pendulums

Problems that involve simple pendulums—in other words, basic, run-of-the-mill, grandfather clock–style pendulums—are actually really similar to problems that involve springs. For example, the formula for the period of a simple pendulum is this:

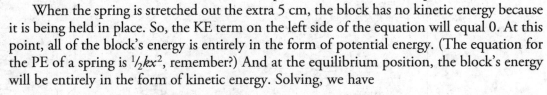

Looks kind of like the period of a mass on a spring, right? In this equation, L is the length of the pendulum, and g is the acceleration attributable to gravity (about 10 m/s²). Of course, if your pendulum happens to be swinging on another planet, g will have a different value.[1]

One interesting thing about this equation: the period of a pendulum does not depend on the mass of whatever is hanging on the end of the pendulum. So if you had a pendulum of length L with a peanut attached to the end, and another pendulum of length L with an elephant attached to the end, both pendulums would have the same period in the absence of air resistance.

A string with a bowling ball tied to its end is attached to the ceiling. The string is pulled back such that it makes a 10° angle with the vertical, and it is then released. When the bowling ball reaches its lowest point, it has a speed of 2 m/s. What is the frequency of this bowling ball pendulum?

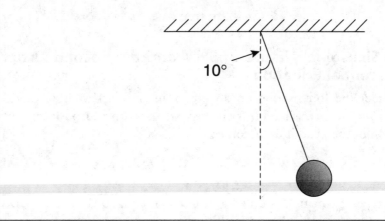

To calculate the period of this pendulum, we must know the length of the string. We can calculate this using conservation of energy. Then, we'll convert the period to a frequency.

Before the string is released, all of the bowling ball's energy is in the form of gravitational PE. If we define the zero of potential to be at the ball's lowest point, then at that point all the bowling ball's energy is in the form of KE. We will use a subscript "a" to represent values before the bowling ball is released and "b" to represent values when the bowling ball is at its lowest point.

$$K_a + U_a = K_b + U_b$$

$$\tfrac{1}{2}mv_a^2 + mgh_a = \tfrac{1}{2}mv_b^2 + mgh_b$$

$$0 + mgh_a = \tfrac{1}{2}mv_b^2 + 0$$

The height of the bowling ball before it is released, h_a, can be calculated using trigonometry.

$$h_a = L - L\cos\theta$$

So, getting back to our previous equation, we have

$$0 + mg(L - L\cos\theta) = \tfrac{1}{2}mv_b^2 + 0$$

---

[1]But even if you did travel to another planet, do you really think you would remember to pack your pendulum?

We know θ and we know v_b, so we can solve for L.

$$L - L \cos\theta = (1/g) \; {}^{1}\!/_{2} v_b^2$$

$$L (1 - \cos\theta) = (1/g) \; {}^{1}\!/_{2} v_b^2$$

$$L = 13.2 \text{ m}$$

Now that we know L, we can find the frequency.

$$T = 2\pi \sqrt{\frac{L}{g}}$$

$$T = 2\pi \sqrt{\frac{13.2}{100}}$$

$T = 7.2$ s; frequency is $1/T$, or 0.14 Hz

The Sinusoidal Nature of SHM and the Second-Order Differential Equation

Consider the force acting on an object in simple harmonic motion: $F_{net} = -kx$. Well, $F_{net} = ma$, and acceleration is the second derivative of position. So the equation for the motion of the pendulum becomes

$$\frac{d^2 x}{dt^2} = \frac{-k}{m} x$$

This type of equation is called a differential equation, where a derivative of a function is proportional to the function itself. Specifically, since the **second** derivative is involved, this is called a "second-order" differential equation.

You don't necessarily need to be able to solve this equation from scratch. However, you should be able to verify that the solution $x = A \cos(\omega t)$ satisfies the equation, where

$$\omega = \sqrt{\frac{k}{m}}$$

(How do you verify this? Take the first derivative to get $dx/dt = -A\omega \sin(\omega t)$; then take the second derivative to get $-A\omega^2 \cos(\omega t)$. This second derivative is, in fact, equal to the original function multiplied by $-k/m$.)

What does this mean? Well, for one thing, the position–time graph of an object in simple harmonic motion is a cosine graph, as you might have been shown in your physics class. But more interesting is the period of that cosine function. The cosine function repeats every 2π radians. So, at time $t = 0$ and at time $t = 2\pi/\omega$, the position is the same. Therefore, the time $2\pi/\omega$ is the period of the simple harmonic motion. And plugging in the ω value shown above, you see that—*voila!*—

$$T = 2\pi \sqrt{\frac{m}{k}}$$

as listed on the equation sheet!

The Compound Pendulum

The basic approach to pendulums detailed above refers to "simple" pendulums for which the dimensions of the hanging mass are irrelevant. If the hanging mass has a size approaching the length of the string, the period of this "compound" pendulum is

$$2\pi \sqrt{\frac{I}{mgd}}$$

where I is the rotational inertia of the hanging mass, m is the hanging mass, and d is the distance from the center of mass to the top of the string. Only use this equation if you have to. The vast majority of Physics C pendulums involve long strings and masses small enough to make the simple pendulum approximation valid. After all, for a "point" mass on the end of the string, the rotational inertia is $I = mL^2$, meaning that even the compound formula reduces to

$$T = 2\pi\sqrt{\frac{L}{g}}$$

❯ Practice Problems

1. A basketball player dribbles the ball so that it bounces regularly, twice per second. Is this ball in simple harmonic motion? Explain.

Multiple Choice:

2. A pendulum has a period of 5 seconds on Earth. On Jupiter, where $g \sim 30$ m/s², the period of this pendulum would be closest to

   (A) 1 s
   (B) 3 s
   (C) 5 s
   (D) 8 s
   (E) 15 s

3. A pendulum and a mass on a spring are designed to vibrate with the same period T. These devices are taken onto the Space Shuttle in orbit. What is the period of each on the Space Shuttle?

	pendulum	mass on a spring
(A)	will not oscillate	T
(B)	T	will not oscillate
(C)	will not oscillate	will not oscillate
(D)	$\sqrt{2} \cdot T$	T
(E)	T	$\sqrt{2} \cdot T$

4. A mass on a spring has a frequency of 2.5 Hz and an amplitude of 0.05 m. In one complete period, what distance does the mass traverse? (This question asks for the actual distance, not the displacement.)

   (A) 0.05 cm
   (B) 0.01 cm
   (C) 20 cm
   (D) 10 cm
   (E) 5 cm

5. Increasing which of the following will increase the period of a simple pendulum?

   I. the length of the string
   II. the local gravitational field
   III. the mass attached to the string

   (A) I only
   (B) II only
   (C) III only
   (D) I and II only
   (E) I, II, and III

Free Response:

6. A mass m is attached to a horizontal spring of spring constant k. The spring oscillates in simple harmonic motion with amplitude A. Answer the following in terms of A.

   (a) At what displacement from equilibrium is the speed half of the maximum value?
   (b) At what displacement from equilibrium is the potential energy half of the maximum value?
   (c) When is the mass farther from its equilibrium position, when its speed is half maximum, or when its potential energy is half maximum?

> Solutions to Practice Problems

1. The ball is *not* in simple harmonic motion. An object in SHM experiences a force that pushes toward the center of the motion, pushing harder the farther the object is from the center; and, an object in SHM oscillates smoothly with a sinusoidal position–time graph. The basketball experiences only the gravitational force, except for the brief time that it's in contact with the ground. Its position–time graph has sharp peaks when it hits the ground.

2. **B**—The period of a pendulum is

$$T = 2\pi\sqrt{\frac{L}{g}}$$

   All that is changed by going to Jupiter is g, which is multiplied by 3. g is in the denominator and under a square root, so the period on Jupiter will be *reduced* by a factor of $\sqrt{3}$. So the original 5-second period is cut by a bit less than half, to about 3 seconds.

3. **A**—The restoring force that causes a pendulum to vibrate is gravity. Because things float in the Space Shuttle rather than fall to the floor, the pendulum will not oscillate at all. However, the restoring force that causes a *spring* to vibrate is the spring force itself, which does not depend on gravity. The period of a mass on a spring also depends on mass, which is unchanged in the Space Shuttle, so the period of vibration is unchanged as well.

4. **C**—The amplitude of an object in SHM is the distance from equilibrium to the maximum displacement. In one full period, the mass traverses this distance four times: starting from max displacement, the mass goes down to the equilibrium position, down again to the max displacement on the opposite side, back to the equilibrium position, and back to where it started from. This is 4 amplitudes, or 0.20 m, or 20 cm.

5. **A**—The period of a pendulum is

$$T = 2\pi\sqrt{\frac{L}{g}}$$

   Because L, the length of the string, is in the numerator, increasing L increases the period. Increasing g will actually *decrease* the period because g is in the denominator; increasing the mass on the pendulum

has no effect because mass does not appear in the equation for period.

6. (a) The maximum speed of the mass is at the equilibrium position, where $PE = 0$, so all energy is kinetic. The maximum potential energy is at the maximum displacement A, because there the mass is at rest briefly and so has no KE. At the equilibrium position all of the PE has been converted to KE, so

$$^1/_2 kA^2 = {}^1/_2 mv^2{}_{max}$$

   Solving for v_{max}, it is found that

$$v_{max} = A\sqrt{\frac{k}{m}}$$

   Now that we have a formula for the maximum speed, we can solve the problem. Call the spot where the speed is half-maximum position 2. Use conservation of energy to equate the energy of the maximum displacement and position 2:

$$\tfrac{1}{2}kA^2 = \tfrac{1}{2}mv_2^2 + \tfrac{1}{2}kx_2^2$$

   The speed v_2 is half of the maximum speed we found earlier, or $\tfrac{1}{2}\left(A\sqrt{\frac{k}{m}}\right)$. Plug that in and solve for x_2:

$$\tfrac{1}{2}kA^2 = \tfrac{1}{2}m\left(\tfrac{1}{2}A\sqrt{\frac{k}{m}}\right)^2 + \tfrac{1}{2}kx_2^2$$

$$\tfrac{1}{2}kA^2 = \tfrac{1}{4}mA^2\frac{k}{m} + \tfrac{1}{2}kx_2^2$$

   The m's and the k's cancel. The result is

$$x_2 = A\sqrt{\frac{3}{4}},$$ or about 86% of the amplitude.

   (b) The total energy is $\tfrac{1}{2}kA^2$. At some position x, the potential energy will be $\tfrac{1}{2}$ of its maximum value. At that point, $\tfrac{1}{2}kx^2 = \tfrac{1}{2}(\tfrac{1}{2}kA^2)$. Canceling and solving for x, it is found that

$$x = \frac{1}{\sqrt{2}}A$$

This works out to about 70% of the maximum amplitude.

(c) Since we solved in terms of A, we can just look at our answers to (a) and (b). The velocity is half maximum at $\sqrt{\frac{3}{4}}$, or 86%, of A; the potential energy is half maximum at $\frac{1}{\sqrt{2}}$ or 71%, of A. Therefore, the mass is farther from equilibrium when velocity is half maximum.

› Rapid Review

- An oscillation is motion that regularly repeats itself over the same path. Oscillating objects are acted on by a restoring force.

- One repetition of periodic motion is called a cycle. The maximum displacement of an oscillating object during a cycle is the object's amplitude. The time it takes for an object to go through a cycle is the period of oscillation.

- Period is related to frequency: $T = 1/f$, and $f = 1/T$.

- When solving problems that involve springs or simple pendulums, be on the lookout for ways to apply conservation of energy. Not every simple harmonic motion problem will require you to use conservation of energy, but many will.

- The position–time graph of an object in simple harmonic motion is a cosine graph. Specifically, the position of the object is found by the equation $x = A \cos(\omega t)$, where

$$\omega = \sqrt{\frac{k}{m}}$$

CHAPTER 17

Electrostatics

IN THIS CHAPTER

Summary: An electric field provides a force on a charged particle. Electric potential, also called voltage, provides energy to a charged particle. Once you know the force or energy experienced by a charged particle, Newtonian mechanics (i.e., kinematics, conservation of energy, etc.) can be applied to predict the particle's motion.

Key Ideas

- ✪ The electric force on a charged particle is qE, regardless of what produces the electric field. The electric potential energy of a charged particle is qV.
- ✪ Positive charges are forced in the direction of an electric field; negative charges, opposite the field.
- ✪ Positive charges are forced from high to low potential; negative charges, low to high.
- ✪ Point charges produce non-uniform electric fields. Parallel plates produce a uniform electric field between them.
- ✪ Electric field is a vector, and electric potential is a scalar.

Relevant Equations

Electric force on a charge in an electric field:

$$F = qE$$

Electric field produced by a point charge[1]:

$$E = \frac{\frac{1}{4\pi\varepsilon_0}Q}{r^2}$$

Electric field produced by parallel plates:

$$E = \frac{V}{d}$$

Electric potential energy in terms of voltage:

$$PE = qV$$

Voltage produced by a point charge:

$$V = \frac{\frac{1}{4\pi\varepsilon_0}Q}{r}$$

Charge stored on a capacitor:

$$Q = CV$$

Capacitance of a parallel plate capacitor:

$$C = \frac{\varepsilon_0 A}{d}$$

Electricity literally holds the world together. Sure, gravity is pretty important, too, but the primary reason that the molecules in your body stick together is because of electric forces. A world without electrostatics would be no world at all.

This chapter introduces a lot of the vocabulary needed to discuss electricity, and it focuses on how to deal with electric charges that aren't moving: hence the name, electro*statics*. We'll look at moving charges in the next chapter, when we discuss circuits.

Electric Charge

All matter is made up of three types of particles: protons, neutrons, and electrons. Protons have an intrinsic property called "positive charge." Neutrons don't contain any charge, and electrons have a property called "negative charge."

The unit of charge is the coulomb, abbreviated C. One proton has a charge of 1.6×10^{-19} coulombs.

Most objects that we encounter in our daily lives are electrically neutral—things like couches, for instance, or trees, or bison. These objects contain as many positive charges as negative charges. In other words, they contain as many protons as electrons.

When an object has more protons than electrons, though, it is described as "positively charged"; and when it has more electrons than protons, it is described as "negatively charged." The reason that big objects like couches and trees and bison don't behave like charged particles is because they contain so many bazillions of protons and electrons that an extra few here or there won't really make much of a difference. So even though they might have a slight electric charge, that charge would be much too small, relatively speaking, to detect.

---

[1]The actual equation sheet for the AP exam includes this equation: $F = \frac{1}{4\pi\varepsilon_0}\frac{q_1 q_2}{r^2}$. To interpret this (and other point charge equations), recognize that this equation for the force between two point charges is an amalgamation of the first two equations above: combine $F = qE$ with $E = \frac{\frac{1}{4\pi\varepsilon_0}Q}{r^2}$ and you get $F = \frac{1}{4\pi\varepsilon_0}\frac{q_1 q_2}{r^2}$.

Tiny objects, like atoms, more commonly carry a measurable electric charge, because they have so few protons and electrons that an extra electron, for example, would make a big difference. Of course, you can have very large charged objects. When you walk across a carpeted floor in the winter, you pick up lots of extra charges and become a charged object yourself . . . until you touch a doorknob, at which point all the excess charge in your body travels through your finger and into the doorknob, causing you to feel a mild electric shock.

Electric charges follow a simple rule: *Like charges repel; opposite charges attract.* Two positively charged particles will try to get as far away from each other as possible, while a positively charged particle and a negatively charged particle will try to get as close as possible.

You can also have something called "induced charge." An induced charge occurs when an electrically neutral object becomes polarized—when negative charges pile up in one part of the object and positive charges pile up in another part of the object. The drawing in Figure 17.1 illustrates how you can create an induced charge in an object.

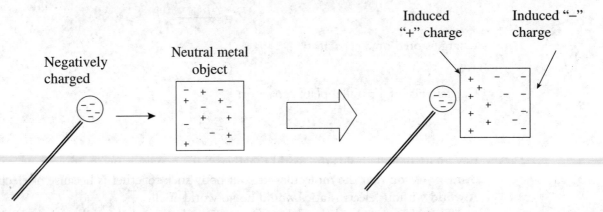

Figure 17.1   Creation of an induced charge.

Electric Fields

Before we talk about electric fields, we'll first define what a field, in general, is.

> **Field:** A property of a region of space that can apply a force to objects found in that region of space

A gravitational field is a property of the space that surrounds any massive object. There is a gravitational field that you are creating and which surrounds you, and this field extends infinitely into space. It is a weak field, though, which means that it doesn't affect other objects very much—you'd be surprised if everyday objects started flying toward each other because of gravitational attraction. The Earth, on the other hand, creates a strong gravitational field. Objects are continually being pulled toward the Earth's surface due to gravitational attraction. However, the farther you get from the center of the Earth, the weaker the gravitational field, and, correspondingly, the weaker the gravitational attraction you would feel.

An **electric field** is a bit more specific than a gravitational field: it only affects charged particles.

> **Electric Field:** A property of a region of space that applies a force to *charged* objects in that region of space. A charged particle in an electric field will experience an electric force.

Unlike a gravitational field, an electric field can either push or pull a charged particle, depending on the charge of the particle. Electric field is a vector; so, electric fields are always drawn as arrows.

Every point in an electric field has a certain value called, surprisingly enough, the "electric field value," or E, and this value tells you how strongly the electric field at that point would affect a charge. The units of E are newtons/coulomb, abbreviated N/C.

Force of an Electric Field

The force felt by a charged particle in an electric field is described by a simple equation:

$$F = qE$$

In other words, the force felt by a charged particle in an electric field is equal to the charge of the particle, q, multiplied by the electric field value, E.

An electron, a proton, and a neutron are each placed in a uniform electric field of magnitude 60 N/C, directed to the right. What is the magnitude and direction of the force exerted on each particle?

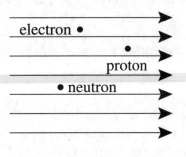

The direction of the force on a positive charge is in the same direction as the electric field; the direction of the force on a negative charge is opposite the electric field.

Let's try this equation on for size. Here's a sample problem:

The solution here is nothing more than plug-and-chug into $F = qE$. Notice that we're dealing with a *uniform* electric field—the field lines are evenly spaced throughout the whole region. This means that, no matter where a particle is within the electric field, it always experiences an electric field of exactly 60 N/C.

Also note our problem-solving technique. To find the magnitude of the force, we plug in *just the magnitude* of the charge and the electric field—no negative signs allowed! To find the direction of the force, use the reasoning in the box above (positive charges are forced in the direction of the E field, negative charges opposite the E field).

Let's start with the electron, which has a charge of 1.6×10^{-19} C (no need to memorize, you can look this up on the constant sheet):

$$F = qE$$
$$F = (1.6 \times 10^{-19} \text{ C})(60 \text{ N/C})$$
$$F = 9.6 \times 10^{-18} \text{ N to the LEFT}$$

Now the proton:

$$F = (1.6 \times 10^{-19} \text{ C})(60 \text{ N/C})$$
$$F = 9.6 \times 10^{-18} \text{ N to the RIGHT}$$

And finally the neutron:

$$F = (0\ C)(60\ N/C) = 0\ N$$

Notice that the proton feels a force in the direction of the electric field, but the electron feels the same force in the opposite direction.

Don't state a force with a negative sign. Signs just indicate the direction of a force, anyway. So, just plug in the values for q and E, then state the direction of the force in words.

Electric Potential

When you hold an object up over your head, that object has gravitational potential energy. If you were to let it go, it would fall to the ground.

Similarly, a charged particle in an electric field can have electrical potential energy. For example, if you held a proton in your right hand and an electron in your left hand, those two particles would want to get to each other. Keeping them apart is like holding that object over your head; once you let the particles go, they'll travel toward each other just like the object would fall to the ground.

In addition to talking about electrical potential energy, we also talk about a concept called electric potential.

> **Electric Potential:** Potential energy provided by an electric field per unit charge; also called **voltage**

Electric potential is a scalar quantity. The units of electric potential are volts. 1 volt = 1 J/C.

Just as we use the term "zero of potential" in talking about gravitational potential, we can also use that term to talk about voltage. We cannot solve a problem that involves voltage unless we know where the zero of potential is. Often, the zero of electric potential is called "ground."

Unless it is otherwise specified, the zero of electric potential is assumed to be far, far away. This means that if you have two charged particles and you move them farther and farther from each another, ultimately, once they're infinitely far away from each other, they won't be able to feel each other's presence.

The electrical potential energy of a charged particle is given by this equation:

$$\boxed{PE = qV}$$

Here, q is the charge on the particle, and V is the voltage.

It is extremely important to note that electric potential and electric field are not the same thing. This example should clear things up:

Three points, labeled A, B, and C, are found in a uniform electric field. At which point will a positron (a positively charged version of an electron) have the greatest electrical potential energy?

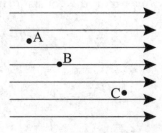

Electric field lines point in the direction that a positive charge will be forced, which means that our positron, when placed in this field, will be pushed from left to right. So, just as an object in Earth's gravitational field has greater potential energy when it is higher off the ground (think "mgh"), our positron will have the greatest electrical potential energy when it is farthest from where it wants to get to. The answer is A.

We hope you noticed that, even though the electric field was the same at all three points, the electric potential was different at each point.

How about another example?

A positron is given an initial velocity of 6×10^6 m/s to the right. It travels into a uniform electric field, directed to the left. As the positron enters the field, its electric potential is zero. What will be the electric potential at the point where the positron has a speed of 1×10^6 m/s?

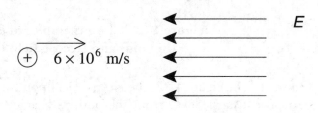

This is a rather simple conservation of energy problem, but it's dressed up to look like a really complicated electricity problem.

As with all conservation of energy problems, we'll start by writing our statement of conservation of energy.

$$K_i + U_i = K_f + U_f$$

Next, we'll fill in each term with the appropriate equations. Here the potential energy is not due to gravity (mgh), nor due to a spring ($1/2\ kx^2$). The potential energy is electric, so it should be written as qV.

$$\tfrac{1}{2}\ mv_i^2 + qV_i = \tfrac{1}{2}\ mv_f^2 + qV_f$$

Finally, we'll plug in the corresponding values. The mass of a positron is exactly the same as the mass of an electron, and the charge of a positron has the same magnitude as the charge of an electron, except a positron's charge is positive. Both the mass and the charge of an electron are given to you on the "constants sheet." Also, the problem told us that the positron's initial potential V_i was zero.

$$\tfrac{1}{2}\ (9.1 \times 10^{-31}\ \text{kg})(6 \times 10^6\ \text{m/s})^2 + (1.6 \times 10^{-19}\ \text{C})(0) =$$
$$\tfrac{1}{2}\ (9.1 \times 10^{-31}\ \text{kg})(1 \times 10^6\ \text{m/s})^2 + (1.6 \times 10^{-19}\ \text{C})(V_f)$$

Solving for V_f, we find that V_f is about 100 V.

For *forces,* a negative sign simply indicates direction. For potentials, though, a negative sign is important. −300 V is less than −200 V, so a proton will seek out a −300 V position in preference to a −200 V position. So, be careful to use proper + and − signs when dealing with potential.

Just as you can draw electric field lines, you can also draw equipotential lines.

> **Equipotential Lines:** Lines that illustrate every point at which a charged particle would experience a given potential

Figure 17.2 shows a few examples of equipotential lines (shown with solid lines) and their relationship to electric field lines (shown with dotted lines):

Figure 17.2   Two examples of equipotential lines (in bold) and electric field lines (dotted).

On the left in Figure 17.2, the electric field points away from the positive charge. At any particular distance away from the positive charge, you would find an equipotential line that circles the charge—we've drawn two, but there are an infinite number of equipotential lines around the charge. If the potential of the outermost equipotential line that we drew was, say, 10 V, then a charged particle placed anywhere on that equipotential line would experience a potential of 10 V.

On the right in Figure 17.2, we have a uniform electric field. Notice how the equipotential lines are drawn perpendicular to the electric field lines. In fact, equipotential lines are always drawn perpendicular to electric field lines, but when the field lines aren't parallel (as in the drawing on the left), this fact is harder to see.

Moving a charge from one equipotential line to another takes energy. Just imagine that you had an electron and you placed it on the innermost equipotential line in the drawing on the left. If you then wanted to move it to the outer equipotential line, you'd have to push pretty hard, because your electron would be trying to move toward, and not away from, the positive charge in the middle.

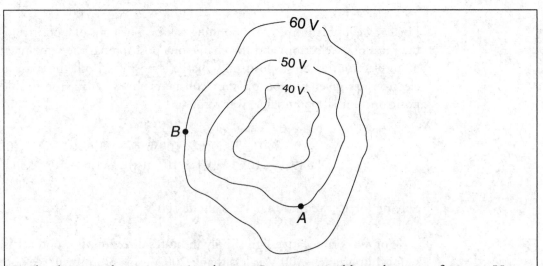

In the diagram above, point *A* and point *B* are separated by a distance of 30 cm. How much work must be done by an external force to move a proton from point *A* to point *B*?

The potential at point B is higher than at point A; so moving the positively charged proton from A to B requires work to change the proton's potential energy. The question here really is asking how much more potential energy the proton has at point B.

Well, potential energy is equal to qV; here, q is 1.6×10^{-19} C, the charge of a proton. The potential energy at point A is $(1.6 \times 10^{-19}$ C$)(50$ V$) = 8.0 \times 10^{-18}$ J; the potential energy at point B is $(1.6 \times 10^{-19}$ C$)(60$ V$) = 9.6 \times 10^{-18}$ J. Thus, the proton's potential is 1.6×10^{-18} J higher at point B, so it takes 1.6×10^{-18} J of work to move the proton there.

Um, didn't the problem say that points A and B were 30 cm apart? Yes, but that's irrelevant. Since we can see the equipotential lines, we know the potential energy of the proton at each point; the distance separating the lines is irrelevant.

Special Geometries for Electrostatics

There are two situations involving electric fields that are particularly nice because they can be described with some relatively easy formulas. Let's take a look:

Parallel Plates

If you take two metal plates, charge one positive and one negative, and then put them parallel to each other, you create a uniform electric field in the middle, as shown in Figure 17.3:

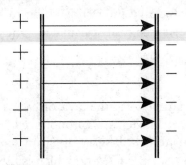

Figure 17.3   Electric field between charged, parallel plates.

The electric field between the plates has a magnitude of

$$E = \frac{V}{d}$$

V is the voltage difference between the plates, and d is the distance between the plates. Remember, this equation only works for parallel plates.

Charged parallel plates can be used to make a **capacitor**, which is a charge-storage device. When a capacitor is made from charged parallel plates, it is called, logically enough, a "parallel-plate capacitor." A schematic of this type of capacitor is shown in Figure 17.4.

The battery in Figure 17.4 provides a voltage across the plates; once you've charged the capacitor, you disconnect the battery. The space between the plates prevents any charges from jumping from one plate to the other while the capacitor is charged. When you want to discharge the capacitor, you just connect the two plates with a wire.

The amount of charge that each plate can hold is described by the following equation:

$$Q = CV$$

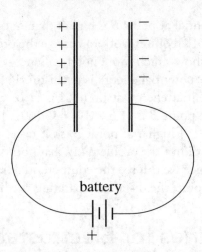

Figure 17.4   Basic parallel-plate capacitor.

Q is the charge on each plate, C is called the "capacitance," and V is the voltage across the plates. The capacitance is a property of the capacitor you are working with, and it is determined primarily by the size of the plates and the distance between the plates, as well as by the material that fills the space between the plates. The units of capacitance are farads, abbreviated F; 1 coulomb/volt = 1 farad.

The only really interesting thing to know about parallel-plate capacitors is that their capacitance can be easily calculated. The equation is:

$$C = \frac{\varepsilon_0 A}{d}$$

In this equation, A is the area of each plate (in m²), and d is the distance between the plates (in m). The term ε_0 (pronounced "epsilon-naught") is called the "permittivity of free space." This term will show up again soon, when we introduce the constant k. The value of ε_0 is 8.84×10^{-12} C/V·m, which is listed on the constants sheet.

Capacitors become important when we work with circuits. So we'll see them again in Chapter 18.

Point Charges

As much as the writers of the AP exam like parallel plates, they *love* point charges. So you'll probably be using these next equations quite a lot on the test.

But, please don't go nuts. . . . The formulas for force on a charge in an electric field ($F = qE$) and a charge's electrical potential energy ($PE = qV$) are your first recourse, your fundamental tools of electrostatics. On the AP exam, most electric fields are NOT produced by point charges! Only use the equations in this section when you have convinced yourself that a point charge is *creating* the electric field or the voltage in question.

First, the value of the electric field at some distance away from a point charge:

$$E = \frac{1}{4\pi\varepsilon_0} \frac{Q}{r^2}$$

Q is the charge of your point charge, ε_0 is the permittivity of free space (on the table of information), and r is the distance away from the point charge.[2] *The field produced by*

---

[2]For calculations, it might be easier to recognize that $\frac{1}{4\pi\varepsilon_0} = 9 \times 10^9 N \frac{m^2}{C^2}$. This value, often labeled as k, shows up repeatedly in point-charge problems.

a positive charge points away from the charge; the field produced by a negative charge points toward the charge. When finding an electric field with this equation, do NOT plug in the sign of the charge or use negative signs at all.

Second, the electric potential at some distance away from a point charge:

$$V = \frac{1}{4\pi\varepsilon_0}\frac{Q}{r}$$

When using this equation, you *must* include a + or − sign on the charge creating the potential. (See Figure 17.5.)

Figure 17.5   Electric field produced by point charges.

And third, the force that one point charge exerts on another point charge:

$$F = \frac{1}{4\pi\varepsilon_0}\frac{Q_1Q_2}{r^2}$$

In this equation, Q_1 is the charge of one of the point charges, and Q_2 is the charge on the other one. This equation is known as Coulomb's Law.

To get comfortable with these three equations, we'll provide you with a rather comprehensive problem.

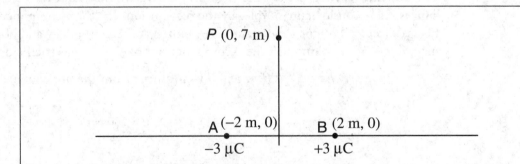

Two point charges, labeled "A" and "B", are located on the *x*-axis. "A" has a charge of −3 μC, and "B" has a charge of +3 μC. Initially, there is no charge at point *P*, which is located on the *y*-axis as shown in the diagram.

(a)   What is the electric field at point *P* due to charges "A" and "B"?
(b)   If an electron were placed at point *P*, what would be the magnitude and direction of the force exerted on the electron?
(c)   What is the electric potential at point *P* due to charges "A" and "B"?

This is a monster problem. But if we take it one part at a time, you'll see that it's really not too bad.

Part 1—Electric Field

Electric field is a vector quantity. So we'll first find the electric field at point P due to charge "A," then we'll find the electric field due to charge "B," and then we'll add these two vector quantities. One note before we get started: to find r, the distance between points P and "A" or between P and "B," we'll have to use the Pythagorean theorem. We won't show you our work for that calculation, but you should if you were solving this on the AP exam.

$$E_{\text{due to "A"}} = \frac{(9\times10^{9})(3\times10^{-6}\,\text{C})}{(\sqrt{53}\ \text{m})^{2}} = 510\,\frac{\text{N}}{\text{C}},\ \text{pointing } \textit{toward } \text{charge A}$$

$$E_{\text{due to "B"}} = \frac{(9\times10^{9})(3\times10^{-6}\,\text{C})}{(\sqrt{53}\ \text{m})^{2}} = 510\,\frac{\text{N}}{\text{C}},\ \text{pointing } \textit{away from } \text{charge B}$$

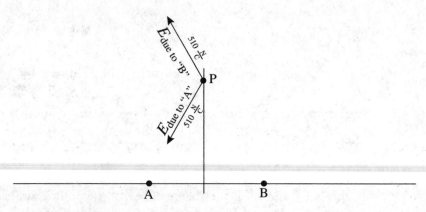

Note that we didn't plug in any negative signs! Rather, we calculated the magnitude of the electric field produced by each charge, and showed the direction on the diagram.

Now, to find the net electric field at point P, we must add the electric field vectors. This is made considerably simpler by the recognition that the y-components of the electric fields cancel . . . both of these vectors are pointed at the same angle, and both have the same magnitude. So, let's find just the x-component of one of the electric field vectors:

$$E_x = E \cos\theta, \text{ where } \theta \text{ is measured from the horizontal.}$$

$E = 510\text{ N/C}$

θ

$E_x\ (= 140\text{ N/C})$

Some quick trigonometry will find $\cos\theta$ . . . since $\cos\theta$ is defined as $\dfrac{\text{adjacent}}{\text{hypotenuse}}$, inspection of the diagram shows that $\cos\theta = \dfrac{2}{\sqrt{53}}$. So, the horizontal electric field $E_x = (510\text{ m})$ $\left(\dfrac{2}{\sqrt{53}}\right)$ . . . this gives 140 N/C.

And now finally, there are *TWO* of these horizontal electric fields adding together to the left—one due to charge "A" and one due to charge "B". The total electric field at point P, then, is

280 N/C, to the left.

Part 2—Force

The work that we put into Part 1 makes this part easy. Once we have an electric field, it doesn't matter what caused the E field—just use the basic equation $F = qE$ to solve for the force on the electron, where q is the charge of the electron. So,

$$F = (1.6 \times 10^{-19} \text{ C}) \, 280 \text{ N/C} = 4.5 \times 10^{-17} \text{ N}.$$

The direction of this force must be OPPOSITE the E field because the electron carries a negative charge; so, **to the right**.

Part 3—Potential

The nice thing about electric potential is that it is a scalar quantity, so we don't have to concern ourselves with vector components and other such headaches.

$$V_{\text{due to "A"}} = \frac{(9 \times 10^9)(-3 \times 10^{-6}\text{C})}{\sqrt{53}\text{m}} = -3700 \text{ V}$$

$$V_{\text{due to "B"}} = \frac{(9 \times 10^9)(+3 \times 10^{-6}\text{C})}{\sqrt{53}\text{m}} = +3700 \text{ V}$$

The potential at point P is just the sum of these two quantities. $V =$ zero!

Notice that when finding the electric potential due to point charges, you must include negative signs . . . negative potentials can cancel out positive potentials, as in this example.

Gauss's Law

A more thorough understanding of electric fields comes from Gauss's law. But before looking at Gauss's law itself, it is necessary to understand the concept of electric flux.

> **Electric flux:** The amount of electric field that penetrates an area
> $$\Phi_E = E \cdot A$$

The electric flux, Φ_E, equals the electric field multiplied by the surface area through which the field penetrates.

Flux only exists if the electric field lines penetrate *straight* through a surface. (Or, if the electric field lines have a component that's perpendicular to a surface.) If an electric field exists parallel to a surface, there is zero flux through that surface. One way to think about this is to imagine that electric field lines are like arrows, and the surface you're considering is like an archer's bull's-eye. There would be flux if the arrows hit the target; but if the archer is standing at a right angle to the target (so that his arrows zoom right on past the target without even nicking it) there's no flux.

In words, Gauss's law states that the net electric flux through a closed surface is equal to the charge enclosed divided by ε_0. This is often written as

$$\int E \cdot dA = \frac{Q_{\text{enclosed}}}{\varepsilon_0}$$

How and When to Use Gauss's Law

Gauss's law is valid the universe over. However, in most cases Gauss's law is not in any way useful—no one expects you to be able to evaluate a three-dimensional integral with a dot product! ONLY use Gauss's law when the problem has spherical, cylindrical, or planar symmetry.

First, identify the symmetry of the problem. Then draw a closed surface, called a "Gaussian surface," that the electric field is everywhere pointing straight through. A Gaussian surface isn't anything real . . . it's just an imaginary closed surface that you'll use to solve the problem. The net electric flux is just E times the area of the Gaussian surface you drew.

> *You should NEVER, ever, try to evaluate the integral $\int E \cdot dA$ in using Gauss's law!*

Here is an example problem.

> Consider a metal sphere of radius R that carries a surface charge density σ. What is the magnitude of the electric field as a function of the distance from the center of the sphere?

There are two possibilities here. One possibility is that the function describing the electric field will be a smooth, continuous function. The other possibility is that the function inside the sphere will be different from the function outside the sphere (after all, they're different environments—inside the sphere you're surrounded by charge, and outside the sphere you're not). So we'll assume that the function is different in each environment, and we'll consider the problem in two parts: inside the sphere and outside the sphere. If it turns out that the function is actually smooth and continuous, then we'll have done some extra work, but we'll still get the right answer.

Inside the sphere, draw a Gaussian sphere of any radius. No charge is enclosed, because in a conductor, all the charges repel each other until all charge resides on the outer edge. So, by Gauss's law since the enclosed charge is zero, the term $E \cdot A$ has to be zero as well. A refers to the area of the Gaussian surface you drew, which sure as heck has a surface area.

The electric field inside the conducting sphere must be zero everywhere. This is actually a general result that you should memorize—the electric field inside a conductor is always zero.

Outside the sphere, draw a Gaussian sphere of radius r. This sphere, whatever its radius, always encloses the full charge of the conductor. What is that charge? Well, σ represents the charge per area of the conductor, and the area of the conductor is $4\pi R^2$. So the charge on the conductor is $\sigma 4\pi R^2$. Now, the Gaussian surface of radius r has area $4\pi r^2$. Plug all of this into Gauss's law:

$$E \cdot 4\pi r^2 = \sigma 4\pi R^2 / \varepsilon_0.$$

All the variables are known, so just solve for electric field: $E = \sigma R^2 / \varepsilon_0 r^2$.

Now we can state our answer, where r is the distance from the center of the charged sphere:

$$E = \begin{cases} 0, when\, 0 \leq r < R \\ \dfrac{\sigma R^2}{\varepsilon_0 r^2}, when\, R \leq r \end{cases}$$

What is interesting about this result? We solved in terms of the charge density σ on the conductor. If we solve instead in terms of Q, the total charge on the conductor, we recover the formula for the electric field of a point charge:

$$E = \frac{1}{4\pi\varepsilon_0} \frac{Q}{r^2}!$$

❯ Practice Problems

Multiple Choice:

Questions 1 and 2

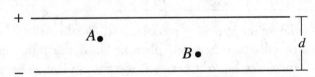

Two identical positive charges Q are separated by a distance a, as shown above.

1. What is the electric field at a point halfway between the two charges?

   (A) kQ/a^2
   (B) $2kQ/a^2$
   (C) zero
   (D) kQQ/a^2
   (E) $2kQ/a$

2. What is the electric potential at a point halfway between the two charges?

   (A) kQ/a
   (B) $2kQ/a$
   (C) zero
   (D) $4kQ/a$
   (E) $8kQ/a$

Questions 3 and 4

The diagram above shows two parallel metal plates that are separated by distance d. The potential difference between the plates is V. Point A is twice as far from the negative plate as is point B.

3. Which of the following statements about the electric potential between the plates is correct?

   (A) The electric potential is the same at points A and B.
   (B) The electric potential is two times larger at A than at B.
   (C) The electric potential is two times larger at B than at A.
   (D) The electric potential is four times larger at A than at B.
   (E) The electric potential is four times larger at B than at A.

4. Which of the following statements about the electric field between the plates is correct?

   (A) The electric field is the same at points A and B.
   (B) The electric field is two times larger at A than at B.
   (C) The electric field is two times larger at B than at A.
   (D) The electric field is four times larger at A than at B.
   (E) The electric field is four times larger at B than at A.

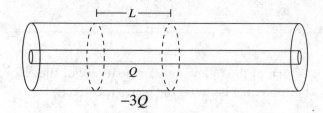

5. A very long cylindrical conductor is surrounded by a very long cylindrical conducting shell, as shown above. A length L of the inner conductor carries positive charge Q. The same length L of the outer shell carries total charge $-3Q$. How much charge is distributed on a length L of the outside surface of the outer shell?

(A) none
(B) $-Q$
(C) $-2Q$
(D) $-3Q$
(E) $-4Q$

Free Response:

6. Two conducting metal spheres of different radii, as shown above, each have charge $-Q$.

(a) Consider one of the spheres. Is the charge on that sphere likely to clump together or to spread out? Explain briefly.
(b) Is charge more likely to stay inside the metal spheres or on the surface of the metal spheres? Explain briefly.
(c) If the two spheres are connected by a metal wire, will charge flow from the big sphere to the little sphere, or from the little sphere to the big sphere? Explain briefly.
(d) Which of the following two statements is correct? Explain briefly.
  i. If the two spheres are connected by a metal wire, charge will stop flowing when the electric field at the surface of each sphere is the same.
  ii. If the two spheres are connected by a metal wire, charge will stop flowing when the electric potential at the surface of each sphere is the same.
(e) Explain how the correct statement you chose from part (d) is consistent with your answer to (c).

› Solutions to Practice Problems

1. C—Electric field is a *vector*. Look at the field at the center due to each charge. The field due to the left-hand charge points away from the positive charge; i.e., to the right; the field due to the right-hand charge points to the left. Because the charges are equal and are the same distance from the center point, the fields due to each charge have equal magnitudes. So the electric field vectors cancel! $E = 0$.

2. D—Electric potential is a *scalar*. Look at the potential at the center due to each charge: Each charge is distance $a/2$ from the center point, so the potential due to each is $kQ/(a/2)$, which works out to $2kQ/a$. The potentials due to both charges are positive, so add these potentials to get $4kQ/a$.

3. B—If the potential difference between plates is, say, 100 V, then we could say that one plate is at +100 V and the other is at zero V. So, the potential *must* change at points in between the plates.

The electric field is uniform and equal to V/d (d is the distance between plates). Thus, the potential increases linearly between the plates, and A must have twice the potential as B.

4. A—The electric field by definition is *uniform* between parallel plates. This means the field must be the same everywhere inside the plates.

5. C—We have cylindrical symmetry, so use Gauss's law. Consider a Gaussian surface drawn within the outer shell. Inside a conducting shell, the electric field must be zero, as discussed in the chapter. By Gauss's law, this means the Gaussian surface we drew must enclose zero net charge. Because the inner cylinder carries charge $+Q$, the inside surface of the shell must carry charge $-Q$ to get zero net charge enclosed by the Gaussian surface. What happens to the $-2Q$ that is left over on the conducting shell? It goes to the outer surface.

6. (a) Like charges repel, so the charges are more likely to spread out from each other as far as possible.

(b) "Conducting spheres" mean that the charges are free to move anywhere within or onto the surface of the spheres. But because the charges try to get as far away from each other as possible, the charge will end up on the surface of the spheres. This is actually a property of conductors—charge will always reside on the surface of the conductor, not inside.

(c) Charge will flow from the smaller sphere to the larger sphere. Following the reasoning from parts (a) and (b), the charges try to get as far away from each other as possible. Because both spheres initially carry the same charge, the charge is more concentrated on the smaller sphere; so the charge will flow to the bigger sphere to spread out. (The explanation that negative charge flows from low to high potential, and that potential is less negative at the surface of the bigger sphere, is also acceptable here.)

(d) The charge will flow until the potential is equal on each sphere. By definition, negative charges flow from low to high potential. So, if the potentials of the spheres are equal, no more charge will flow.

(e) The potential at the surface of each sphere is $-kQ/r$, where r is the radius of the sphere. Thus, the potential at the surface of the smaller sphere is initially more negative, and the charge will initially flow low-to-high potential to the larger sphere.

› Rapid Review

- Matter is made of protons, neutrons, and electrons. Protons are positively charged, neutrons have no charge, and electrons are negatively charged.

- Like charges repel, opposite charges attract.

- An induced charge can be created in an electrically neutral object by placing that object in an electric field.

- Electric field lines are drawn from positive charges toward negative charges. Where an electric field is stronger, the field lines are drawn closer together.

- The electric force on an object depends on both the object's charge and the electric field it is in.

- Unless stated otherwise, the zero of electric potential is at infinity.

- Equipotential lines show all the points where a charged object would feel the same electric force. They are always drawn perpendicular to electric field lines.

- The electric field between two charged parallel plates is constant. The electric field around a charged particle depends on the distance from the particle.

- Gauss's law says that the net electric flux through a closed surface is equal to the charge enclosed divided by ε_0. To solve a problem using Gauss's law, look for planar, cylindrical, or spherical symmetry.

CHAPTER 18

Circuits

IN THIS CHAPTER

Summary: Electric charge flowing through a wire is called current. An electrical circuit is built to control current. In this chapter, you will learn how to predict the effects of current flow.

Key Ideas

✪ The current in series resistors is the same through each, whereas the voltage across series resistors adds to the total voltage.
✪ The voltage across parallel resistors is the same across each, whereas the current through parallel resistors adds to the total current.
✪ The brightness of a light bulb depends on the power dissipated by the bulb.
✪ A capacitor blocks current once it has been connected for a while.
✪ Physics C students need to know that the time constant of an RC circuit is *RC*.

Relevant Equations

Definition of current:

$$I = \frac{dQ}{dt}$$

Resistance of a wire in terms of its properties:

$$R = \rho \frac{L}{A}$$

Ohm's law:

$$V = IR$$

Power in a circuit:

$$P = IV$$

Time constant for an RC circuit:

$$\tau = RC$$

In the last chapter, we talked about situations where electric charges don't move around very much. Isolated point charges, for example, just sit there creating an electric field. But what happens when you get a lot of charges all moving together? That, at its essence, is what goes on in a circuit.

Besides discussing circuits in general, this chapter presents a powerful problem-solving technique: the *V-I-R* chart. As with the chart of variables we used when solving kinematics problems, the *V-I-R* chart is an incredibly effective way to organize a problem that involves circuits. We hope you'll find it helpful.

Current

A circuit is simply any path that will allow charge to flow.

> **Current:** The flow of electric charge. In a circuit, the current is the amount of charge passing a given point per unit time.

Technically, a current is defined as the flow of positive charge. We don't think this makes sense, because electrons—and not protons or positrons—are what flow in a circuit. But physicists have their rationale, and no matter how wacky, we won't argue with it.

In more mathematical terms, current is defined as follows:

$$I = \frac{\Delta Q}{\Delta t}$$

What this means is that the current, I, equals the amount of charge flowing past a certain point divided by the time interval during which you're making your measurement. This definition tells us that current is measured in coulombs/second. 1 C/s = 1 ampere, abbreviated as 1 A.

Resistance and Ohm's Law

You've probably noticed that just about every circuit drawn in your physics book contains a battery. The reason most circuits contain a battery is because batteries create a potential difference between one end of the circuit and the other. In other words, if you connect the

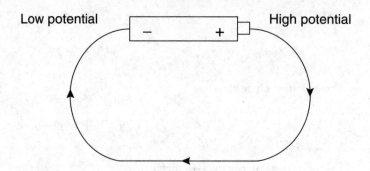

Low potential   High potential

Figure 18.1   Flow of charge in a wire connected to a battery.

terminals of a battery with a wire, the part of the wire attached to the "+" terminal will have a higher electric potential than the part of the wire attached to the "−" terminal. And positive charge flows from high potential to low potential. So, in order to create a current, you need a battery. (See Figure 18.1.)

In general, the greater the potential difference between the terminals of the battery, the more current flows.

The amount of current that flows in a circuit is also determined by the resistance of the circuit.

Resistance: A property of a circuit that resists the flow of current

---

Resistance is measured in ohms. 1 ohm is abbreviated as 1 Ω.

If we have some length of wire, then the resistance of that wire can be calculated. Three physical properties of the wire affect its resistance:

- The material the wire is made out of: the **resistivity**, ρ, of a material is an intrinsic property of that material. Good conducting materials, like gold, have low resistivities.[1]
- The length of the wire, L: the longer the wire, the more resistance it has.
- The cross-sectional area A of the wire: the wider the wire, the less resistance it has.

We put all of these properties together in the equation for resistance of a wire:

$$R = \rho \frac{L}{A}$$

Now, this equation is useful only when you need to calculate the resistance of a wire from scratch. Usually, on the AP exam or in the laboratory, you will be using resistors that have a pre-measured resistance.

Resistor: Something you put in a circuit to change the circuit's resistance

---

[1]Resistivity would be given on the AP exam if you need a value. Nothing here to memorize.

Resistors are typically ceramic, a material that doesn't allow current to flow through it very easily. Another common type of resistor is the filament in a light bulb. When current flows into a light bulb, it gets held up in the filament. While it's hanging out in the filament, it makes the filament extremely hot, and the filament gives off light.

The way that a resistor (or a bunch of resistors) affects the current in a circuit is described by Ohm's law.

$$\text{Ohm's law: } V = IR$$

V is the voltage across the part of the circuit you're looking at, I is the current flowing through that part of the circuit, and R is the resistance in that part of the circuit. Ohm's law is the most important equation when it comes to circuits, so make sure you know it well.

When current flows through a resistor, electrical energy is being converted into heat energy. The rate at which this conversion occurs is called the power dissipated by a resistor. This power can be found with the equation

$$P = IV$$

This equation says that the power, P, dissipated in part of a circuit equals the current flowing through that part of the circuit multiplied by the voltage across that part of the circuit.

Using Ohm's law, it can be easily shown that $IV = I^2R = V^2/R$. It's only worth memorizing the first form of the equation, but any one of these could be useful.

Resistors in Series and in Parallel

In a circuit, resistors can either be arranged in series with one another or parallel to one another. Before we take a look at each type of arrangement, though, we need first to familiarize ourselves with circuit symbols, shown in Figure 18.2.

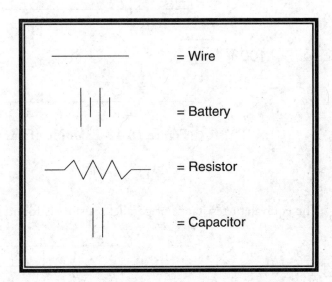

Figure 18.2 Common circuit symbols.

First, let's examine resistors in series. In this case, all the resistors are connected in a line, one after the other after the other:

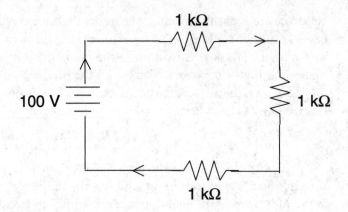

Figure 18.3   Example of series resistors.

To find the equivalent resistance of series resistors, we just add up all the individual resistors.

$$R_{eq} = R_1 + R_2 + R_3 \dots$$

For the circuit in Figure 18.3, $R_{eq} = 3000\ \Omega$. In other words, using three 1000 Ω resistors in series produces the same total resistance as using one 3000 Ω resistor.

Parallel resistors are connected in such a way that you create several paths through which current can flow. For the resistors to be truly in parallel, the current must split, then immediately come back together.

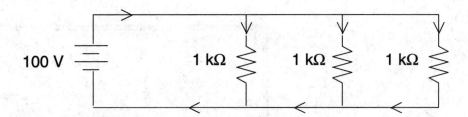

Figure 18.4   Example of parallel resistors.

The equivalent resistance of parallel resistors is found by this formula:

$$\frac{1}{R_{eq}} = \frac{1}{R_1} + \frac{1}{R_2} + \frac{1}{R_3} \dots$$

For the circuit in Figure 18.4, the equivalent resistance is 333 Ω. So hooking up three 1000 Ω resistors in parallel produces the same total resistance as using one 333 Ω resistor. (Note that the equivalent resistance of parallel resistors is *less than* any individual resistor in the parallel combination.)

A Couple of Important Rules

Rule #1—When two resistors are connected in SERIES, the amount of current that flows through one resistor equals the amount of current that flows through the other resistor.

Rule #2—When two resistors are connected in PARALLEL, the voltage across one resistor is the same as the voltage across the other resistor, and is equal to the total voltage across the parallel combination.

The *V-I-R* Chart

Here it is—the trick that will make solving circuits a breeze. Use this method on your homework. Use this method on your quizzes and tests. But most of all, use this method on the AP exam. It works.

The easiest way to understand the *V-I-R* chart is to see it in action, so we'll go through a problem together, filling in the chart at each step along the way.

Find the voltage across each resistor in the circuit shown below.

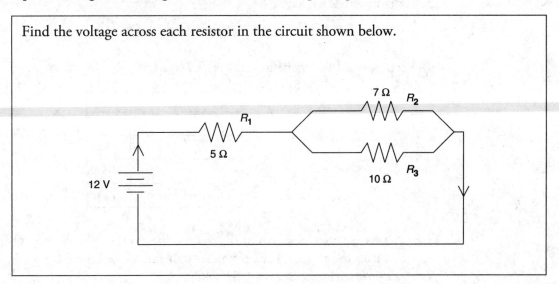

We start by drawing our *V-I-R* chart, and we fill in the known values. Right now, we know the resistance of each resistor, and we know the total voltage (it's written next to the battery).

	V	I	R
R_1			$5\,\Omega$
R_2			$7\,\Omega$
R_3			$10\,\Omega$
Total	$12\,V$		

Next, we simplify the circuit. This means that we calculate the equivalent resistance and redraw the circuit accordingly. We'll first find the equivalent resistance of the parallel part of the circuit:

$$\frac{1}{R_{eq}} = \frac{1}{7\,\Omega} + \frac{1}{10\,\Omega}.$$

Use your calculator to get $1/R_{eq} = (0.24)$.

Taking the reciprocal and rounding to 1 significant figure, we get

$$R_{eq} = 4 \; \Omega.$$

So we can redraw our circuit like this:

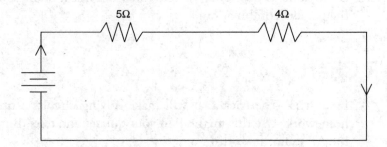

Next, we calculate the equivalent resistance of the entire circuit. Following our rule for resistors in series, we have

$$R_{eq} = 4 \; \Omega + 5 \; \Omega = 9 \; \Omega.$$

We can now fill this value into the *V-I-R* chart.

	V	I	R
R_1			5Ω
R_2			7Ω
R_3			10Ω
Total	12 V		9Ω

Notice that we now have two of the three values in the "Total" row. Using Ohm's law, we can calculate the third. That's the beauty of the *V-I-R* chart: *Ohm's law is valid whenever two of the three entries in a row are known.*

Then we need to put on our thinking caps. We know that all the current that flows through our circuit will also flow through R_1 (You may want to take a look back at the original drawing of our circuit to make sure you understand why this is so). Therefore, the *I* value in the "R_1" row will be the same as the *I* in the "Total" row. We now have two of the three values in the "R_1" row, so we can solve for the third using Ohm's law.

	V	I	R
R_1	6.5 V	1.3 A	5Ω
R_2			7Ω
R_3			10Ω
Total	12 V	1.3 A	9Ω

Finally, we know that the voltage across R_2 equals the voltage across R_3, because these resistors are connected in parallel. The total voltage across the circuit is 12 V, and the voltage across R_1 is 6.5 V. So the voltage that occurs between R_1 and the end of the circuit is

$$12 \; V - 6.5 \; V = 5.5 \; V.$$

Therefore, the voltage across R_2, which is the same as the voltage across R_3, is 5.5 V. We can fill this value into our table. Finally, we can use Ohm's law to calculate I for both R_2 and R_3. The finished *V-I-R* chart looks like this:

	V	I	R
R_1	6.5 V	1.3 A	5 Ω
R_2	5.5 V	0.8 A	7 Ω
R_3	5.5 V	0.6 A	10 Ω
Total	12 V	1.3 A	9 Ω

To answer the original question, which asked for the voltage across each resistor, we just read the values straight from the chart.

Now, you might be saying to yourself, "This seems like an awful lot of work to solve a relatively simple problem." You're right—it is.

However, there are several advantages to the *V-I-R* chart. The major advantage is that, by using it, you force yourself to approach every circuit problem exactly the same way. So when you're under pressure—as you will be during the AP exam—you'll have a tried-and-true method to turn to.

Also, if there are a whole bunch of resistors, you'll find that the *V-I-R* chart is a great way to organize all your calculations. That way, if you want to check your work, it'll be very easy to do.

Finally, free-response problems that involve circuits generally ask you questions like these.

(a) What is the voltage across each resistor?
(b) What is the current flowing through resistor #4?
(c) What is the power dissipated by resistor #2?

By using the *V-I-R* chart, you do all your calculations once, and then you have all the values you need to solve any question that the AP writers could possibly throw at you.

Tips for Solving Circuit Problems Using the *V-I-R* Chart

- First, enter all the given information into your chart. If resistors haven't already been given names (like "R_1"), you should name them for easy reference.
- Next simplify the circuit to calculate R_{eq}, if possible.
- Once you have two values in a row, you can calculate the third using Ohm's law. *You CANNOT use Ohm's law unless you have two of the three values in a row.*
- Remember that if two resistors are in series, the current through one of them equals the current through the other. And if two resistors are in parallel, the voltage across one equals the voltage across the other.

Kirchoff's Laws

Kirchoff's laws help you solve complicated circuits. They are especially useful if your circuit contains two batteries.

Kirchoff's laws say:

1. At any junction, the current entering equals the current leaving.
2. The sum of voltages around a closed loop is 0.

The first law is called the "junction rule," and the second is called the "loop rule." To illustrate the junction rule, we'll revisit the circuit from our first problem. (See Figure 18.5.)

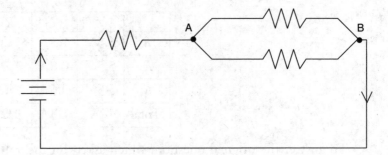

Figure 18.5   Circuit illustrating Kirchoff's junction rule.

According to the junction rule, whatever current enters Junction "A" must also leave Junction "A." So let's say that 1.25 A enters Junction "A," and then that current gets split between the two branches. If we measured the current in the top branch and the current in the bottom branch, we would find that the total current equals 1.25 A. And, in fact, when the two branches came back together at Junction "B," we would find that exactly 1.25 A was flowing out through Junction "B" and through the rest of the circuit.

Kirchoff's junction rule says that charge is conserved: you don't lose any current when the wire bends or branches. This seems remarkably obvious, but it's also remarkably essential to solving circuit problems.

Kirchoff's loop rule is a bit less self-evident, but it's quite useful in sorting out difficult circuits.

As an example, we'll show you how to use Kirchoff's loop rule to find the current through all the resistors in the circuit.

We will follow the steps for using Kirchoff's loop rule:

- Arbitrarily choose a direction of current. Draw arrows on your circuit to indicate this direction.

- Follow the loop in the direction you chose. When you cross a resistor, the voltage is $-IR$, where R is the resistance, and I is the current flowing through the resistor. This is just an application of Ohm's law. (If you have to follow a loop *against* the current, though, the voltage across a resistor is written $+IR$.)

- When you cross a battery, if you trace from the − to the + add the voltage of the battery, subtract the battery's voltage if you trace from + to −.

- Set the sum of your voltages equal to 0. Solve. If the current you calculate is negative, then the direction you chose was wrong—the current actually flows in the direction opposite to your arrows.

In the case of Figures 18.6a and 18.6b, we'll start by collapsing the two parallel resistors into a single equivalent resistor of 170 Ω. You don't *have* to do this, but it makes the mathematics much simpler.

Next, we'll choose a direction of current flow. But which way? In this particular case, you can probably guess that the 9-V battery will dominate the 1.5-V battery, and thus the current will be clockwise. But even if you aren't sure, just choose a direction and stick with it—if you get a negative current, you chose the wrong direction.

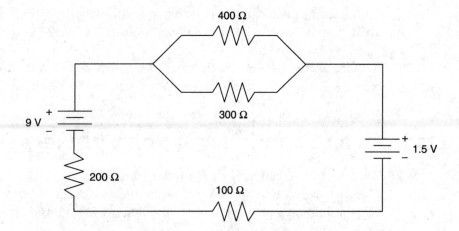

Figure 18.6a   Example circuit for using Kirchoff's loop rule.

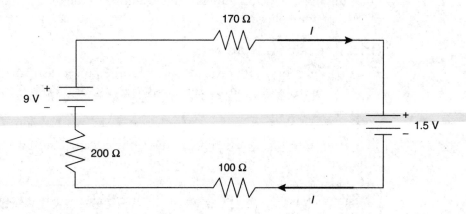

Figure 18.6b   Circuit ready for analysis via Kirchoff's loop rule.

Here is the circuit redrawn with the parallel resistors collapsed and the assumed direction of current shown. Because there's now only one path for current to flow through, we have labeled that current I.

Now let's trace the circuit, starting at the top left corner and working clockwise:

- The 170 Ω resistor contributes a term of $-(170\ \Omega)\ I$.
- The 1.5-V battery contributes the term of -1.5 volts.
- The 100 Ω resistor contributes a term of $-(100\ \Omega)\ I$.
- The 200 Ω resistor contributes a term of $-(200\ \Omega)\ I$.
- The 9-V battery contributes the term of $+9$ volts.

Combine all the individual terms, and set the result equal to zero. The units of each term are volts, but units are left off below for algebraic clarity:

$$0 = (-170)I + (-1.5) + (-100)I + (-200)I + (+9).$$

By solving for I, the current in the circuit is found to be 0.016 A; that is, 16 milliamps, a typical laboratory current.

The problem is not yet completely solved, though—16 milliamps go through the 100 Ω and 200 Ω resistors, but what about the 300 Ω and 400 Ω resistors? We can find that the voltage across the 170 Ω equivalent resistance is (0.016 A)(170 Ω) = 2.7 V. Because the voltage across parallel resistors is the same for each, the current through each is just 2.7 V divided by the resistance of the actual resistor: 2.7 V/300 Ω = 9 mA, and 2.7 V/400 Ω = 7 mA. Problem solved!

Oh, and you might notice that the 9 mA and 7 mA through each of the parallel branches adds to the total of 16 mA—as required by Kirchoff's junction rule.

Circuits from an Experimental Point of View

When a real circuit is set up in the laboratory, it usually consists of more than just resistors—light bulbs and motors are common devices to hook to a battery, for example. For the purposes of computation, though, we can consider pretty much any electronic device to act like a resistor.

But what if your purpose is *not* computation? Often on the AP exam, as in the laboratory, you are asked about observational and measurable effects. The most common questions involve the brightness of light bulbs and the measurement (not just computation) of current and voltage.

Brightness of a Bulb

The brightness of a bulb depends solely on the power dissipated by the bulb. (Remember, power is given by any of the equations I^2R, IV, or V^2/R). You can remember that from your own experience—when you go to the store to buy a light bulb, you don't ask for a "400-ohm" bulb, but for a "100-watt" bulb. And a 100-watt bulb is brighter than a 25-watt bulb. But be careful—a bulb's power can change depending on the current and voltage it's hooked up to. Consider this problem.

A light bulb is rated at 100 W in the United States, where the standard wall outlet voltage is 120 V. If this bulb were plugged in in Europe, where the standard wall outlet voltage is 240 V, which of the following would be true?

(A) The bulb would be one-quarter as bright.
(B) The bulb would be one-half as bright.
(C) The bulb's brightness would be the same.
(D) The bulb would be twice as bright.
(E) The bulb would be four times as bright.

Your first instinct might be to say that because brightness depends on power, the bulb is exactly as bright. But that's not right! The power of a bulb can change.

The resistance of a light bulb is a property of the bulb itself, and so will not change no matter what the bulb is hooked to.

Since the resistance of the bulb stays the same while the voltage changes, by V^2/R, the power goes up, and the bulb will be brighter. How much brighter? Since the voltage in Europe is doubled, and because voltage is squared in the equation, the power is multiplied by 4—choice E.

Ammeters and Voltmeters

Ammeters measure current, and voltmeters measure voltage. This is pretty obvious, because current is measured in amps, voltage in volts. It is *not* necessarily obvious, though, how to connect these meters into a circuit.

Remind yourself of the properties of series and parallel resistors—voltage is the same for any resistors in parallel with each other. So if you're going to measure the voltage across a resistor, you must put the voltmeter in *parallel* with the resistor. In Figure 18.7, the meter labeled V_2 measures the voltage across the 100 Ω resistor, while the meter labeled V_1 measures the potential difference between points A and B (which is also the voltage across R_1).

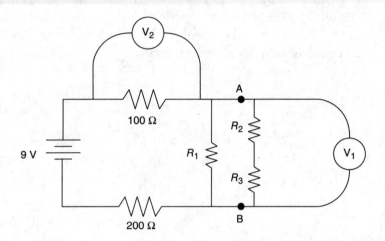

Figure 18.7   Measuring voltage with a voltmeter.

Current is the same for any resistors in *series* with one another. So, if you're going to measure the current through a resistor, the ammeter must be in series with that resistor. In Figure 18.8, ammeter A_1 measures the current through resistor R_1, while ammeter A_2 measures the current through resistor R_2.

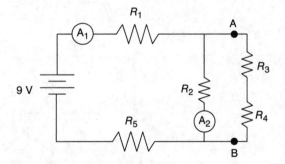

Figure 18.8   Measuring current with an ammeter.

As an exercise, ask yourself, is there a way to figure out the current in the other three resistors based only on the readings in these two ammeters? The answer is in the footnote.[2]

---

[2] The current through R_5 must be the same as through R_1, because both resistors carry whatever current came directly from the battery. The current through R_3 and R_4 can be determined from Kirchoff's junction rule: subtract the current in R_2 from the current in R_1, and that's what's left over for the right-hand branch of the circuit.

RC Circuits: Steady-State Behavior

When you have both resistors and capacitors in a circuit, the circuit is called an "RC circuit." If you remember, we introduced capacitors in Chapter 17, when we talked about charged, parallel plates.

The simplest problems with capacitors in circuits involve "steady-state behavior." This just means that the circuit has been connected for a while. In these cases, the only thing you'll generally need to worry about is how to deal with capacitors in series and in parallel.

When capacitors occur in series, you add them inversely. The charge stored on each capacitor in series must be the same.

$$\frac{1}{C_{eq}} = \frac{1}{C_1} + \frac{1}{C_2} + \frac{1}{C_3} + \dots$$

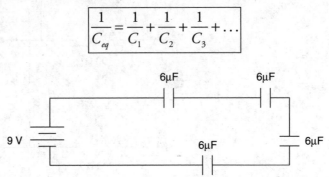

Figure 18.9   Example of capacitors in series.

For the circuit in Figure 18.9, the equivalent capacitance is $C_{eq} = 1.5\ \mu F$.

When capacitors occur in parallel, you add them algebraically. The voltage across each capacitor in parallel must be the same.

$$C_{eq} = C_1 + C_2 + C_3 + \dots$$

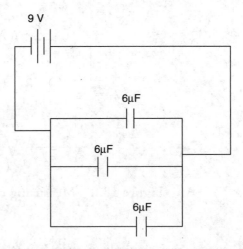

Figure 18.10   Example of capacitors in parallel.

The equivalent capacitance for the circuit in Figure 18.10 is $18\ \mu F$.

You should also know that the energy stored by a capacitor is

$$E = \frac{1}{2}\,CV^2$$

Once the circuit has been connected for a long time, capacitors stop current from flowing. To find the charge stored on or the voltage across a capacitor, just use the equation for capacitors, $Q = CV$.

For example, imagine that you hook up a 10-V battery to a 5 Ω resistor in series with an uncharged 1 F capacitor. (1 F capacitors are rarely used in actual electronics application—most capacitances are micro- or nanofarads—but they are commonly used for physics class demonstrations!) When the circuit is first hooked up, the capacitor is empty—it is ready and waiting for as much charge as can flow to it. Thus, initially, the circuit behaves as if the capacitor weren't there. In this case, then, the current through the resistor starts out at 10 V/5 Ω = 2 A.

But, after a long time, the capacitor blocks current. The resistor might as well not be there; we might as well just have a capacitor right across the battery. After a long time, the capacitor takes on the voltage of the battery, 10 V. (So the charge stored on the capacitor is $Q = CV = 10$ C.)

RC Circuits: Transitional Behavior

Okay, the obvious question here is, "What happens during the in-between times, while the capacitor is charging?" That's a more complicated question, one that is approached in Physics C. It's easiest if we start with a discussion of a capacitor *discharging*. (See Figure 18.11.)

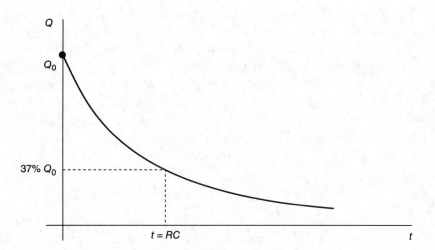

Figure 18.11   Graph of a capacitor discharging.

Consider a circuit with just a resistor R and a capacitor C. (That's what we mean by an RC circuit.) The capacitor is initially charged with charge Q_0. Apply Kirchoff's voltage rule:

$$-IR + V_c = 0$$

where V_c is the voltage across the capacitor, equal to Q/C by the equation for capacitors.

By definition, current is the time derivative of charge,

$$I = \frac{dQ}{dt}$$

So substituting this value for I into the Kirchoff equation we wrote above, and rearranging a bit, we get

$$\frac{dQ}{dt} = \frac{Q}{RC}$$

This is a differential equation. On the AP exam you will only rarely have to carry out the algorithmic solution to such an equation; however, you must recognize that the solution will have an exponential term, and you should be able to use limiting case reasoning to guess at the precise form of the solution. See the section on air resistance in Chapter 10 for details.

Here, the charge on the capacitor as a function of time is $Q = Q_0 e^{-t/RC}$. What does this mean?

Well, look at the limiting cases. At the beginning of the discharge, when $t = 0$, the exponential term becomes $e^0 = 1$; so $Q = Q_0$, as expected. After a long time, the exponential term becomes very small (e gets raised to a large negative power), and the charge goes to zero on the capacitor. Of course—that's what is meant by discharging.

And in between times? Try graphing this on your calculator. You get a function that looks like exponential decay.

What's cool here is that the product RC has special meaning. The units of RC are seconds: this is a time. RC is called the time constant of the RC circuit. The time constant gives us an idea of how long it will take to charge or discharge a capacitor. (Specifically, after one time constant the capacitor will have $1/e = 37\%$ of its original charge remaining; if the capacitor is charging rather than discharging, it will have charged to 63% of its full capacity.)

So there's no need to memorize the numerous complicated exponential expressions for charge, voltage, and current in an RC circuit. Just remember that all these quantities vary exponentially, and approach the "after a long time" values asymptotically.

What does the graph of charge vs. time for a *charging* capacitor look like? (See Figure 18.12.) Think about it a moment. At $t = 0$, there won't be any charge on the capacitor, because you haven't started charging it yet. And after a long time, the capacitor will be fully charged, and you won't be able to get more charge onto it. So the graph must start at zero and increase asymptotically.

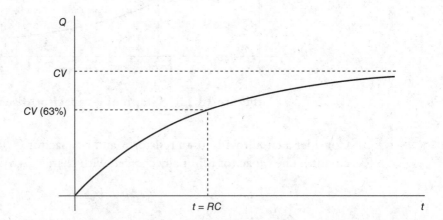

Figure 18.12   Graph of a capacitor charging.

The charge asymptotically approaches the maximum value, which is equal to CV (V is the final voltage across the capacitor). After one time constant, the charge is $1/e = 37\%$ away from its maximum value.

Inductors in Circuits

An inductor makes use of induced EMF (see Chapter 19) to resist changes in current in a circuit. If part of a circuit is coiled, then the magnetic field produced by the coils induces a "back EMF" in the rest of the circuit . . . that EMF depends on how fast the current is changing, by Faraday's law. An inductor in a circuit is drawn as a little coil, as shown in Figure 18.13.

Figure 18.13   Symbol for an inductor in a circuit.

The voltage drop across an inductor is

$$V = L\frac{dI}{dt}$$

where L is called the inductance of the inductor. Inductance is measured in units of henrys.

What does this equation mean? If the current is changing rapidly, as when a circuit is first turned on or off, the voltage drop across the inductor is large; if the current is barely changing, as when a circuit has been on for a long time, the inductor's voltage drop is small.

We can think of an inductor as storing energy in the magnetic field it creates. When current begins to flow through the inductor, it stores up as much energy as it can. After a while, it has stored all the energy it can, so the current just goes through the inductor without trouble. The energy stored in an inductor is found by this equation.

$$E = \frac{1}{2}LI^2$$

For the AP Physics C exam, you need to understand circuits with inductors and resistors, as well as circuits with inductors and capacitors.

Other Circuits

RL Circuits

RL circuits contain just an inductor and a resistor, and perhaps a battery, as shown in Figure 18.14.

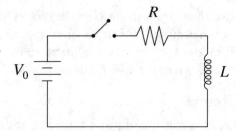

Figure 18.14   An RL circuit.

Imagine that we connect the switch in the circuit in Figure 18.15 at time $t = 0$. At that point, the current will change rapidly from zero to some nonzero value. So, because $\dfrac{dI}{dt}$

is large, the inductor has a large voltage drop, the resistor has very little voltage drop, and the current cannot immediately reach its maximum value. After a while, though, the current changes less rapidly, the voltage drop across the inductor becomes small, the voltage drop across the resistor gets bigger, and the current in the circuit becomes large.

A graph of current vs. time for this circuit is shown in Figure 18.15.

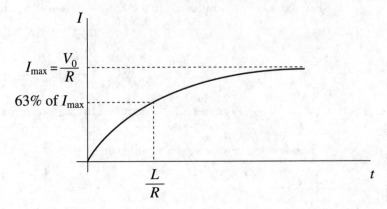

Figure 18.15   Graph of current vs. time for a simple RL circuit.

What would happen if we disconnected the battery? Well, the inductor would discharge its energy through the resistor. At first, the inductor would resist the decrease in current; but after a long time, the current would reach zero, as shown in Figure 18.16.

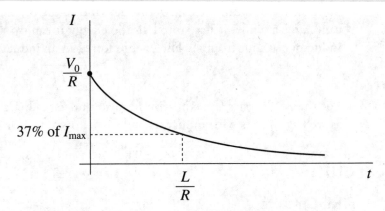

Figure 18.16   Graph of current vs. time for a simple RL circuit once the battery is disconnected.

Note that the current in an RL circuit looks much like that in an RC circuit. In fact, we can define a time constant for an RL circuit, just as we did for the RC circuit, as the time for the current to lose 63% of its value (or to reach 37% of its maximum value when increasing). The time constant for an RL circuit is L/R.

LC Circuits

In a circuit consisting of just a capacitor and an inductor, both the capacitor and inductor try to store energy. They take turns storing the energy in the circuit—the capacitor charges, then discharges, then charges again . . .

In fact, the charge on the capacitor oscillates from maximum to minimum sinusoidally with period $2\pi\sqrt{LC}$. You may have to write the solution to a second-order differential equation, just like you did for the mass on a spring in Chapter 16.

› Practice Problems

Multiple Choice:

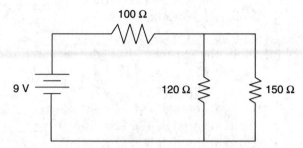

1. A 100 Ω, 120 Ω, and 150 Ω resistor are connected to a 9-V battery in the circuit shown above. Which of the three resistors dissipates the most power?

   (A) the 100 Ω resistor
   (B) the 120 Ω resistor
   (C) the 150 Ω resistor
   (D) both the 120 Ω and 150 Ω
   (E) all dissipate the same power

2. A 1.0-F capacitor is connected to a 12-V power supply until it is fully charged. The capacitor is then disconnected from the power supply, and used to power a toy car. The average drag force on this car is 2 N. About how far will the car go?

   (A) 36 m
   (B) 72 m
   (C) 144 m
   (D) 24 m
   (E) 12 m

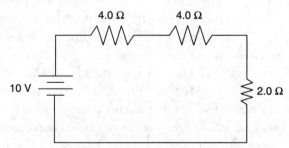

3. Three resistors are connected to a 10-V battery as shown in the diagram above. What is the current through the 2.0 Ω resistor?

   (A) 0.25 A
   (B) 0.50 A
   (C) 1.0 A
   (D) 2.0 A
   (E) 4.0 A

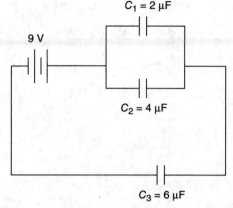

4. Three capacitors are connected as shown in the diagram above. $C_1 = 2\mu F$; $C_2 = 4\mu F$; $C_3 = 6\mu F$. If the battery provides a potential of 9 V, how much charge is stored by this system of capacitors?

   (A) 3.0 μC
   (B) 30 μC
   (C) 2.7 μC
   (D) 27 μC
   (E) 10 μC

5. What is the resistance of an ideal ammeter and an ideal voltmeter?

	Ideal Ammeter	Ideal Voltmeter
(A)	zero	infinite
(B)	infinite	zero
(C)	zero	zero
(D)	infinite	infinite
(E)	1 Ω	1 Ω

Free Response:

6.

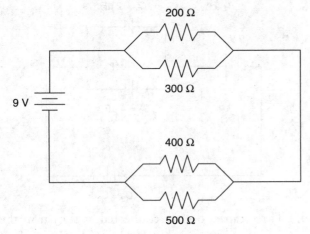

(a) Simplify the above circuit so that it consists of one equivalent resistor and the battery.

(b) What is the total current through this circuit?

(c) Find the voltage across each resistor. Record your answers in the spaces below.
   Voltage across 200 Ω resistor: _____
   Voltage across 300 Ω resistor: _____
   Voltage across 400 Ω resistor: _____
   Voltage across 500 Ω resistor: _____

(d) Find the current through each resistor. Record your answers in the spaces below.
   Current through 200 Ω resistor: _____
   Current through 300 Ω resistor: _____
   Current through 400 Ω resistor: _____
   Current through 500 Ω resistor: _____

(e) The 500 Ω resistor is now removed from the circuit. State whether the current through the 200 Ω resistor would increase, decrease, or remain the same. Justify your answer.

› Solutions to Practice Problems

1. **A**—On one hand, you could use a V-I-R chart to calculate the voltage or current for each resistor, then use $P = IV$, I^2R, or V^2/R to find power. On the other hand, there's a quick way to reason through this one. Voltage changes across the 100 Ω resistor, then again across the parallel combination. Because the 100 Ω resistor has a bigger resistance than the parallel combination, the voltage across it is larger as well. Now consider each resistor individually. By power = V^2/R, the 100 Ω resistor has both the biggest voltage and the smallest resistance, giving it the most power.

2. **A**—The energy stored by a capacitor is $\frac{1}{2}CV^2$. By powering a car, this electrical energy is converted into mechanical work, equal to force times parallel displacement. Solve for displacement, you get 36 m.

3. **C**—To use Ohm's law here, simplify the circuit to a 10-V battery with the 10 Ω equivalent resistance. We can use Ohm's law for the entire circuit to find that 1.0 A is the total current. Because all the resistors are in series, this 1.0 A flows through each resistor, including the 2 Ω resistor.

4. **D**—First, simplify the circuit to find the equivalent capacitance. The parallel capacitors add to 6 μF. Then the two series capacitors combine to 3 μF. So we end up with 9 V across a 3 μF equivalent capacitance. By the basic equation for capacitors, $Q = CV$, the charge stored on these capacitors is 27 μC.

5. **A**—An ammeter is placed in series with other circuit components. In order for the ammeter not to itself resist current and change the total current in the circuit, you want the ammeter to have as little resistance as possible—in the ideal case, zero resistance. But a voltmeter is placed in parallel with other circuit components. If the voltmeter has a low resistance, then current will flow through the voltmeter instead of through the rest of the circuit. Therefore, you want it to have as high a resistance as possible, so the voltmeter won't affect the circuit being measured.

6. (a) Combine each of the sets of parallel resistors first. You get 120 Ω for the first set, 222 Ω for the second set, as shown in the diagram below. These two equivalent resistances add as series resistors to get a total resistance of 342 Ω.

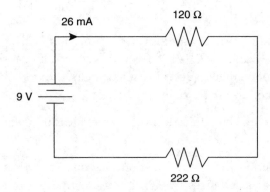

(b) Now that we've found the total resistance and we were given the total voltage, just use Ohm's law to find the total current to be 0.026 A (also known as 26 mA).

(c) and (d) should be solved together using a V-I-R chart. Start by going back one step to when we began to simplify the circuit: a 9-V battery, a 120 Ω combination, and a 222 Ω combination, shown above. The 26-mA current flows through each of these . . . so use V = IR to get the voltage of each: 3.1 V and 5.8 V, respectively.

Now go back to the original circuit. We know that voltage is the same across parallel resistors. So both the 200 Ω and 300 Ω resistors have a 3.1-V voltage across them. Use Ohm's law to find that 16 mA goes through the 200 Ω resistor, and 10 mA through the 300 Ω. Similarly, both the 400 Ω and 500 Ω resistors must have 5.8 V across them. We get 15 mA and 12 mA, respectively.

Checking these answers for reasonability: the total voltage adds to 8.9 V, or close enough to 9.0 V with rounding. The current through each set of parallel resistors adds to just about 26 mA, as we expect.

(e) Start by looking at the circuit as a whole. When we remove the 500 Ω resistor, we actually *increase* the overall resistance of the circuit because we have made it more difficult for current to flow by removing a parallel path. The total voltage of the circuit is provided by the battery, which provides 9.0 V no matter what it's hooked up to. So by Ohm's law, if total voltage stays the same while total resistance increases, total current must *decrease* from 26 mA.

Okay, now look at the first set of parallel resistors. Their equivalent resistance doesn't change, yet the total current running through them decreases, as discussed above. Therefore, the voltage across each resistor decreases, and the current through each decreases as well.

❯ Rapid Review

- Current is the flow of positive charge. It is measured in amperes.

- Resistance is a property that impedes the flow of charge. Resistance in a circuit comes from the internal resistance of the wires and from special elements inserted into circuits known as "resistors."

- Resistance is related to current and voltage by Ohm's law: $V = IR$.

- When resistors are connected in series, the total resistance equals the sum of the individual resistances. And the current through one resistor equals the current through any other resistor in series with it.

- When resistors are connected in parallel, the inverse of the total resistance equals the sum of the inverses of the individual resistances. The voltage across one resistor equals the voltage across any other resistor connected parallel to it.

> **Exam tip from an AP Physics veteran:**
> Many AP problems test your ability to use Ohm's law correctly. Ohm's law cannot be used unless the voltage, current, and resistance all refer to the same circuit element; on a *V-I-R* chart, this means that Ohm's law can only be used across a single row of the chart.
> —*Chat, college junior and physics major*

- The *V-I-R* chart is a convenient way to organize any circuit problem.

- Kirchoff's junction rule says that any current coming into a junction will leave the junction. This is a statement of conservation of charge. Kirchoff's loop rule says that the sum of the voltages across a closed loop equals zero. This rule is helpful especially when solving problems with circuits that contain more than one battery.

- Ammeters measure current, and are connected in series; voltmeters measure voltage, and are connected in parallel.

- When capacitors are connected in series, the inverse of the total capacitance equals the sum of the inverses of the individual capacitances. When they are connected in parallel, the total capacitance just equals the sum of the individual capacitances.

- A capacitor's purpose in a circuit is to store charge. After it has been connected to a circuit for a long time, the capacitor becomes fully charged and prevents the flow of current.

- A capacitor gains or loses charge exponentially. The "time constant" of an RC circuit is equal to the resistance times the capacitance, and gives a characteristic time for the charging or discharging to occur.

- An inductor resists the change of current in a circuit. In an RL circuit, when the battery is first connected, the current increases asymptotically from zero up to a final value of *V/R*. When the battery is disconnected, the current decreases asymptotically to zero with a time constant of $\frac{L}{R}$. In an LC circuit, the charge on the capacitor oscillates from maximum to minimum sinusoidally with period $2\pi\sqrt{LC}$.

CHAPTER 19

Magnetism

IN THIS CHAPTER

Summary: Magnetic fields produce forces on moving charges; moving charges, such as current-carrying wires, can create magnetic fields. This chapter discusses the production and the effects of magnetic fields.

Key Ideas

✪ The force on a moving charge due to a magnetic field is qvB.
✪ The direction of the magnetic force on a moving charge is given by a right-hand rule, and is NOT in the direction of the magnetic field.
✪ Current-carrying wires produce magnetic fields.
✪ When the magnetic flux through a wire changes, a voltage is induced.
✪ An inductor inhibits the change in the current running through it. After a long time, the inductor acts as a bare wire.

Relevant Equations

Force on a charged particle in a magnetic field:

$$F = qvB$$

Force on a current-carrying wire:

$$F = ILB$$

Magnetic field due to a long, straight, current-carrying wire:

$$B = \frac{\mu_0 I}{2\pi r}$$

Magnetic flux:

$$\Phi_B = BA$$

Induced EMF:

$$\varepsilon = N\frac{\Delta\Phi}{\Delta t}$$

Induced EMF for a rectangular wire moving into or out of a magnetic field:

$$\varepsilon = BLv$$

Time constant for an LR circuit:

$$\tau = \frac{L}{R}$$

When most people think of magnets, they imagine horseshoe-shaped objects that can pick up bits of metal. Or maybe they visualize a refrigerator door. But not a physics ace like you! You know that magnetism is a wildly diverse topic, involving everything from bar magnets to metal coils to mass spectrometers. Perhaps you also know that magnetism is a subject filled with countless "right-hand rules," many of which can seem difficult to use or just downright confusing. So our goal in this chapter—besides reviewing all of the essential concepts and formulas that pertain to magnetism—is to give you a set of easy-to-understand, easy-to-use right-hand rules that are guaranteed to earn you points on the AP exam.

Magnetic Fields

All magnets are dipoles, which means that they have two "poles," or ends. One is called the north pole, and the other is the south pole. Opposite poles attract, and like poles repel.

You can never create a magnet with just a north pole or just a south pole. If you took the magnet in Figure 19.1

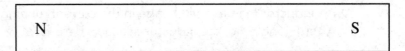

Figure 19.1   Bar magnet.

and cut it down the middle, you would not separate the poles. Instead, you would create two magnets like those shown in Figure 19.2.

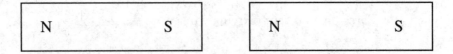

Figure 19.2   Cutting the bar magnet in Figure 19.1 in half just gives you two smaller bar magnets. You can never get an isolated north or south pole.

A magnet creates a magnetic field. (See Figure 19.3.) Unlike electric field lines, which either go from a positive charge to a negative charge or extend infinitely into space, magnetic field lines form loops. These loops point away from the north end of a magnet, and toward the south end. Near the magnet the lines point nearly straight into or out of the pole.

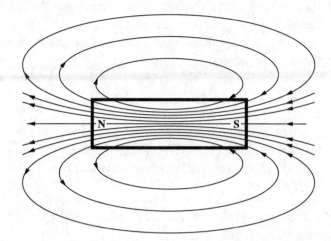

Figure 19.3   Magnetic field lines created by a bar magnet.

Just as we talk about the value of an electric field at a certain point, we can also talk about the value of a magnetic field at a certain point. The value of a magnetic field is a vector quantity, and it is abbreviated with the letter B. The value of a magnetic field is measured in teslas.

Often, the writers of the AP exam like to get funky about how they draw magnetic field lines. Rather than putting a magnetic field in the plane of the page, so that the field would point up or down or left or right, the AP writers will put magnetic fields perpendicular to the page. This means that the magnetic field either shoots out toward you or shoots down into the page.

When a magnetic field line is directed out of the page, it is drawn as shown in Figure 19.4a,

Figure 19.4a   Symbol for a magnetic field line directed out of the page.

and when a magnetic field line is directed into the page, it is drawn as shown in Figure 19.4b.

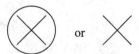

Figure 19.4b   Symbol for a magnetic field line directed into the page.

Supposedly, the drawing in Figure 19.4a is intended to look like the tip of an arrow coming out of a page, and the drawing in Figure 19.4b is intended to look like the tail of an arrow going into a page.[1] These symbols can be used to describe other ideas, such as electric fields going into or out of the page, or currents flowing into or out of the page, but they are most often used to describe magnetic fields.

---

[1]If you're not too impressed by these representations, just remember how physicists like to draw hippopotomuses. There's a reason why these science folks weren't accepted into art school.

Long, Straight, Current-Carrying Wires

Bar magnets aren't the only things that create magnetic fields—current-carrying wires do also. Of course, you can also create a magnetic field using a short, curvy, current-carrying wire, but the equations that describe that situation are a little more complicated, so we'll focus on long, straight, current-carrying wires.

The magnetic field created by a long, straight, current-carrying wire loops around the wire in concentric circles. The direction in which the magnetic field lines loop is determined by a right-hand rule.

(Incidentally, our versions of the right-hand rules may not be the same as what you've learned in physics class. If you're happy with the ones you already know, you should ignore our advice and just stick with what works best for you.)

> Right-hand rule: To find the direction of the B field produced by long, straight, current-carrying wires.
>
> Pretend you are holding the wire with your right hand. Point your thumb in the direction of the current. Your fingers wrap around your thumb the same way that the magnetic field wraps around the wire.

Here's an example. A wire is directed perpendicular to the plane of this page (that is, it's coming out straight toward you). The current in this wire is flowing out of the page. What does the magnetic field look like?

To solve this, we first pretend that we are grabbing the wire. If it helps, take your pencil and place it on this page, with the eraser touching the page and the point of the pencil coming out toward you. This pencil is like the wire. Now grab the pencil with your right hand. The current is coming out of the page, so make sure that you have grabbed the pencil in such a way that your thumb is pointing away from the page. If it looks like you're giving someone a "thumbs-up sign," then you're doing this correctly. Finally, look at how your fingers are wrapped around the pencil. From a bird's-eye view, it should look like your fingers are wrapping counterclockwise. So this tells us the answer to the problem, as shown in Figure 19.5.

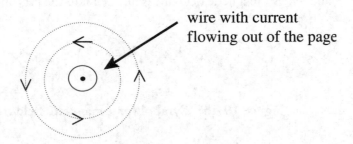

wire with current flowing out of the page

Figure 19.5   Magnetic field (dotted lines) generated by a long, straight, current-carrying wire oriented perpendicular to the plane of the page.

Here's another example. What does the magnetic field look like around a wire in the plane of the page with current directed upward?

We won't walk you through this one; just use the right-hand rule, and you'll be fine. The answer is shown in Figure 19.6.

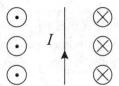

**Figure 19.6   Magnetic field around a wire in the
plane of the page with current directed upward.**

The formula that describes the magnitude of the magnetic field created by a long, straight, current-carrying wire is the following:

$$B = \frac{\mu_0 I}{2\pi r}$$

In this formula, B is the magnitude of the magnetic field, μ_0 is a constant called the "permeability of free space" ($\mu_0 = 4\pi \times 10^{-7}$ T·m/A), I is the current flowing in the wire, and r is the distance from the wire.

Moving Charged Particles

The whole point of defining a magnetic field is to determine the forces produced on an object by the field. You are familiar with the forces produced by bar magnets—like poles repel, opposite poles attract. We don't have any formulas for the amount of force produced in this case, but that's okay, because this kind of force is irrelevant to the AP exam.

Instead, we must focus on the forces produced by magnetic fields on charged particles, including both isolated charges and current-carrying wires. (After all, current is just the movement of positive charges.)

A magnetic field exerts a force on a charged particle if that particle is moving perpendicular to the magnetic field. A magnetic field does not exert a force on a stationary charged particle, nor on a particle that is moving parallel to the magnetic field.

$$F = qvB$$

The magnitude of the force exerted on the particle equals the charge on the particle, q, multiplied by the velocity of the particle, v, multiplied by the magnitude of the magnetic field.

This equation is sometimes written as $F = qvB(\sin\theta)$. The θ refers to the angle formed between the velocity vector of your particle and the direction of the magnetic field. So, if a particle moves in the same direction as the magnetic field lines, $\theta = 0°$, $\sin 0° = 0$, and *that particle experiences no magnetic force!*

Nine times out of ten, you will not need to worry about this "$\sin\theta$" term, because the angle will either be zero or 90°. However, if a problem explicitly tells you that your particle is *not* traveling perpendicular to the magnetic field, then you will need to throw in this extra "$\sin\theta$" term.

Right-hand rule: To find the force on a charged particle.

Point your right hand, with fingers extended, in the direction that the charged particle is traveling. Then, bend your fingers so that they point in the direction of the magnetic field.

- If the particle has a POSITIVE charge, your thumb points in the direction of the force exerted on it.
- If the particle has a NEGATIVE charge, your thumb points opposite the direction of the force exerted on it.

The key to this right-hand rule is to remember the sign of your particle. This next problem illustrates how important sign can be.

An electron travels through a magnetic field, as shown below. The particle's initial velocity is 5×10^6 m/s, and the magnitude of the magnetic field is 0.4 T. What are the magnitude and direction of the particle's acceleration?

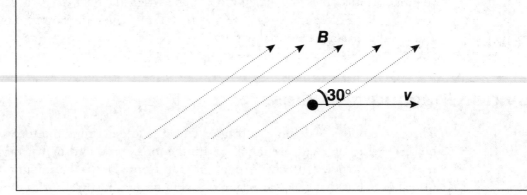

This is one of those problems where you're told that the particle is *not* moving perpendicular to the magnetic field. So the formula we use to find the magnitude of the force acting on the particle is

$$F = qvB(\sin \theta)$$
$$F = (1.6 \times 10^{-19} \text{ C})(5 \times 10^6 \text{ m/s})(0.4 \text{ T})(\sin 30°)$$
$$F = 1.6 \times 10^{-13} \text{ N}.$$

Note that we never plug in the negative signs when calculating force. The negative charge on an electron will influence the direction of the force, which we will determine in a moment. Now we solve for acceleration:

$$F_{net} = ma$$
$$a = 1.8 \times 10^{17} \text{ m/s}^2.$$

Wow, you say . . . a bigger acceleration than anything we've ever dealt with. Is this unreasonable? After all, in less than a second the particle would be moving faster than the speed of light, right? The answer is still reasonable. In this case, the acceleration is perpendicular to the velocity. This means the acceleration is *centripetal*, and the particle must move in a circle at constant speed. But even if the particle were speeding up at this rate, either the acceleration wouldn't act for very long, or relativistic effects would prevent the particle from traveling faster than light.

Finally, we solve for direction using the right-hand rule. We point our hand in the direction that the particle is traveling—to the right. Next, we curl our fingers upward, so that they point in the same direction as the magnetic field. Our thumb points out of the page. BUT WAIT!!! We're dealing with an electron, which has a negative charge. So the force acting on our particle, and therefore the particle's acceleration, points in the opposite direction. The particle is accelerating into the page.

Magnetic Force on a Wire

A current is simply the flow of positive charges. So, if we put a current-carrying wire perpendicular to a magnetic field, we have placed moving charges perpendicular to the field, and these charges experience a force. The wire can be pulled by the magnetic field!

The formula for the force on a long, straight, current-carrying wire in the presence of a magnetic field is

$$F = ILB$$

This equation says that the force on a wire equals the current in the wire, I, multiplied by the length of the wire, L, multiplied by the magnitude of the magnetic field, B, in which the wire is located.

Sometimes you'll see this equation written as $F = ILB(\sin \theta)$. Just like the equation for the force on a charge, the θ refers to the angle between the wire and the magnetic field. You normally don't have to worry about this θ because, in most problems, the wire is perpendicular to the magnetic field, and $\sin 90° = 1$, so the term cancels out.

The direction of the force on a current-carrying wire is given by the same right-hand rule as for the force on a charged particle because current is simply the flow of positive charge.

What would happen if you had two long, straight, current-carrying wires side by side? This is a question that the writers of the AP exam love to ask, so it is a great idea to learn how to answer it.

The trick that makes answering this question very easy is that you have to draw the direction of the magnetic field that one of the wires creates; then consider the force on the other wire. So, for example . . .

Two wires are placed parallel to each other. The direction of current in each wire is indicated above. How will these wires interact?

(A) They will attract each other.
(B) They will repel each other.
(C) They will not affect each other.
(D) This question cannot be answered without knowing the length of each wire.
(E) This question cannot be answered without knowing the current in each wire.

Let's follow our advice and draw the magnetic field created by the left-hand wire.

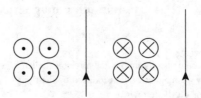

Now, a wire's field cannot produce a force on itself. The field that we drew is *caused by* the left wire, but produces a force on the right-hand wire. Which direction is that force? Use the right-hand rule for the force on a charged particle. The charges are moving up, in the direction of the current. So point up the page, and curl your fingers toward the magnetic field, into the page. The right wire is forced to the LEFT. Newton's third law says that the force on the left wire by the right wire will be equal and opposite.[2] So, the wires attract, answer A.

Often, textbooks give you advice such as, "Whenever the current in two parallel wires is traveling in the same direction, the wires will attract each other, and vice versa." Use it if you like, but this advice can easily be confused.

Mass Spectrometry: More Charges Moving Through Magnetic Fields

A magnetic field can make a charged particle travel in a circle. Here's how it performs this trick.

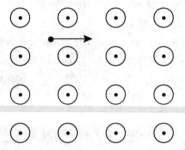

Figure 19.7a   Positively charged particle moving in a magnetic field directed out of the page.

Let's say you have a proton traveling through a uniform magnetic field coming out of the page, and the proton is moving to the right, like the one we drew in Figure 19.7a. The magnetic field exerts a downward force on the particle (use the right-hand rule). So the path of the particle begins to bend downward, as shown in Figure 19.7b.

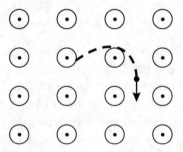

Figure 19.7b   Curving path of a positively charged particle moving in a magnetic field directed out of the page.

---

[2]You could also figure out the force on the left wire by using the same method we just used for the force on the right wire: draw the magnetic field produced by the right wire, and use the right-hand rule to find the direction of the magnetic force acting on the left wire.

Now our proton is moving straight down. The force exerted on it by the magnetic field, using the right-hand rule, is now directed to the left. So the proton will begin to bend leftward. You probably see where this is going—a charged particle, traveling perpendicular to a uniform magnetic field, will follow a circular path.

We can figure out the radius of this path with some basic math. The force of the magnetic field is causing the particle to go in a circle, so this force must cause centripetal acceleration. That is, $qvB = mv^2/r$.

We didn't include the "$\sin \theta$" term because the particle is always traveling perpendicular to the magnetic field. We can now solve for the radius of the particle's path:

$$r = \frac{mv}{qB}$$

The real-world application of this particle-in-a-circle trick is called a mass spectrometer. A mass spectrometer is a device used to determine the mass of a particle.

A mass spectrometer, in simplified form, is drawn in Figure 19.8.

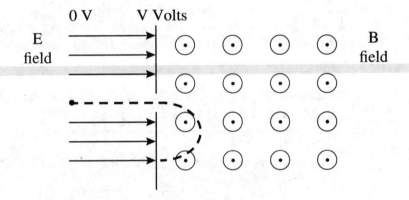

Figure 19.8   Basic mass spectrometer.

A charged particle enters a uniform electric field (shown at the left in Figure 19.8). It is accelerated by the electric field. By the time it gets to the end of the electric field, it has acquired a high velocity, which can be calculated using conservation of energy. Then the particle travels through a tiny opening and enters a uniform magnetic field. This magnetic field exerts a force on the particle, and the particle begins to travel in a circle. It eventually hits the wall that divides the electric-field region from the magnetic-field region. By measuring where on the wall it hits, you can determine the radius of the particle's path. Plugging this value into the equation we derived for the radius of the path, you can calculate the particle's mass, $r = mv/qB$.

You may see a problem on the free-response section that involves a mass spectrometer. These problems may seem intimidating, but, when you take them one step at a time, they're not very difficult.

Induced EMF

A changing magnetic field produces a current. We call this occurrence **electromagnetic induction**.

So let's say that you have a loop of wire in a magnetic field. Under normal conditions, no current flows in your wire loop. However, if you change the magnitude of the magnetic field, a current will begin to flow.

We've said in the past that current flows in a circuit (and a wire loop qualifies as a circuit, albeit a simple one) when there is a potential difference between the two ends of the circuit. Usually, we need a battery to create this potential difference. But we don't have a battery hooked up to our loop of wire. Instead, the changing magnetic field is doing the same thing as a battery would. So rather than talking about the voltage of the battery in this circuit, we talk about the "voltage" created by the changing magnetic field. The technical term for this "voltage" is **induced EMF**.

> **Induced EMF:** The potential difference created by a changing magnetic field that causes a current to flow in a wire. EMF stands for Electro-Motive Force, but is *NOT* a force.

For a loop of wire to "feel" the changing magnetic field, some of the field lines need to pass through it. The amount of magnetic field that passes through the loop is called the **magnetic flux**. This concept is pretty similar to electric flux.

> **Magnetic Flux:** The number of magnetic field lines that pass through an area

The units of flux are called webers; 1 weber = 1 T·m². The equation for magnetic flux is

$$\Phi_B = BA$$

In this equation, Φ_B is the magnetic flux, B is the magnitude of the magnetic field, and A is the area of the region that is penetrated by the magnetic field.

Let's take a circular loop of wire, lay it down on the page, and create a magnetic field that points to the right, as shown in Figure 19.9.

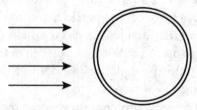

Figure 19.9   Loop of wire in the plane of a magnetic field.

No field lines go through the loop. Rather, they all hit the edge of the loop, but none of them actually passes through the center of the loop. So we know that our flux should equal zero.

Okay, this time we will orient the field lines so that they pass through the middle of the loop. We'll also specify the loop's radius = 0.2 m, and that the magnetic field is that of the Earth, $B = 5 \times 10^{-5}$ T. This situation is shown in Figure 19.10.

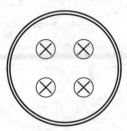

Figure 19.10   Loop of wire with magnetic field lines going through it.

Now all of the area of the loop is penetrated by the magnetic field, so A in the flux formula is just the area of the circle, πr^2.

The flux here is

$$\Phi_B = (5 \times 10^{-5})(\pi)\,(0.2^2) = 6.2 \times 10^{-6} \text{ T·m}^2.$$

Sometimes you'll see the flux equation written as $BA\cos\theta$. The additional cosine term is only relevant when a magnetic field penetrates a wire loop at some angle that's not 90°. The angle θ is measured between the magnetic field and the "normal" to the loop of wire . . . if you didn't get that last statement, don't worry about it. Rather, know that the cosine term goes to 1 when the magnetic field penetrates directly into the loop, and the cosine term goes to zero when the magnetic field can't penetrate the loop at all.

Because a loop will only "feel" a changing magnetic field if some of the field lines pass through the loop, we can more accurately say the following: *A changing magnetic **flux** creates an induced EMF.*

Faraday's law tells us exactly how much EMF is induced by a changing magnetic flux.

$$\boxed{\varepsilon = \frac{N \cdot \Delta\Phi_B}{\Delta t}}^3$$

ε is the induced EMF, N is the number of loops you have (in all of our examples, we've only had one loop), and Δt is the time during which your magnetic flux, Φ_B, is changing.

Up until now, we've just said that a changing magnetic flux creates a current. We haven't yet told you, though, in which direction that current flows. To do this, we'll turn to **Lenz's Law**.

Lenz's Law: States that the direction of the induced current opposes the increase in flux

---

When a current flows through a loop, that current creates a magnetic field. So what Lenz said is that the current that is induced will flow in such a way that the magnetic field it creates points opposite to the direction in which the already existing magnetic flux is changing.

---

[3]But the calculus version of the induced EMF formula states: $\varepsilon = -N\dfrac{d\Phi}{dt}$. If you're given magnetic flux as a function of time, then take the *negative* time derivative to find the induced EMF.

Sound confusing?[4] It'll help if we draw some good illustrations. So here is Lenz's Law in pictures.

We'll start with a loop of wire that is next to a region containing a magnetic field (Figure 19.11a). Initially, the magnetic flux through the loop is zero.

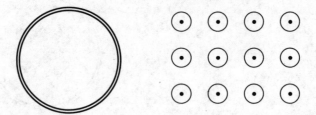

Figure 19.11a   Loop of wire next to a region containing a magnetic field pointing out of the page.

Now, we will move the wire into the magnetic field. When we move the loop toward the right, the magnetic flux will increase as more and more field lines begin to pass through the loop. The magnetic flux is increasing out of the page—at first, there was no flux out of the page, but now there is some flux out of the page. Lenz's Law says that the induced current will create a magnetic field that opposes this increase in flux. So the induced current will create a magnetic field into the page. By the right-hand rule, the current will flow clockwise. This situation is shown in Figure 19.11b.

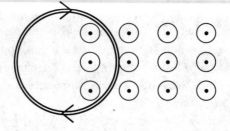

Figure 19.11b   Current induced in loop of wire as it moves into a magnetic field directed out of the page.

After a while, the loop will be entirely in the region containing the magnetic field. Once it enters this region, there will no longer be a changing flux, because no matter where it is within the region, the same number of field lines will always be passing through the loop. Without a changing flux, there will be no induced EMF, so the current will stop. This is shown in Figure 19.11c.

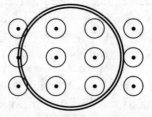

Figure 19.11c   Loop of wire with no current flowing, because it is not experiencing a changing magnetic flux.

---

[4]"Yes."

To solve a problem that involves Lenz's Law, use this method:

- Point your right thumb in the initial direction of the magnetic field.
- Ask yourself, "Is the flux increasing or decreasing?"
- If the flux is decreasing, then just curl your fingers (with your thumb still pointed in the direction of the magnetic field). Your fingers show the direction of the induced current.
- If flux is increasing in the direction you're pointing, then flux is decreasing in the other direction. So, point your thumb in the opposite direction of the magnetic field, and curl your fingers. Your fingers show the direction of the induced current.

Induced EMF in a Rectangular Wire

Consider the example in Figures 19.11a–c with the circular wire being pulled through the uniform magnetic field. It can be shown that if instead we pull a *rectangular* wire into or out of a uniform field B at constant speed v, then the induced EMF in the wire is found by

$$\varepsilon = BLv$$

Here, L represents the length of the side of the rectangle that is NOT entering or exiting the field, as shown below in Figure 19.12.

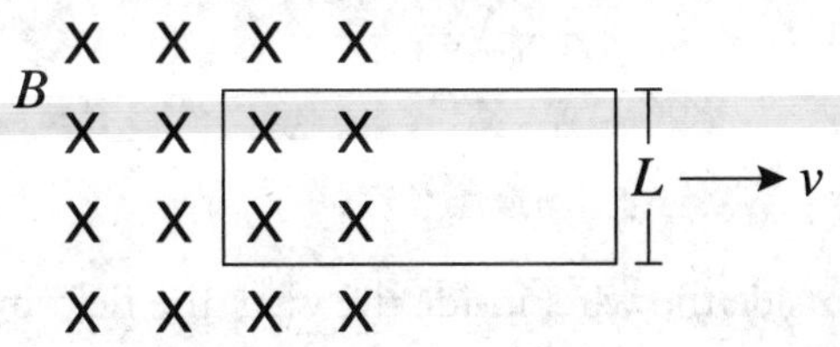

Figure 19.12   Rectangular wire moving through a uniform magnetic field.

Some Words of Caution

We say this from personal experience. First, when using a right-hand rule, use big, easy-to-see gestures. A right-hand rule is like a form of advertisement: it is a way that your hand tells your brain what the answer to a problem is. You want that advertisement to be like a billboard—big, legible, and impossible to misread. Tiny gestures will only lead to mistakes. Second, when using a right-hand rule, *always* use your right hand. *Never use your left hand!* This will cost you points!

Exam tip from an AP Physics veteran:
Especially if you hold your pencil in your right hand, it's easy accidentally to use your left hand. Be careful!

—*Jessica, college sophomore*

The Biot-Savart Law and Ampere's Law

So far we've only discussed two possible ways to create a magnetic field—use a bar magnet, or a long, straight, current-carrying wire. And of these, we only have an equation to find the magnitude of the field produced by the wire.

Biot-Savart Law

The Biot-Savart law provides a way, albeit a complicated way, to find the magnetic field produced by pretty much any type of current. It's not worth worrying about using the law because it's got a horrendously complicated integral with a cross product included. Just know the conceptual consequence: a little element of wire carrying a current produces a magnetic field that (a) wraps around the current element via the right-hand rule, and (b) decreases in magnitude as $1/r^2$, r being the distance from the current element.

So why does the magnetic field caused by a long, straight, current-carrying wire drop off as $1/r$ rather than $1/r^2$? Because the $1/r^2$ drop-off is for the magnetic field produced just by a teeny little bit of current-carrying wire (in calculus terminology, by a differential element of current). When we include the contributions of every teeny bit of a very long wire, the net field drops off as $1/r$.

Ampere's Law

Ampere's law gives an alternative method for finding the magnetic field caused by a current. Although Ampere's law is valid everywhere that current is continuous, it is only *useful* in a few specialized situations where symmetry is high. There are three important results of Ampere's law:

1. The magnetic field produced by a very long, straight current is

$$B = \frac{\mu_0 I}{2\pi r}$$

   outside the wire; inside the wire, the field increases linearly from zero at the wire's center.

2. A solenoid is set of wound wire loops. A current-carrying solenoid produces a magnetic field. Ampere's law can show that the magnetic field due to a solenoid is shaped like that of a bar magnet; and the magnitude of the magnetic field inside the solenoid is approximately uniform, $B_{solenoid} = \mu_0\, nI$. (Here I is the current in the solenoid, and n is the number of coils per meter in the solenoid.)

3. The magnetic field produced by a wire-wrapped torus (a "donut" with wire wrapped around it [see Figure 19.13]) is zero everywhere outside the torus, but nonzero within the torus. The direction of the field inside the torus is around the donut.

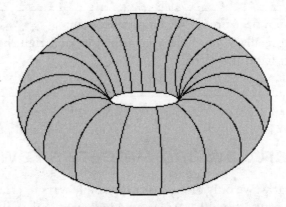

Figure 19.13   A wire-wrapped torus.

Maxwell's Equations

Okay, we'll get this out of the way right now: *You will not have to solve Maxwell's equations on the AP Physics exam.* These four equations include integrals the likes of which you will not be able to solve until well into college physics, if then. However, you *can* understand the basic point of each equation, and, most importantly, understand the equations' greatest consequence.

Accelerating charges produce oscillations of electric and magnetic fields. These oscillations propagate as waves, with speed

$$c = \frac{1}{\sqrt{\mu_0 \varepsilon_0}}$$

Maxwell obtained this wave speed as a mathematical result from the equations. He noticed that, when the experimentally determined constants were plugged in, the speed of his "electromagnetic waves" was identical to the speed of light.[5] Maxwell's conclusion was that light must be an electromagnetic wave.

What are Maxwell's equations? We're not even going to write them out, for fear that you might throw down your book in trepidation. If you're really interested in the integral or differential form of the equations, you will find them in your physics book (or on a rather popular T-shirt). While we won't write the equations, we'll gladly summarize what they are and what they mean.

- *Maxwell equation 1* is simply Gauss's law: the net electric flux through a closed surface is proportional to the charge enclosed by that surface.
- *Maxwell equation 2* is sometimes called Gauss's law for magnetism: the net magnetic flux through a closed surface must always be zero. The consequence of this equation is that magnetic poles come in north/south pairs—you cannot have an isolated north magnetic pole.
- *Maxwell equation 3* is simply Faraday's law: a changing magnetic flux through a loop of wire induces an EMF.
- *Maxwell equation 4* is partly Ampere's law, but with an addition called "displacement current" that allows the equation to be valid in all situations. The principal consequence is that just as a changing magnetic field can produce an electric field, a changing electric field can likewise produce a magnetic field.

---

[5] Which had first been accurately measured in the late 1600s using observations of the moons of Jupiter.

› Practice Problems

Multiple Choice:

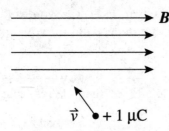

1. A point charge of +1 μC moves with velocity v into a uniform magnetic field B directed to the right, as shown above. What is the direction of the magnetic force on the charge?

(A) to the right and up the page
(B) directly out of the page
(C) directly into the page
(D) to the right and into the page
(E) to the right and out of the page

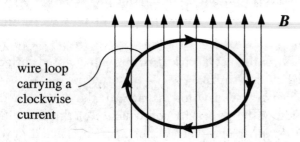

2. A uniform magnetic field B points up the page, as shown above. A loop of wire carrying a clockwise current is placed at rest in this field as shown above, and then let go. Which of the following describes the motion of the wire immediately after it is let go?

(A) The wire will expand slightly in all directions.
(B) The wire will contract slightly in all directions.
(C) The wire will rotate, with the top part coming out of the page.
(D) The wire will rotate, with the left part coming out of the page.
(E) The wire will rotate clockwise, remaining in the plane of the page.

3. An electron moves to the right in a uniform magnetic field that points into the page. What is the direction of the electric field that could be used to cause the electron to travel in a straight line?

(A) down toward the bottom of the page
(B) up toward the top of the page
(C) into the page
(D) out of the page
(E) to the left

Free Response:

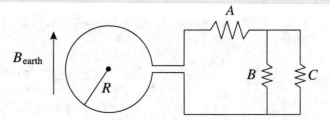

4. A circular loop of wire of negligible resistance and radius $R = 20$ cm is attached to the circuit shown above. Each resistor has resistance 10 Ω. The magnetic field of the Earth points up along the plane of the page in the direction shown, and has magnitude $B = 5.0 \times 10^{-5}$ T.

The wire loop rotates about a horizontal diameter, such that after a quarter rotation the loop is no longer in the page, but perpendicular to it. The loop makes 500 revolutions per second, and remains connected to the circuit the entire time.

(a) Determine the magnetic flux through the loop when the loop is in the orientation shown.
(b) Determine the maximum magnetic flux through the loop.
(c) Estimate the average value of the induced EMF in the loop.
(d) Estimate the average current through resistor C.

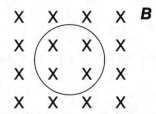

5. A loop of wire is located inside a uniform magnetic field, as shown above. Name at least four things you could do to induce a current in the loop.

› Solutions to Practice Problems

1. **C**—Use the right-hand rule for the force on charged particles. You point in the direction of the velocity, and curl your fingers in the direction of the magnetic field. This should get your thumb pointing into the page. Because this is a positive charge, no need to switch the direction of the force.

2. **C**—Use the right-hand rule for the force on a wire. Look at each part of this wire. At the leftmost and rightmost points, the current is along the magnetic field lines. Thus, these parts of the wire experience no force. The topmost part of the wire experiences a force out of the page (point to the right, fingers curl up the page, the thumb points out of the page). The bottommost part of the wire experiences a force *into* the page. So, the wire will rotate.

3. **A**—Use the right-hand rule for the force on a charge. Point in the direction of velocity, curl the fingers into the page, the thumb points up the page . . . but this is a *negative* charge, so the force on the charge is down the page. Now, the electric force must cancel the magnetic force for the charge to move in a straight line, so the electric force should be up the page. (E and B *fields* cannot cancel, but forces sure can.) The direction of an *electric* force on a negative charge is opposite the field; so the field should point down, toward the bottom of the page.

4. (a) Flux equals zero because the field points along the loop, not ever going straight through the loop.
    (b) Flux is maximum when the field *is* pointing straight through the loop; that is, when the loop is perpendicular to the page. Then flux will be just $BA = 5.0 \times 10^{-5}$ T·$\pi(0.20$ m$)^2 = 6.3 \times 10^{-6}$ T·m². (Be sure your units are right!)
    (c) Induced EMF for this one loop is change in flux over time interval. It takes 1/500 of a second for the loop to make one complete rotation; so it takes $^1/_4$ of that, or 1/2000 of a second, for the loop to go from zero to maximum flux. Divide this change in flux by 1/2000 of a second . . . this is 6.3×10^{-6} T·m²/0.0005 s = 0.013 V. (That's 13 mV.)
    (d) Now we can treat the circuit as if it were attached to a battery of voltage 13 mV. The equivalent resistance of the parallel combination of resistors B and C is 5 Ω; the total resistance of the circuit is 15 Ω. So the current in the whole circuit is 0.013 V/15 W = 8.4×10^{-4} A. (This can also be stated as 840 μA.) The current splits evenly between resistors B and C since they're equal resistances, so we get 420 μA for resistor C.

5. The question might as well be restated, "Name four things you could do to change the flux through the loop," because only a changing magnetic flux induces an EMF.

    (a) Rotate the wire about an axis in the plane of the page. This will change the θ term in the expression for magnetic flux, $BA \cos \theta$.
    (b) Pull the wire out of the field. This will change the area term, because the magnetic field lines will intersect a smaller area of the loop.
    (c) Shrink or expand the loop. This also changes the area term in the equation for magnetic flux.
    (d) Increase or decrease the strength of the magnetic field. This changes the B term in the flux equation.

› Rapid Review

- Magnetic fields can be drawn as loops going from the north pole of a magnet to the south pole.

- A long, straight, current-carrying wire creates a magnetic field that wraps around the wire in concentric circles. The direction of the magnetic field is found by a right-hand rule.

- Similarly, loops of wire that carry current create magnetic fields. The direction of the magnetic field is, again, found by a right-hand rule.

- A magnetic field exerts a force on a charged particle if that particle is moving perpendicular to the magnetic field.

- When a charged particle moves perpendicular to a magnetic field, it ends up going in circles. This phenomenon is the basis behind mass spectrometry.

- A changing magnetic flux creates an induced EMF, which causes current to flow in a wire.

- Lenz's Law says that when a changing magnetic flux induces a current, the direction of that current will be such that the magnetic field it induces is pointed in the opposite direction of the original change in magnetic flux.

- The Biot–Savart law has as its consequence that a little element of wire carrying a current produces a magnetic field that (1) wraps around the current element via the right-hand rule, and (2) decreases in magnitude as $1/r^2$, r being the distance from the current element. This is applicable to Physics C only.

- Ampere's law has as its consequence that (1) the magnetic field produced by a very long, straight current is

$$B_{wire} = \frac{\mu_0 I}{2\pi r}$$

outside the wire; inside the wire, the field increases linearly from zero at the wire's center, and (2) the magnetic field produced by a wire-wrapped torus is zero everywhere outside the torus, but nonzero within the torus. The direction of the field inside the torus is around the donut.

STEP 5

Build Your Test-Taking Confidence

PHYSICS C—Mechanics Practice Exam 1—Multiple-Choice Questions

PHYSICS C—Mechanics Practice Exam 1—Free-Response Questions

PHYSICS C—Electricity and Magnetism Practice Exam 1—Multiple-Choice Questions

PHYSICS C—Electricity and Magnetism Practice Exam 1—Free-Response Questions

PHYSICS C—Mechanics Practice Exam 1—Multiple-Choice Solutions

PHYSICS C—Mechanics Practice Exam 1—Free-Response Solutions

PHYSICS C—Electricity and Magnetism Practice Exam 1—Multiple-Choice Solutions

PHYSICS C—Electricity and Magnetism Practice Exam 1—Free-Response Solutions

Physics C—Mechanics Practice Exam 1—Multiple-Choice Questions

ANSWER SHEET

1 Ⓐ Ⓑ Ⓒ Ⓓ Ⓔ	13 Ⓐ Ⓑ Ⓒ Ⓓ Ⓔ	25 Ⓐ Ⓑ Ⓒ Ⓓ Ⓔ
2 Ⓐ Ⓑ Ⓒ Ⓓ Ⓔ	14 Ⓐ Ⓑ Ⓒ Ⓓ Ⓔ	26 Ⓐ Ⓑ Ⓒ Ⓓ Ⓔ
3 Ⓐ Ⓑ Ⓒ Ⓓ Ⓔ	15 Ⓐ Ⓑ Ⓒ Ⓓ Ⓔ	27 Ⓐ Ⓑ Ⓒ Ⓓ Ⓔ
4 Ⓐ Ⓑ Ⓒ Ⓓ Ⓔ	16 Ⓐ Ⓑ Ⓒ Ⓓ Ⓔ	28 Ⓐ Ⓑ Ⓒ Ⓓ Ⓔ
5 Ⓐ Ⓑ Ⓒ Ⓓ Ⓔ	17 Ⓐ Ⓑ Ⓒ Ⓓ Ⓔ	29 Ⓐ Ⓑ Ⓒ Ⓓ Ⓔ
6 Ⓐ Ⓑ Ⓒ Ⓓ Ⓔ	18 Ⓐ Ⓑ Ⓒ Ⓓ Ⓔ	30 Ⓐ Ⓑ Ⓒ Ⓓ Ⓔ
7 Ⓐ Ⓑ Ⓒ Ⓓ Ⓔ	19 Ⓐ Ⓑ Ⓒ Ⓓ Ⓔ	31 Ⓐ Ⓑ Ⓒ Ⓓ Ⓔ
8 Ⓐ Ⓑ Ⓒ Ⓓ Ⓔ	20 Ⓐ Ⓑ Ⓒ Ⓓ Ⓔ	32 Ⓐ Ⓑ Ⓒ Ⓓ Ⓔ
9 Ⓐ Ⓑ Ⓒ Ⓓ Ⓔ	21 Ⓐ Ⓑ Ⓒ Ⓓ Ⓔ	33 Ⓐ Ⓑ Ⓒ Ⓓ Ⓔ
10 Ⓐ Ⓑ Ⓒ Ⓓ Ⓔ	22 Ⓐ Ⓑ Ⓒ Ⓓ Ⓔ	34 Ⓐ Ⓑ Ⓒ Ⓓ Ⓔ
11 Ⓐ Ⓑ Ⓒ Ⓓ Ⓔ	23 Ⓐ Ⓑ Ⓒ Ⓓ Ⓔ	35 Ⓐ Ⓑ Ⓒ Ⓓ Ⓔ
12 Ⓐ Ⓑ Ⓒ Ⓓ Ⓔ	24 Ⓐ Ⓑ Ⓒ Ⓓ Ⓔ	

Physics C—Mechanics Practice Exam 1—Multiple-Choice Questions

Time: 45 minutes. You may refer to the constants sheet and the equation sheet, both of which are found in the appendix. You may use a calculator.

1. A cannon is mounted on a truck that moves forward at a speed of 5 m/s. The operator wants to launch a ball from a cannon so the ball goes as far as possible before hitting the level surface. The muzzle velocity of the cannon is 50 m/s. At what angle from the horizontal should the operator point the cannon?

   (A) 5°
   (B) 41°
   (C) 45°
   (D) 49°
   (E) 85°

2. A car moving with speed v reaches the foot of an incline of angle θ. The car coasts up the incline without using the engine. Neglecting friction and air resistance, which of the following is correct about the magnitude of the car's horizontal acceleration a_x and vertical acceleration a_y?

   (A) $a_x = 0$; $a_y < g$
   (B) $a_x = 0$; $a_y = g$
   (C) $a_x < g$; $a_y < g$
   (D) $a_x < g$; $a_y = g$
   (E) $a_x < g$; $a_y > g$

3. A bicycle slows down with an acceleration whose magnitude increases linearly with time. Which of the following velocity–time graphs could represent the motion of the bicycle?

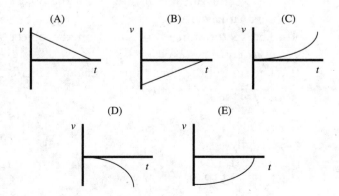

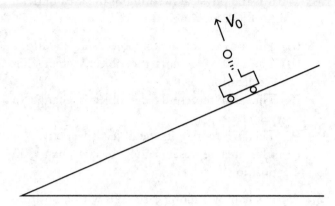

4. A cart is sliding down a low friction incline. A device on the cart launches a ball, forcing the ball perpendicular to the incline, as shown above. Air resistance is negligible. Where will the ball land relative to the cart, and why?

   (A) The ball will land in front of the cart, because the ball's acceleration component parallel to the plane is greater than the cart's acceleration component parallel to the plane.
   (B) The ball will land in front of the cart, because the ball has a greater magnitude of acceleration than the cart.
   (C) The ball will land in the cart, because both the ball and the cart have the same component of acceleration parallel to the plane.
   (D) The ball will land in the cart, because both the ball and the cart have the same magnitude of acceleration.
   (E) The ball will land behind the cart, because the ball slows down in the horizontal direction after it leaves the cart.

GO ON TO THE NEXT PAGE

5. The quantity "jerk," j, is defined as the time derivative of an object's acceleration,

$$j = \frac{da}{dt} = \frac{d^3x}{dt^3}.$$

What is the physical meaning of the area under a graph of jerk vs. time?

(A) The area represents the object's acceleration.
(B) The area represents the object's change in acceleration.
(C) The area represents the object's change in velocity.
(D) The area represents the object's velocity.
(E) The area represents the object's change in position.

6. A particle moves along the x-axis with a position given by the equation $x(t) = 5 + 3t$, where x is in meters, and t is in seconds. The positive direction is east. Which of the following statements about the particle is FALSE.

(A) The particle is east of the origin at $t = 0$.
(B) The particle is at rest at $t = 0$.
(C) The particle's velocity is constant.
(D) The particle's acceleration is constant.
(E) The particle will never be west of position $x = 0$.

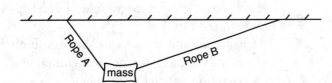

7. A mass hangs from two ropes at unequal angles, as shown above. Which of the following makes correct comparisons of the horizontal and vertical components of the tension in each rope?

	Horizontal Tension	Vertical Tension
(A)	greater in rope B	greater in rope B
(B)	equal in both ropes	greater in rope A
(C)	greater in rope A	greater in rope A
(D)	equal in both ropes	equal in both ropes
(E)	greater in rope B	equal in both ropes

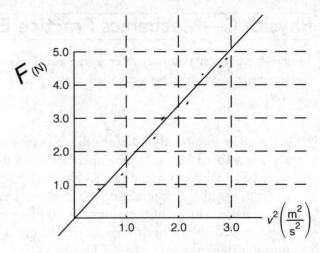

8. The force of air resistance F on a mass is found to obey the equation $F = bv^2$, where v is the speed of the mass, for the range of speeds investigated in an experiment. A graph of F vs. v^2 is shown above. What is the value of b?

(A) 0.83 kg/m
(B) 1.7 kg/m
(C) 3.0 kg/m
(D) 5.0 kg/m
(E) 1.0 kg/m

9. A box sits on an inclined plane without sliding. As the angle of the plane (measured from the horizontal) increases, the normal force

(A) increases linearly
(B) decreases linearly
(C) does not change
(D) decreases nonlinearly
(E) increases nonlinearly

10. Which of the following conditions are necessary for an object to be in static equilibrium?

I. The vector sum of all torques on the object must equal zero.
II. The vector sum of all forces on the object must equal zero.
III. The sum of the object's potential and kinetic energies must be zero.

(A) I only
(B) II only
(C) III only
(D) I and II only
(E) I, II, and III

GO ON TO THE NEXT PAGE

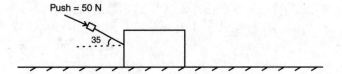

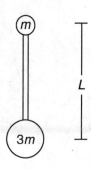

11. A student pushes a big 16-kg box across the floor at constant speed. He pushes with a force of 50 N angled 35° from the horizontal, as shown in the diagram above. If the student pulls rather than pushes the box at the same angle, while maintaining a constant speed, what will happen to the force of friction?

(A) It must increase.
(B) It must decrease.
(C) It must remain the same.
(D) It will increase only if the speed is greater than 3.1 m/s.
(E) It will increase only if the speed is less than 3.1 m/s.

12. Consider a system consisting only of the Earth and a bowling ball, which moves upward in a parabola above Earth's surface. The downward force of Earth's gravity on the ball, and the upward force of the ball's gravity on the Earth, form a Newton's third law force pair. Which of the following statements about the ball is correct?

(A) The ball must be in equilibrium since the upward forces must cancel downward forces.
(B) The ball accelerates toward the Earth because the force of gravity on the ball is greater than the force of the ball on the Earth.
(C) The ball accelerates toward the Earth because the force of gravity on the ball is the only force acting on the ball.
(D) The ball accelerates away from Earth because the force causing the ball to move upward is greater than the force of gravity on the ball.
(E) The ball accelerates away from Earth because the force causing the ball to move upward plus the force of the ball on the Earth are together greater than the force of gravity on the ball.

13. A mass m is attached to a mass $3m$ by a rigid bar of negligible mass and length L. Initially, the smaller mass is located directly above the larger mass, as shown above. How much work is necessary to flip the rod 180° so that the larger mass is directly above the smaller mass?

(A) $4mgL$
(B) $2mgL$
(C) mgL
(D) $4\pi mgL$
(E) $2\pi mgL$

14. A ball rolls horizontally with speed v off of a table a height h above the ground. Just before the ball hits the ground, what is its speed?

(A) $\sqrt{2gh}$

(B) $v\sqrt{2gh}$

(C) $\sqrt{v^2 + 2gh}$

(D) v

(E) $v + \sqrt{2gh}$

GO ON TO THE NEXT PAGE

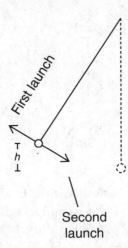

15. A pendulum is launched into simple harmonic motion in two different ways, as shown above, from a point that is a height h above its lowest point. During both launches, the bob is given an initial speed of 3.0 m/s. On the first launch, the initial velocity of the bob is directed upward along the pendulum's path, and on the second launch it is directed downward along the pendulum's path. Which launch will cause the pendulum to swing with the larger amplitude?

(A) the first launch
(B) the second launch
(C) Both launches produce the same amplitude.
(D) The answer depends on the initial height h.
(E) The answer depends on the length of the supporting rope.

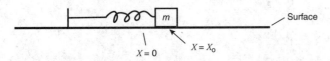

16. The mass M is moving to the right with velocity v_0 at position $x = x_0$. Neglect friction. The spring has force constant k. What is the total mechanical energy of the block at this position?

(A) $\frac{1}{2}mv_0^2$
(B) $\frac{1}{2}mv_0^2 + \frac{1}{2}kx_0^2$
(C) $\frac{1}{2}mv_0^2 + \frac{1}{2}kx_0^2 + mgx_0$
(D) $mgx_0 + \frac{1}{2}mv_0^2$
(E) $mgx_0 + \frac{1}{2}kx_0^2$

17. A sphere, a cube, and a cylinder, all of equal mass, are released from rest from the top of a short incline. The surface of the incline is extremely slick, so much so that the objects do not rotate when released, but rather slide with negligible friction. Which reaches the base of the incline first?

(A) the sphere
(B) the cube
(C) the cylinder
(D) All reach the base at the same time.
(E) The answer depends on the relative sizes of the objects.

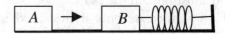

18. Block B is at rest on a smooth tabletop. It is attached to a long spring, which is in turn anchored to the wall. Block A slides toward and collides with block B. Consider two possible collisions:

Collision I: Block A bounces back off of block B.
Collision II: Block A sticks to block B.

Which of the following is correct about the speed of block B immediately after the collision?

(A) It is faster in case II than in case I ONLY if block B is heavier.
(B) It is faster in case I than in case II ONLY if block B is heavier.
(C) It is faster in case II than in case I regardless of the mass of each block.
(D) It is faster in case I than in case II regardless of the mass of each block.
(E) It is the same in either case regardless of the mass of each block.

GO ON TO THE NEXT PAGE

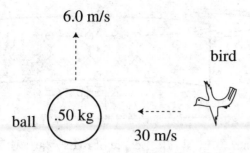

19. A 0.30-kg bird is flying from right to left at 30 m/s. The bird collides with and sticks to a 0.50-kg ball that is moving straight up with speed 6.0 m/s. What is the magnitude of the momentum of the ball/bird combination immediately after collision?

(A) 12.0 N·s
(B) 9.5 N·s
(C) 9.0 N·s
(D) 6.0 N·s
(E) 3.0 N·s

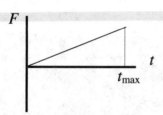

20. The force F on a mass is shown above as a function of time t. Which of the following methods can be used to determine the impulse experienced by the mass?

I. multiplying the average force by t_{max}
II. calculating the area under the line on the graph
III. taking the integral $\int_{0}^{t_{max}} F \cdot dt$

(A) II only
(B) III only
(C) II and III only
(D) I and II only
(E) I, II, and III

21. A projectile is launched on level ground in a parabolic path so that its range would normally be 500 m. When the projectile is at the peak of its flight, the projectile breaks into two pieces of equal mass. One of these pieces falls straight down, with no further horizontal motion. How far away from the launch point does the other piece land?

(A) 250 m
(B) 375 m
(C) 500 m
(D) 750 m
(E) 1000 m

Questions 22 and 23

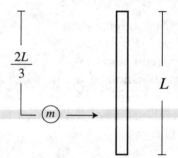

A rigid rod of length L and mass M is floating at rest in space far from a gravitational field. A small blob of putty of mass $m < M$ is moving to the right, as shown above. The putty hits and sticks to the rod a distance $2L/3$ from the top end.

22. How will the rod/putty contraption move after the collision?

(A) The contraption will have no translational motion, but will rotate about the rod's center of mass.
(B) The contraption will have no translational motion, but will rotate about the center of mass of the rod and putty combined.
(C) The contraption will move to the right and rotate about the position of the putty.
(D) The contraption will move to the right and rotate about the center of mass of the rod and putty combined.
(E) The contraption will move to the right and rotate about the rod's center of mass.

GO ON TO THE NEXT PAGE

23. What quantities are conserved in this collision?

(A) linear and angular momentum, but not kinetic energy
(B) linear momentum only
(C) angular momentum only
(D) linear and angular momentum, and linear but not rotational kinetic energy
(E) linear and angular momentum, and linear and rotational kinetic energy

24. A car rounds a banked curve of uniform radius. Three forces act on the car: a friction force between the tires and the road, the normal force from the road, and the weight of the car. Which provides the centripetal force which keeps the car in circular motion?

(A) the friction force alone
(B) the normal force alone
(C) the weight alone
(D) a combination of the normal force and the friction force
(E) a combination of the friction force and the weight

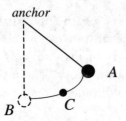

25. A ball of mass m anchored to a string swings back and forth to a maximum position A, as shown above. Point C is partway back to the vertical position. What is the direction of the mass's acceleration at point C?

(A) along the mass's path toward point B
(B) toward the anchor
(C) away from the anchor
(D) between a line toward the anchor and a line along the mass's path
(E) along the mass's path toward point A

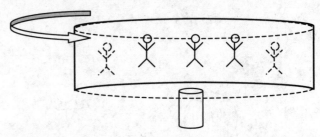

26. In a carnival ride, people of mass m are whirled in a horizontal circle by a floorless cylindrical room of radius r, as shown in the diagram above. If the coefficient of friction between the people and the tube surface is μ, what minimum speed is necessary to keep the people from sliding down the walls?

(A) $\sqrt{\mu r g}$

(B) $\sqrt{\dfrac{rg}{\mu}}$

(C) $\sqrt{\dfrac{\mu}{rg}}$

(D) $\sqrt{\dfrac{1}{\mu r g}}$

(E) $\sqrt{\mu m g}$

GO ON TO THE NEXT PAGE

Questions 27 and 28

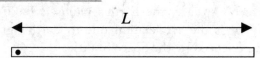

The uniform, rigid rod of mass m, length L, and rotational inertia I shown above is pivoted at its left-hand end. The rod is released from rest from a horizontal position.

27. What is the linear acceleration of the rod's center of mass the moment after the rod is released?

(A) $\dfrac{mgL^2}{2I}$

(B) $\dfrac{mgL^2}{4I}$

(C) $\dfrac{mgL^2}{I}$

(D) $\dfrac{mgL}{2I}$

(E) $\dfrac{2mgL^2}{I}$

28. What is the linear speed of the rod's center of mass when the mass passes through a vertical position?

(A) $\sqrt{\dfrac{mgL^3}{8I}}$

(B) $\sqrt{\dfrac{mg\pi L^3}{4I}}$

(C) $\sqrt{\dfrac{mg\pi L^3}{8I}}$

(D) $\sqrt{\dfrac{mgL^3}{4I}}$

(E) $\sqrt{\dfrac{mgL^3}{2I}}$

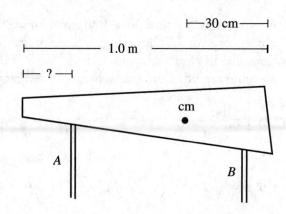

29. The 1.0-m-long nonuniform plank, shown above, has weight 1000 N. It is to be supported by two rods, A and B, as shown above. The center of mass of the plank is 30 cm from the right edge. Each support bears half the weight of the plank. If support B is 10 cm from the right-hand edge, how far from the left-hand edge should support A be?

(A) 0 cm
(B) 10 cm
(C) 30 cm
(D) 50 cm
(E) 70 cm

30. A mass m on a spring oscillates on a horizontal surface with period T. The total mechanical energy contained in this oscillation is E. Imagine that instead a new mass $4m$ oscillates on the same spring with the same amplitude. What is the new period and total mechanical energy?

	Period	Total Mechanical Energy
(A)	T	E
(B)	$2T$	E
(C)	$2T$	$2E$
(D)	T	$4E$
(E)	$2T$	$16E$

GO ON TO THE NEXT PAGE

31. A mass m is attached to a horizontal spring of spring constant k. The spring oscillates in simple harmonic motion with amplitude A. What is the maximum speed of this simple harmonic oscillator?

(A) $2\pi\sqrt{\dfrac{m}{k}}$

(B) $2\pi A\sqrt{\dfrac{m}{k}}$

(C) $2\pi A\sqrt{\dfrac{k}{m}}$

(D) $A\sqrt{\dfrac{k}{m}}$

(E) $A\sqrt{\dfrac{m}{k}}$

32. An empty bottle goes up and down on the surface of the ocean, obeying the position function $x = A\cos(\omega t)$. How much time does this bottle take to travel once from its lowest position to its highest position?

(A) $\dfrac{2\pi}{\omega}$

(B) $\dfrac{\pi}{\omega}$

(C) $\dfrac{4\pi}{\omega}$

(D) $\dfrac{\pi}{2\omega}$

(E) $\dfrac{\pi}{4\omega}$

33. The Space Shuttle orbits 300 km above the Earth's surface; the Earth's radius is 6400 km. What is the acceleration due to Earth's gravity experienced by the Space Shuttle?

(A) 4.9 m/s²
(B) 8.9 m/s²
(C) 9.8 m/s²
(D) 10.8 m/s²
(E) zero

34. An artificial satellite orbits Earth just above the atmosphere in a circle with constant speed. A small meteor collides with the satellite at point P in its orbit, increasing its speed by 1%, but not changing the instantaneous direction of the satellite's velocity. Which of the following describes the satellite's new orbit?

(A) The satellite now orbits in an ellipse, with P as the farthest approach to Earth.
(B) The satellite now orbits in an ellipse, with P as the closest approach to Earth.
(C) The satellite now orbits in a circle of larger radius.
(D) The satellite now orbits in a circle of smaller radius.
(E) The satellite cannot maintain an orbit, so it flies off into space.

35. Mercury orbits the sun in about one-fifth of an Earth year. If 1 AU is defined as the distance from the Earth to the sun, what is the approximate distance between Mercury and the sun?

(A) (1/25) AU
(B) (1/9) AU
(C) (1/5) AU
(D) (1/3) AU
(E) (1/2) AU

STOP. End of Physics C—Mechanics Practice Exam 1—Multiple-Choice Questions

Physics C—Mechanics Practice Exam 1—Free-Response Questions

Time: 45 minutes. You may refer to the constants sheet and the equation, both of which are found in the appendix. You may use a calculator.

CM 1

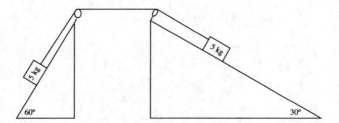

Two 5-kg masses are connected by a light string over two massless, frictionless pulleys. Each block sits on a frictionless inclined plane, as shown above. The blocks are released from rest.

(a) Determine the magnitude of the acceleration of the blocks.

Now assume that the 30° incline provides a resistive force which depends on speed v. This resistive force causes the entire system's acceleration to be given by the expression

$$a = 1.8 - 0.03v$$

where a speed v in m/s gives an acceleration in m/s². The blocks are again released from rest.

(b) i. On the axes below, sketch a graph of the speed of the 5 kg block as a function of time. Label important values, including any asymptotes and intercepts.

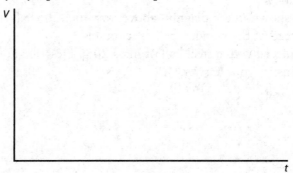

ii. Explain how the expression for acceleration leads to the graph you drew.

(c) Explain how to figure out the terminal speed of the 5 kg block.

(d) The terminal speed is 60 m/s – that's a typical speed in automobile racing. Explain briefly why this result is physically reasonable, even though the blocks are on a track in a physics laboratory.

GO ON TO THE NEXT PAGE

CM 2

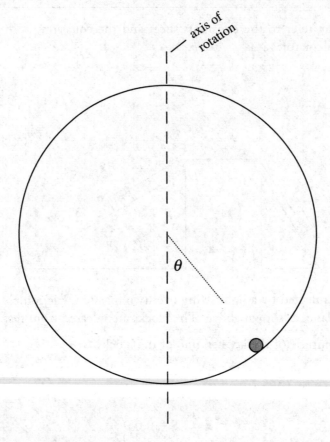

A hollow glass sphere of radius 8.0 cm rotates about a vertical diameter with frequency 5 revolutions per second. A small wooden ball of mass 2.0 g rotates inside the sphere, as shown in the diagram above.

(a) Draw a free-body diagram indicating the forces acting on the wooden ball when it is at the position shown in the picture above.

(b) Calculate the angle θ, shown in the diagram above, to which the ball rises.

(c) Calculate the linear speed of the wooden ball as it rotates.

(d) The wooden ball is replaced with a steel ball of mass 20 g. Describe how the angle θ to which the ball rises will be affected. Justify your answer.

GO ON TO THE NEXT PAGE

CM 3

A heavy ball of mass m is attached to a light but rigid rod of length L. The rod is pivoted at the top and is free to rotate in a circle in the plane of the page, as shown above.

(a) The mass oscillates to a maximum angle θ. On the picture of the mass m below, draw a vector representing the direction of the NET force on the mass while it is at angle θ. Justify your choice of direction.

●

(b) Is the magnitude of the net force at the maximum displacement equal to $mg \sin\theta$ or $mg \cos\theta$? Choose one and justify your choice.

(c) Derive an expression for the ball's potential energy U as a function of the angle θ. Assume that a negative angle represents displacement from the vertical in the clockwise direction.

(d) On the axes below, sketch a graph of the mass's potential energy U as a function of the angle θ for angles between $-90°$ and $+360°$. Label maximum and minimum values on the vertical axis.

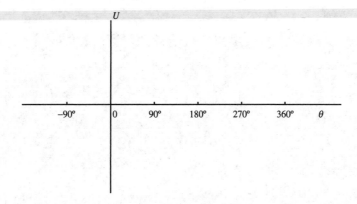

(e) The pendulum is considered a classic example of simple harmonic motion when it undergoes small-amplitude oscillation. With specific reference to the graph you made in part (d), explain why the assumption of simple harmonic motion is valid.

STOP. End of Physics C—Mechanics Practice Exam 1—Free-Response Questions

Physics C—Electricity and Magnetism Practice Exam 1—Multiple-Choice Questions

ANSWER SHEET

1 (A) (B) (C) (D) (E)	13 (A) (B) (C) (D) (E)	25 (A) (B) (C) (D) (E)
2 (A) (B) (C) (D) (E)	14 (A) (B) (C) (D) (E)	26 (A) (B) (C) (D) (E)
3 (A) (B) (C) (D) (E)	15 (A) (B) (C) (D) (E)	27 (A) (B) (C) (D) (E)
4 (A) (B) (C) (D) (E)	16 (A) (B) (C) (D) (E)	28 (A) (B) (C) (D) (E)
5 (A) (B) (C) (D) (E)	17 (A) (B) (C) (D) (E)	29 (A) (B) (C) (D) (E)
6 (A) (B) (C) (D) (E)	18 (A) (B) (C) (D) (E)	30 (A) (B) (C) (D) (E)
7 (A) (B) (C) (D) (E)	19 (A) (B) (C) (D) (E)	31 (A) (B) (C) (D) (E)
8 (A) (B) (C) (D) (E)	20 (A) (B) (C) (D) (E)	32 (A) (B) (C) (D) (E)
9 (A) (B) (C) (D) (E)	21 (A) (B) (C) (D) (E)	33 (A) (B) (C) (D) (E)
10 (A) (B) (C) (D) (E)	22 (A) (B) (C) (D) (E)	34 (A) (B) (C) (D) (E)
11 (A) (B) (C) (D) (E)	23 (A) (B) (C) (D) (E)	35 (A) (B) (C) (D) (E)
12 (A) (B) (C) (D) (E)	24 (A) (B) (C) (D) (E)	

Physics C—Electricity and Magnetism Practice Exam 1— Multiple-Choice Questions

Time: 45 minutes. You may refer to the constants sheet and the equation sheet, both of which are found in the appendix. You may use a calculator.

1. Experimenter A uses a very small test charge q_0, and experimenter B uses a test charge $2q_0$ to measure an electric field produced by two parallel plates. A finds a field that is

   (A) greater than the field found by B
   (B) the same as the field found by B
   (C) less than the field found by B
   (D) either greater or less than the field found by B, depending on the accelerations of the test charges
   (E) either greater or less than the field found by B, depending on the masses of the test charges

2. A solid conducting sphere has radius R and carries positive charge Q. Which of the following graphs represents the electric field E as a function of the distance r from the center of the sphere?

   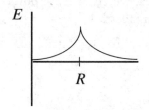

   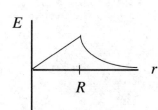   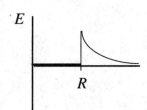

   (E)

   E

   R

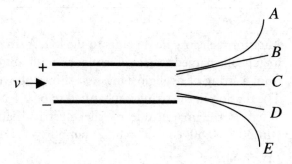

3. An electron moving at constant velocity enters the region between two charged plates, as shown above. Which of the paths above correctly shows the electron's trajectory after leaving the region between the charged plates?

   (A) A
   (B) B
   (C) C
   (D) D
   (E) E

4. Two isolated particles, A and B, are 4 m apart. Particle A has a net charge of $2Q$, and B has a net charge of Q. The ratio of the magnitude of the electric force on A to that on B is

   (A) 4:1
   (B) 2:1
   (C) 1:1
   (D) 1:2
   (E) 1:4

GO ON TO THE NEXT PAGE

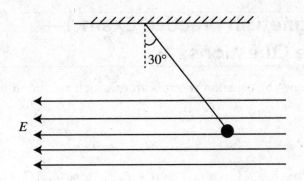

5. A uniform electric field points to the left. A small metal ball charged to −2 mC hangs at a 30° angle from a string of negligible mass, as shown above. The tension in the string is measured to be 0.1 N. What is the magnitude of the electric field? (sin 30° = 0.50; cos 30° = 0.87; tan 30° = 0.58.)

(A) 25 N/C
(B) 50 N/C
(C) 2,500 N/C
(D) 5,000 N/C
(E) 10,000 N/C

6. A thin semicircular conductor of radius R holds charge $+Q$. What is the magnitude and direction of the electric field at the center of the circle?

(A) $\dfrac{kQ}{R^2}$ ↑

(B) $\dfrac{kQ}{R^2}$ ↓

(C) $\dfrac{kQ}{\pi R^2}$ ↑

(D) $\dfrac{kQ}{\pi R^2}$ ↓

(E) The electric field is zero at the center.

7. Above an infinitely large plane carrying charge density σ, the electric field points up and is equal to $\sigma/2\varepsilon_o$. What is the magnitude and direction of the electric field below the plane?

(A) $\sigma/2\varepsilon_o$, down
(B) $\sigma/2\varepsilon_o$, up
(C) σ/ε_o, down
(D) σ/ε_o, up
(E) zero

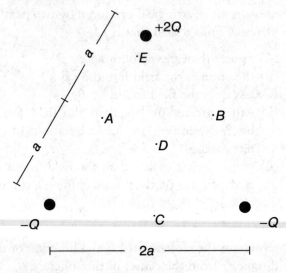

8. Three charges are arranged in an equilateral triangle, as shown above. At which of these points is the electric potential smallest?

(A) A
(B) B
(C) C
(D) D
(E) E

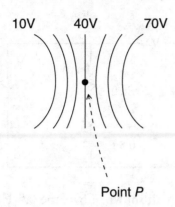

Point P

9. The diagram shows a set of equipotential surfaces. At point *P*, what is the direction of the electric field?

(A) left
(B) right
(C) up the page
(D) down the page
(E) either left or right, which one cannot be determined

10. A metal sphere carries charge *Q*; a nonconducting sphere of equal size carries the same charge *Q*, uniformly distributed throughout the sphere. These spheres are isolated from each other. Consider the electric field at the center of the spheres, within the spheres, and outside the spheres. Which of these electric fields will be the same for both spheres, and which will be different?

	At the Center	Elsewhere Within the Sphere	Outside the Sphere
(A)	Same	Same	Same
(B)	Same	Same	Different
(C)	Same	Different	Same
(D)	Different	Different	Same
(E)	Different	Different	Different

11. Under what conditions is the net electric flux through a closed surface proportional to the enclosed charge?

(A) under any conditions
(B) only when the enclosed charge is symmetrically distributed
(C) only when all nearby charges are symmetrically distributed
(D) only when there are no charges outside the surface
(E) only when enclosed charges can be considered to be point charges

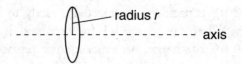

radius *r*

axis

12. A hollow metal ring of radius *r* carries charge *q*. Consider an axis straight through the center of the ring. At what point(s) along this axis is/are the electric field equal to zero?

(A) only at the center of the ring
(B) only at the center of the ring, and a very long distance away
(C) only a very long distance away
(D) only at the center of the ring, a distance *r* away from the center, and a very long distance away
(E) everywhere along this axis

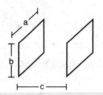

13. A parallel plate capacitor consists of identical rectangular plates of dimensions *a* × *b*, separated by a distance *c*. To cut the capacitance of this capacitor in half, which of these quantities should be doubled?

(A) *a*
(B) *b*
(C) *c*
(D) *ab*
(E) *abc*

14. Two identical capacitors are hooked in parallel to an external circuit. Which of the following quantities must be the same for both capacitors?

I. the charge stored on the capacitor
II. the voltage across the capacitor
III. the capacitance of the capacitor

(A) I only
(B) II only
(C) II and III only
(D) I and III only
(E) I, II, and III

GO ON TO THE NEXT PAGE

15. A 2 µF capacitor is connected directly to a battery. When the capacitor is fully charged, it stores 600 µC of charge. An experimenter replaces the 2 µF capacitor with three 18 µF capacitors in series connected to the same battery. Once the capacitors are fully charged, what charge is stored on each capacitor?

(A) 100 µC
(B) 200 µC
(C) 600 µC
(D) 1200 µC
(E) 1800 µC

16. A spherical conductor carries a net charge. How is this charge distributed on the sphere?

(A) The charge is evenly distributed on the surface.
(B) The charge resides on the surface only; the distribution of charge on the surface depends on what other charged objects are near the sphere.
(C) The charge moves continually within the sphere.
(D) The charge is distributed uniformly throughout the sphere.
(E) The charge resides within the sphere; the distribution of charge within the sphere depends on what other charged objects are near the sphere.

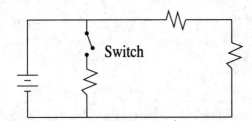

17. Three resistors are connected to a battery as shown in the diagram above. The switch is initially open. When the switch is closed, what happens to the total voltage, current, and resistance in the circuit?

	Voltage	Current	Resistance
(A)	increases	increases	increases
(B)	does not change	does not change	does not change
(C)	does not change	decreases	increases
(D)	does not change	increases	decreases
(E)	decreases	decreases	decreases

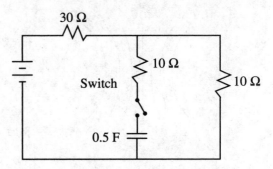

18. In the circuit shown above, the 0.5-F capacitor is initially uncharged. The switch is closed at time $t = 0$. What is the time constant (the time for the capacitor to charge to 63% of its maximum charge) for the charging of this capacitor?

(A) 5 s
(B) 10 s
(C) 20 s
(D) 30 s
(E) 40 s

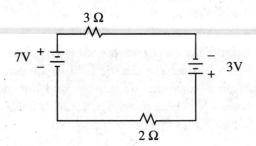

19. In the circuit shown above, what is the current through the 3 Ω resistor?

(A) 0 A
(B) 0.5 A
(C) 1.0 A
(D) 1.5 A
(E) 2.0 A

20. A light bulb rated at 100 W is twice as bright as a bulb rated at 50 W when both are connected in parallel directly to a 100-V source. Now imagine that these bulbs are instead connected in series with each other. Which is brighter, and by how much?

(A) The bulbs have the same brightness.
(B) The 100-W bulb is twice as bright.
(C) The 50-W bulb is twice as bright.
(D) The 100-W bulb is four times as bright.
(E) The 50-W bulb is four times as bright.

GO ON TO THE NEXT PAGE

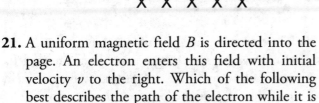

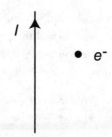

21. A uniform magnetic field B is directed into the page. An electron enters this field with initial velocity v to the right. Which of the following best describes the path of the electron while it is still within the magnetic field?

   (A) It moves in a straight line.
   (B) It bends upward in a parabolic path.
   (C) It bends downward in a parabolic path.
   (D) It bends upward in a circular path.
   (E) It bends downward in a circular path.

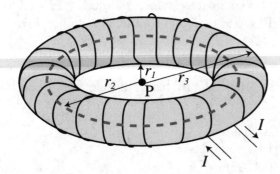

22. Wire is wound around an insulated circular donut, as shown above. A current I flows in the wire in the direction indicated by the arrows. The inner, average, and outer radii of the donut are indicated by r_1, r_2, and r_3, respectively. What is the magnitude and direction of the magnetic field at point P, the center of the donut?

   (A) zero

   (B) $\dfrac{\mu_o I}{2r_1}$

   (C) $\dfrac{\mu_o I}{2r_2}$

   (D) $\dfrac{\mu_o I}{2r_3}$

   (E) $\dfrac{\mu_o I}{2\pi r_2}$

23. A wire carries a current toward the top of the page. An electron is located to the right of the wire, as shown above. In which direction should the electron be moving if it is to experience a magnetic force toward the wire?

   (A) into the page
   (B) out of the page
   (C) toward the bottom of the page
   (D) toward the top of the page
   (E) to the right

24. Which of the following statements about electric and magnetic fields is FALSE:

   (A) A charge moving along the direction of an electric field will experience a force, but a charge moving along the direction of a magnetic field will not experience a force.
   (B) All charges experience a force in an electric field, but only moving charges can experience a force in a magnetic field.
   (C) A positive charge moves in the direction of an electric field; a positive charge moves perpendicular to a magnetic field.
   (D) All moving charges experience a force parallel to an electric field and perpendicular to a magnetic field.
   (E) A negative charge experiences a force opposite the direction of an electric field; a negative charge experiences a force perpendicular to a magnetic field.

25. Which of these quantities decreases as the inverse square of distance for distances far from the objects producing the fields?

   (A) the electric field produced by a finite-length charged rod
   (B) the electric field produced by an infinitely long charged cylinder
   (C) the electric field produced by an infinite plane of charge
   (D) the magnetic field produced by an infinitely long, straight current-carrying wire
   (E) the magnetic field produced by a wire curled around a torus

GO ON TO THE NEXT PAGE

26. A proton enters a solenoid. Upon entry, the proton is moving in a straight line along the axis of the solenoid. Which of the following is a correct description of the proton's motion within the solenoid?

(A) The proton will be bent in a parabolic path.
(B) The proton will be bent in a circular path.
(C) The proton will continue in its straight path at constant velocity.
(D) The proton will continue in its straight path and slow down.
(E) The proton will continue in its straight path and speed up.

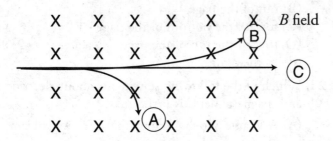

27. A uniform magnetic field points into the page. Three subatomic particles are shot into the field from the left-hand side of the page. All have the same initial speed and direction. These particles take paths A, B, and C, as labeled in the diagram above. Which of the following is a possible identity for each particle?

	A	B	C
(A)	antiproton	proton	electron
(B)	antiproton	positron	neutron
(C)	proton	electron	neutron
(D)	positron	antiproton	neutron
(E)	electron	proton	neutron

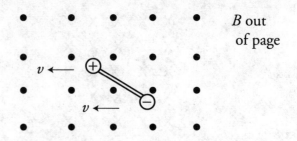

28. The electric dipole shown above consists of equal-magnitude charges and has an initial leftward velocity v in a uniform magnetic field pointing out of the page, as shown above. The dipole experiences

(A) a clockwise net torque, and a net force to the left
(B) a counterclockwise net torque, and a net force to the left
(C) no net torque, and a net force to the left
(D) a counterclockwise net torque, and no net force
(E) a clockwise net torque, and no net force

29. A beam of electrons has speed 10^7 m/s. It is desired to use the magnetic field of the Earth, 5×10^{-5} T, to bend the electron beam into a circle. What will be the radius of this circle?

(A) 1 nm
(B) 1 μm
(C) 1 mm
(D) 1 m
(E) 1 km

30. A very small element of wire of length dL carries a current I. What is the direction of the magnetic field produced by this current element at point P, shown above?

(A) to the right
(B) toward the top of the page
(C) into the page
(D) out of the page
(E) there is no magnetic field produced at point P by this element.

GO ON TO THE NEXT PAGE

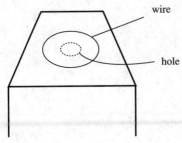

wire

hole

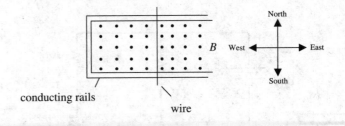

B West ← → East

North

South

conducting rails

wire

31. A loop of wire surrounds a hole in a table, as shown above. A bar magnet is dropped, north end down, from far above the table through the hole. Let the positive direction of current be defined as counterclockwise as viewed from above. Which of the following graphs best represents the induced current I in the loop?

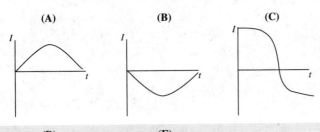

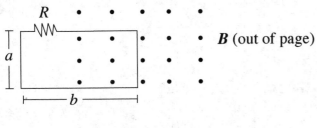

33. A conducting wire sits on smooth metal rails, as shown above. A variable magnetic field points out of the page. The strength of this magnetic field is increased linearly from zero. Immediately after the field starts to increase, what will be the direction of the current in the wire and the direction of the wire's motion?

	Current in the Wire	Motion of the Wire
(A)	north	no motion
(B)	north	east
(C)	north	west
(D)	south	west
(E)	south	east

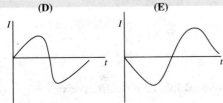

R

a

b

B (out of page)

v

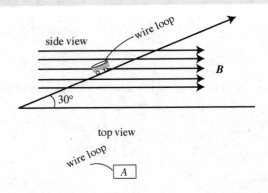

side view

wire loop

B

30°

top view

wire loop

A

32. A rectangular loop of wire has dimensions $a \times b$ and includes a resistor R. This loop is pulled with speed v from a region of no magnetic field into a uniform magnetic field B pointing through the loop, as shown above. What is the magnitude and direction of the current through the resistor?

(A) Bav/R, left-to-right
(B) Bbv/R, left-to-right
(C) Bav/R, right-to-left
(D) Bbv/R, right-to-left
(E) Bba/R, right-to-left

34. A uniform magnetic field B points parallel to the ground. A toy car is sliding down a frictionless plane inclined at 30°. A loop of wire of resistance R and cross-sectional area A lies in the flat plane of the car's body, as shown above. What is the magnetic flux through the wire loop?

(A) zero
(B) $BA \cos 30°$
(C) $BA \cos 60°$
(D) BA
(E) $(BA \cos 60°)/R$

GO ON TO THE NEXT PAGE

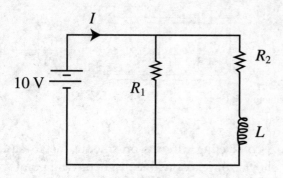

35. If the two equal resistors R_1 and R_2 are connected in parallel to a 10-V battery with no other circuit components, the current provided by the battery is I. In the circuit shown above, an inductor of inductance L is included in series with R_2. What is the current through R_2 after the circuit has been connected for a long time?

(A) zero
(B) $(1/4)\,I$
(C) $(1/2)\,I$
(D) I

(E) $I\dfrac{R_1 + R_2}{LR_2}$

STOP. End of Physics C—Electricity and Magnetism Practice Exam 1—Multiple-Choice Questions

Physics C—Electricity and Magnetism Practice Exam 1— Free-Response Questions

Time: 45 minutes. You may refer to the constants sheet and the equation sheet, both of which are found in the appendix. You may use a calculator.

E&M 1

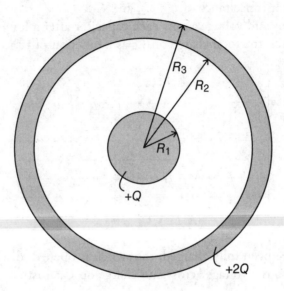

A metal sphere of radius R_1 carries charge $+Q$. A concentric spherical metal shell, of inner radius R_2 and outer radius R_3, carries charge $+2Q$.

(a) Let r represent the distance from the center of the spheres. Calculate the electric field as a function of r in each of the following four regions:
1. between $r = 0$ and $r = R_1$
2. between $r = R_1$ and $r = R_2$
3. between $r = R_2$ and $r = R_3$
4. between $r = R_3$ and $r = 0$

(b) How much charge is on each surface of the outer spherical shell? Justify your answer.
(c) Determine the electric potential of the outer spherical shell.
(d) Determine the electric potential of the inner metal sphere.

GO ON TO THE NEXT PAGE

E&M 2

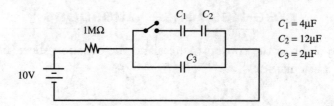

$C_1 = 4\mu F$
$C_2 = 12\mu F$
$C_3 = 2\mu F$

A 1 MΩ resistor is connected to the network of capacitors shown above. The circuit is hooked to a 10-V battery. The capacitors are initially uncharged. The battery is connected, and the switch is closed at time $t = 0$.

(a) Determine the equivalent capacitance of C_1, C_2, and C_3.

(b) Determine the charge on and voltage across each capacitor after a long time has elapsed.

(c) On the axes below, sketch the total charge on C_3 as a function of time.

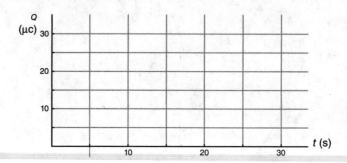

(d) After the capacitors have been fully charged, the switch is opened, disconnecting C_1 and C_2 from the circuit. What happens to the voltage across and charge on C_3? Justify your answer.

GO ON TO THE NEXT PAGE

E&M 3

In the laboratory, far from the influence of other magnetic fields, the Earth's magnetic field has a value of 5.00×10^{-5} T. A compass in this lab reads due north when pointing along the direction of Earth's magnetic field.

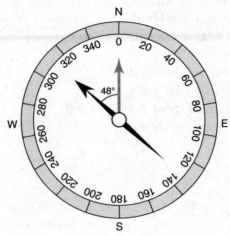

A long, straight current-carrying wire is brought close to the compass, deflecting the compass to the position shown above, 48° west of north.

(a) Describe one possible orientation of the wire and the current it carries that would produce the deflection shown.

(b) Calculate the magnitude B_{wire} of the magnetic field produced by the wire that would cause the deflection shown.

(c) The distance d from the wire to the compass is varied, while the current in the wire is kept constant; a graph of B_{wire} vs. d is produced. On the axes below, sketch the shape of this graph.

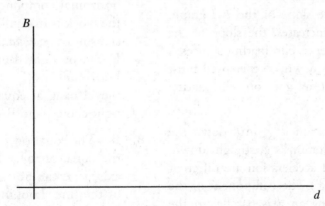

(d) It is desired to adjust this plot so that the graph becomes a straight line. The vertical axis is to remain B_{wire}, the magnetic field produced by the wire. How could the quantity graphed on the horizontal axis be adjusted to produce a straight-line graph? Justify your answer.

(e) The current carried by the wire is 500 mA. Determine the slope of the line on the graph suggested in part (d).

STOP. End of Physics C—Electricity and Magnetism Practice Exam 1—Free-Response Questions

Physics C—Mechanics Practice Exam 1—Multiple-Choice Solutions

1. **D**—A projectile has its maximum range when it is shot at an angle of 45° relative to the ground. The cannon's initial velocity relative to the ground in this problem is given by the vector sum of the man's 5 m/s forward motion and the cannon's 50 m/s muzzle velocity. To get a resultant velocity of 45°, the man must shoot the cannon at only a slightly higher angle, as shown in the diagram below.

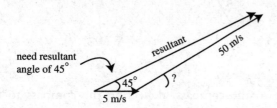

2. **C**—The car stays on the plane, and slows down as it goes up the plane. Thus, the net acceleration is in the direction down the plane, which has both a nonzero horizontal and vertical component. The car is not in free fall, so its vertical acceleration is less than g.

3. **E**—Acceleration is the slope of the v–t graph. Because acceleration increases, the slope of the v–t graph must get steeper, eliminating choices A and B. The bike slows down, so the speed must get closer to zero as time goes on, eliminating choices C and D.

4. **C**—The cart's acceleration is $g \sin\theta$, down the plane, the ball's acceleration is g, straight down. (So the magnitudes of acceleration are different and choice D is wrong.) The component of the ball's acceleration along an axis parallel to the plane is also $g \sin\theta$, equal to the ball's acceleration component.

5. **B**—The area under a jerk–time graph is the quantity jdt. The derivative

$$j = \frac{da}{dt}$$

can be interpreted as a change in acceleration over a time interval,

$$j = \frac{\Delta a}{\Delta t}.$$

Solving algebraically, $j\Delta t$ is Δa, meaning the change in acceleration.

6. **B**—At $t = 0$, $x = +5$ m, so the particle is east of the origin to start with. The velocity is given by the derivative of the position function, $v(t) = 3$ m/s. This is a constant velocity; the acceleration is thus zero (and constant), but at $t = 0$ the velocity is also 3 m/s, so choice B is false.

7. **B**—Consider the horizontal and vertical forces separately. The only horizontal forces are the horizontal components of the tensions. Because the block is in equilibrium, these horizontal tensions must be *equal*, meaning only choices B and D can be right. But the ropes can't have equal horizontal AND vertical tensions, otherwise they'd hang at equal angles. So D can't be the right choice, and B must be right.

8. **B**—The equation $F = bv^2$ is of the form $y = mx$, the equation of a line. Here F is the vertical axis, v^2 is the horizontal axis, so b is the slope of the line. Looking at the graph, the slope is 5.0 N/3.0 m²/s² = 1.7 kg/m.

9. **D**—Because no forces act perpendicular to the incline except for the normal force and the perpendicular component of weight, and there is no acceleration perpendicular to the incline, the normal force is equal to the perpendicular component of weight, which is $mg \cos\theta$. As the angle increases, the cosine of the angle decreases. This decrease is nonlinear because a graph of F_N vs. θ would show a curve, not a line.

10. **D**—In equilibrium, the net force and the net torque must both be zero. *Static* equilibrium means the object is stationary, so kinetic energy must be zero. However, potential energy can take on any value—a sign suspended above a roadway is in static equilibrium, yet has potential energy relative to Earth's surface.

11. **B**—The friction force is equal to the coefficient of friction times the normal force. The coefficient of friction is a property of the surfaces in contact, and thus will not change here. However, the normal force decreases when the cart is pulled rather than pushed—the surface must apply more force to the box when there is a downward component to the applied force than when there is an upward component. Speed is irrelevant because equilibrium in the vertical direction is maintained regardless.

12. **C**—The ball accelerates *toward* the Earth because, although it is moving upward, it must be slowing down. The only force acting on the ball is Earth's gravity. Yes, the ball exerts a force on the Earth, but that force acts on the Earth, not the ball. According to Newton's third law, force pairs always act on different objects, and thus can never cancel.

13. **B**—The work done on an object by gravity is independent of the path taken by the object and is equal to the object's weight times its vertical displacement. Gravity must do *3mgL* of work to raise the large mass, but must do $mg(-L)$ of work to lower the small mass. The net work done is thus *2mgL*.

14. **C**—Use conservation of energy. Position 1 will be the top of the table; position 2 will be the ground. $PE_1 + KE_1 = PE_2 + KE_2$. Take the PE at the ground to be zero. Then $\frac{1}{2}mv_2^2 = \frac{1}{2}mv_1^2 + mgh$. The *m*s cancel. Solving for v_2, you get choice C. (Choice E is wrong because it's illegal algebra to take a squared term out of a square root when it is added to another term.)

15. **C**—Consider the conservation of energy. At the launch point, the potential energy is the same regardless of launch direction. The kinetic energy is also the same because KE depends on speed alone and not direction. So, both balls have the same amount of kinetic energy to convert to potential energy, bringing the ball to the same height in every cycle.

16. **B**—Total mechanical energy is defined as kinetic energy plus potential energy. The KE here is $\frac{1}{2}mv_0^2$. The potential energy is provided entirely by the spring—gravitational potential energy requires a *vertical* displacement, which doesn't occur here. The PE of the spring is $\frac{1}{2}kx_0^2$.

17. **D**—When an object rotates, some of its potential energy is converted to rotational rather than linear kinetic energy, and thus it moves more slowly than a non-rotating object when it reaches the bottom of the plane. However, here none of the objects rotate! The acceleration does not depend on mass or size.

18. **D**—Momentum must be conserved in the collision. If block *A* bounces, it changes its momentum by a larger amount than if it sticks. This means that block *B* picks up more momentum (and thus more speed) when block *A* bounces. The mass of the blocks is irrelevant because the comparison here is just between bouncing and not bouncing. So *B* goes faster in collision I regardless of mass.

19. **B**—The momentum of the bird before collision is 9 N·s to the left; the momentum of the ball is initially 3 N·s up. The momentum after collision is the *vector* sum of these two initial momentums. With a calculator you would use the Pythagorean theorem to get 9.5 N·s; without a calculator you should just notice that the resultant vector must have magnitude less than 12 N·s (the algebraic sum) and more than 9 N·s.

20. **E**—Impulse is defined on the equation sheet as the integral of force with respect to time, so III is right. The meaning of this integral is to take the area under a *F* vs. *t* graph, so II is right. Because the force is increasing linearly, the average force will be halfway between zero and the maximum force, and the rectangle formed by this average force will have the same area as the triangle on the graph as shown, so I is right.

21. **D**—The center of mass of the projectile must maintain the projectile path and land 500 m from the launch point. The first half of the projectile fell straight down from the peak of its flight, which is halfway to the maximum range, or 250 m from the launch point. So the second half of equal mass must be 250 m beyond the center of mass upon hitting the ground, or 750 m from the launch point.

22. D—By conservation of linear momentum, there is momentum to the right before collision, so there must be momentum to the right after collision as well. A free-floating object rotates about its center of mass; because the putty is attached to the rod, the combination will rotate about its combined center of mass.

23. A—Linear and angular momentum are conserved in *all* collisions (though often angular momentum conservation is irrelevant). Kinetic energy, though, is only conserved in an elastic collision. Because the putty sticks to the rod, this collision cannot be elastic. Some of the kinetic energy must be dissipated as heat.

24. D.

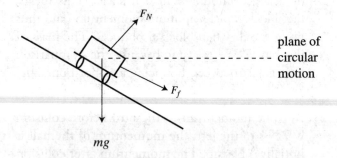

The centripetal force must act toward the center of the car's circular path. This direction is NOT down the plane, but rather is purely horizontal. The friction force acts down the plane and thus has a horizontal component; the normal force acts perpendicular to the plane and has a horizontal component. So BOTH F_N and F_f contribute to the centripetal force.

25. D—The mass's acceleration has two components here. Some acceleration must be centripetal (i.e., toward the anchor) because the mass's path is circular. But the mass is also speeding up, so it must have a tangential component of acceleration toward point *B*. The vector sum of these two components must be in between the anchor and point *B*.

26. B—The free-body diagram for a person includes F_N toward the center of the circle, mg down, and the force of friction up:

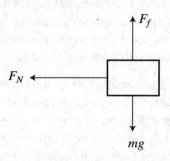

Because the person is not sliding down, $mg = F_f$. And because the motion of the person is circular, the normal force is a centripetal force, so $F_N = mv^2/r$. The force of friction by definition is μF_N. Combining these equations, we have $mg = \mu mv^2/r$; solve for v to get answer choice B. Note: Without any calculation, you could recognize that only choices A and B have units of speed, so you would have had a good chance at getting the answer right just by guessing one of these two!

27. B—Use Newton's second law for rotation, $\tau_{net} = I a$. The only torque about the pivot is the rod's weight, acting at the rod's center; this torque is thus $mgL/2$. So the angular acceleration, a, of the rod is $mgL/2I$. But the question asks for a linear acceleration, $a = ra$, where r is the distance to the center of rotation. That distance here is $L/2$. So combining, you get $a = (L/2)(mgL/2I) = mgL^2/4I$.

28. D—We cannot use rotational kinematics here because the net torque, and thus the angular acceleration, is not constant. Use conservation of energy instead. The potential energy at the release point is $mg(L/2)$ ($L/2$ because the rod's center of mass is that far vertically above its lowest point). This potential energy is converted entirely into rotational kinetic energy $\frac{1}{2}I\omega^2$. The rod's angular velocity ω is equal to $v/(L/2)$, where v is the linear speed of the center of mass that we're solving for. Plugging in, you get $mgL/2 = \frac{1}{2}I(v^2/[L/2]^2)$. Solving for v, choice D emerges from the mathematics.

29. D—Choose any point at all as the fulcrum; say, the center of mass. Rod *B* supports 500 N, and is located 20 cm from the fulcrum, producing a total counterclockwise torque of 10,000 N·cm. Rod *A* also supports 500 N; call its distance from the fulcrum "*x*". So 10,000 = 500*x*, and *x* = 20 cm. This means Rod *A* is located 20 cm left of the center of mass, or 50 cm from the left edge.

30. B—The period of a mass on a spring is

$$2\pi\sqrt{\frac{m}{k}}$$

with the mass under the square root. So when the mass is quadrupled, the period is only multiplied by two. The total mechanical energy is the sum of potential plus kinetic energy. At the greatest displacement from equilibrium (i.e., at the amplitude), the mass's speed is zero and all energy is potential; potential energy of a spring is $\frac{1}{2}kx^2$ and does not depend on mass. So, because the amplitude of oscillation remains the same, the total mechanical energy does not change.

31. D—The maximum potential energy of the mass is at the amplitude, and equal to $\frac{1}{2}kA^2$. This is entirely converted to kinetic energy at the equilibrium position, where the speed is maximum. So set $\frac{1}{2}kA^2 = \frac{1}{2}mv_{max}^2$. Solving for v_{max}, you get choice D. (Note: Only choices C and D have units of velocity! So guess between these if you have to!)

32. B—The bottle's lowest position is $x = -A$, and its highest position is $x = +A$. When $t = 0$, cos (0) = 1 and the bottle is at $x = +A$. So, find the time when the cosine function goes to −1. This is when $\omega t = \pi$, so $t = \pi/\omega$.

33. B—Don't try to calculate the answer by saying $mg = GMm/r^2$! Not only would you have had to memorize the mass of the Earth, but you have no calculator and you only have a minute or so, anyway. So think: the acceleration must be less than 9.8 m/s², because that value is calculated at the surface of the Earth, and the Shuttle is farther from Earth's center than that. But the added height of 300 km is a small fraction (~5%) of the Earth's radius. So the gravitational acceleration will not be THAT much less. The best choice is thus 8.9 m/s². (By the way, acceleration is not zero—if it were, the Shuttle would be moving in a straight line, and not orbiting.)

34. B—The orbit can no longer be circular—circular orbits demand a specific velocity. Because the satellite gains speed while at its original distance from the planet, the orbit is now elliptical. Because the direction of the satellite's motion is still tangent to the former circular path, in the next instant the satellite will be farther from Earth than at point *P*, eliminating answer choice A. The satellite will not "fly off into space" unless it reaches escape velocity, which cannot be 1% greater than the speed necessary for a low circular orbit.

35. D—Kepler's third law states that for all planets in the same system, their period of orbit squared is proportional to the average distance from the sun cubed. Using units of years and AU, for Earth, $(1 \text{ year})^2 = (1 \text{ AU})^3$. For Mercury, we have $(\frac{1}{5} \text{ year})^2 = (? \text{ AU})^3$. Solving for the question mark, you find that the distance from Mercury to the sun is the cube root of $\frac{1}{25}$ AU, which is closest to $\frac{1}{3}$ AU.

Physics C—Mechanics Practice Exam 1—Free-Response Solutions

Notes on grading your free-response section

For answers that are numerical, or in equation form:

*For each part of the problem, look to see if you got the right answer. If you did, and you showed any reasonable (and correct) work, give yourself full credit for that part. It's okay if you didn't explicitly show EVERY step, as long as some steps are indicated and you got the right answer. However:

*If you got the WRONG answer, then look to see if you earned partial credit. Give yourself points for each step toward the answer as indicated in the rubrics below. Without the correct answer, you must show each intermediate step explicitly in order to earn the point for that step. (See why it's so important to show your work?)

*If you're off by a decimal place or two, not to worry—you get credit anyway, as long as your approach to the problem was legitimate. This isn't a math test. You're not being evaluated on your rounding and calculator-use skills.

*You do not have to simplify expressions in variables all the way. Square roots in the denominator are fine; fractions in nonsimplified form are fine. As long as you've solved properly for the requested variable, and as long as your answer is algebraically equivalent to the rubric's, you earn credit.

*Wrong, but consistent: Often you need to use the answer to part (a) in order to solve part (b). But you might have the answer to part (a) wrong. If you follow the correct procedure for part (b), plugging in your incorrect answer, then you will usually receive *full credit* for part (b). The major exceptions are when your answer to part (a) is unreasonable (say, a car moving at 10^5 m/s, or a distance between two cars equal to 10^{-100} meters), or when your answer to part (a) makes the rest of the problem trivial or irrelevant.

For answers that require justification:

*Obviously your answer will not match the rubric word-for-word. If the general gist is there, you get credit.

*But the reader is not allowed to interpret for the student. If your response is vague or ambiguous, you will NOT get credit.

*If your response consists of both correct and incorrect parts, you will usually not receive credit. It is not possible to try two answers, hoping that one of them is right. ☺ (See why it's so important to be concise?)

CM 1

(a)

1 pt: Write Newton's second law for the direction along the plane for each block.
For the right block, $T - mg\sin 30° = ma$
For the left block $mg\sin 60° - T = ma$

1 pt: for including consistent directions for both equations

1 pt: for including a trig function in both equations, even if it's the wrong function

1 pt: solve these equations simultaneously to get the acceleration

1 pt: answer is $a = 1.8$ m/s^2. (An answer of $a = -1.8$ m/s^2 is incorrect because the magnitude of a vector cannot be negative.)
(Alternatively you can just recognize that $mg\sin 60°$ pulls left, while $mg\sin 30°$ pulls right, and use Newton's second law directly on the combined system. Be careful, though, because the mass of the ENTIRE system is 10 kg, not 5 kg!)

(b)

i.

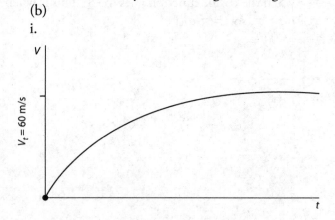

1 pt: for a graph that starts at $v = 0$, has exponential form, and sort of levels off to a maximum speed.

1 pt: for indicating that the asymptote represents the terminal speed, or 60 m/s.

ii.

1 pt: since acceleration is dv/dt, we have a differential equation: $dv/dt = 1.8 - 0.03v$. We need to find the expression for v.

1 pt: In a differential equation where the derivative is proportional to the function itself, the solution has an exponential term.

1 pt: In the solution e is raised to the $-0.03t$ power because 0.03 is what multiplies the v.

1 pt: Since the blocks start at rest and speed up, the solution includes $(1 - e^{-0.03t})$ not just $e^{-0.03t}$. [Those previous three points could be earned for a direct algorithmic solution for v, using separation of variables and integration.]

1 pt: For large t, the exponential term goes to zero, and so $(1 - e^{-0.03t})$ should be multiplied by the terminal velocity. That's why there's an asymptote.

(c)

1 pt: The terminal velocity is when acceleration equals zero.

1 pt: solve the equation $0 = 1.8 - 0.03v$. (You get 60 m/s.)

(d)

1 pt: The blocks only reach this terminal speed after a long time. An incline in a physics lab can't be more than a couple of meters long, meaning the blocks don't have the time and space to reach 60 m/s.

CM 2

F_N

mg

(a)

1 pt: The weight of the ball acts down.

1 pt: The normal force acts up and left, perpendicular to the surface of the glass.

1 pt: No other forces act.

(b)

1 pt: The normal force can be broken into vertical and horizontal components, where the vertical is $F_N \cos \theta$ and the horizontal is $F_N \sin \theta$. (The vertical direction goes with cosine here because θ is measured from the vertical.)

1 pt: The net vertical force is zero because the ball doesn't rise or fall on the glass. Setting up forces equal to down, $F_N \cos \theta = mg$.

1 pt: The horizontal force is a centripetal force, so $F_N \sin \theta = mv^2/r \sin \theta$.

1 pt: For using $r \sin \theta$ and not just r. (Why? Because you need to use the radius of the actual circular motion, which is not the same as the radius of the sphere.)

1 pt: The tangential speed "v" is the circumference of the circular motion divided by the period. Since period is $1/f$, and because the radius of the circular motion is $r \sin \theta$, this speed $v = 2\pi r \sin \theta f$.

1 pt: Now divide the vertical and horizontal force equations to get rid of the F_N term:

$$\sin \theta / \cos \theta = v^2 / r \sin \theta g.$$

1 pt: Plug in the speed and the $\sin \theta$ terms cancel, leaving $\cos \theta = g / 4\pi^2 r f^2$.

1 pt: Plugging in the given values (including $r = 0.08$ m), $\theta = 83°$.

(c)

1 pt: From part (a), the linear speed is $2\pi r \sin \theta f$.

1 pt: Plugging in values, the speed is 2.5 m/s. (If you didn't get the point in part (a) for figuring out how to calculate linear speed, but you do it right here, then you can earn the point here.)

(d)

1 pt: The angle will not be affected.

1 pt: Since the mass of the ball does not appear in the equation to calculate the angle in part (b), the mass does not affect the angle.

CM 3

F_{net}

(a)

1 pt: The net force is at an angle down and to the left, perpendicular to the rod.

1 pt: Because the ball is instantaneously at rest, the direction of the velocity in the next instant must also be the direction of the acceleration; this direction is along the arc of the ball's motion.

(b)

1 pt: The magnitude of the net force is $mg \sin \theta$.

1 pt: It's easiest to use a limiting argument: When $\theta = 90°$, then the net force would be simply the weight of the ball, mg. $mg \sin 90° = mg$, while $mg \cos 90° = $ zero; hence the correct answer.

(c)

1 pt: The force on the mass is $-mg \sin \theta$, the negative arising because the force is always opposite the displacement.

1 pt: Potential energy is derived from force by

$$U = -\int F dx.$$

1 pt: The distance displaced $x = L\theta$.

1 pt: The differential dx becomes $L\, d\theta$.

1 pt: The integral becomes $\int mgL \sin \theta \, d\theta$, which evaluates to $-mgL \cos \theta$. (Here the constant of integration can be taken to be any value at all because the zero of potential energy can be chosen arbitrarily.)

[Alternate solution: Using geometry, it can be found that the height of the bob above the lowest point is $L - L \cos \theta$. Thus, the potential energy is $mgh = mg(L - L \cos \theta)$. This gives the same answer, but has defined the arbitrary constant of integration as mgL.]

(d)

1 pt: The graph should look like some sort of sine or cosine function, oscillating smoothly. The graph may be shifted up or down and still receive full credit.

1 pt: The graph should have an amplitude of mgL, though the graph can be shifted arbitrarily up or down on the vertical axis.

1 pt: The graph should have a minimum at $\theta = 0$.

1 pt: The graph should have a maximum at $\theta = 180°$.

(e)

1 pt: For simple harmonic motion, the restoring force must be linearly proportional to the displacement, like $F = -kx$. This yields an energy function that is quadratic: $-(-kx) \cdot dx$ integrates to give $U = \frac{1}{2}kx^2$. The graph of the energy of a simple harmonic oscillator is, thus, parabolic.

1 pt: Near the $\theta = 0$ position, the graph in part (e) is shaped much like a parabola, only deviating from a parabolic shape at large angles; so the pendulum is a simple harmonic oscillator as long as the energy graph approximates a parabola.

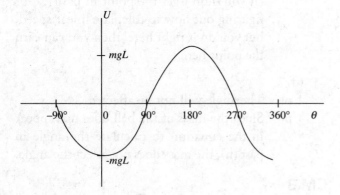

AP Physics C—Mechanics
Full Exam Scoring

Multiple Choice: Number Correct_____(35 max)

Free Response: Question 1_____(15 max)
Question 2_____(15 max)
Question 3_____(15 max)

Total Free Response_____(45 max)

$1.286 \times$ Multiple Choice + Free Response = Raw Score_____(90 max)

59–90	5
45–58	4
35–44	3
23–34	2
0–22	1

Physics C—Electricity and Magnetism Practice Exam 1— Multiple-Choice Solutions

1. **B**—An electric field exists regardless of the amount of charge placed in it, and regardless of whether any charge at all is placed in it. So both experimenters must measure the same field (though they will measure different forces on their test charges).

2. **D**—You could use Gauss's law to show that the field outside the sphere has to decrease as $1/r^2$, eliminating choices B and E. But it's easier just to remember that an important result of Gauss's law is that the *electric field inside a conductor is always zero everywhere,* so D is the only possibility.

3. **B**—While in the region between the plates, the negatively charged electron is attracted to the positive plate, so bends upward. But after leaving the plates, there is no more force acting on the electron. Thus, the electron continues in motion in a straight line by Newton's first law.

4. **C**—This is a Newton's third law problem! The force of *A* on *B* is equal (and opposite) to the force of *B* on *A*. Or, we can use Coulomb's law: The field due to *A* is $k(2Q)/(4 \text{ m})^2$. The force on *B* is $QE = k2QQ/(4 \text{ m})^2$. We can do the same analysis finding the field due to *B* and the force on *A* to get the same result.

5. **A**—The charge is in equilibrium, so the horizontal component of the tension must equal the electric force. This horizontal tension is 0.1 N times sin 30° (not cosine because 30° was measured from the *vertical*), or 0.05 N. The electric force is *qE,* where *q* is 0.002 C. So the electric field is 0.050 N/0.002 C. Reduce the expression by moving the decimal to get 50/2, or 25 N/C.

6. **D**—The answer could, in principle, be found using the integral form of Coulomb's law. But you can't do that on a one-minute multiple-choice problem. The electric field will point down the page—the field due to a positive charge points away from the charge, and there's an equal amount of charge producing a rightward field as a leftward field, so horizontal fields cancel. So, is the answer B or D? Choice B is not correct because electric fields add as vectors. Only the vertical component of the field due to each little charge element contributes to the net electric field, so the net field must be *less than* kQ/R^2.

7. **A**—Use the symmetry of the situation to see the answer. Because the infinitely large plane looks the same on the up side as the down side, its electric field must look the same, too—the field must point away from the plane and have the same value.

8. **C**—Another way to look at this question is, "Where would a small positive charge end up if released near these charges?" because positive charges seek the smallest potential. The positive charge would be repelled by the +2*Q* charge and attracted to the −*Q* charges, so would end up at point *C*. Or, know that potential due to a point charge is *kq/r*. Point *C* is closest to both −*Q* charges, so the *r* terms will be smallest, and the negative contribution to the potential will be largest; point *C* is farthest from the +2*Q* charge, so the *r* term will be large, and the positive contribution to the potential will be smallest.

9. **A**—A positive charge is forced from high to low potential, which is generally to the left; and the force on a positive charge is in the direction of the electric field. At point *P* itself the electric field is directly to the left because an electric field is always perpendicular to equipotential surfaces.

10. **C**—The charge on the metal sphere distributes uniformly on its surface. Because the nonconducting sphere also has a uniform charge distribution, by symmetry the electric fields will cancel to zero at the center. Outside the spheres we can use Gauss's law: $E \cdot A = Q_{enclosed}/\varepsilon_o$. Because the charge enclosed by a Gaussian surface outside either sphere will be the same, and the spheres are the same size, the electric field will be the same everywhere outside either sphere. But within the sphere? A Gaussian surface drawn inside the conducting sphere encloses no charge, while a Gaussian surface inside the nonconducting sphere does enclose some charge. The fields inside must *not* be equal.

11. **A**—That's what Gauss's law says: net flux through a closed surface is equal to the charge enclosed divided by ε_o. Though Gauss's law is only *useful* when all charge within or without a Gaussian surface is symmetrically distributed, Gauss's law is *valid* always.

12. **B**—The electric field at the center of the ring is zero because the field caused by any charge element is canceled by the field due to the charge on the other side of the ring. The electric field decreases as $1/r^2$ by Coulomb's law, so a long distance away from the ring the field goes to zero. The field is nonzero near the ring, though, because each charge element creates a field pointing away from the ring, resulting in a field always along the axis.

13. **C**—Capacitance of a parallel-plate capacitor is $\varepsilon_o A/d$, where A is the area of the plates, and d is the separation between plates. To halve the capacitance, we must halve the area or double the plate separation. The plate separation in the diagram is labeled c, so double distance c.

14. **E**—We are told that the capacitors are identical, so their capacitances must be equal. They are hooked in parallel, meaning the voltages across them must be equal as well. By $Q = CV$, the charge stored by each must also be equal.

15. **E**—First determine the voltage of the battery by $Q = CV$. This gives $V = 600\ \mu C/2\ \mu F = 300$ V. This voltage is hooked to the three series capacitors, whose equivalent capacitance is 6 μF (series capacitors add inversely, like parallel resistors). So the total charge stored now is (6 μF)(300 V) = 1800 μC. This charge is *not* split evenly among the capacitors, though! Just as the current through series resistors is the same through each and equal to the total current through the circuit, the charge on series capacitors is the same and equal to the total.

16. **B**—The charge does reside on the surface, and, if the conductor is alone, will distribute evenly. But, if there's another nearby charge, then this charge can repel or attract the charge on the sphere, causing a redistribution.

17. **D**—The voltage must stay the same because the battery by definition provides a constant voltage. Closing the switch adds a parallel branch to the network of resistors. Adding a parallel resistor *reduces* the total resistance. By Ohm's law, if voltage stays the same and resistance decreases, total current must increase.

18. **C**—The time constant for an RC circuit is equal to RC. The resistance used is the resistance encountered by charge that's flowing to the capacitor; in this case, 40 Ω. So $RC = 20$ s.

19. **E**—Assume that the current runs clockwise in the circuit, and use Kirchoff's loop rule. Start with the 7-V battery and trace the circuit with the current: $+ 7V - I(3\Omega) + 3V - I(2\Omega) = 0$. Solve for I to get 2.0 A.

20. **C**—The intrinsic property of the light bulb is *resistance*; the power dissipated by a bulb depends on its voltage and current. When the bulbs are connected to the 100-V source, we can use the expression for power $P = V^2/R$ to see that the bulb rated at 50 watts has twice the resistance of the other bulb. Now in series, the bulbs carry the same current. Power is also I^2R; thus the 50-watt bulb with twice the resistance dissipates twice the power, and is twice as bright.

21. E—The electron bends downward by the right-hand rule for a charge in a B field—point to the right, curl fingers into the page, and the thumb points up the page. But the electron's negative charge changes the force to down the page. The path is a circle because the direction of the force continually changes, always pointing perpendicular to the electron's velocity. Thus, the force on the electron is a centripetal force.

22. A—This is one of the important consequences of Ampere's law. The magnetic field inside the donut is always along the axis of the donut, so the symmetry demands of Ampere's law are met. If we draw an "Amperian Loop" around point P but inside r_1, this loop encloses no current; thus the magnetic field must be zero.

23. C—The magnetic field due to the wire at the position of the electron is into the page. Now use the other right-hand rule, the one for the force on a charged particle in a magnetic field. If the charge moves down the page, then the force on a positive charge would be to the right, but the force on a (negative) electron would be left, toward the wire.

24. C—A positive charge experiences a force in the direction of an electric field, and perpendicular to a magnetic field; but the direction of a force is not necessarily the direction of motion.

25. A—The electric field due to *any* finite-sized charge distribution drops off as $1/r^2$ a long distance away because if you go far enough away, the charge looks like a point charge. This is not true for infinite charge distributions, though. The magnetic field due to an infinitely long wire is given by

$$\frac{\mu_\circ I}{2\pi r}$$

not proportional to $1/r^2$; the magnetic field produced by a wire around a torus is zero outside the torus by Ampere's law.

26. C—The magnetic field produced by a single loop of wire at the center of the loop is directly out of the loop. A solenoid is a conglomeration of many loops in a row, producing a magnetic field that is uniform and along the axis of the solenoid. So, the proton will be traveling parallel to the magnetic field. By $F = qvB \sin\theta$, the angle between the field and the velocity is zero, producing no force on the proton. The proton continues its straight-line motion by Newton's first law.

27. E—By the right-hand rule for the force on a charged particle in a magnetic field, particle C must be neutral, particle B must be positively charged, and particle A must be negatively charged. Charge B must be more massive than charge A because it resists the change in its motion more than A. A proton is positively charged and more massive than the electron; the neutron is not charged.

28. E—The force on the positive charge is upward; the force on the negative charge is downward. These forces will tend to rotate the dipole clockwise, so only A or E could be right. Because the charges and velocities are equal, the magnetic force on each $= qvB$ and is the same. So, there is no net force on the dipole. (Yes, no net force, even though it continues to move to the left.)

29. D—The centripetal force keeping the electrons in a circle is provided by the magnetic force. So set $qvB = mv^2/r$. Solve to get $r = (mv)/(qB)$. Just look at orders of magnitude now: $r = (10^{-31}\text{ kg})(10^7\text{m/s})/(10^{-19}\text{ C})(10^{-5}\text{ T})$. This gives $r = 10^{24}/10^{24} = 10^0$ m ~ 1 m.

30. E—An element of current produces a magnetic field that wraps around the current element, pointing out of the page above the current and into the page below. But right in front (or anywhere along the axis of the current), the current element produces no magnetic field at all.

31. D—A long way from the hole, the magnet produces very little flux, and that flux doesn't change much, so very little current is induced. As the north end approaches the hole, the magnetic field points down. The flux is *increasing* because the field through the wire gets stronger with the approach of the magnet; so, point your right thumb upward (in the direction of *decreasing* flux) and curl your fingers. You find the current flows counterclockwise, defined as positive. Only A or D could be correct. Now consider what happens when the magnet leaves the loop. The south end descends away from the loop. The magnetic field still points down, into the south end of the magnet, but now the flux is *decreasing*. So point your right thumb down (in the direction of decreasing flux) and curl your fingers. Current now flows clockwise, as indicated in choice D. (While the magnet is going through the loop, current goes to zero because the magnetic field of the bar magnet is reasonably constant near the center of the magnet.)

32. A—You remember the equation for the induced EMF in a moving rectangular loop, $\varepsilon = Blv$. Here l represents the length of the wire that doesn't change within the field; dimension a in the diagram. So the answer is either A or C. To find the direction of induced current, use Lenz's law: The field points out of the page, but the flux through the loop is *increasing* as more of the loop enters the field. So, point your right thumb into the page (in the direction of decreasing flux) and curl your fingers; you find the current is clockwise, or left to right across the resistor.

33. D—Start by finding the direction of the induced current in the wire using Lenz's law: the magnetic field is out of the page. The flux *increases* because the field strength increases. So point your right thumb into the page, and curl your fingers to find the current flowing clockwise, or south in the wire. Now use the right-hand rule for the force on moving charges in a magnetic field (remembering that a current is the flow of positive charge). Point down the page, curl your fingers out of the page, and the force must be to the west.

34. C—There is clearly nonzero flux because the field does pass through the wire loop. The flux is not BA, though, because the field does not go *straight* through the loop—the field hits the loop at an angle. So is the answer $BA \cos 30°$, using the angle of the plane; or $BA \cos 60°$, using the angle from the vertical? To figure it out, consider the extreme case. If the incline were at zero degrees, there would be zero flux through the loop. Then the flux would be $BA \cos 90°$, because $\cos 90°$ is zero, and $\cos 0°$ is one. So don't use the angle of the plane, use the angle from the vertical, $BA \cos 60°$.

35. C—The inductor resists changes in current. But after a long time, the current reaches steady state, meaning the current does not change; thus the inductor, after a long time, might as well be just a straight wire. The battery will still provide current I, of which half goes through each equal resistor.

Physics C—Electricity and Magnetism Practice
Exam 1—Free-Response Solutions

E&M 1

(a)

1 pt: Inside a conductor, the electric field must always be zero. $E = 0$.

1 pt: Because we have spherical symmetry, use Gauss's law.

1 pt: The area of a Gaussian surface in this region is $4\pi r^2$. The charge enclosed by this surface is Q.

1 pt: So, $E = Q_{enclosed}/\varepsilon_o A = Q/4\pi \varepsilon_o r^2$.

1 pt: Inside a conductor, the electric field must always be zero. $E = 0$.

2 pts: Just as in part 2, use Gauss's law, but now the charge enclosed is $3Q$. $E = 3Q/4\pi \varepsilon_o r^2$.

(b)

1 pt: $-Q$ is on the inner surface.

1 pt: $+3Q$ is on the outer surface.

1 pt: Because $E = 0$ inside the outer shell, a Gaussian surface inside this shell must enclose zero charge, so $-Q$ must be on the inside surface to cancel the $+Q$ on the small sphere. Then to keep the total charge of the shell equal to $+2Q$, $+3Q$ must go to the outer surface.

(c)

1 pt: Because we have spherical symmetry, the potential due to both spheres is $3Q/4\pi \varepsilon_o r$, with potential equal to zero an infinite distance away.

1 pt: So at position R_3, the potential is $3Q/4\pi \varepsilon_o R_3$. (Since $E = 0$ inside the shell, V is the same value everywhere in the shell.)

(d)

1 pt: Integrate the electric field between R_1 and R_2 to get $V = Q/4\pi \varepsilon_o r + a$ constant of integration.

1 pt: To find that constant, we know that $V(R_2)$ was found in part (c), and is $3Q/4\pi \varepsilon_o R_3$. Thus, the constant is

$$\frac{3Q}{4\pi\varepsilon_o R_3} - \frac{Q}{4\pi\varepsilon_o R_2}.$$

1 pt: Then, potential at $R_1 = Q/4\pi \varepsilon_o R_1 +$ the constant of integration.

E&M 2

(a)

1 pt: The series capacitors add inversely,

$$\frac{1}{4\ \mu F} + \frac{1}{12\ \mu F} = \frac{1}{C_{eq}},$$

so C_{eq} for the series capacitors is 3 μF.

1 pt: The parallel capacitor just adds in algebraically, so the equivalent capacitance for the whole system is 5 μF.

(b)

1 pt: After a long time, the resistor is irrelevant; no current flows because the fully charged capacitors block direct current.

1 pt: The voltage across C_3 is 10 V (because there's no voltage drop across the resistor without any current).

1 pt: By $Q = CV$ the charge on C_3 is 20 μC.

1 pt: Treating C_1 and C_2 in series; the equivalent capacitance is 3 μF, the voltage is 10 V (in parallel with C_3).

1 pt: The charge on the equivalent capacitance of C_1 and C_2 is 30 μC; thus the charge on $C_1 = 30$ μC, and the charge on C_2 is also 30 μC (charge on series capacitors is the same).

1 pt: Using $Q = CV$, the voltage across C_1 is 7.5 V.

1 pt: Using $Q = CV$, the voltage across C_2 is 2.5 V.

(c)

1 pt: For a graph that starts at $Q = 0$.

1 pt: For a graph that asymptotically approaches 20 μC (or whatever charge was calculated for C_3 in part b).

1 pt: For calculating the time constant of the circuit, $RC = 5$ s.

1 pt: For the graph reaching about 63% of its maximum charge after one time constant.

(d)

1 pt: For recognizing that the voltage does not change.

1 pt: For explaining that if voltage changed, then Kirchoff's voltage rule would not be valid around a loop including C_3 and the battery (or explaining that voltage is the same across parallel components, so if one is disconnected the other's voltage is unaffected).

E&M 3

(a)

1 pt: For placing the wire along a north–south line.

1 pt: The wire could be placed above the compass, with the current traveling due north. (The wire also could be placed underneath the compass, with current traveling due south.) (Points can also be earned for an alternative correct solution: for example, the wire could be placed perpendicular to the face of the compass (just south of it), with the current running up.)

(b)

1 pt: The B field due to Earth plus the B field caused by the wire, when added together as vectors, must give a resultant direction of 48° west of north.

1 pt: Placing these vectors tail-to-tip, as shown below, $\tan 48° = B_{wire}/B_{Earth}$.

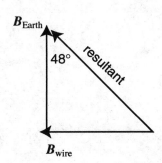

1 pt: So $B_{wire} = B_{Earth}\tan 48° = 5.6 \times 10^{-5}$ T.

(c)

1 pt: The magnetic field due to a long, straight, current-carrying wire is given by

$$B = \frac{\mu_o I}{2\pi r},$$

where r is the distance from the wire to the field point, represented in this problem by d.

1 pt: So B is proportional to $1/d$; this results in a hyperbolic graph.

1 pt: This graph should be asymptotic to both the vertical and horizontal axes.

(d)

1 pt: Place $1/d$ on the horizontal axis.

2 pts: The equation for the field due the wire can be written

$$B = \left(\frac{\mu_o I}{2\pi}\right)\left(\frac{1}{d}\right).$$

Everything in the first set of parentheses is constant. So, this equation is of the form $y = mx$, which is the equation of a line, if $1/d$ is put on the x-axis of the graph. (1 point can be earned for a partially complete explanation. On this problem, no points can be earned for justification if the answer is incorrect.)

(e)

1 pt: The slope of the graph, from the equation above, is

$$\frac{\mu_o I}{2\pi}.$$

1 pt: For plugging in values correctly, including 0.5 A or 500 mA.

1 pt: For units on the slope equivalent to magnetic field times distance (i.e., T·m, T·cm, mT·m, etc.).

1 pt: For a correct answer, complete with correct units: 1.0×10^{-7} Tm, or 1.0×10^{-4} mT·m.

AP Physics C—Electricity and Magnetism
Full Exam Scoring

Multiple-Choice: Number Correct_____(35 max)

Free-Response: Question 1_____(15 max)
                 Question 2_____(15 max)
                 Question 3_____(15 max)

Total Free-Response_____(45 max)

$1.286 \times$ Multiple-Choice + Free-Response = Raw Score_____(90 max)

56–90	5
44–55	4
32–43	3
23–34	2
0–22	1

Physics C—Mechanics Practice Exam 2—Multiple-Choice Questions

ANSWER SHEET

1 Ⓐ Ⓑ Ⓒ Ⓓ Ⓔ
2 Ⓐ Ⓑ Ⓒ Ⓓ Ⓔ
3 Ⓐ Ⓑ Ⓒ Ⓓ Ⓔ
4 Ⓐ Ⓑ Ⓒ Ⓓ Ⓔ
5 Ⓐ Ⓑ Ⓒ Ⓓ Ⓔ
6 Ⓐ Ⓑ Ⓒ Ⓓ Ⓔ
7 Ⓐ Ⓑ Ⓒ Ⓓ Ⓔ
8 Ⓐ Ⓑ Ⓒ Ⓓ Ⓔ
9 Ⓐ Ⓑ Ⓒ Ⓓ Ⓔ
10 Ⓐ Ⓑ Ⓒ Ⓓ Ⓔ
11 Ⓐ Ⓑ Ⓒ Ⓓ Ⓔ
12 Ⓐ Ⓑ Ⓒ Ⓓ Ⓔ

13 Ⓐ Ⓑ Ⓒ Ⓓ Ⓔ
14 Ⓐ Ⓑ Ⓒ Ⓓ Ⓔ
15 Ⓐ Ⓑ Ⓒ Ⓓ Ⓔ
16 Ⓐ Ⓑ Ⓒ Ⓓ Ⓔ
17 Ⓐ Ⓑ Ⓒ Ⓓ Ⓔ
18 Ⓐ Ⓑ Ⓒ Ⓓ Ⓔ
19 Ⓐ Ⓑ Ⓒ Ⓓ Ⓔ
20 Ⓐ Ⓑ Ⓒ Ⓓ Ⓔ
21 Ⓐ Ⓑ Ⓒ Ⓓ Ⓔ
22 Ⓐ Ⓑ Ⓒ Ⓓ Ⓔ
23 Ⓐ Ⓑ Ⓒ Ⓓ Ⓔ
24 Ⓐ Ⓑ Ⓒ Ⓓ Ⓔ

25 Ⓐ Ⓑ Ⓒ Ⓓ Ⓔ
26 Ⓐ Ⓑ Ⓒ Ⓓ Ⓔ
27 Ⓐ Ⓑ Ⓒ Ⓓ Ⓔ
28 Ⓐ Ⓑ Ⓒ Ⓓ Ⓔ
29 Ⓐ Ⓑ Ⓒ Ⓓ Ⓔ
30 Ⓐ Ⓑ Ⓒ Ⓓ Ⓔ
31 Ⓐ Ⓑ Ⓒ Ⓓ Ⓔ
32 Ⓐ Ⓑ Ⓒ Ⓓ Ⓔ
33 Ⓐ Ⓑ Ⓒ Ⓓ Ⓔ
34 Ⓐ Ⓑ Ⓒ Ⓓ Ⓔ
35 Ⓐ Ⓑ Ⓒ Ⓓ Ⓔ

Physics C—Mechanics Practice Exam 2—Multiple-Choice Questions

Time: 45 minutes. You may refer to the constants sheet and the equation sheet, both of which are found in the appendix. You may use a calculator.

1. A jet airplane has mass 300,000 kg. In order to take off, it accelerates uniformly over a horizontal distance of 3000 m, reaching a top speed of 80 m/s. Neglecting drag forces, which of the following is closest to the average horizontal force provided by the airplane's engines?

    (A) 10^6 N
    (B) 10^4 N
    (C) 10^3 N
    (D) 10^5 N
    (E) 10^0 N

2. On a one-dimensional track, a large cart in motion collides with a small cart at rest. The carts bounce off each other. Which of the following is true about linear momentum and kinetic energy?

    (A) Momentum may or may not be conserved; kinetic energy may or may not be conserved.
    (B) Momentum must be conserved; kinetic energy must be conserved.
    (C) Momentum may or may not be conserved; kinetic energy must be conserved.
    (D) Momentum must be conserved; kinetic energy may or may not be conserved.
    (E) Momentum must be conserved; kinetic energy must not be conserved.

3. The escape velocity for a rocket from Earth's surface is 11 km/s. What is the escape velocity for a rocket on the surface of a planet whose mass is the same as Earth's but whose radius is half that of Earth?

    (A) 2.8 km/s
    (B) 6.5 km/s
    (C) 7.8 km/s
    (D) 11 km/s
    (E) 15.4 km/s

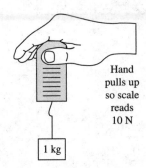

Hand pulls up so scale reads 10 N

1 kg

4. A 1-kg block hangs from a string at rest. A person holds a spring scale attached vertically to the string, pulling upward so that the scale reads 10 N. What is the tension in the string?

    (A) 19 N
    (B) 9 N
    (C) 0 N
    (D) 10 N
    (E) 20 N

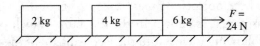

2 kg — 4 kg — 6 kg → $F = 24$ N

5. Three blocks A, B, and C are connected by taut light strings on a frictionless surface, as shown earlier. A rightward force $F = 24$ N is applied to block C. Which of the following correctly ranks the accelerations a_A, a_B, and a_C of each block?

    (A) $a_A > a_B > a_C$
    (B) $a_C > a_B > a_A$
    (C) $a_A = a_B > a_C$
    (D) $a_A = a_B = a_C$
    (E) $a_C > a_B = a_A$

6. A 250-g cart rolls to the right at 100 cm/s and collides with a 500-g cart, which is initially rolling left at 75 cm/s. The carts stick together. What is the speed of the carts right after they collide?

    (A) 75 cm/s
    (B) 83 cm/s
    (C) 25 cm/s
    (D) 17 cm/s
    (E) 50 cm/s

GO ON TO THE NEXT PAGE

7. An object of mass m is constrained to move along the x-axis only. It experiences a potential energy function $U = \frac{1}{2}kx^2 - bx$, where U is in joules and x is in meters. Which of the following represents the net force F on the object?

(A) $b - kx$

(B) $kx - b$

(C) $\frac{kx^3}{6} - bx^2$

(D) $bx^2 - \frac{kx^3}{6}$

(E) $kx + b$

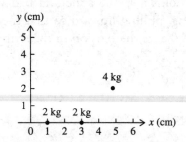

8. Three objects, of mass 2 kg, 2 kg, and 4 kg, are arranged as shown in the diagram. Which of the following is closest to the y-coordinate of the three objects' center of mass?

(A) 2.0 cm

(B) 3.5 cm

(C) 1.5 cm

(D) 0.5 cm

(E) 1.0 cm

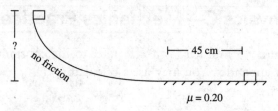

9. A block is released from rest at the top of a ramp on which friction is negligible. At the bottom of the ramp, the block encounters a rough, level surface on which the coefficient of kinetic friction with the block is 0.20. The block slides to rest after traveling 45 cm on the rough surface, as shown in the diagram. From what height vertically above the rough surface was the block released?

(A) 9 cm

(B) 22.5 cm

(C) The answer cannot be determined without knowing the mass of the block.

(D) 225 cm

(E) 90 cm

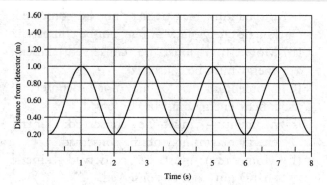

Questions 10 and 11: A 0.20-kg object is attached to a spring, which hangs vertically. A motion detector placed underneath the object records the position-time data shown earlier.

10. At which of the following times is the object's acceleration downward and at its maximum magnitude?

(A) 1.5 s

(B) 2.0 s

(C) 0.0 s

(D) 1.0 s

(E) 0.5 s

GO ON TO THE NEXT PAGE

11. What is the spring constant of the spring?

(A) 0.9 N/m
(B) 5.0 N/m
(C) 2.5 N/m
(D) 2.0 N/m
(E) 3.9 N/m

12. Which of the following quantities, if any, is a scalar quantity?

(A) A velocity of −2.0 m/s
(B) A potential energy of −2.0 J
(C) A momentum of −2.0 N·s
(D) A displacement of −2.0 m
(E) None of the above is a scalar quantity.

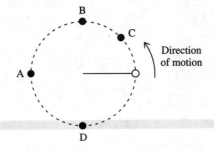

13. A ball of mass m is attached to a light string, as shown earlier. The ball is whirled counterclockwise in a vertical circle at constant speed. At which labeled position is the tension in the string largest?

(A) A
(B) B
(C) C
(D) D
(E) None of the above; the tension is constant throughout.

14. An object moves along the x-axis according to the potential energy function $U(x) = ax^2 - b$, where a and b are positive constants. Which of the following lists all of the positions in which the particle is in stable equilibrium?

(A) $x = 0$ only
(B) $x = 0$, $x = b$, and $x = -b$
(C) $x = b$ and $x = -b$
(D) $x = 0$, $x = a/b$, and $x = -a/b$
(E) $x = a/b$ and $x = -a/b$

15. A 200-W motor lifts an object at a constant speed of 0.5 m/s. The object ends up 100 m east of where it started and elevated 100 m vertically from its starting point after 20 seconds of elapsed time. What is the mass of the object?

(A) $2\sqrt{2}$ kg

(B) $4\sqrt{2}$ kg

(C) 0.2 kg

(D) 4 kg

(E) 8 kg

16. The velocity of a particle moving along the x-axis is given as a function of time by the expression $v(t) = 4t^2 - 3t + 2$, where v is in units of m/s and t in s. About how far did the particle move between $t = 0$ and $t = 2$ s?

(A) 9 m
(B) 12 m
(C) 24 m
(D) 19 m
(E) 13 m

Questions 17–19: A moon executes an elliptical orbit about its planet. Point P is where the moon is closest to the planet; point A is where the moon is farthest from the planet.

17. As the moon moves from point P to point A and then back to its original position, what happens to its angular momentum about the central planet?

(A) It increases, then decreases
(B) It decreases, then increases
(C) It decreases the entire way.
(D) It remains constant.
(E) It increases the entire way.

18. As the moon moves from point P to point A and then back to its original position, what happens to the potential energy of the moon-planet system?

(A) It increases, then decreases
(B) It decreases, then increases
(C) It decreases the entire way.
(D) It remains constant.
(E) It increases the entire way.

GO ON TO THE NEXT PAGE

19. As the planet moves from point P to point A and then back to its original position, what happens to the magnitude of the force of the moon on the planet?

(A) It increases, then decreases
(B) It decreases, then increases
(C) It decreases the entire way.
(D) It remains constant.
(E) It increases the entire way.

20. Block A has mass 4 kg; block B has mass 2 kg. Each block experiences an identical but unknown net force for a time of 3 s. Which of the following correctly compares block A's change in linear momentum Δp_A to block B's change in linear momentum Δp_B?

(A) $\Delta p_A = \Delta p_B \neq 0$
(B) $\Delta p_A = (1/12)\Delta p_B$
(C) $\Delta p_A = \Delta p_B = 0$
(D) $\Delta p_A = (1/2)\Delta p_B$
(E) $\Delta p_A = (1/6)\Delta p_B$

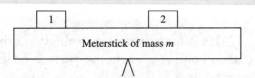

Meterstick of mass m

21. A meterstick of nonnegligible mass m is pivoted at its center, as shown. Two blocks, block 1 and block 2, are placed on top of the meterstick. When the meterstick is released from the rest at the position shown, it begins to rotate clockwise. Which of the following statements about the masses of the two blocks is correct?

(A) It cannot be determined which block has greater mass, because the lever arms associated with the torques provided by each block are different.
(B) The blocks are of equal mass, because the magnitude of the angular acceleration of each block is the same.
(C) Block 1 has greater mass, because the lever arm associated with the torque it provides is larger than that of block 2.
(D) Block 2 has greater mass, because more torque is provided by block 2 with a smaller lever arm.
(E) The blocks are of equal mass, because the meterstick's mass is not negligible.

22. In an amusement park ride, people of mass m stand with their backs to the inside of a large cylinder of radius R. The maximum coefficient of static friction between a person's clothes and the cylinder wall is μ. The cylinder rotates fast enough that the floor can drop away and the riders remain "stuck" to the wall without falling. What is the minimum period of rotation for which the riders will "stick" to the wall?

(A) $\dfrac{\mu}{Rg}$

(B) μmg

(C) $\sqrt{\dfrac{\mu}{Rg}}$

(D) $2\pi\sqrt{\dfrac{R\mu}{g}}$

(E) $2\pi\mu mg$

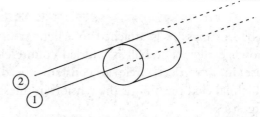

23. The solid disk shown has mass M and radius R. The rotational inertia of the disk about axis 1, which passes through the disk's center, is $(1/2)MR^2$. What is the rotational inertia of the disk about axis 2, which is tangential to the disk's edge?

(A) $(3/2)MR^2$
(B) $(2/5)MR^2$
(C) MR^2
(D) $(1/3)MR^2$
(E) $(2/3)MR^2$

GO ON TO THE NEXT PAGE

24. A 0.50-kg lab cart on a frictionless surface is attached to a spring, as shown in the figure. The rightward direction is considered positive. The spring is neither compressed nor stretched at position $x = 0$. The cart is released from rest at position $x = +0.25$ m at time $t = 0$. Which of the following graphs represents the force applied by the spring as a function of x?

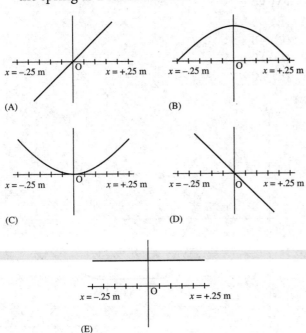

(A)   (B)

(C)   (D)

(E)

Questions 25 and 26: A ball is thrown off a cliff, with an initial velocity directed at an angle θ downward and to the right.

25. Which of the following is correct about the ball's acceleration from when the ball is released until it hits the ground?

(A) It remains constant and is directed at the angle θ.
(B) It remains constant and is directed downward.
(C) It increases and its direction changes.
(D) It increases and is directed downward.
(E) It increases and is directed at the angle θ.

26. Which of the following graphs represents the vertical position y of the ball as a function of time, where upward is the positive direction?

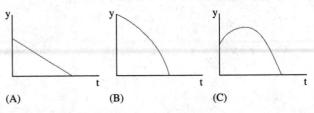

(A)   (B)   (C)

(D)   (E)

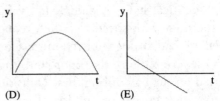

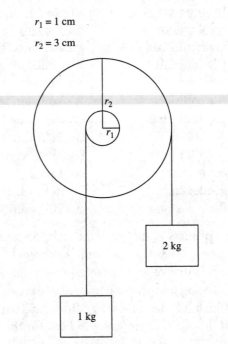

27. A double-pulley consists of pulleys of two different radii attached together such that they rotate together. The radius r_1 of the inner pulley is 1 cm, and the radius r_2 of the outer pulley is 3 cm. A 1-kg object and a 2-kg object are hung from the pulley as shown in the diagram. How much torque must be applied in order to hold the pulley at rest?

(A) 50 N·cm
(B) 7 N·cm
(C) 70 N·cm
(D) 5 N·cm
(E) 30 N·cm

GO ON TO THE NEXT PAGE

28. Identical balls A and B are thrown straight upward with initial speeds v_A and v_B, respectively. Ball A goes three times higher than ball B. What is the relationship between v_A and v_B?

(A) $v_A = 6v_B$
(B) $v_A = 9v_B$
(C) $v_A = 1.7v_B$
(D) $v_A = 2.4v_B$
(E) $v_A = 3v_B$

29. Two identical balls, A and B, fall vertically and hit the floor with speed v_1. Ball A rebounds with speed v_2; ball B does not rebound. Consider the impulse exerted on the floor and the impulse exerted on the ball during these collisions. Which case(s) cause greater magnitude of impulse?

Impulse exerted on the floor	Impulse exerted on the ball
(A) greater in ball B's collision	greater in ball B's collision
(B) greater in ball A's collision	greater in ball A's collision
(C) greater in ball A's collision	greater in ball B's collision
(D) equal in both collisions	equal in both collisions
(E) greater in ball B's collision	greater in ball A's collision

30. A cart of mass m moves to the right on a level surface along the x-axis. The only horizontal force on the cart is that of air resistance, which can be modeled as being linearly proportional to the cart's speed v. Which of the following differential equations could describe Newton's second law for this cart?

(A) $\dfrac{dv}{dt} = -\dfrac{b}{m}v$

(B) $\dfrac{dv}{dt} = \dfrac{b}{m}v$

(C) $\dfrac{dv}{dt} = g - \dfrac{b}{m}v$

(D) $\dfrac{d^2x}{dt^2} = -\dfrac{b}{m}x$

(E) $\dfrac{d^2x}{dt^2} = \dfrac{b}{m}x$

31. Train A is initially traveling east with speed 10 m/s, slowing down with acceleration 5 m/s². Train B is initially at rest a distance of 200 m from train A's starting location. Train B speeds up to the west with identical acceleration 5 m/s². How long does it take for the trains to pass each other?

(A) 80 s
(B) 5 s
(C) 40 s
(D) 10 s
(E) 20 s

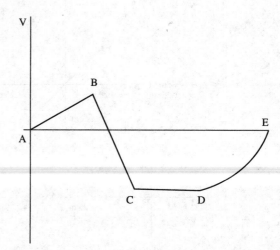

32. An object moves along the x-axis with a velocity v given as a function of time t as shown in the graph. During which section(s) of the graph is the object's acceleration constant, but not zero?

(A) AB and BC only
(B) AB, BC, and DE only
(C) CD only
(D) DE only
(E) AB only

33. A particle of mass m is released from rest at position $x = 0$ at time $t = 0$. The velocity v of the particle is given by the equation $v = \dfrac{3t^2}{m}$. Which of the following functions could represent the net force on the particle?

(A) $6t^3$
(B) t^3
(C) $3t$
(D) $6t$
(E) $(3/2)t$

GO ON TO THE NEXT PAGE

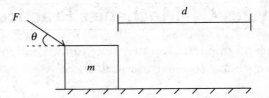

34. A ball can move to the left or right along a track, where right is considered positive. A graph of the ball's velocity as a function of time is shown. Which of the following describes the ball's motion?

(A) The ball slows down to the right, then speeds up to the right.
(B) The ball slows down to the right, then speeds up to the left.
(C) The ball speeds up and then slows down.
(D) The ball slows down to the left, then speeds up to the left.
(E) The ball slows down to the left, then speeds up to the right.

35. A block of mass m experiences a force F, which pushes down and to the right at an angle θ, as shown. The block encounters a rough surface of coefficient of kinetic friction μ. As the block moves a distance d, how much work is done by the net force on the block?

(A) $(F\cos\theta - \mu mg)d$
(B) $(F - \mu mg)d$
(C) Fd
(D) $Fd\cos\theta$
(E) $(F\cos\theta - \mu[mg + F\sin\theta])d$

STOP. End of Physics C—Mechanics Practice Exam 2—Multiple-Choice Questions

Physics C—Mechanics Practice Exam 2—Free-Response Questions

Time: 45 minutes. You may refer to the constants sheet and the equation sheet, both of which are found in the appendix. You may use a calculator.

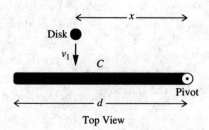

Top View

1. An end of a uniform rod of length d and mass M is attached to a frictionless horizontal surface by a frictionless pivot, as shown. Point C marks the midpoint of the rod. The rod is initially motionless, but is free to rotate about the pivot.

   (a) Derive an expression for the rotational inertia of the rod about the pivot in terms of given variables and fundamental constants.

   (b) Student 1 slides a clay disk of mass m_1 perpendicular to the rod with speed v_1, as shown. The disk sticks to the rod a distance x from the pivot. Derive an expression for the angular speed ω of the rod-disk system immediately after the collision.

   (c) Student 2 slides a rubber disk of mass m_1 perpendicular to the rod, also with speed v_1. However, this rubber disk bounces off the rod. After which collision, if either, does the rod rotate with greater angular speed?

   _____ after colliding with the clay disk
   _____ after colliding with the rubber disk
   _____ both collisions result in the same angular speed for the rod
   _____ which collision produces greater angular speed for the rod cannot be determined

   Justify your answer.

   For the following two questions, consider collisions involving the clay disk and assume $M \gg m_1$.

   (d) In order to maximize the angular speed of the rod-disk system after collision, should the disk hit the rod left of, right of, or at point C? Briefly justify your answer.

   (e) How, if at all, would your answer to (d) change if the rod's mass distribution were nonuniform, with linear mass density getting larger farther from the pivot? Justify your answer.

GO ON TO THE NEXT PAGE

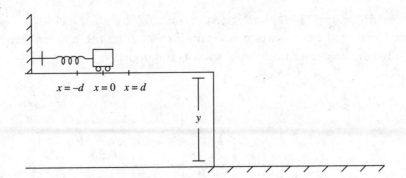

$x = -d \quad x = 0 \quad x = d$

y

2. An object of mass m is attached to a spring of spring constant k, as shown in the diagram. The object rests on a horizontal frictionless surface. The spring is compressed a distance d from the equilibrium position, where $x = 0$. The object is then released from rest to oscillate in simple harmonic motion.

(a) Derive a differential equation that can be used to solve for the block's position x as a function of time t.

(b) Write an expression for the block's position x as a function of time that satisfies the differential equation in (a) and the conditions in the problem statement.

(c) The block loses its attachment to the spring when it is at the equilibrium position while moving to the right in its oscillation. The block falls off the table a height y above the ground. Derive an expression for the horizontal distance R that the block lands from the table.

(d) Instead consider that the block lost its attachment to the spring when it was moving to the right in its oscillation, but a distance $\frac{1}{2}d$ to the right of the equilibrium position. How, if at all, does the distance R change?

____ R becomes larger   ____ R becomes smaller   ____ R remains the same

Justify your answer.

(e) On the axes provided, sketch a graph of horizontal position x versus time for the block that loses attachment a distance $\frac{1}{2}d$ to the right of the equilibrium position. Let $t = 0$ be the moment when the spring is fully compressed; continue the graph until the block hits the floor.

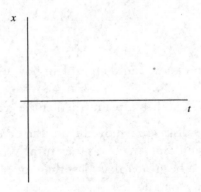

GO ON TO THE NEXT PAGE

(f) On the axes provided, sketch a graph of speed versus time for the block that loses attachment a distance $\frac{1}{2}d$ to the right of the equilibrium position. Let $t = 0$ be the moment when the spring is fully compressed; continue the graph until the block hits the floor.

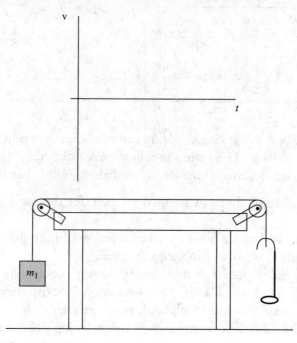

3. In the laboratory, a block of unknown mass m_1 is attached via a light rope and pulleys to a hanger of known mass m_2. The pulleys are of negligible mass and turn with negligible friction. The block and hanger are released from rest in the configuration shown.

(a) Describe a procedure for measuring the acceleration of the hanger. You should use equipment usually found in a high school laboratory.

(b) Is the magnitude of the acceleration of the block greater than, less than, or equal to the magnitude of the acceleration of the hanger? Justify your answer.

Now m_2 is varied by placing disks of different masses on the hanger. For each value of m_2, the acceleration a of the hanger is measured. A graph is produced with m_2g on the vertical axis and a on the horizontal axis.

(c) Is this graph linear?

____ yes   ____ no

- If yes, explain how you know and then explain how you would use a line of best fit to determine the mass m_1.
- If no, explain why not and then explain whether the graph would be concave-up or concave-down.

(d) In a final experiment, the disks are removed from the hanger, and the pulleys are replaced with pulleys that do experience significant friction as they turn. Will the acceleration of the hanger in this final experiment be measured to be greater than, less than, or equal to the acceleration of the hanger in the original experiment? Justify your answer.

STOP. End of Physics C—Mechanics Practice Exam 2—Free-Response Questions

Physics C—Electricity and Magnetism Practice Exam 2—Multiple-Choice Questions

ANSWER SHEET

1 Ⓐ Ⓑ Ⓒ Ⓓ Ⓔ   13 Ⓐ Ⓑ Ⓒ Ⓓ Ⓔ   25 Ⓐ Ⓑ Ⓒ Ⓓ Ⓔ
2 Ⓐ Ⓑ Ⓒ Ⓓ Ⓔ   14 Ⓐ Ⓑ Ⓒ Ⓓ Ⓔ   26 Ⓐ Ⓑ Ⓒ Ⓓ Ⓔ
3 Ⓐ Ⓑ Ⓒ Ⓓ Ⓔ   15 Ⓐ Ⓑ Ⓒ Ⓓ Ⓔ   27 Ⓐ Ⓑ Ⓒ Ⓓ Ⓔ
4 Ⓐ Ⓑ Ⓒ Ⓓ Ⓔ   16 Ⓐ Ⓑ Ⓒ Ⓓ Ⓔ   28 Ⓐ Ⓑ Ⓒ Ⓓ Ⓔ
5 Ⓐ Ⓑ Ⓒ Ⓓ Ⓔ   17 Ⓐ Ⓑ Ⓒ Ⓓ Ⓔ   29 Ⓐ Ⓑ Ⓒ Ⓓ Ⓔ
6 Ⓐ Ⓑ Ⓒ Ⓓ Ⓔ   18 Ⓐ Ⓑ Ⓒ Ⓓ Ⓔ   30 Ⓐ Ⓑ Ⓒ Ⓓ Ⓔ
7 Ⓐ Ⓑ Ⓒ Ⓓ Ⓔ   19 Ⓐ Ⓑ Ⓒ Ⓓ Ⓔ   31 Ⓐ Ⓑ Ⓒ Ⓓ Ⓔ
8 Ⓐ Ⓑ Ⓒ Ⓓ Ⓔ   20 Ⓐ Ⓑ Ⓒ Ⓓ Ⓔ   32 Ⓐ Ⓑ Ⓒ Ⓓ Ⓔ
9 Ⓐ Ⓑ Ⓒ Ⓓ Ⓔ   21 Ⓐ Ⓑ Ⓒ Ⓓ Ⓔ   33 Ⓐ Ⓑ Ⓒ Ⓓ Ⓔ
10 Ⓐ Ⓑ Ⓒ Ⓓ Ⓔ   22 Ⓐ Ⓑ Ⓒ Ⓓ Ⓔ   34 Ⓐ Ⓑ Ⓒ Ⓓ Ⓔ
11 Ⓐ Ⓑ Ⓒ Ⓓ Ⓔ   23 Ⓐ Ⓑ Ⓒ Ⓓ Ⓔ   35 Ⓐ Ⓑ Ⓒ Ⓓ Ⓔ
12 Ⓐ Ⓑ Ⓒ Ⓓ Ⓔ   24 Ⓐ Ⓑ Ⓒ Ⓓ Ⓔ

Physics C—Electricity and Magnetism Practice Exam 2—Multiple-Choice Questions

Time: 45 minutes. You may refer to the constants sheet and the equation sheet, both of which are found in the appendix. You may use a calculator.

1. A object of charge q moves at constant speed v in a uniform magnetic field B in a circular path of radius R. How much work is done by the field on the object in each revolution?

   (A) $qvBR$
   (B) $\pi R^2 qvB$
   (C) $2\pi R^2 qvB$
   (D) zero
   (E) $2\pi qvBR$

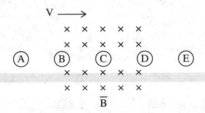

2. A uniform magnetic field B points into the page and is limited to the region shown. A circular loop of wire is pulled to the right such that it maintains a steady speed. At which labeled position is the current in the wire at its largest counterclockwise value?

   (A) A
   (B) B
   (C) C
   (D) D
   (E) E

Questions 3 and 4: Two point objects produce electric potentials at the origin. Object 1, located along the positive x-axis, produces an electric potential of +100 V at the origin; Object 2, located along the negative y-axis, produces an electric potential of +100 V at the origin.

3. What is the net electric potential at the origin?

   (A) +200 V
   (B) 0 V
   (C) $+100\sqrt{2}$ V
   (D) The answer cannot be determined without knowing the relative distances of the charges from the origin.
   (E) (+200 V) (cos 45°)

4. The magnitude of the charge on object 1 is twice the magnitude of the charge on object 2. What is the ratio of object 1's distance from the origin to object 2's distance from the origin?

   (A) 2:1
   (B) 1:1
   (C) 1:4
   (D) 4:1
   (E) 1:2

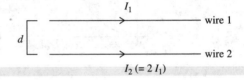

Questions 5–7:

Two isolated and identical long, straight, parallel wires carry currents I_1 and I_2 in the directions shown in the top view. The wires are separated by a distance d. The magnitude of current in wire 2 initially is twice the magnitude of current in wire 1. The top wire experiences a force F_1 due to the bottom wire.

GO ON TO THE NEXT PAGE

5. In the laboratory, I_2 is held constant while I_1 is changed to different values both greater and less than I_2. A force probe measures the force F_1 on the top wire for each different I_1. Which of the following graphs represents F_1 as a function of I_1?

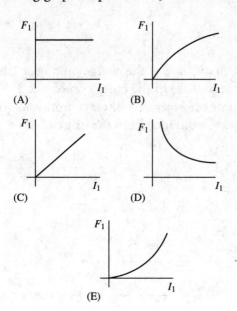

(A) (B)

(C) (D)

(E)

6. Which of the following indicates the magnitude and direction of the force F_2 on wire 2 due to wire 1?

(A) Half F_1 and downward
(B) Twice F_1 and downward
(C) Equal to F_1 and upward
(D) Equal to F_1 and downward
(E) Half F_1 and upward

7. Now the distance d is doubled while the currents I_1 and I_2 remain the same. In terms of F_1, what is the new force of wire 2 on wire 1?

(A) $2F_1$
(B) $(1/8)\ F_1$
(C) $(1/4)\ F_1$
(D) $(1/2)\ F_1$
(E) F_1

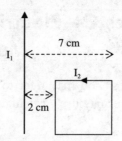

8. A very long, straight wire carries a current of I_1 in a direction toward the top of the page, as shown in the diagram. A rectangular coil with two sides parallel to the straight wire carries a current I_2. The near side of the rectangular coil is 2 cm away from the straight wire; the far side is 7 cm from the straight wire. Which of the following correctly sketches the magnetic field magnitude B as a function of the distance x along the *top* segment of the rectangular wire loop?

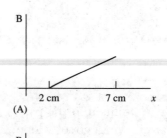

(A) (B)

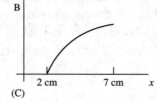

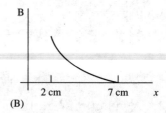

(C) (D)

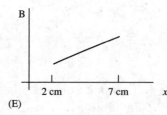

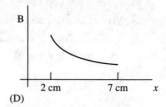

(E)

GO ON TO THE NEXT PAGE

9. A magnetic field that is aimed perpendicular to the plane of a wire loop varies as a function of time given by the equation $B(t) = 4t$. Which of the following sketches the emf produced in the loop as a function of time?

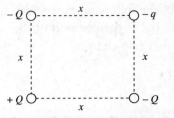

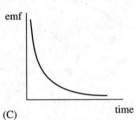

(A)

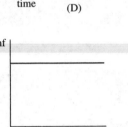

(B)

(C)   (D)

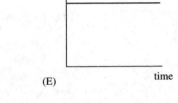

(E)

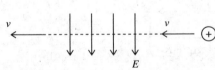

10. A positively charged object moves to the left at constant speed v. The object enters a region containing uniform magnetic and electric fields and continues to move in a straight line at constant speed. The electric field E is directed down toward the bottom of the page, as shown. What is the direction of the magnetic field?

(A) Into the page
(B) Down toward the bottom of the page
(C) Up toward the top of the page
(D) To the right
(E) Out of the page

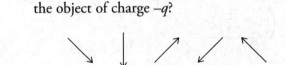

Questions 11–13: Four objects with charge $+Q$, $-Q$, and $-q$ are placed at the corners of a square of side x, as shown in the diagram.

11. What is the direction of the net electric force on the object of charge $-q$?

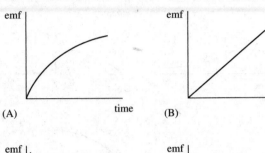

12. Which of the following represents the magnitude of the electric field due to the other three charges at the location of the $-q$ charge?

(A) $\dfrac{\sqrt{2}kQ}{x^2}$

(B) $\dfrac{5kQ}{x^2}$

(C) $\dfrac{\left(2\sqrt{2}-1\right)kQ}{x^2}$

(D) $\dfrac{kQ}{x^2}$

(E) $\dfrac{3kQ}{2x^2}$

GO ON TO THE NEXT PAGE

13. Which of the following expressions gives the electric potential at the position of the $-q$ charge due to the other two charges?

(A) $\dfrac{-kQ}{\sqrt{2}x}$

(B) $\dfrac{-kQ}{x}$

(C) $\dfrac{3kQ}{x}$

(D) $\dfrac{\left(1-2\sqrt{2}\right)kQ}{x}$

(E) $\dfrac{\left(2\sqrt{2}-1\right)kQ}{x}$

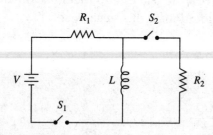

Questions 14–16: A battery with voltage V, two resistors R_1 and R_2, two switches S_1 and S_2, and an inductor L are connected in a circuit as shown. The resistance of R_2 is twice that of R_1. At time $t = 0$, the switches have been open for a long time and the inductor stores no energy. At time $t = 0$, switch S_1 is closed. At time $t = t_1$ switch S_1 is opened and, simultaneously, switch S_2 is closed.

14. Which of the following expressions represents the voltage across the resistor R_1 as a function of time before t_1?

(A) $Ve^{-\frac{t}{RL}}$

(B) $V(1-e^{-\frac{tR}{L}})$

(C) V

(D) $V(1-e^{-\frac{t}{RL}})$

(E) $Ve^{-\frac{tR}{L}}$

15. Which of the following graphs represents the current I through the inductor as a function of time?

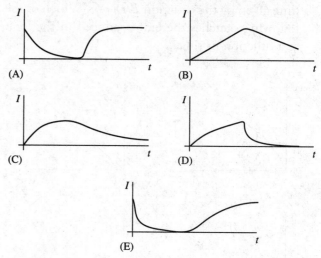

16. What is the maximum energy stored in the inductor?

(A) $\dfrac{LV^2}{2R_1^2}$

(B) zero

(C) $\dfrac{LV^2}{2R_2^2}$

(D) $\dfrac{LV^2}{2\left(\dfrac{R_1 R_2}{R_1 + R_2}\right)^2}$

(E) $\dfrac{LV^2}{2(R_1 + R_2)^2}$

17. Two identical resistors are connected in parallel to a battery of voltage V, dissipating power P. Next, the same resistors are instead connected in series to the same battery. What is the new total voltage and total power in the new circuit?

(A) $4V, P/4$
(B) V, P
(C) $4V, 4P$
(D) $V, 4P$
(E) $V, P/4$

GO ON TO THE NEXT PAGE

18. In a region of space, the electric field is zero everywhere. Which of the following MUST be true about the electric potential in this region?

(A) It must be the same value, either positive or negative, everywhere.
(B) It must be zero everywhere.
(C) It must be the same positive value everywhere.
(D) It must be zero at at least one point in the region.
(E) It must be the same negative value everywhere.

Questions 19 and 20: Two parallel plate capacitors, each with capacitance C, are connected in series with one another as part of a larger circuit. Each stores charge Q and has voltage difference V between its plates. These two capacitors are then replaced by a single equivalent capacitor and reconnected to the same larger circuit.

19. What is the capacitance of the replacement capacitor?

(A) C
(B) $C/2$
(C) $2C$
(D) $3C/2$
(E) $C/\sqrt{2}$

20. What is the charge on and voltage across the replacement capacitor?

	charge	voltage
(A)	$2Q$	$V/2$
(B)	$2Q$	$2V$
(C)	Q	$2V$
(D)	Q	V
(E)	Q	$V/2$

21. Two large oppositely charged parallel plates are initially separated by a distance d. The uniform electric field between the plates has magnitude E. Next, the magnitude of the charge on each plate is doubled, while the separation distance d is doubled. What is the new electric field magnitude?

(A) E
(B) $E/4$
(C) $E/2$
(D) $4E$
(E) $2E$

22. Four objects with charge $+Q$ are arranged on the corners of a square, as shown. Three of the objects are fixed in place; the one at the top right of the square is free to move and is released from rest. No external forces act on the four-object system. Which of the following correctly describes the motion of the free object?

(A) It moves up and to the right with increasing acceleration, always speeding up.
(B) It moves down and left until it hits the bottom-right object.
(C) It moves up and to the right with decreasing acceleration until it eventually comes to rest.
(D) It oscillates about its original position.
(E) It moves up and to the right with decreasing acceleration, always speeding up.

23. Two hollow metal spheres of different radii initially carry different charges: the larger sphere 1 carries charge $+q_1$, and the smaller sphere 2 carries charge $-q_2$. When the spheres are connected by a long conducting wire, charge will flow until:

(A) The electric field at each sphere's surface is the same
(B) The charge residing on the surface of each sphere is equal
(C) The electric field at each sphere's center is the same
(D) The charge residing on the surface of each sphere is zero
(E) The electric potential at each sphere's surface is the same

Questions 24 and 25: A parallel-plate capacitor is filled with air. Each plate has area 10 cm². The separation between plates is 2.0 cm. The top place stores +200 nC of charge, and the bottom plate stores –200 nC of charge.

24. An insulating material of dielectric constant κ is inserted between the plates. What happens to the capacitance of the capacitor?

(A) (0.44 pF) $/ \kappa$
(B) (0.44 pF)$\cdot\kappa$
(C) (0.44 pF)
(D) (0.44 pF)$\cdot\kappa^2$
(E) (0.44 pF) $/ \kappa^2$

GO ON TO THE NEXT PAGE

25. The original capacitor is again filled with air. Now the plates are replaced with new plates of area 20 cm² but the same charge and separation. How is the potential difference across the plates affected?

(A) The potential difference is quadrupled.
(B) The potential difference is cut in half.
(C) The potential difference is doubled.
(D) The potential difference is unchanged.
(E) The potential difference is reduced to ¼ of its previous value.

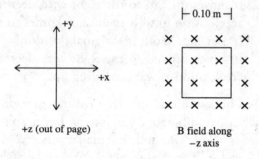

26. A square loop of wire with side length 0.10 m is situated in the plane of the page. A uniform magnetic field **B** points into the page, along the z-axis, as shown in the diagram. Which of the following manipulations would increase the magnetic flux through the wire loop?

(A) Increase the side length of the square loop
(B) Rotate the loop about the z-axis
(C) Decrease the magnetic field strength
(D) Rotate the loop about the x-axis
(E) Rotate the loop about the y-axis

27. A solid, nonconducting sphere carries a uniform volume charge distribution r. Which of the following is a correct statement?

(A) All positions in the sphere are at the same electric potential.
(B) All charge that is not bound to an atom resides on the surface of the sphere.
(C) The net charge enclosed by any Gaussian surface entirely within the conductor must be zero.
(D) The electric field just outside the sphere is directed perpendicular to the sphere's surface.
(E) The electric field magnitude inside the sphere is zero.

28. A proton moving to the right encounters an electric field that points up. What is the direction of the electric force on the proton once the proton enters the electric field?

(A) At an angle down and to the right
(B) Down
(C) At an angle up and to the right
(D) Right
(E) Up

29. A solid conducting sphere of radius R contains a distribution of charge −Q along its surface. Although the electric field at the sphere's center is zero, the electric potential is not. Why not?

(A) Because the electric potential is defined as equal to zero only at a position very far away from the sphere, the potential cannot be zero anywhere else.
(B) Because the electric field is only zero right at the sphere's center, a changing electric field nearby must create a changing electric potential nearby, too.
(C) Because in the formula for electric potential R is in the denominator; when R = 0 the potential is not zero, it is undefined.
(D) Because a negative charge would be forced away from the sphere toward V = 0 far away, the potential at the sphere's surface is nonzero; and in a conductor, the potential is uniform throughout.
(E) Because a positive test charge placed at the sphere's center would be attracted to the surface, and positive charges are forced high-to-low potential.

GO ON TO THE NEXT PAGE

30. Can a negatively charged conductor apply an attractive force on an uncharged insulator?

(A) YES – If the uncharged insulator is small enough, the r term in the denominator of Coulomb's law would become small, making the whole expression large and creating a measurable force.

(B) NO – Because charge can't move freely along the insulator's surface, charge separation by induction cannot occur.

(C) NO – Because one of the q terms in Coulomb's law would be zero, it's impossible for a negatively charged object to apply an electric force on an uncharged object.

(D) YES – The positive charges can induce a local negative charge on the near surface of the insulator.

(E) YES – The electrons in the negatively charged conductor can attract the protons in the insulator.

31. Two objects, each with charge $+Q$, are a fixed distance d apart. Each applies an electric force F to the other. Next, an object with charge $-(1/8)Q$ is placed on the midpoint between the first two objects. The new electric force experienced by each of the positively charged objects is:

(A) $(3/4)F$
(B) $3F$
(C) $(1/2)F$
(D) F
(E) zero

32. The electric potential along the y-axis is given by $V = -3y^2 - 2y - 3$, where y is in meters and V is in volts. At what position on the y-axis is the electric field equal to zero?

(A) $+0.33$ m
(B) -3 m
(C) 0 m
(D) -0.33 m
(E) $+3$ m

33. A long straight wire of circular cross-section with radius a carries a uniform areal current density j. What is the value of the line integral of the magnetic field around the circumference of the wire?

(A) $\mu_0 j \pi a$

(B) $2\mu_0 j \pi a$

(C) $2\mu_0 j \pi a^2$

(D) $\mu_0 j$

(E) $\mu_0 j \pi a^2$

Questions 34 and 35: A 120-V source is connected to three resistors, as shown in the diagram. The resistance of R_3 is twice the resistance of R_2, which is twice the resistance of R_1.

34. Which of the following ranks the power P_1, P_2, and P_3 dissipated by each resistor?

(A) $P_1 > P_3 > P_2$
(B) $P_2 > P_3 > P_1$
(C) $P_1 = P_2 = P_3$
(D) $P_3 > P_2 > P_1$
(E) $P_1 > P_2 > P_3$

35. Which of the following is correct about the equivalent resistance of this circuit?

(A) It is between the resistances of R_2 and R_3.
(B) It is greater than the resistance of R_3.
(C) It is between the resistances of R_1 and R_2.
(D) It is less than the resistance of R_1.
(E) It is equal to the resistance of R_2.

STOP. End of Physics C—Electricity and Magnetism Practice Exam 2—Multiple-Choice Questions

Physics C—Electricity and Magnetism Practice Exam 2— Free-Response Questions

Time: 45 minutes. You may refer to the constants sheet and the equation sheet, both of which are found in the appendix. You may use a calculator.

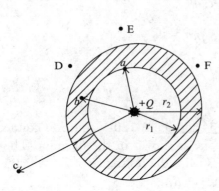

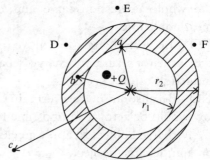

1. (15 points)

   A point object carrying positive charge $+Q$ sits in the hollow center of a spherical conducting shell, as shown in the diagram. The inner radius of the shell is r_1, and the outer radius is r_2. Positions A, B, and C are located distances a, b, and c from the shell's center, respectively.

   (a) Determine the magnitude of the electric field at each of the following positions:
      i. Position C
      ii. Position B
      iii. Position A

   (b) Draw a vector indicating the direction and relative magnitude of the electric field at positions D, E, and F. If the electric field is zero, indicate so explicitly.

   (c) Determine the electric potential at each of the following positions:
      i. Position C
      ii. Position B
      iii. Position A

   (d) i. What charge resides on the inner surface of the shell? Justify your answer.
      ii. What charge resides on the outer surface of the shell? Justify your answer.

   (e) Now the charged point object is relocated such that it is off-center, as shown in the diagram.
      i. Describe any changes to the magnitude or direction of the electric fields at positions B and C with the relocated central object. Justify your answer.
      ii. Describe any changes to the amount, sign, or distribution of charge residing on the inner and outer surface of the conducting shell. Justify your answer.

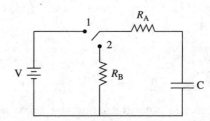

2. An uncharged capacitor is connected to the circuit shown, where $R_A > R_B$. Initially the switch is open, connected neither to position 1 nor to position 2. At time $t = 0$, the switch is thrown to position 1.

   (a) i. What is the current through resistor R_1 immediately after $t = 0$?
      ii. What is the voltage across the capacitor a long time after $t = 0$?
      Now, at time t_2, which is a long time after $t = 0$, the switch is thrown to position 2.

GO ON TO THE NEXT PAGE

(b) i. Which resistor, if either, takes a larger current immediately after time t_2? Justify your answer briefly.

ii. Which resistor, if either, takes a larger voltage immediately after time t_2? Justify your answer briefly.

iii. What is the voltage across the capacitor a long time after time t_2?

(c) i. Show how to use Kirchhoff's rules to write (but do NOT solve) a differential equation for the charge Q on the capacitor as a function of time for all times after t_2.

ii. On the axes provided, sketch a graph of the charge on the capacitor Q as a function of time, beginning at t_2 and ending a long time afterward.

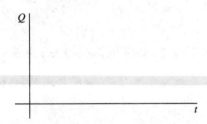

iii. On the axes provided, sketch the magnitude of current through R_A as a function of time, beginning at t_2 and ending a long time afterward.

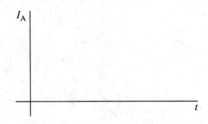

(d) A student in the laboratory is assigned to verify the current graph in (c) iii. experimentally. The student proposes the following procedure:

I'll hook a digital multimeter set to measure current in series with R_A. I'll start a stopwatch simultaneously with throwing the switch to position 2. I'll call out every 10 s, when my partner will record the ammeter reading.

Explain under what conditions, if any, this procedure will effectively provide evidence for the time-dependent current of the circuit as predicted in (c) iii.

3. (15 points)

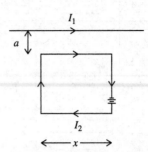

A very long wire carries current I_1. Nearby, a square wire loop of side x carries a current I_2, which is produced by a very small battery within the loop as shown. The top side of the square loop is located a distance a from the long wire.

(a) i. In terms of given variables and fundamental constants, calculate the magnitude of the total force applied by the long wire on the wire loop.

ii. Draw a vector indicating the direction of the magnetic force calculated in (a) i.

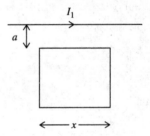

Now the battery in the square loop is removed, and the loop is placed at the same location. For the following, use values $a = 0.02$ m, $x = 0.05$ m, and $I_1 = 0.50$ A.

(b) Calculate the magnetic flux through the square loop.

(c) Calculate the induced current in the square loop.

GO ON TO THE NEXT PAGE

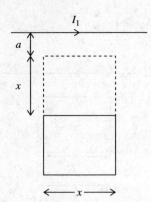

(d) Finally, the square loop is moved from its initial position to a new position, a distance $a + x$ from the long wire. It takes 2 s for the wire to change locations. Using the values $I_1 = 0.50$ A, $a = 0.020$ m, and $x = 0.050$ m, calculate the average EMF induced in the square loop while it changes positions.

STOP. End of Physics C—Electricity and Magnetism Practice Exam 2—Free-Response Questions

Physics C—Mechanics Practice Exam 2—Multiple-Choice Solutions

1. **D**—The airplane's acceleration can be found from kinematics, using $v^2 = v_0^2 + 2a\Delta x$ with $v_0 = 0$. This gives $a = (80 \text{ m/s})^2/2(3000 \text{ m}) = 1.1$ m/s/s. The net force is ma, so multiply by the 300,000-kg mass to get about 310,000 N. That's 3×10^5 N.

2. **D**—In collisions, momentum generally must be conserved because no net external force acts. But kinetic energy could be converted into internal energy in the collision. Without data to check or an explicit statement of an elastic collision, kinetic energy may or may not be conserved.

3. **E**—For an object of mass m launched with escape velocity, its total mechanical energy at the surface of the planet is kinetic plus potential, or

   $\frac{1}{2}mv^2 + \left(-G\dfrac{Mm}{r}\right)$. When the object gets very far

   from the planet, its kinetic energy is zero (because escape velocity is the *minimum* speed necessary to leave the planet) and its potential energy is also zero (by definition, any position a long way from the planet has zero potential energy). So set the previous expression equal to zero and solve for v

   to get $v = \sqrt{\dfrac{2GM}{r}}$. Now apply semi-quantitative

   reasoning—the numerator does not change, but the planet's radius gets cut in half. The radius is in the denominator and under the square root,

   meaning the speed is multiplied by $\dfrac{1}{\sqrt{\frac{1}{2}}} = \sqrt{2} = 1.4$.

   Or, you can intuit that the gravitational field at the surface of the planet will be stronger because the planet's radius is smaller. That would increase, not decrease, the escape velocity. Probably it's easier the conceptual way.

4. **D**—The block is in equilibrium, at rest. Thus the weight equals the tension, which is 10 N. The scale simply reads this tension. (If you wanted to do a free body diagram of the scale, it would include a 10 N tension pulling down, and the 10 N force of the hand pulling up.)

5. **D**—The blocks are attached together. Acceleration is the change in speed every second. In 1 second, all the blocks must change speed by the same amount; if they didn't, one of the blocks would become unattached. The objects experience different net forces because they are of different mass, but the accelerations must be the same.

6. **D**—The total momentum before collision is (250 g)(100 m/s) = 25,000 g·cm/s to the right and (500 g)(75 cm) = 37,500 g·cm/s to the left. Subtracting, this gives 12,500 g·cm/s total momentum to the left. That's the same momentum as after collision, by conservation. After collision, because the carts stick, the total momentum of 12,500 g·cm/s is the total mass of 750 g times the speed. Dividing, the speed is 17 cm/s.

7. **A**—Take the negative derivative of a potential energy function to get force. Here, the force is $-kx + b$.

8. **E**—Ignore the x direction entirely. In the y direction, there's 4 kg at $y = 0$ and 4 kg at $y = 2$ cm. These equal masses have a center of mass directly in between, at $y = 1$ cm.

9. **A**—The energy conversion here is gravitational potential energy (mgh) to work done by friction (equal to friction force times distance, where friction force is mu times the normal force): $mgh = \mu mgd$. Solving, $h = \mu d$. Here μ is 0.20 and $d = 0.45$ m. That's 0.09 m, or 9 cm.

10. **D**—The vertical axis of the graph indicates that up is the positive direction. The slope of this graph is velocity. When an object slows down, its acceleration is in the opposite direction of its motion; when an object speeds up, its acceleration is in the same direction as its motion. So we want a negative slope that gets steeper (meaning downward, increasing velocity) or a positive slope that gets shallower (meaning upward, decreasing velocity). That's near the top of the peaks of the graph, like at $t = 1.0$ s.

11. D—The period of an object oscillating on a spring is $2\pi\dfrac{\sqrt{m}}{\sqrt{k}}$. The graph shows the period of oscillation—the time for one complete cycle—to be 2.0 s. The mass is given as 0.20 kg. Plug into the equation earlier to get $k = 2.0$ N/m.

12. C—Displacement, velocity, and momentum are vector quantities because their direction matters. When using a negative sign with these, the negative indicates a direction. However, all forms of energy are scalar quantities, just amounts with no direction. The negative sign on potential energy simply means an amount of potential energy less than zero.

13. D—The net force is ma, which in circular motion is mv^2/r. Because speed, radius, and mass don't change throughout the motion, the net force is constant. To find the net force, add or subtract the individual forces on the ball. At the peak, both the tension in the string and the weight pull down: $F_{net} = T + mg$. At the bottom, though, the tension pulls up while the weight pulls down: $F_{net} = T - mg$. With F_{net} and mg constants, the tension at the bottom must be greater—at the bottom, tension is $F_{net} + mg$, whereas at the top, tension is $F_{net} - mg$.

14. A—Stable equilibrium is where the U vs. x graph has a local minimum. This function is an upward-opening parabola, so anywhere where the derivative is zero is a local minimum. Set the derivative $2ax = 0$; solving, $x = 0$.

15. D—Power P is work done per time. The motor must do work to change the object's potential energy by mgh, where h is 100 m. (Not $100\sqrt{2}$ m, because the h in this formula represents vertical height only. No work is done to carry the object horizontally.) The relevant equation becomes $P = \dfrac{mgh}{t}$, where t is the 20-s time interval. Solving, $m = \dfrac{Pt}{gh}$. That's (200 W)(20 s) / (10 m/s/s) (100 m) = 4 kg.

16. A—To get displacement, integrate the velocity function. The limits of the definite integral should be 0 to 2 s. The integral gives $\left. 4\dfrac{t^3}{3} - 3\dfrac{t^2}{2} + 2t \right|_0^2$. This evaluates to 8.7 m, closest to A.

17. D—The only force on the moon is the force of the planet. This force acts on a line directly through the planet's center; thus, this force provides no torque about the planet. Because no torque acts on the moon, the moon's angular momentum is conserved.

18. A—The formula for the moon-planet potential energy is $-G\dfrac{Mm}{d}$, where M is the planet's mass, m is the moon's mass, and d is the distance between them. The zero of potential energy is taken by convention to be when the moon is a very long way from the planet. As the moon gets closer to the planet, the d term in the denominator decreases. This increases the absolute value of the $G\dfrac{Mm}{d}$ term. But that term is negative, that is, below zero; a smaller d means a smaller potential energy.

19. B—The magnitude of the force of the planet on the moon is $G\dfrac{Mm}{d^2}$. As the moon gets closer to the planet, the d term in the denominator decreases, increasing the amount of the force.

20. A—Force times time is impulse. Both objects experienced the same nonzero force for the same time, so experience the same impulse. Impulse is change in momentum.

21. **D**—Because the pivot is at the meterstick's center of mass, the meterstick's weight provides no torque. The angular acceleration is clockwise; thus, clockwise torques are greater than counterclockwise torques. These torques are equal to the weight of each object times the object's distance from the pivot. Object 2 provides a greater torque, yet its lever arm (the distance from the pivot) is smaller. Thus, object 2 must be more massive.

22. **D**—The centripetal force mv^2/r is the normal force F_n. The friction force, also equal to μF_n, balances the weight. The leads to the equation $\mu \dfrac{mv^2}{r} = mg$. The speed of an object in circular motion is the circumference over the period T, so replace v with $\dfrac{2\pi r}{T}$. Now manipulate algebraically to solve for T.

23. **A**—Use the parallel axis theorem: $I = I_{cm} + Mh^2$, where h is the distance between parallel axes. The rotational inertia through the object's center of mass is $(1/2)MR^2$. The distance between the two axes is R. So $I = (1/2)MR^2 + MR^2 = (3/2)MR^2$.

24. **D**—When the displacement is positive—that is, to the right—the force of the spring is negative, that is, to the left. The magnitude of the force of a spring is kx and so is linear in x. Only choice **D** is linear, with negative force for positive displacement.

25. **B**—Regardless of how it's thrown, once released, the ball is in free-fall: no forces except gravity act on the ball. All objects in free-fall experience a constant acceleration of 10 m/s/s downward.

26. **B**—The slope of the position-time graph is the velocity. Initially, the slope must be nonzero and negative because the ball moves down. And then the graph curves; the slope gets steeper because the ball's speed increases.

27. **A**—The torque provided by each string is force times lever arm. The lever arm in this case is the radius of the pulley. So clockwise torque is (20 N)(3 cm) = 60 N·cm. The counterclockwise torque is (10 N)(1 cm) = 10 N·cm. The net torque is thus (60 − 10) = 50 N·cm.

28. **C**—Use kinematics equation $v_f^2 = v_o^2 + 2a\Delta x$. The ball comes to rest at its peak, $v_f = 0$. So $v_0 = \sqrt{2a\Delta x}$. Here the maximum height Δx is under a square root. So three times higher means $\sqrt{3}$ times bigger speed, and the square root of 3 is 1.7.

29. **B**—Impulse is change in momentum. Both balls lose the same amount of momentum in hitting the floor and coming to rest; however, ball A changes its momentum even more in order to rebound. So ball A changes its momentum by a larger amount, therefore experiencing the greater impulse. Impulse is also force times time of collision. By Newton's third law, the force of the ball on the floor is equal to the force of the floor on the ball, and the same collision takes the same amount of time. So if ball A experiences more impulse in its collision, so does the floor.

30. **A**—Translated to equations, the problem says $F = -bv$, where b is some positive constant. (The term bv is negative, because the force of air resistance must act opposite the direction of velocity.) We know net force $F = ma$, and a is the time derivative of velocity. So rewrite: $m\dfrac{dv}{dt} = -bv$. Rearrange algebraically to get.

31. **E**—The equation for train A's position is derived from $\Delta x = v_0 t + \frac{1}{2}at^2$: $x = 10t - 2.5t^2$, with $x = 0$ at its original location and calling positive x to the east. That makes train A's initial velocity positive and its acceleration negative. Train B's position is given by $x = 200 - 2.5t^2$. This works because at time $t = 0$ $x = 200$; then after 1 s, $x = 197.5$ m, so is moving west as expected. Now set both expressions for x equal to each other: $10t - 2.5t^2 = 200 - 2.5t^2$. This solves to give $t = 20$ s.

32. **A**—Acceleration is the slope of a velocity-time graph. The acceleration is constant when the graph is a line: AB, BC, and CD. But CD's section is horizontal, indicating zero acceleration.

33. **D**—Net force is ma, where a is the time derivative of the velocity function. This derivative gives $v = \dfrac{6t}{m}$. So ma is $6t$.

34. A—Here the graph is always above the horizontal axis; this means the motion is always in the positive direction (i.e., right). The vertical axis values get closer to zero, reach zero, and then get farther from zero. Thus, the speed gets closer then farther from zero: the car slows down and speeds up.

35. E—The net force on the block includes the horizontal component of F to the right and the friction force to the left. That's $F\cos\theta$ to the right. To the left, the force of friction is μF_n, where the normal force F_n in this case is the weight mg plus the vertical component of F in order to maintain vertical equilibrium. So the friction force to the left is $\mu(mg + F\sin\theta)$. The net force is now $F\cos\theta - \mu(mg + F\sin\theta)$. And this net force is parallel to the displacement d, so multiply these to get the net work: $[F\cos\theta - \mu(mg + F\sin\theta)]d$.

Physics C—Mechanics Practice Exam 2—Free-Response Solutions

Notes on grading your free-response section

For answers that are numerical, or in equation form:

*For each part of the problem, look to see if you got the right answer. If you did, and you showed any reasonable (and correct) work, give yourself full credit for that part. It's okay if you didn't explicitly show EVERY step, as long as some steps are indicated and you got the right answer. However:

*If you got the WRONG answer, then look to see if you earned partial credit. Give yourself points for each step toward the answer as indicated in the rubrics below. Without the correct answer, you must show each intermediate step explicitly in order to earn the point for that step. (See why it's so important to show your work?)

*If you're off by a decimal place or two, not to worry—you get credit anyway, as long as your approach to the problem was legitimate. This isn't a math test. You're not being evaluated on your rounding and calculator-use skills.

*You do not have to simplify expressions in variables all the way. Square roots in the denominator are fine; fractions in nonsimplified form are fine. As long as you've solved properly for the requested variable, and as long as your answer is algebraically equivalent to the rubric's, you earn credit.

*Wrong, but consistent: Often you need to use the answer to part (a) in order to solve part (b). But you might have the answer to part (a) wrong. If you follow the correct procedure for part (b), plugging in your incorrect answer, then you will usually receive *full credit* for part (b). The major exceptions are when your answer to part (a) is unreasonable (say, a car moving at 10^5 m/s, or a distance between two cars equal to 10^{-100} meters), or when your answer to part (a) makes the rest of the problem trivial or irrelevant.

For answers that require justification:

*Obviously your answer will not match the rubric word-for-word. If the general gist is there, you get credit.

*But the reader is not allowed to interpret for the student. If your response is vague or ambiguous, you will NOT get credit.

*If your response consists of both correct and incorrect parts, you will usually not receive credit. It is not possible to try two answers, hoping that one of them is right. ☺ (See why it's so important to be concise?)

1.

(a)

The rotational inertia is given by $I = \int x^2 \, dm$.

To evaluate the integral, set λ as the constant mass per unit length. Replace dm with $\lambda \, dx$, giving $\lambda \int_0^d x^2 \, dx$. This evaluates to $\dfrac{\lambda d^3}{3}$. Here, λ is m/d, making the final result $I = (1/3)md^2$.

1 point for using the correct general calculus expression for I

1 point for replacing dm with $\lambda \, dx$

1 point for setting up an integral with an $x^2 \, dx$ term and limits from 0 to d

1 point for correctly evaluating a correct integral

1 point for recognizing that λ is m/d

1 point for the correct answer

(b)

Angular momentum is conserved. Before, the total angular momentum is just that of the disk, $m_1 v_1 x$. Afterward, the total angular momentum is the sum of the disk and rod's $I\omega$, which is $\left(\frac{1}{3}Md^2 + m_1 x^2\right)\omega$. Set the expressions equal and solve to get $\omega = \dfrac{m_1 v_1 x}{\left(\frac{1}{3}Md^2 + m_1 x^2\right)\omega}$.

1 point for a correct expression for total momentum before collision

1 point for a correct expression for I of the rod-disk system

1 point for setting expressions for total momentum before collision equal to total momentum after.
1 point for the correct expression for ω

(c)
The rubber disk provides greater angular speed after collision. In both cases the angular momentum before the collision is the same. However, the rubber disk rebounds, which means it has negative momentum after the collision. That means that the rod must have even more positive momentum after the collision in order to subtract the rubber disk's momentum and still get the same total momentum.

1 point for correct answer
1 point for correct justification

(d)
To the left of point C. Angular momentum for the disk is m_1v_1x, and the bigger x, the bigger the total angular momentum that can be transferred into the rod-disk after the collision.

1 point for correct answer and justification

(e)
The answer wouldn't change. The total angular momentum of the system before collision is still m_1v_1x. That angular momentum is still transferred to the system after the collision. Because this angular momentum depends on x but not on properties of the rod, the rod's linear density is irrelevant.

1 point for correct answer
1 point for correct justification

2.

(a)
The net force is ma, and also is equal to $-kx$ because it's provided by a spring. Acceleration is $\frac{d^2x}{dt^2}$. Combine to get $\frac{d^2x}{dt^2} = -\frac{k}{m}x$.

1 point for setting ma equal to the force of the spring
1 point for substituting $\frac{d^2x}{dt^2}$ for a

(b)
The solution to a second-order differential equation is a cosine function. Initially, the compression is maximum and equal to d. So write $x = d\cos(\omega t)$. But ω isn't given in the problem statement. Take two derivatives to get $\frac{d^2x}{dt^2} = -d\omega^2\cos(\omega t)$. In order for this expression to match the one in (a), ω must be equal to $\sqrt{\frac{k}{m}}$. The final answer is thus $x = d\cos(\sqrt{\frac{k}{m}}t)$.

1 point for writing an expression with a cosine or sine term
1 point for a correct answer

(c)
First, find the speed of the block when it loses contact with the spring. This requires energy conservation, because the block's acceleration while attached to the spring is not constant. Spring potential energy is converted to kinetic energy: $\frac{1}{2}kd^2 = \frac{1}{2}mv^2$. The speed of the block is $d\sqrt{\frac{k}{m}}$. Then when the block leaves the table, it falls for a time given by vertical kinematics with $v_0 = 0$: $y = \frac{1}{2}gt^2$. Solve to get the time $t = \sqrt{\frac{2y}{g}}$.

Horizontally, the block's speed doesn't change; so multiply speed by time to get distance traveled in the air, $R = d\sqrt{\frac{2ky}{mg}}$.

1 point for using energy to get the block's speed
1 point for using vertical kinematics to get time
1 point for the correct expression in terms of given variables

(d)
R becomes smaller. In the first case, all of the spring energy was transferred to the block's kinetic energy. In the new case, the spring stores some energy at release. So the block has less kinetic energy, moves at a slower speed, and covers less horizontal distance in the same time of flight.

1 point for the correct answer
1 point for a correct justification

(e)

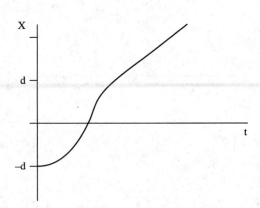

Initially the positon-time graph is sinusoidal, because the block was in simple harmonic motion. When the block is released, it moves at constant speed, represented by an unchanging slope (i.e., a straight line). That slope doesn't change, even after the block leaves the table, because no further horizontal forces act on the block.

1 point for the correct sinusoidal shape before release from the spring
1 point for a straight line, tangent to the sinusoid, immediately after release
1 point for continuing the straight line until the end

(f)

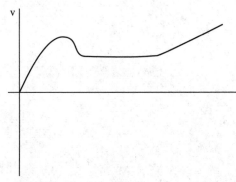

Initially the speed is zero; the velocity-time graph is sinusoidal, because the block was in simple harmonic motion. When the block is released, its speed doesn't change until the block leaves the table. Then, the block gains speed—the vertical velocity increases, so the Pythagorean sum of vertical and horizontal velocities must also increase even though horizontal velocity doesn't change.

1 point for the correct sinusoidal shape before release from the spring

1 point for a horizontal line continuous with the sinusoid after release
1 point for increasing speed when the block leaves the table

3.

(a)
Many approaches. My favorite: Place a sonic motion detector beneath the hanger. Use the detector to make a velocity-time graph while the hanger is in motion. The slope of that graph is the hanger's acceleration.

1 point for measuring quantities that could lead to a determination of acceleration
1 point for a plausible procedure
1 point for a detailed procedure
1 point for explaining how to get acceleration from measured quantities
1 point for multiple data points (note that any use of a graph satisfies this requirement)

(b)
Equal. Acceleration is the change in an object's speed in some about of time. The objects are connected; if one speeds up, so does the other by the same amount. (Otherwise, they would become disconnected or the rope would go slack.)

1 point for the correct answer
1 point for a correct justification

(c)

The relevant equation here comes from applying Newton's second law to the two-object system. The net force is $m_2g - m_1g$; the system mass is $m_1 + m_2$. Because the graph has m_2g on the vertical axis, solve for m_2g: $m_2g = (m_1 + m_2)a + m_1g$. Because a appears linearly (i.e., not squared or square rooted) in the numerator, the graph is linear: **yes**. Identify each term with a term in the equation for a line, $y = mx + b$. The y variable is m_2g. The x variable is a. This leaves the slope of the graph as $(m_1 + m_2)$. The b term is the y-intercept and is m_1g. To get m_1, find the vertical intercept of the best-fit line and divide by g.

1 point for recognizing that the graph is linear
1 point for explaining why the graph is linear
1 point for using Newton's second law correctly to get an expression relating m_2g and a

1 point for using the vertical intercept to get m_1

1 point for explaining in words or mathematics why the vertical intercept is used to get m_1

(d)

The newly measured acceleration would be **less**. Now the net force on the system isn't just $m_2g - m_1g$; there's another force, the friction force, that acts opposite the direction of motion. Because the objects are released from rest, that's also opposite the direction of acceleration. So the net force would be smaller than before. Because $a = F_{net} / m$ and the system mass hasn't changed, the acceleration would be smaller.

1 point for choosing "less"

1 point for explicitly explaining why the net force would be less

1 point for relating less net force to less acceleration using Newton's second law

AP Physics C—Mechanics
Full Exam Scoring

Multiple Choice: Number Correct_____(35 max)

Free-Response: Question 1_____(15 max)
                Question 2_____(15 max)
                Question 3_____(15 max)

Total Free-Response_____(45 max)

$1.286 \times$ Multiple Choice + Free-Response = Raw Score_____(90 max)

59–90	5
45–58	4
35–44	3
23–34	2
0–22	1

Physics C—Electricity and Magnetism Practice Exam 2—Multiple-Choice Solutions

1. **D**—The magnetic force on the object is indeed qvB. However, that force is always perpendicular to the direction of motion. (This is true for all magnetic forces on moving charged objects.) Work is equal to force times the distance traveled parallel to that force—because the force and motion are never parallel to one another, no work is done.

2. **B**—An emf is only induced in a wire when the flux through the wire is changing; thus the answer must be B or D, where the wire is entering or leaving the magnetic field. To find the direction of the induced current, use Lenz's law—point the right thumb in the direction of the magnetic field, and ask if the flux is decreasing. At position D the flux is decreasing; so curl the fingers to find that at D the current is clockwise. At position B the flux is not decreasing; so flip the direction of the thumb and curl the fingers. That gives a counterclockwise current.

3. **A**—Electric potential is a scalar; thus, electric potentials at a point due to multiple objects are added together.

4. **A**—The potential due to a point charge is $\dfrac{kQ}{d}$, where d is the distance from the charge. Both objects produce the same potential. So the equation with the bigger charge in the numerator must also have a bigger distance in the denominator and by the same factor because the equation has no squares or square roots.

5. **C**—The force of a magnetic field on a current carrying wire is $F = ILB$. Here the I is I_1 because wire 1 is experiencing the force; B is the magnetic field produced by wire 2 at the location of wire 1. That magnetic field is $B = \dfrac{\mu_0 I_2}{2\pi d}$. Combining the equations, we find that $F_1 = \dfrac{I_1 L \mu_0 I_2}{2\pi d}$. All values here are constant except I_1, which is in the numerator and to the first power; the graph is therefore linear.

6. **C**—Newton's third law demands that the force of wire 1 on wire 2 be equal to the force of wire 2 on wire 1; so the magnitude of F_2 is equal to F_1. Wire 1 produces a magnetic field into the page at the location of wire 2 (by the second right-hand rule: point the thumb along I_1 and curl the fingers—the fingers point into the page at the location of wire 2). Then by the first right-hand rule (point in the direction of current, curl the fingers toward the magnetic field, the thumb gives the direction of force), the force on wire 2 is upward, toward wire 1.

7. **D**—Combining the equations for the magnetic field produced by wire 2 at the location of wire 1, and for the force exerted by that magnetic field on wire 1, we get $F_1 = \dfrac{I_1 L \mu_0 I_2}{2\pi d}$. Here d is in the denominator and to the first power, so doubling d simply halves F_1.

8. **D**—The magnetic field produced by a current-carrying wire is given by $\dfrac{\mu_0 I}{2\pi r}$, where r is the distance from the wire. So B goes inversely with x here, meaning only B or D could be right. The magnetic field does not go to zero just because a wire ends 7 cm away from another wire.

9. **E**—Emf is the time derivative of magnetic flux. Here, because the area of the loop and the angle of the magnetic field relative to the loop don't change, the time derivative of the magnetic field determines the flux. The time derivative of $4t$ is simply a constant 4—the emf doesn't vary in time.

10. **E**—The electric force on a positive charge is in the direction of the electric field, so downward. To create equilibrium allowing for constant speed, the magnetic force must be upward. Using the first right-hand rule, the fingers point left for the velocity and the thumb points up for the force, so the fingers indicating the magnetic field direction curl out of the page.

11. **D**—The force components are away from the negative charges and toward the positive charge. The negative charges produce equal components right and up, with a resultant 45 degrees up and right. The positive charge produces a force 45 degrees down and left. Because the positive charge is farther from $-q$ than the other charges, the force it produces is smaller, and thus the net force is up and right.

12. **C**—The top-left and bottom-right charges each produce an electric field component of magnitude $\dfrac{kQ}{x^2}$ directed toward those charges. These perpendicular components add pythagoreanly to $\dfrac{\sqrt{2}kQ}{x^2}$ down and left, toward the $+Q$ charge. That $+Q$ charge produces an electric field pointing up and right of magnitude $\dfrac{kQ}{(\sqrt{2}x)^2}$. Because this field is in the opposite direction of the field due to the other two charges, the two fields subtract. Finding a common denominator and subtracting yields choice.

13. **D**—Each of the $-Q$ charges produces a potential of $\dfrac{-kQ}{x}$ at the position in question. (Potentials add or subtract algebraically; negative charges produce negative potentials.) The $+Q$ charge is $\sqrt{2}x$ away and so produces a potential of $\dfrac{+kQ}{\sqrt{2}x}$. Get a common denominator and add together $\dfrac{+kQ}{\sqrt{2}x}$ $\dfrac{-kQ}{x}$ $\dfrac{-kQ}{x}$ to get choice.

14. **B**—An inductor resists change in current. Initially, when we close S_1, the current needs to change rapidly from zero to something; so the inductor stores energy initially, leaving zero voltage for the resistor. After a long time, though, when the current reaches a steady state, the circuit behaves as if the inductor weren't there, meaning the voltage across R_1 is just V. Both choices B and D meet these limiting conditions—plug in $t = 0$ and you get a voltage of zero. But the time constant for an RL circuit is L/R, not RL. Thus, the correct choice is not D, but B.

15. **D**—Without the inductor, the current would go from zero to a maximum value instantaneously when S_1 was closed. With the inductor, the current increases to a maximum gradually with an exponential relationship. So only C and D get the first part of the current right. Then the current decreases back to zero exponentially—both C and D show that. What's the difference? The time constant for changes in the current is given by L/R. The bigger the resistance, the shorter the time it takes to reach the steady-state current. Because R_2 is bigger than R_1, the drop in current after the second switch is closed is faster than the rise in current initially.

16. **A**—The energy stored by an inductor is $\dfrac{LI^2}{2}$. What current I is used? We need the maximum current. That's V/R_1, when S_1 has been closed for a long time but before S_2 is closed. When S_2 is open, the resistor R_2 has no effect on the circuit. After S_2 is closed, the current in the inductor drops, so it cannot be the maximum.

17. **E**—Voltage is provided by a battery; with rare exceptions, this voltage does not depend on what the battery is attached to. Power is V^2/R. The equivalent resistance of the circuit quadruples with the new arrangement. (Originally identical resistors R in parallel give equivalent resistance $R/2$; in series, the equivalent resistance is $2R$.) So the numerator of the power equation doesn't change while the denominator quadruples, causing power to be cut by ¼.

18. **A**—Pretend a positive charge is in fact located in this region. No electric field means no electric force on this charge. Because positive charges are forced high-to-low potential and there's no force on this charge, there can't be "high" and "low" potentials—the potential must be uniform. Uniform potential has the same effect whether it's a uniform potential of zero, +5 V, –10 V, or whatever—only the difference in potential from one position to another is relevant here.

19. **B**—The equivalent resistance of series capacitors is given by $\frac{1}{C_{eq}} = \frac{1}{C_1} + \frac{1}{C_2}$. The shortcut is that the equivalent capacitance of two equal capacitors in series is half of each individual capacitance.

20. **C**—Even though each of the original capacitors stored charge Q, the equivalent capacitor also stores charge Q: capacitors in series each carry the same charge, which is equal to the total charge stored. In the initial situation, each capacitor took voltage $V = Q/C$. Now the equivalent capacitor takes voltage $(Q)/(C/2) = 2Q/C$ = twice the voltage across each individual capacitor.

21. **E**—Start with the equation for capacitance of a parallel plate capacitor, $C = \frac{\varepsilon_0 A}{d}$. Doubling d causes the capacitance C to be cut in half. Next, look at the relationship between charge and voltage for a capacitor: $Q = CV$. Here, Q is doubled and C is halved, meaning that V must be increased by a factor of 4. Finally, the electric field between the plates is given by $E = V/d$. The numerator increases by a factor of 4, while the denominator only increases by a factor of 2. So E is doubled.

22. **E**—The acceleration depends on the net force. The net force on the free object decreases as it gets farther from the other objects, because the distance term in the denominator of Coulomb's law gets larger. But the free object will always experience a force up and to the right. A net force in the direction of motion always causes an object to speed up, not to slow down.

23. **E**—Positive charge is forced high-to-low potential; negative charge is forced low-to-high potential. When there's no difference in electric potential, then charge is not forced to flow.

24. **B**—The capacitance of a parallel plate capacitor filled with a vacuum (or air, which is close enough) is $C = \varepsilon_0 \frac{A}{d}$, which works out to 0.44 pF – 0.44×10^{-12} F in this case. The capacitance is multiplied by the dielectric constant of the material filling the capacitor. Note that there's no need to plug in values into the capacitance equation.

25. **B**—The potential difference (i.e., the voltage) across a capacitor is given by $Q = CV$. In this case the charge across the plates is unaffected. The capacitance is given by $C = \varepsilon_0 \frac{A}{d}$; because A is in the numerator and to the first power, the capacitance doubles when the area of the plates doubles. Back to $Q = CV$, the same Q with doubled C gives half the previous V.

26. **A**—Magnetic flux is BA, where B is the magnetic field strength and A is the area of the loop that is directly penetrated by the magnetic field. So we need to either increase the magnetic field strength or increase the area of the loop directly penetrated by the field. The rotations do not increase that area: rotating about the x- or y-axis would reduce the area of the loop available to the magnetic field penetration. Rotation about the z-axis wouldn't change that area. But increasing the actual physical area of the loop would increase the A term.

27. D—Choices (A), (B), (C), and (E) are valid only for a conducting sphere. However, (D) is correct in this case, too, because the charge distribution is uniform; the symmetry of the charge distribution means that at any position on the surface, the charges in the sphere produce horizontal electric field components that cancel. Only the vertical (i.e., perpendicular to the surface) component remains.

28. E—A positively charged object is forced in the same direction as the electric field. The direction of motion has nothing to do with the direction of force.

29. D—It is correct that electric potential is zero a very long distance away from the sphere, but so what. The electric potential at the surface is given by $V = -kQ/R$; it is negative because it is produced by a negative charge. A negative charge near the surface of the sphere would be forced low-to-high potential, which would be from the negative-potential surface toward zero potential far away. But within the conducting sphere, the electric field is zero, meaning the potential cannot change. The potential at the sphere's center is ALSO $V = -kQ/R$.

30. B—Charge separation by induction happens in conductors, in which charge can flow freely along the conductor's surface. This phenomenon allows an uncharged *conductor* to experience attraction to another charged object. However, in an insulator, charges cannot flow freely, so there can't even be a local area in which negative charges attract positive charges.

31. C—Consider the leftmost object. It experiences two electric forces, one from the $+Q$ charge and one from the $-(1/8)Q$ charge. Write Coulomb's law for each of these forces, and subtract because the forces act in opposite directions: $\dfrac{kQQ}{d^2} - \dfrac{k\frac{1}{8}QQ}{\left(\frac{1}{2}d\right)^2}$.

Simplify the expression to get $\dfrac{1}{2}\dfrac{kQQ}{d^2}$, which is half of the force of the two $+Q$ charges on each other.

32. D—The electric field is related to the electric potential by $E = -\dfrac{dV}{dy}$. The negative derivative of the V function is $6y + 2$; set that equal to zero to get $y = -(1/3)$.

33. E—Ampere's law says that the line integral of the magnetic field around a closed line is $\mu_0 I_{enclosed}$. How much current is enclosed by the circumference of the wire? The areal current density j times the area enclosed. The cross-sectional area enclosed here is just the area of the circular wire, πa^2.

34. E—The power dissipated by a resistor is given by V^2/R. Here the voltage across each resistor is the same, because all are in parallel with each other. Mathematically, then, the smallest resistance will take the largest power. Distance from the battery is irrelevant.

35. D—You don't need the equation for equivalent resistance of parallel resistors. No matter the values, the equivalent resistance of parallel resistors is always less than the smallest resistor.

Physics C—Electricity and Magnetism Practice Exam 2— Free-Response Solutions

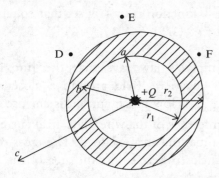

1. (15 points)

A point object carrying positive charge $+Q$ sits in the hollow center of an uncharged spherical conducting shell, as shown in the diagram. The inner radius of the shell is r_1, and the outer radius is r_2. Positions A, B, and C are located distances a, b, and c from the shell's center, respectively.

(a) Determine the magnitude of the electric field at each of the following positions:
  i. Position C
     Because the conductor itself has no charge, the charge enclosed by a Gaussian surface of radius c is just Q. Then the reasoning in part i gives $Q/4\pi\varepsilon_0 c^2$ or kQ/c^2.

1 pt for correct answer
  ii. Position B
     Fact: The electric field inside a conductor is zero.

1 pt for correct answer
  iii. Position A
     Draw a spherical Gaussian surface with radius a. It encloses charge Q and has surface area $4\pi a2$. By the symmetry of the problem, the integral in Gauss's law becomes multiplication: $EA = Q_{enclosed}/\varepsilon_0$. The electric field is then $Q/4\pi\varepsilon_0 a2$; this is equivalent to $kQ/a2$ using k as the Coulomb's law constant.

1 pt for correct answer

(b) Draw a vector indicating the direction and relative magnitude of the electric field at positions D, E, and F. If the electric field is zero, indicate so explicitly.

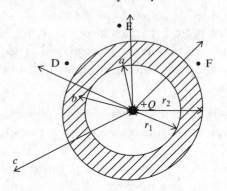

1 pt for each vector pointing away from the center of the sphere
1 pt for vectors at D and F being longer than the vector at E

(c) Determine the electric potential at each of the following positions:
  i. Position C
     The electric potential a long distance away is zero. Because the electric field outside the shell has the same form as that due to a point charge, so does the electric potential: $+kQ/c$.

1 pt for the correct answer
  ii. Position B
     The electric potential at the outer surface of the shell is $+kQ/r_2$. Because the electric field is zero within the shell, the potential cannot change within the shell—it's still the same potential as at either surface. So $+kQ/r_2$.

1 pt for correct answer
  iii. Position A
     The electric potential inside a spherical shell of charge is equal to kq/r, where r is the radius of the shell. The electric potential due to a point charge is also kq/r, where this r represents the distance from the charge. At position A, we have three things contributing to

the potential: the point charge $+Q$ at the center, the ring of charge $-Q$ on the inside surface, and the ring $+Q$ on the outside surface. Superimpose these three to get a total potential of $+kQ/a - kQ/r_1 + kQ/r_2$.

Note that this works out to give the same potential at the inside surface $(+kQ/r_2)$ as at the outer surface.

1 pt for correct answer

(d)

    i. A spherical Gaussian surface drawn inside the shell must enclose zero charge, because the electric field inside the shell is zero. We know such a shell encloses $+Q$ from the point object, so the inner surface must carry charge $-Q$ to make the total charge inside that Gaussian surface zero.

1 pt for correct answer

1 pt for a correct justification

    ii. What charge resides on the outer surface of the shell? Justify your answer.

We know the shell is uncharged. With $-Q$ on the inner surface, $+Q$ must be on the outer surface to give a net charge of zero on the shell.

1 pt for an answer consistent with i and correct justification

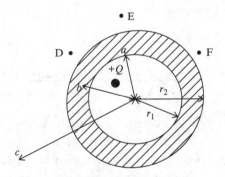

(e) Now the charged point object is relocated such that it is off-center, as shown in the diagram.

    i. Describe any changes to the magnitude or direction of the electric fields at positions B and C with the relocated central object. Justify your answer.

The electric field at B is still zero, because B is still inside a conductor. No change.

        The electric field at C is unchanged, because the electric field outside a con-

ductor is perpendicular to the conductor's surface; the symmetry of the problem *outside* the shell is unchanged. A Gaussian sphere drawn through C still encloses the same charge, so no change.

1 pt for correct justification for no change in electric field at B

1 pt for correct justification that there is no change in the electric field at C

    ii. Describe any changes to the amount, sign, or distribution of charge residing on the inner and outer surface of the conducting shell. Justify your answer.

The same amount and sign of charge must reside on each surface, according to Gauss's law, in order to get an electric field of zero inside the conductor. However, whereas the outer surface's charge will still be uniformly distributed, the charge on the inner surface will be differently distributed—the point object will induce a denser negative charge on the part of the surface closest to the object.

1 pt justifying the same amount and sign of charge on each surface with Gauss's law

1 pt justifying the different distribution on the inner surface

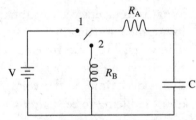

2. An uncharged capacitor of capacitance C is connected to the circuit shown, where $R_A > R_B$. Initially the switch is open, connected neither to position 1 nor to position 2. At time $t = 0$, the switch is thrown to position 1.

(a)

    i. What is the current through resistor R_1 immediately after $t = 0$?

The uncharged capacitor will initially allow current to flow as if the circuit consisted of just the battery and resistor. So by Ohm's law the current is V/R_A.

1 pt for correct answer

ii. What is the voltage across the capacitor a long time after $t = 0$?

After a long time the capacitor will be charged, and thus will block current. Zero.

1 pt for correct answer

Now, at time t_2, which is a long time after $t = 0$, the switch is thrown to position 2.

(b)

i. Which resistor, if either, takes a larger current immediately after time t_2? Justify your answer briefly.

The resistors are in series—they take the same current by definition (or by Kirchhoff's junction rule).

1 pt for answer and brief justification

ii. Which resistor, if either, takes a larger voltage immediately after time t_2? Justify your answer briefly.

In the instant after closing the switch, the capacitor is charged, meaning it has a voltage across it and will act briefly as a battery. Both resistors take the same current as each other. By Ohm's law, then, the bigger resistor takes the bigger voltage. So R_A.

1 pt for correct answer
1 pt for justification

iii. What is the voltage across the capacitor a long time after time t_2?

The voltage is given by Q/C, where Q is the charge on the capacitor. This charge drains over time, so the voltage will also drop, reducing to zero after a long time.

1 pt for correct answer

(c)

i. Show how to use Kirchhoff's rules to write (but do NOT solve) a differential equation for the charge Q on the capacitor as a function of time for all times after t_2.

The sum of the voltage changes will equal zero. Trace the circuit starting with the capacitor, which raises the voltage by Q/C. Each resistor drops the voltage by IR: $Q/C - IR_1 - IR_2 = 0$.

Current is dQ/dt; replace I to get $Q/C - (R_1 + R_2)\, dQ/dt = 0$

And that is a differential equation for Q. All the variables except for Q and t are constants.

1 pt for writing any equation that tries to sum voltage changes to zero

1 pt for the correct Kirchhoff's equation: $Q/C - IR_1 - IR_2 = 0$

1 pt replacing I with dQ/dt

ii. On the axes provided, sketch a graph of the charge on the capacitor Q as a function of time, beginning at t_2 and ending a long time afterward.

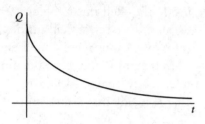

1 pt starting with nonzero Q and ending close to zero Q

1 pt showing something like exponential decay

iii. On the axes provided, sketch the magnitude of current through R_A as a function of time, beginning at t_2 and ending a long time afterward.

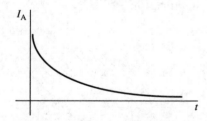

The current is initially large—see (d). The current drops to zero—see (e). In between, the current in any RC circuit changes by an exponential function.

1 pt starting with nonzero I and ending close to zero I

1 pt showing something like exponential decay

(d) A student in the laboratory is assigned to verify the current graph in (c) iii. experimentally. The student proposes the following procedure:

The time constant $(R_1 + R_2)C$ for the capacitor's discharge has to be comparable with the 10-s stopwatch call-out time.

1 pt for referencing the time constant of the circuit

1 pt for correctly relating the time constant to the 10-s stopwatch time, that is, they should be somewhat similar

3. (15 points)

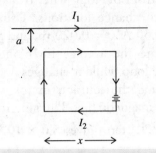

A very long wire carries current I_1. Nearby, a square wire loop of side x carries a current I_2, which is produced by a very small battery within the loop as shown. The top side of the square loop is located a distance a from the long wire.

(a)

   i. In terms of given variables and fundamental constants, calculate magnitude of the total force applied by the long wire on the wire loop.

   The magnetic field produced by I_1 at the location of the wire loop is always into the page, by the right-hand rule associated with $B = \dfrac{\mu_0 I}{2\pi d}$. Thus, by the right-hand rule associated with $F = ILB$, the force on the left-hand side of the loop is to the left; the force on the right-hand side of the loop is to the right. These forces are equal in magnitude, because each element of the loop is the same distance from the long wire. So the side forces cancel.

The force on the top wire is upward and equal to $I_2 x B$, where $B = \dfrac{\mu_0 I_1}{2\pi a}$. The force on the bottom wire is downward and equal to $I_2 x B$, where $B = \dfrac{\mu_0 I_1}{2\pi(a + x)}$.

Subtract the two forces to get $F = I_2 x \dfrac{\mu_0 I_1}{2\pi a} - I_2 x \dfrac{\mu_0 I_1}{2\pi(x + a)}$. No need to simplify—any equivalent form is acceptable.

1 pt for subtracting just force on top and bottom wire portions

1 pt for correct use of $B = \dfrac{\mu_0 I}{2\pi d}$

1 pt for correct use of $F = ILB$

1 pt for combining equations and substituting a and $x + a$ for d, and x for L

   ii. Draw a vector indicating the direction of the magnetic force calculated in (a) i.

1 pt for the correct answer

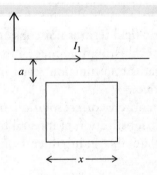

Now the battery in the square loop is removed, and the loop is placed at the same location.

(b) Calculate the magnetic flux through the square loop.

Magnetic flux is $\int B \cdot dA$. Here replace B with

$B = \dfrac{\mu_0 I_1}{2\pi r}$ and dA with $x \cdot dr$, where r is a variable representing distance from the long wire: $x \displaystyle\int_{a}^{x+a} \dfrac{\mu_0 I_1}{2\pi r} dr$. Take the integral to get

$\dfrac{x \mu_0 I_1}{2\pi} \ln r$, evaluated from a to $x + a$. That's $\dfrac{x \mu_0 I_1}{2\pi} \ln\left(\dfrac{x+a}{a}\right)$. Any form of answer is acceptable, as long as the integral is actually evaluated—no integral notation on the final answer.

1 pt for substituting $B = \dfrac{\mu_0 I_1}{2\pi r}$ into any form of the magnetic flux equation

1 pt for attempting to use calculus rather than straight multiplication because the magnetic field term is not constant

1 pt for evaluating the integral to some sort of logarithmic function, even if not entirely correct

1 pt for entirely correct solution, including correct substitution of integral limits

(c) Calculate the induced emf in the square loop.

Induced emf is the time derivative of the magnetic flux. This flux does not change in time, because the field and the area of the loop that the field penetrates don't change in time. So zero induced current.

1 pt for using any form of the emf equation, either in words or variables (not just writing it, using it)

1 pt for explaining or showing that the ΔBA term is zero (i.e., the magnetic flux doesn't change in time)

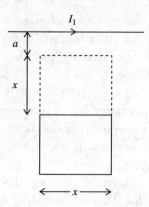

(d) Finally, the square loop is moved from its initial position to a new position, a distance $a + x$ from the long wire. It takes 2 s for the wire to change locations. Using the values $I_1 = 0.50$ A, $a = 0.020$ m, and $x = 0.050$ m, calculate the average EMF induced in the square loop while it changes positions.

Using the solution in (c), we know the initial magnetic flux. Plugging into the result, the $\dfrac{x \mu_0 I_1}{2\pi}$ term gives 5.0×10^{-9} in standard units. The natural log term becomes $\ln (7/2) = 1.3$. So the initial flux is 6.3×10^{-9} Tm^2.

The final flux is calculated using the same formula, just plugging in the different locations of the loop: $x + x + a$ and $x + a$. That's 0.12 m and 0.07 m. The natural log term this time becomes $\ln (12/7) = 0.53$. So the final flux is 2.7×10^{-9} Tm^2.

Subtract final minus initial flux to get the change in flux of 3.6×10^{-9} Tm^2.

But induced emf is change in flux divided by the time interval over which the flux changed—divide by 2 s to get the final answer: the induced emf is 1.8×10^{-9} V (i.e., 1.8 nV).

1 pt for plugging the correct values into whatever equation they came up with in (c) for the initial flux.

1 pt for plugging the correct values into whatever equation they came up with in (c) for the final flux

1 pt for dividing any defined change in flux by 2 s

1 pt for the correct numerical answer (i.e., somewhere between 1.5 and 2.0 nV); the answer must have correct units, but may be in any form

AP Physics C—Electricity and Magnetism
Full Exam Scoring

Multiple-Choice: Number Correct_____(35 max)

Free-Response: Question 1_____(15 max)
Question 2_____(15 max)
Question 3_____(15 max)

Total Free-Response_____(45 max)

$1.286 \times$ Multiple-Choice + Free-Response = Raw Score_____(90 max)

56–90	5
44–55	4
32–43	3
23–34	2
0–22	1

Appendixes

1 amu	u	1.7×10^{-27} kg
mass of proton	m_p	1.7×10^{-27} kg
mass of neutron	m_n	1.7×10^{-27} kg
mass of electron	m_e	9.1×10^{-31} kg
charge of proton	e	1.6×10^{-19} C
Avogadro's number	N	6.0×10^{-23} mol^{-1}
Universal gas constant	R	8.3 J/(mol·K)
Boltzmann's constant	k_B	1.4×10^{-23} J/K
Speed of light	c	3.0×10^8 m/s
Planck's constant	h	6.6×10^{-34} J·s
	h	4.1×10^{-15} eV·s
Planck's constant · speed of light	hc	1.99×10^{-25} J·m
	hc	1.24×10^3 eV·nm
Permittivity of free space	ε_o	8.9×10^{-12} C^2/N·m^2
Coulomb's law constant	k	9.0×10^9 N·m^2/C^2
Permeability of free space	μ_o	$4\pi \times 10^{-7}$ T·m/A
Universal gravitation constant	G	6.7×10^{-11} N·m^2/kg^2
Earth's free fall acceleration	g	9.8 m/s^2
1 atmosphere of pressure	atm	1.0×10^5 Pa
1 electron-volt	eV	1.6×10^{-19} J

PHYSICS C EQUATIONS

Read Chapter 6 about memorizing equations for more help with learning not only what the equations say, but also what they mean.

You'll notice that the C equation sheet often expresses relationships in calculus terms. Don't let that confuse you; for example, though impulse is expressed as an integral of force with respect to time, you should also interpret that as force times time if the force is constant, or as the area under a force vs. time graph.

Remember, your textbook might use slightly different symbols.

MECHANICS

$$v_f = v_o + at$$

$$x - x_o = v_o t + \tfrac{1}{2}at^2$$

$$v_f^2 = v_0^2 + 2a(x - x_o)$$

$$F_{net} = ma$$

$$F = \frac{dp}{dt}$$

$$I = \Delta p = \int F \cdot dt$$

$$p = mv$$

$$F_f = \mu F_N$$

$$W = \int F \cdot dx$$

$$K = \tfrac{1}{2}mv^2$$

$$P = \frac{dW}{dt}$$

$$P = F \cdot v$$

$$U_g = mgh$$

$$a_c = \frac{v^2}{r} = \omega^2 r$$

$$\tau = F \cdot d$$

$$\tau_{net} = Ia$$

$$I = \int r^2 dm = \sum m_i r_i^2$$

$$Mx_{cm} = \sum m_i x_i$$

$$v = r\omega$$

$$L = I\omega = mvr$$

$$K = \tfrac{1}{2}I\omega^2$$

$$\omega_f = \omega_0 + at$$

$$\Delta\theta = \omega_0 t + \tfrac{1}{2}at^2$$

$$F = -kx$$

$$U_s = \tfrac{1}{2}kx^2$$

$$T = \frac{2\pi}{\omega} = \frac{1}{f}$$

$$T = 2\pi\sqrt{\frac{m}{k}}$$

$$T = 2\pi\sqrt{\frac{L}{g}}$$

$$F_G = G\frac{m_1 m_2}{r^2}$$

$$U_G = -G\frac{m_1 m_2}{r}$$

ELECTRICITY AND MAGNETISM

$$F = \frac{1}{4\pi\varepsilon_o}\frac{q_1 q_2}{r^2}$$

$$\frac{1}{C_s} = \sum \frac{1}{C_i}$$

$$F = ILB\sin\theta$$

$$F = qE$$

$$I = \frac{dQ}{dt}$$

$$B_s = \mu_o nl$$

$$\oint E \cdot dA = \frac{Q_{enclosed}}{\varepsilon_0}$$

$$PE_C = \frac{1}{2}CV^2$$

$$\phi_m = \int B \cdot dA$$

$$E = -\frac{dV}{dr}$$

$$R = \rho\frac{L}{A}$$

$$\varepsilon = -\frac{d\phi_m}{dt}$$

$$U_E = qV = \frac{1}{4\pi\varepsilon_o}\frac{q_1 q_2}{r}$$

$$V = IR$$

$$\varepsilon = Blv$$

$$V = \frac{1}{4\pi\varepsilon_o}\sum \frac{q_i}{r_i}$$

$$R_s = \sum R_i$$

$$\varepsilon = -L\frac{dI}{dt}$$

$$Q = CV$$

$$\frac{1}{R_p} = \sum \frac{1}{R_i}$$

$$PE_L = \frac{1}{2}LI^2$$

$$C = \kappa\varepsilon_0\frac{A}{d}$$

$$P = IV$$

$$C_p = \sum C_i$$

$$F = qvB\sin\theta$$

$$\oint B \cdot dl = \mu_0 I_c$$

FOUR-MINUTE DRILL PROMPTS

The lists that follow are designed to help you study equations. Each prompt refers to a specific equation on the AP Equations sheet (we've listed the prompts in the same order in which the equations appear on the Equations sheet). So, for example, the prompt "Net force" refers to the equation, "$F_{net} = ma$."

There are several ways to use these prompts. First, you can use them as a self-test: For each prompt, write down the corresponding equation on a separate sheet of paper. Then check the equations you wrote down against the AP Equations sheet to see if you got any wrong. You can also use these prompts when you study with a friend: Have your friend read the prompts to you, and you respond by reciting the appropriate equation. Try to go through the list as fast as possible without making a mistake. Last, your physics teacher can use these prompts to lead your class through a four-minute drill, which is an activity we describe in Chapter 6.

Mechanics

1st kinematics equation
2nd kinematics equation
3rd kinematics equation
Net force
Force in terms of momentum
Impulse
Definition of momentum
Force of friction
Work
Kinetic energy
Power
Power—alternate expression
Gravitational potential energy near a planet
Centripetal acceleration
Torque
Newton's second law for rotation
Definition of rotational inertia
Position of the center of mass
Conversion between linear and angular velocity
Angular momentum
Rotational kinetic energy
1st rotational kinematics equation
2nd rotational kinematics equation

Force of a spring (The negative sign reminds you that the spring force is a restoring force, always acting toward the equilibrium point.)
Potential energy of a spring
Period in terms of angular frequency and standard frequency
Period of a mass on a spring
Period of a pendulum
Gravitational force between two massive objects
Gravitational potential energy between two massive objects (Don't use unless an object is far away from a planet's surface.)

Electricity and Magnetism

Electric force between two point charges
Definition of electric field
Gauss's law (Though you should never actually take an integral when using this.)
How to find electric field in terms of potential
Potential energy in terms of potential, and then potential energy between two point charges (This line on the equation sheet really has two different equations. $PE = qV$ is always valid, but $PE = kqq/r$ is only valid between two point charges.)
The electric potential at some point due to surrounding point charges
Definition of capacitance
Capacitance of a parallel-plate capacitor with a dielectric substance of constant κ added
How to add parallel capacitors
How to add series capacitors
Definition of current
Energy stored on a capacitor
Resistance of a wire
Ohm's law
How to add series resistors
How to add parallel resistors
Power in an electrical circuit
Magnetic force on a charge
Ampere's law
Magnetic force on a wire
Magnetic field of a solenoid
Magnetic flux
Induced EMF
Voltage across an inductor
Energy stored in an inductor

The Internet offers some great resources for preparing for the AP Physics exam.

Your textbook may have an associated Web site . . . if so, check it out! For example, Paul A. Tipler's Physics C-level text provides this Web site: http://www.whfreeman.com/tipler4e/

- Of course, the official site of the College Board, www.collegeboard.com, has administrative information and test-taking hints, as well as contact information for the organization that actually is in charge of the exam.
- Did you enjoy your first taste of physics? If so, you can try your hand at physics debating. The United States Association for Young Physicists Tournaments hosts a national tournament which consists of "physics fights," or debates, over experimental research projects. Check out www.usaypt.org for details.
- The author writes the country's leading physics teaching blog, available at jacobsphysics.blogspot.com. Students and teachers can obtain and share ideas at this site.
- Having trouble solving calculus problems associated with Physics C, especially differential equations? Don't spend a lot of time solving these. Use www.wolfranalpha.com to get the solution spit out for you. Sure, you can't use this on the exam, but it's worth using on homework to speed or check your solutions. Physics is generally more about setting up the problem correctly than carrying out the mathematics anyway.

acceleration—the change in an object's velocity divided by the time it took to make that change; equal to the derivative (slope) of an object's velocity–time function

amplitude—the maximum displacement from the equilibrium position during a cycle of periodic motion; also, the height of a wave

angular momentum—the amount of effort it would take to make a rotating object stop spinning

atom—the fundamental unit of matter; includes protons and neutrons in a small nucleus, surrounded by electrons

atomic mass unit (amu)—the mass of a proton; also the mass of a neutron

average speed—the distance an object travels divided by the time it took to travel that distance

capacitor—a charge-storage device, often used in circuits

centrifugal force—a made-up force; when discussing circular motion, only talk about "centripetal" forces

centripetal force—the force keeping an object in uniform circular motion

coefficient of friction—the ratio of the friction force to the normal force. The coefficient of static friction is used when an object has no velocity relative to the surface it is in contact with; the coefficient of kinetic friction is used for a moving object

concave lens—a translucent object that makes the light rays passing through it diverge

conservative force—a force that acts on an object without causing the dissipation of that object's energy in the form of heat

current—the flow of positive charge in a circuit; the amount of charge passing a given point per unit time

dipole—something, usually a set of charges, with two nonidentical ends

direction—the orientation of a vector

displacement—a vector quantity describing how far an object moved

elastic collision—a collision in which kinetic energy is conserved

electric field—a property of a region of space that affects charged objects in that particular region

electric flux—the amount of electric field that penetrates a certain area

electric potential—potential energy provided by an electric field per unit charge

electromagnetic induction—the production of a current by a changing magnetic field

electron—a subatomic particle that carries a negative charge

energy—the ability to do work

equilibrium—when the net force and net torque on an object equal zero

equipotential lines—lines that illustrate every point at which a charged particle would experience a given potential

field—a property of a region of space that can affect objects found in that particular region

free-body diagram—a picture that represents one or more objects, along with the forces acting on those objects

frequency—the number of cycles per second of periodic motion; also, the number of wavelengths of a wave passing a certain point per second

friction—a force acting parallel to two surfaces in contact; if an object moves, the friction force always acts opposite the direction of motion

fulcrum—the point about which an object rotates

g—free-fall acceleration near the Earth's surface, about 10 m/s^2

induced EMF—the potential difference created by a changing magnetic flux that causes a current to flow in a wire; EMF stands for "electro-motive force," but the units of EMF are *volts.*

inductance—the property of an inductor that describes how good it is at resisting changes in current in a circuit

inductor—a coil in a circuit that makes use of induced EMF to resist changes in current in the circuit

inelastic collision—a collision in which kinetic energy is not conserved, as opposed to an elastic collision, in which the total kinetic energy of all objects is the same before and after the collision

inertia—the tendency for a massive object to resist a change in its velocity

internal energy—the sum of the kinetic energies of each molecule of a substance

ion—an electrically charged atom or molecule

kinetic energy—energy of motion

Kirchoff's laws—in a circuit, 1) at any junction, the current entering equals the current leaving; 2) the sum of the voltages around a closed loop is zero

Lenz's law—the direction of the current induced by a changing magnetic flux creates a magnetic field that opposes the change in flux

magnetic field—a property of a region of space that causes magnets and moving charges to experience a force

magnetic flux—the amount of magnetic field that penetrates an area

magnitude—how much of a quantity is present; see "scalar" and "vector"

mass spectrometer—a device used to determine the mass of a particle

rotational inertia—the rotational equivalent of mass

momentum—the amount of "oomph" an object has in a collision, equal to an object's mass multiplied by that object's velocity

net force—the vector sum of all the forces acting on an object

normal force—a force that acts perpendicular to the surface on which an object rests

nucleus—the small, dense core of an atom, made of protons and neutrons

oscillation—motion of an object that regularly repeats itself over the same path

parallel—the arrangement of elements in a circuit so that the charge that flows through one element does not flow through the others

perfectly inelastic collision—a collision in which the colliding objects stick together after impact

period—the time it takes for an object to pass through one cycle of periodic motion; also, the time for a wave to propagate by a distance of one wavelength

potential energy—energy of position

power—the amount of work done divided by the time it took to do that work; also, in a circuit, equal to the product of the current flowing through a resistor and the voltage drop across that resistor

resistance—a property of a circuit that resists the flow of current

resistor—something put in a circuit to increase its resistance

restoring force—a force that restores an oscillating object to its equilibrium position

scalar—a quantity that has a magnitude but no direction

series—the arrangement of elements in a circuit so that they are connected in a line, one after the other

time constant—a value related to how long it takes to charge or discharge a capacitor, or for current to flow in an inductor

torque—the application of a force at some distance from a fulcrum; if the net torque on an object isn't zero, the object's rotational velocity will change

vector—a quantity that has both magnitude and direction

velocity—how fast an object's displacement changes; equal to the derivative (slope) of an object's position–time function

weight—the force due to gravity; equal to the mass of an object times g, the gravitational field

work—the product of the distance an object travels and the components of the force acting on that object directed parallel to the object's direction of motion

work-energy theorem—the net work done on an object equals that object's change in kinetic energy

BIBLIOGRAPHY

Your AP Physics textbook may have seemed difficult to read early in the year. But now that you have heard lectures, solved problems, and read our guide, try reading your text again—you'll be amazed at how much more clear the text has become.

If you'd like to look at another textbook, here is one that we recommend:

- Tipler, P. A., Mosca, G. (2007). *Physics for Scientists and Engineers* (6th ed.). New York: W. H. Freeman.

You might also find this book helpful:

- Hewitt, P. G. (2009). *Conceptual Physics* (11th ed.). San Francisco: Addison Wesley.

(Hewitt's is the classic text for readable, non-mathematical expositions of physics principles. If you are having trouble seeing the meaning behind the mathematics, check out this book.)

Just for fun, we also recommend these books . . . they might not help you too much for the AP exam, but they're great reads.

- Feynman, R. (1997). *Surely you're joking, Mr. Feynman!* New York: W. W. Norton. (Collected stories of the 20th century's most charismatic physicist. If you ever thought that physicists were a bunch of stuffy nerds without personality, you should definitely read this book. One of our all-time favorites!)
- Hawking, S. (1998). *A Brief History of Time.* New York: Bantam. (The canonical introduction to cosmology at a layperson's level.)
- Lederman, L. (1993). *The God Particle.* New York: Dell. (Written by a Nobel Prize–winning experimental physicist, this book not only discusses what kinds of strange subatomic particles exist, but goes through the amazing and interesting details of how these particles are discovered.)
- Walker, J. (2007). *The Flying Circus of Physics* (2nd ed.). New Jersey: Wiley. (This book provides numerous conceptual explanations of physics phenomena that you have observed. The classic "Physics of the world around you" book.)

THE PANTHEON OF PIZZA

Pizza is the traditional food of the physics study group. Why? Probably because it's widely available, relatively inexpensive, easily shareable, and doesn't cause arguments the way "let's order bean curd" might.

If you have not yet experienced the late-night physics group study session, you should. Physics is more fun with friends than alone, and you learn more productively with other people around. Ideally, you'll find a mix of people in which sometimes they are explaining things to you, but sometimes you are explaining things to them. Explaining physics to friends is the absolute best way to cement your own knowledge.

But if you don't already have a regular study group, how do you go about creating one? Use pizza as bait. "Hey, let's get together in my mom's basement to do the problem set" is like a party invitation from Bill Nye the Science Guy. But, "Hey, we're ordering seven large pizzas with extra cheese and a variety of toppings; why don't you come by and do your problem set with us?" sounds more like you're headed to *Encore* on the Vegas Strip.[1]

Over the years I've eaten enough pizza to fill several dozen dumpsters—and dumpsters have been an appropriate receptacle for much of that pizza. Given the choice between a five-star restaurant and a pizza place, I'd usually choose the five stars. Usually. I know of four—just four—pizza places I would prefer to anything recommended by Squilliam Fancyson.

These four make up the Pantheon of Pizza.

Please understand the rules of access to the Pantheon:

1. I must have eaten at a member restaurant at least twice. This unfortunately rules out the heavenly *Pepper's Pizza* in Chapel Hill, North Carolina.[2]
2. I must have such an affinity for their pepperoni-and-extra-cheese pizza that my mouth waters upon the mere mention of a potential visit to the restaurant.

That's it. It's my pantheon, so it's my choice who gets in.

That said, please do send your own corrections, additions, oversights, etc. You can contact me via Woodberry Forest School. If you make a good enough case for a particular pizza place possibly joining the Pantheon, I may attempt to make a pilgrimage.

The Pantheon

5. Homeslice, Kansas City, Missouri. Imagine you've been grading AP exams for eight hours in the heart of downtown Kansas City. Imagine you're hungry, on foot, and that you are not up for the two-mile hike to Gates Barbecue tonight. (I don't have to imagine. This is my life for several days each June.) Grab some friends and walk a few blocks toward the basketball arena, then turn right. The airy restaurant with the high tables and the Royals pregame on the TVs is Homeslice. Their defining pizza feature is fresh mozzarella, made each day in-house. One of the owners came out to earnestly tell our table the origin story of

---

[1] Sorry. I certainly do *not* intend to dis Bill Nye the Science Guy. He is demonstrably cool.
[2] Now, alas, I hear they've closed down for good. Sigh.

this fresh mozzarella, the recent genesis of their restaurant, and how AP readers are appreciated as customers, but can't top concert attendees of any genre. Nevertheless…the proof in the pizza is the eating of the same. The spices are just right; the large thin pepperoni slices taste excellent and add flavor to the entire pie. Bring whatever you don't finish back to the physics lounge in the basement of the Crowne Plaza hotel. Please.

4. Broadway Joe's Pizza, Riverdale, New York. This tiny shop below the #1 line train station in the North Bronx has everything you could ask for in a New York pizzeria—street noise, no air conditioning but instead a fan running all summer, the Yankees game on the television, and Broadway Joe himself behind the counter. Okay, I'm sure that there are hundreds of such places throughout New York City, all of which probably have tremendous pizza. But Broadway Joe's is the one I walk to every year during the AP Physics Teachers' Summer Institute that I run at Manhattan College. Bonus points to Mr. Joe for recognizing me each year: "Hey, you're the teacher who wants a small[3] pepperoni and extra cheese." Ten minutes later, out pops the classic New York–style pie with deciliters of cheese piled on top of a foldable crust. I can never finish the small by myself, but I so, so want to.

3. Thyme Market, Culpeper, Virginia. When I moved to central Virginia, I initially despaired at the food choices. But then we discovered Pizza Monday at Thyme Market. Even an unjuiced Alex Rodriguez[4] could knock a baseball across the length of Culpeper's Main Street, but it contains the heavenly brick oven from which its $5 pies spring forth each Monday, plus a lot of money for toppings, plus another $5 if you come on a day other than Monday. But it's well worth the cash and the trip. This is one of the few pizza places ever in which "extra cheese" provides a bit too much gooeyness. The pepperoni itself is the best of any in the Pantheon—just the right size, on top of the cheese, a bit of thickness to it, and baked until the edges begin to get crispy. While you're in the restaurant, try a bite of the "Culpeper Crack"–branded cheese spread that's always available to sample. The pizza may be only $5 per pie, but you'll spend an order of magnitude more than that after you buy up multiple tubs of the Crack to take home.

2. Big Ed's Pizza, Oak Ridge, Tennessee. I encountered Big Ed's in conjunction with the United States Invitational Young Physicists Tournament, which was held in Oak Ridge for several years due to the presence of Oak Ridge National Laboratory. My friend and fellow physics teacher Peggy insisted that it was worth waiting in the crowd outside the door for a table, and she was right. The pizza was, of course, fabulous: New York–style foldable crust, with plenty of cheese and a multitude thereof of pepperonis. What sold me on Big Ed's, more so than even the T-shirts with a cartoony drawing of Big Ed himself, was the Kneeling Bench. The kitchen is separated from the dining area by a high wooden façade. But in the middle of the façade are two holes, with benches underneath. I was instructed to kneel on a bench, cup my hands communion-style, and put them through the hole. Lo, a generous portion of shredded mozzarella was placed in my hands by unknown beneficiaries. I had to go through this ritual a second time—I probably had as much cheese from my trips to the Kneeling Bench as from the pizza itself.

1. Langel's Pizza, Highland, Indiana. Most people who sample Chicago-style deep-dish pizza go to the big chains that have sprouted up across the Chicagoland area. Burrito Girl[5] grew up in a small suburb in northwest Indiana, and so she is well aware of the famous fancy chains. Yet the first pizza place that Burrito Girl took me to consisted of

---

[3]Don't be deceived. A "small" pie at Broadway Joe's could last for three straight late nights of Minecraft. Just one extra-large could sustain the entire rat population along the banks of the East River.

[4]… if such a thing exists.

[5]My wife and sidekick, also known as the mild-mannered Shari.

about six booths sandwiched between an exotic reptiles store and a sports bar. I ordered, and I endured the requisite progression of helpfulness, skepticism, and then outright horror that waitresses in Chicago pizza places bestow upon me when I order extra cheese. Yes, I want extra cheese, even though the pizza is stuffed with seemingly an entire cowday's worth of cheese already. Really. I've done this before, and lived to tell the tale. Please?

At Langel's, the extra cheese oozes and stretches beyond the mere constraints of slices. It takes a full 20 minutes before the cheese is congealed enough to hold the shape in which you cut it. But it's the sauce that makes Langel's the best pizza in the known universe. This deepdish pizza does not come in layers, but rather mixed all about, which means that the sauce can be appreciated throughout every bite. The pepperoni is fine, but I actually recommend just getting a pure extra-cheese pie. You'll have enough for lunch right now, dinner tonight, and probably breakfast tomorrow. Too bad they don't deliver within a 1,200-km radius.